Heaven and Earth in Luke-Acts

Ming Gao

© 2017 by Ming Gao

Published 2017 by Langham Monographs
An imprint of Langham Creative Projects

Langham Partnership
PO Box 296, Carlisle, Cumbria CA3 9WZ, UK
www.langham.org

ISBNs:
978-1-78368-347-5 Print
978-1-78368-349-9 Mobi
978-1-78368-348-2 ePub
978-1-78368-350-5 PDF

Ming Gao has asserted his right under the Copyright, Designs and Patents Act, 1988 to be identified as the Author of this work.

All rights reserved. No part of this publication may be reproduced, stored in a retrieval system or transmitted, in any form or by any means, electronic, mechanical, photocopying, recording or otherwise, without the prior written permission of the publisher or the Copyright Licensing Agency.

All Scripture quotations, unless otherwise indicated, are taken from the Holy Bible, New International Version®, NIV®. Copyright ©1973, 1978, 1984, 2011 by Biblica, Inc.™ Used by permission of Zondervan.

British Library Cataloguing in Publication Data
A catalogue record for this book is available from the British Library

ISBN: 978-1-78368-347-5

Cover & Book Design: projectluz.com

Langham Partnership actively supports theological dialogue and an author's right to publish but does not necessarily endorse the views and opinions set forth here or in works referenced within this publication, nor can we guarantee technical and grammatical correctness. Langham Partnership does not accept any responsibility or liability to persons or property as a consequence of the reading, use or interpretation of its published content.

In this insightful study, Dr Gao situates the heaven motif within the theological landscape of Lukan writings and provides a strong argument for a dynamic reading of this motif as a symbol of the unfolding of cosmic warfare at the dawn of God's eschatological kingdom on earth. Through the lens of this heaven motif, Dr Gao is also able to provide a fresh reading of a number of passages in both Luke and Acts. Those who are interested in the theology of Luke will find this volume a helpful dialogue partner, and those who are interested in the power of the Lukan message for the contemporary reader will not be disappointed with it.

David W. Pao, PhD
Professor of New Testament and Chair of the New Testament Department,
Trinity Evangelical Divinity School, Deerfield, IL, USA

Dr Gao insightfully illumines how the concept of "heaven and earth" is integral to the storyline of Luke-Acts, from Christ's birth to his ascension. While doing so, he forces you to observe how what transpires in the heavens has ramifications on earth. Heaven is not merely a static place of angelic bliss; it is both a headquarters and battleground where God enacts his triumphant plan to establish his kingdom. I have been enriched by this impressive study, and I am delighted to know that many others will be through its publication.

Andrew T. Abernethy, PhD
Associate Professor of Old Testament, Wheaton College, Wheaton, IL, USA

Dedication
to Irene and Carol
and
in memory of my Father and Mother

Contents

Abstract xi

Acknowledgments xiii

Abbreviations xvii

Chapter 1 1
  Introduction
    Heaven Language in Luke-Acts 1
    Literature Review 5
    Thesis Statement 10
    Methodology 11

Chapter 2 17
  The Invasion of the Heavenly Glory on Earth – Luke 2:14
    Introduction 17
    Narrative Analysis of the Infancy Narrative 18
    Structural Analysis of Luke 2:8–20 20
    The Heavenly Hymn: Luke 2:14 24
      Textual Issue 24
      A Study of "Highest" (ὕψιστος) 24
      Who/What Is This Heavenly Glory? 27
      Heaven and Peace in Luke 2:14 33
      Summary 33
    The Heaven Motif and the Peace Motif 34
      Peace Motif in Recent Lukan Scholarship 34
      The Term Peace (εἰρήνη) in Luke-Acts 36
      "Peace" (εἰρήνη) in Luke 2:14 37
      The Relationship between the Heaven Motif and the
        Peace Motif 42
      Summary 46
    The Outworking of the Heaven Motif by the Peace Motif in
      Luke-Acts 47
      Heavenly Glory Manifested by Peace in the Ministry of Jesus 47
      Heavenly Glory Presented by Peace in the Mission
        of the Disciples 51
      Heavenly Glory Manifested in the Ecclesial Dimension 57
    Conclusion 65

Chapter 3 69
  The Victory of God in Heaven and Its Impact on Earth –
  The Fall of Satan From Heaven in Luke 10:18
    Introduction 69
    The Fall of Satan in Luke 10:18 70
      Views on the Vision of Satan's Fall 71
      The Victory of God in Heaven...100
      The Agent of the Victory of God 105
      The Victory of God over Satan in Heaven and Its Impact
        on Earth..108
      Summary 113
    Exorcisms in Luke...114
      Exorcisms 114
      The Theological Significance of Exorcisms: *Luke 11:14–23*......115
      Individual Exorcism Narrative 126
      Summary 134
    Conclusion 135

Chapter 4 137
  The Ascension of Jesus – Luke 24:50–53 and Acts 1:9–11
    Introduction 137
    The Ascension of Jesus 138
      Scholarship on the Ascension of Jesus 138
      Double Accounts, One Event (*Luke 24:50–53* and
        Acts 1:9–11) 144
      Literary Function...149
      Ascension and Resurrection 150
      Luke's Theological Concerns 156
    Ascension and Exaltation of Jesus..161
      Εἰς Τὸν Οὐρανὸν..161
      "At the Right Hand of God" 165
      Summary 169
    The Cosmic Lord 169
      The Cosmic God/Lord...169
      Visions from Heaven: The Inclusion of the Gentiles 175
      Cosmic Lordship of Christ: Anti-Idol Polemic........................187
    Conclusion 208

Chapter 5 211
   Heaven Must Receive Jesus Until the Restoration of All – Acts 3:21
      Introduction 211
      Acts 3:21 212
         Temporal Markers in *Acts 3:17–26* 212
         Temporal Phrases 218
         The First and Second Comings of Jesus in *Acts 3:17–26* 239
         Acts 3:21 241
         Summary 243
      Luke 17:22–37 244
         Temporal Markers 245
         The Context of *Luke 17:22–37* 247
         Summary 247
      Luke 21:25–28 248
         Temporal Markers 248
         Summary 249
      Acts 2:17–21 249
         Temporal Markers 249
         The Last Days – Inaugurated 250
         Summary 253
      Conclusion 253
      Excursus: Lukan Eschatology 256
         Review of Scholarship 257
         Conclusion 263

Chapter 6 267
   Summary and Conclusion
      Summary 267
      Conclusion 269
      Implications for the Study of the Lukan Ecclesiology 270
      Implications for the Study of Luke-Acts 271
      Implications for Evangelization 271
      Implications for the Persecuted Church 271
      Implication for Contextualization 272
      Areas for Further Research 272

Bibliography 275

Abstract

Is heaven simply a place where God is or the symbol of God's power? The answer to both questions is probably "no." This project is a narrative-critical and redaction-critical study of the much-overlooked heaven motif in Luke-Acts. Examinations are made into programmatic passages that contain the heaven motif (Luke 2:14; 10:18; 24:50–53; Acts 1:9–11; 3:21), considering their immediate and broader literary contexts as well as their Jewish and Greco-Roman contexts.

First, our examination of Luke 2:14 demonstrates that the heavenly hymn concerns both heaven and earth. The glory of the highest heaven has been manifested on earth by the eschatological peace/salvation. The heavenly glory brings the eschatological peace down to earth. Second, our study of Luke 10:18 demonstrates that the fall of Satan from heaven points to the victory of God in heaven. Jesus saw a vision of this fall when his disciples were performing exorcisms. Exorcisms are thus lethal attacks on Satan and his dominion. The victory of God in heaven and its impact on earth is the realization of the eschatological kingdom of God. Third, our investigation of Luke 24:50–53 and Acts 1:9–11 demonstrates that the heaven reference here points to yet another stage of Luke's narrative: the exaltation of Jesus. The cosmic Lord has challenged human opponents and the idols of the nations, thus confirming the universal lordship of God. The purpose of the challenge of human opponents is for the realization of the kingdom of God on earth. By critiquing idols, a call for turning away from idols to the cosmic Lord has been made. Finally, our examination of Acts 3:21 demonstrates that the reference to heaven here points to the unfulfilled nature of the kingdom of God. Heaven must keep Jesus for a certain period of time until the completion of the restoration of all the Jews and Gentiles who should obtain salvation. Then heaven will release Jesus for his final return, the Parousia.

Therefore, this study shows that heaven is not simply a static place where God is or the symbol of God's power. Heaven is not a static place at all but is dynamic and points to the unfolding of cosmic warfare, the effects of which are to be felt on earth. Heaven points to the arrival of God's eschatological kingdom on earth.

Acknowledgments

Many have contributed to this project. First of all, I would like to thank Dr David W. Pao, my mentor, who has been so generous to give me precious time and invaluable guidance. Especially when I was stuck, it was his excellent Lukan scholarship that brought me through. He has always been available and reachable. His quick responses are far beyond my expectations! His sharp and insightful comments/critiques are so very helpful. His creative and rigorous scholarship has provided me a role model to follow. His regular preaching at our church (CCFC-South Lake) is always insightful and powerful, not only nourishing me (and also my wife) but also setting a model for expository preaching. Dr Pao's classes on the Lukan writings and seminar on Luke-Acts were fascinating and benefited me a lot. He and his wife, Dr Ho Pao, also showed loving-kindness to my family when we dealt with family illnesses.

I also give my thanks to Dr Grant R. Osborne. As a New Testament scholar, he attracted me to pursue doctoral study at Trinity. Many years ago, when I was in China, I read some of his books, especially the encyclopedic *The Hermeneutical Spiral*, which inspired me to pursue biblical studies. His Biblical Interpretation seminar at Singapore Bible College further convinced me to pursue biblical studies at Trinity. His classes at Trinity affirmed that my choice was correct. I also want to share a touching moment. It was Dr Osborne's short address at the section dedicated to his 70th birthday at the 2012 annual meeting of the Evangelical Theological Society in Milwaukee, WI, that really touched my heart. He said emotionally, "As a teacher, I have such a privilege to impact the lives of my students through teaching!" Many people were moved to tears, me included. His dedication of nearly forty years of teaching at Trinity has impacted so many lives, mine included. Dr Osborne's active involvement in teaching and training Chinese pastors and church leaders often encouraged my heart and fueled me to finish my studies soon and then go back to China to serve our Lord. Dr Osborne's careful examination and critical comments on this project have been greatly appreciated.

Dr Richard E. Averbeck, the PhD program director, is always encouraging. Each conversation with him turned out to be a pleasant one. His biblical scholarship with an expertise in counseling makes him an ideal program director! His concern and love for China have often encouraged me! I am so thankful for his involvement in training Chinese pastors then and now. His examination and invaluable comments on this project have been greatly appreciated. Dr Averbeck, thank you so much!

I have benefited from many other professors at Trinity. Among them are: Dr Willem A. VanGemeren, who taught an OT seminar on the Book of Isaiah. He helped me see the gospel in the OT. Dr Robert Yarbrough taught me the meaning of "pastoral" in his Pastoral Epistles seminar. Dr D. A. Carson's seminar on Mystery in the NT led me taste how unfathomable God's salvific love is. Dr Kevin J. Vanhoozer's Theological Prolegomena seminar provided me the foundation of how to be an evangelical scholar. Dr Graham Cole's Atonement seminar let me taste the importance of the atonement from a theologian's perspective. Dr Scott Manetsch's seminar on the Reformation opened a window to glimpse the greatness of the Giants (Luther, Calvin and others). Other professors have extended their kindness and care to me, even if I did not have a chance to take a class with them, such as Dr Greg Scharf, Dr Te-Li Lau, and Dr Tite Tiénou.

Many thanks go to my classmates for their friendship. To name a few: David Sloan, Andy Abernathy, Todd Patterson, Hans Sun, Jared Compton, David Feiser, Jacob Rosenberg, Nelson Morales, Yacouba Sanon, Yun Gab Choi, Sun Wook Kim, May Young, Jillian Rose. Of special mention is Chin Hong Yee, a dear friend and a classmate, whom I knew when I studied at Singapore Bible College. He came to Trinity the same year that I did. We have had many classes together. He is always available to me so I can share my ups and downs. Thank you, Chin Hong!

Dr Hae-Won Kim, May Young, John Simons and Scott Swingle at the Doctoral Office offered kind help to make my study at Trinity go smoothly and to make my journey at Trinity a pleasant one. To them I give my thanks!

The Dean of Students, Felix Theonugraha; the Dean of Students, Heather Rosenberg; and the Coordinator of International Students, Kate Reed, are so kind and helpful that they not only made my study smooth but also made my journey at Trinity memorable. Thank you so much!

Of special mention are the two scholarships: Langham Partenership and Scholarleader International without which it would have been impossible for me to pursue and accomplish my study in the States.

Many friends and families here in the States, in Singapore, and in China have supported me and my family financially and spiritually. Especially families in Trinity Chinese Fellowship offered much help on the occasion of my family illness. To you all, I give my thanks.

My thanks go to Irene, my darling wife, for her love, support and sacrifice (she even sacrificed the opportunity to pursue her doctoral studies at Trinity), without which it would have been impossible for me to finish this project. To her I owe a lot! I give thanks to Carol, my "Sweetie," who often cheers me on! The most frequent question she asks is, "Daddy, are you going to library?" My answer is always "Yes." I owe her a lot! To both of them I dedicate this dissertation.

I give my thanks to my mother, a role model in terms of prayer and faith. She regularly fasted one day a week to pray! She simply believed whatever the Bible says! I give my thanks to my father, a brave man who never gave up! He is a hero living in my heart forever! Both of them went away with our Lord during my study at Trinity. In memory of my mom and dad I dedicate this dissertation! They must be very pleased at the completion of my study in the States. They will be very happy that soon Irene, Carol and I will go back to our home country, China, to serve our Lord there!

Thanks to my dear siblings – six sisters and two brothers – and their families for their love and prayers! I am so blessed by them.

Above all, I give my thanks to the Lord who saved me, sustained me to go through my study journey and chose me to serve him!

To Him be all glory, honor, and praise!

Amen!

Abbreviations

The following abbrevations supplement those in *The SBL Handbook of Style: For Ancient Near Eastern, Biblical, And Early Christian Studies* (Patrick H. Alexander et al. eds. [Peabody: Hendrickson, 1999]).

BECNT	Baker Exegetical Commentary on the New Testament
BK	*Bibel und Kirche*
CBC	Collegeville Bible Commentary
COQD	Christian Origins and the Question of God
FCBS	Fortress Classics in Biblical Studies
IBC	International Bible Commentary
JPThSup	Journal of Pentecostal Theology Supplement
LNTS	Library of New Testament Studies
NIBC	New International Biblical Commentary
NovTSup	Supplements to Novum Testamentum
NTC	New Testament Commentary
NTT	New Testament Theology
PNTC	The Pillar New Testament Commentary
ThS	*Theology in Scotland*
ZECNT	Zondervan Exegetical Commentary on the New Testament

CHAPTER 1

Introduction

Heaven Language in Luke-Acts

Heaven language (οὐρανός) is widely used by almost all New Testament authors.[1] Luke uses οὐρανός,[2] its cognate words,[3] and a synonym,[4] forty times in his Gospel and twenty-nine times in the Book of Acts.[5] These

---

1. In the New Testament, the word οὐρανός (*heaven*) occurs 273 times in 255 verses throughout most of the NT, except in 1–3 John and the book of Jude. The data are based on Bible Works 8.0.

2. There are generally three categories of οὐρανός. First, οὐρανός refers to the invisible, transcendent place above where God dwells along with his angels and the righteous dead. This usage occurs forty times in Luke–Acts (Luke 2:15; 3:21, 22; 6:23; 9:16, 54; 10:15, 18, 20; 11:13, 16; 12:56; 15:7, 18, 21; 17:29; 18:13, 22; 19:38; 20:4, 5; 21:11; 22:43; 24:51; Acts 1:10, 11 [x3]; 2:2, 19, 34; 3:21; 7:42, 49, 55, 56; 9:3; 10:11, 16; 11:5, 9, 10; 22:6). Second, οὐρανός referring to "the starry heaven, the firmament or sky above, the atmosphere where birds fly" occurs eight times (Luke 4:25; 8:5; 9:58; 12:56; 13:9; 17:24 [x2]; 21:26; Acts 2:5; 4:12; 10:12; 11:6). Third, οὐρανός, used together with γῆ, as a merism, refers to the whole world, heaven and earth (Luke 10:21; 16:17; 21:33 Acts 4:24; 14:15; 17:24). This study will focus on the first category.

3. These include the adjective οὐράνιος (heavenly) (Luke 2:13, Acts 26:19) and the adverb οὐρανόθεν (from heaven) (Acts 14:17; 26:13).

4. The term ὕψιστος (*highest*) is used by Luke as a synonym for heaven in Luke 2:14 and Luke 19:38. Another term, "ὕψος," should be also considered a synonym for heaven (Luke 1:78; 24:49). With this in mind, Pennington overlooks this term in his analysis. See Jonathan T. Pennington, *Heaven and Earth in the Gospel of Matthew*, NovTSup 126 (Grand Rapids: Baker, 2009), 68.

5. Unless otherwise indicated, the Greek text of the Bible is from the following source: Kurt Aland and Eberhard Nestle, *Novum Testamentum Graece* (Stuttgart: Deutsche Bibelgesellschaft, 2001). There are four textual issues in Luke (11:2; 11:13; 21:11; 24:51) and one in Acts 1:11. See Bruce Manning Metzger, *A Textual Commentary on the Greek New Testament* (London: United Bible Society, 1994), 154, 158, 172, 189–190, 283.

numbers are striking.⁶ Luke's use of heaven language is different from that of other synoptic gospel writers.⁷ He utilizes heaven language differently than Matthew in that he seems to avoid using it in places where Matthew is fond of using it,⁸ and he uniquely uses heaven words eleven times in some crucial narratives.⁹ Unlike Matthew, Luke uses only eleven instances from

---

6. In Matthew, there are ninety occurrences; in the book of Revelation, fifty-five; in Mark's gospel and John's, nineteen; in Pauline Epistles (from the book of Romans to Philemon), thirty-three; in the book of Hebrews, sixteen; and in the General Epistles, eleven.

7. References to heaven in Luke could be classified into four categories: (1) From Mark's gospel, there are ten occurrences (Luke 3:21, 22; 9:16; 11:16; 12:19; 18:22; 20:4, 5; 21:26, 33; (2) from "Q," nine occurrences (Luke 6:23; 9:58; 10:15, 21; 11:13; 12:33, 56; 15:7; 16:17); (3) from the Lukan source "L," eleven references occur (Luke 2:13, 15; 4:25; 9:54; 10:18, 20; 15:18, 21; 18:13; 19:38; 22:3; 24:51); (4) Six are considered to be Lukan redaction: Luke 8:5; 17:24[x2], 29; 19:38; 21:11). We will take the view of the two-source hypothesis and its modification proposed by Streeter. "Q" determinations are based on Paul Hoffmann, et al., *The Critical Edition of Q: Synopsis Including the Gospels of Matthew and Luke, Mark and Thomas with English, German, and French Translations of Q and Thomas* (Louvain: Peeters, 2000). For synoptic issues, see Rudolf Karl Bultmann, *The History of the Synoptic Tradition* (Oxford: Basil Blackwell, 1968), 1–374; Scot McKnight, *Interpreting the Synoptic Gospels* (Grand Rapids: Baker, 1988), 19–44; Peter Stuhlmacher, ed., *The Gospel and the Gospels* (Grand Rapids: Eerdmans, 1991); David Alan Black and David R. Beck, eds., *Rethinking the Synoptic Problem* (Grand Rapids: Baker, 2001); Martin Mosse, *The Three Gospels: New Testament History Introduced by the Synoptic Problem* (Paternoster Biblical Monographs; Milton Keynes: Paternoster, 2007), 1–90; Robert A. Derrenbacker, Jr., *Ancient Compositional Practices and the Synoptic Problem*, BETL (Leuven: Peeters, 2005), 120–256; Paul Foster, Gregory, Andrew, et al., eds., *New Studies in the Synoptic Problem: Oxford Conference, April 2008: Essays in Honour of Christopher M Tuckett* (ibid., 2011), 51–85; Burnett Hillman Streeter, *The Four Gospels: A Study of Origins* (New York: Macmillan, 1925), 150–270; Bernard Orchard and Harold Riley, *The Order of the Synoptics: Why Three Synoptic Gospels?* (Macon, GA: Mercer Univ Press, 1987), 3–99; Robert H. Stein, *The Synoptic Problem* (Grand Rapids: Baker, 1987), 29–160; Grant R. Osborne, "History and Theology in the Synoptic Gospels," *TrinJ* 24 (2003): 5–22.

8. First, Matthew likes to use "kingdom of heaven" which occurs thirty-two times. See Robert L. Mowery, "The Matthean References to the Kingdom: Different Terms for Different Audiences," *ETL* 70 (1994): 398–405. Unlike Matthew's frequent use of "kingdom of heaven," Luke, instead, uses "the kingdom of God" thirty-three times in his Gospel and six times in Acts. Second, Matthew uses "Father in heaven" and "heavenly Father" twenty times. However, Luke uses "heavenly Father" only once in Luke 11:13. Matthew's two favorite phrases occur fifty-two times (52/90). In other words, apart from the occurrences of these two phrases, only thirty-eight heaven references occur in Matthew. This is nearly equivalent to Luke's gospel in which the term "heaven" occures thirty-seven times.

9. There are seventeen occurrences in Luke, but not in Matthew (Luke 2:13,15; 4:25; 8:5; 9:54; 10:18, 20; 15:18, 21; 17: 24 [x2], 29; 18:13; 19:38; 21:11; 22:43; 24:51). My count is different from that of Pennington's. He misses two instances in Luke 17:24. Pennington, *Heaven and Earth in Matthew*, 73. Out of the seventeen occurrences, eleven are considered to be Lukan. See footnote 7.

Mark's gospel.[10] Matthew uses nearly all of the occurrences of "heaven" in Mark's gospel (17/19).[11] Luke uses the other eight "heaven" occurrences for a wider range of concerns and purposes than Mark does.

Moving to the Book of Acts, the word οὐρανός and its cognates appear twenty-nine times.[12] Not only is this high number impressive, but the cluster distribution is also suggestive in that these occurrences of "heaven" concern the following crucial narratives: the ascension of Jesus (Acts 1), the coming of the Holy Spirit (Acts 2), the history of Israel (Acts 7) and the mission to the Gentiles (Acts 9, 10, and 11).[13] The analysis of these occurrences shows that Luke uses heaven language in clusters in the significant events in Acts.

This statistical analysis of heaven language shows that Luke uses heaven language frequently, and he uses "heaven" occurrences for his own concerns and purposes in his gospel compared to the way this language is used in Matthew and Mark. Luke also utilizes heaven references in significant narratives in the Book of Acts. The following analysis will show that heaven is an important motif in Luke-Acts.

In addition, other terms that often appear in passages where heaven is mentioned should be noted. First, the term for "angel/heavenly being" (ἄγγελος) often appears in the following passages: the birth of Jesus (Luke

---

10. For the comparison see Kurt Aland, *Synopsis of the Four Gospels: Greek-English Edition of the Synopsis Quattuor Evangeliorum with the Text of the Revised Standard Version* (New York: United Bible Societies, 1973); Burton Hamilton Throckmorton, ed., *Gospel Parallels: A Synopsis of the First 3 Gospels* (Thomas Nelson, 1967). Out of these eleven instances, two occurrences link with episodes that have significant theological importance appearing in both Mark and Luke. These are the baptism of Jesus (Mark 1:9–11 and Luke 3:21–22) and the ascension of Jesus (Mark 16:19 and Luke 24:50–51). There are twenty-four occurrences of heaven appearing in Luke but not in Mark. This means Luke uses nearly two-thirds (twenty-four out of thirty-eight) of his "heaven" occurrences for his own purposes. In these instances, Luke develops his own concerns such as the birth of Jesus (Luke 2:15 including ὕψιστος in 2:14); the mission of the seventy(-two) (Luke 10:18, 20); the parable of the lost sheep, coin and son (Luke 15:7, 18, 21); and Jesus's entering into Jerusalem (Luke 19:38).

11. The two exceptions are Mark 7:34 and 16:19.

12. Acts is ranked fourth in the entire New Testament for the number of occurrences it contains. The first is Matthew (ninety), then Revelation (fifty-five), and, third, Luke's Gospel (thirty-eight).

13. *Heaven* occurs four times each in Acts 1, 2, 7 and 11. It occurs three times in Acts 10. The total number of these occurrences occupies 73 percent (nineteen out of twenty-six) of all the instances. The other occurrences seem to appear sporadically in six chapters in Acts, including 3:21; 4:12, 24; 9:3; 14:15; 17:24 and 22:6.

2:8–21);[14] the fall of Satan (Luke 10:18);[15] the ascension account (Acts 1:1–11);[16] Stephen's speech (Acts 7:30, 35, 38, 53); Paul's vision (Acts 9:1–9 and its recounting in 22:6–16 and 26:12–18) and Peter's vision (Acts 10:3, 7, 22; 11:3).[17] Second, the term for "light/flashing" (φῶς/ἀστραπὴν) often appears in passages that use heaven language, such as the birth narrative (Luke 2:8–21), the fall of Satan passage (Luke 10:18) and Paul's vision (Acts 9:3; 22:6, 9, 11, 13). Third, the term for "voice" (φωνή) or "to speak" (λέγω) often occurs in the following heaven passages: such as the angel's speaking (Luke 2:8–20, 24:1–12; Acts 1:6–11) and the voice from heaven (Luke 3:21–22; 9: 28–36; Acts 9:4, 7; 22:7, 9, 14, 22; 26:14; Acts 10:13, 15; 11:7, 9). Thus, the terms angel/heavenly figure, light/flash/glory, and voice/speaking often appear with the term for heaven as a pattern. The cluster of terms for heaven language, the heavenly figure, and the phenomenon of light and sound constitute the heaven motif.[18]

This study of the patterns in which terms for heaven occur shows that Luke uses heaven as a motif in his two-volume work. This motif occurs frequently in crucial narratives: the infancy narrative (Luke 2:14); the baptism of Jesus (Luke 3:21—2); the fall of Satan (Luke 10:18); the ascension narratives (Luke 24:50–53 and Acts 1:9–11); the vision of Stephen (Acts 7:55–56); the vision of Paul (Acts 9:1–9; 22:6–16; and 26:12–18); the vision of Peter (Acts 10:9–16 and 11:4–10).

Acts 3:21 needs to be mentioned in particular though it does not contain terms like "light/flashing" or "speaking/voice." First, this passage has the reference to heaven. It says, "Whom [Jesus] heaven must receive" (ὃν δεῖ οὐρανὸν μὲν δέξασθαι). Besides, this passage contains the heavenly figure that is the exalted Jesus. The resurrected Jesus has ascended and been exalted in heaven. Further, heaven is anthropomorphized. We will illustrate this point

---

14. See Luke 2:9, 10, 13, 15, 21.

15. Here, instead of the appearance of an angel, the heavenly being is Satan (Σατανᾶς).

16. Here, it seems that there is no angel who appears. However, "the men in white clothes" are angels. See Luke 24:4, which says, "two men stood in dazzling apparel"; also see Matt 28:2–7, which says, "an angel"; and, finally, see John 20:12, which says, "two angels in white."

17. Instead of the appearance of angles, the Lord reveals himself to Paul and talks to him.

18. For the definition of motif, see William Flint Thrall and Addison Hibbard, *A Handbook to Literature* (New York: Odyssey, 1960), 294.

in its due course. Thus, Acts 3:21 should be considered one of the passages that contain the heaven motif.

Even with the understanding that no single motif or theme could encompass all the purposes, intentions, and theological concerns of the author, it seems that the heaven motif functions as a significant thread that runs through the fabric of Luke-Acts.

Literature Review

A review of literature on Luke-Acts provides a fitting context for this study. The historical-critical period is a good starting point.[19] Hans Conzelmann, a leading figure who applied redaction criticism to the study of Luke-Acts, is known for his seminal work: *Die Mitte der Zeit* (*The Middle of Time*), translated as *The Theology of St. Luke*.[20] He later published his commentary on the Book of Acts.[21] Applying redaction criticism in *The Theology of St. Luke*, he compared Luke with Mark and Matthew and concluded that Luke, working with his sources (Mark, Q, and others), composed his gospel

---

19. Wilhelm Martin Leberecht de Wette (1780–1849) was the first among scholars to challenge the historicity of Acts and to launch historical studies on Acts. Wilhelm Martin Leberecht De Wette and Frederick Frotheringham, *An Historico-Critical Introduction to the Canonical Books of the New Testament* (Boston: Crosby, 1858). In response to the denial of Luke's historicity and to Baur, many scholars have defended Luke. James Smith, *The Voyage and Shipwreck of St Paul* (Grand Rapids: Baker, 1978), 1–250. William Mitchell Ramsay, *The Bearing of Recent Discovery on the Trustworthiness of the New Testament* (New York: Hodder and Stoughton, 1915), 35–105. Ferdinand Christian Baur, the greatest leader of the Tübingen School, followed de Wette and proposed that Acts was written to defend Paul's mission to the Gentiles. See Peter C. Hodgson, *The Formation of Historical Theology: A Study of Ferdinand Christian Baur* (New York: Harper and Row, 1966), 196–210. Martin Dibelius championed "form criticism" (*Formgeschichtliche Methode*) and applied this method to the interpretation of the book of Acts. He examined Acts with his "form-criticism" (or "style-criticism"), and he concluded that Paul's itinerary gave the author the frame work to which Luke added his own tradition and inserted other traditions. See Martin Dibelius, *Die Formgeschichte des Evangeliums* (Tübingen: JCB Mohr, 1961); Martin Dibelius and K. C. Hanson, *The Book of Acts: Form, Style, and Theology*, FSBS (Minneapolis: Fortress, 2004), 3–152. Ernst Haenchen was the first scholar to apply Dibelius's form criticism while writing a commentary on Acts. His nearly 600-page commentary on Acts is a good showcase of Dibelius' methodology. Ernst Haenchen, *The Acts of the Apostles* (Philadelphia: Westminster, 1971). Form-critical analysis focuses on the transmission of the biblical text, and therefore it has no interest in "heaven" occurrences.

20. Hans Conzelmann, *Die Mitte der Zeit: Studien zur Theologie des Lukas* (Tübingen: Mohr Siebeck, 1954). Hans Conzelmann, *The Theology of St Luke*, trans. George Buswell (New York: Harper & Row, 1960).

21. Hans Conzelmann, *Acts of the Apostles* (Philadelphia: Fortress, 1987).

and Acts to deal with one particular situation of the church – the delay of the Parousia.²² His major contribution was to point out that Luke was a theologian rather than a historian.²³ Redaction studies that focused on the editorial process should have detected the Lukan significance of heaven language, but they have not.²⁴

Recent works related to the heaven language in Luke-Acts have been written by Matthew Sleeman, Steve Walton and others.²⁵ A brief discussion of these works is appropriate.

Matthew Sleeman studied the usage of "heaven" in Acts.²⁶ Sleeman, a geographer,²⁷ used Soja's geographical theory to interpret the Book of Acts.

---

22. Conzelmann, *Theology*, 131–132. His treatment of Luke 21 as a redaction of Mark 13 is a good example of his redaction criticism. See ibid., 125–131.

23. David Alan Black and David S. Dockery, eds., *New Testament Criticism & Interpretation* (Grand Rapids: Zondervan, 1991), 202; Norman Perrin, *What Is Redaction Criticism,* Guides to Biblical Scholarship (Philadelphia: Fortress, 1969), 28–33.

24. Another pioneer in redaction criticism was Henry Joel Cadbury. His redaction method can be seen in his book: Henry Joel Cadbury, *Making of Luke-Acts* (New York: Macmillan, 1958). He was also known by his literary studies of Luke-Acts. See, Henry Joel Cadbury, *The Style and Literary Method of Luke. I, The Diction of Luke and Acts*, HTS 6, (Cambridge: Harvard University Press, 1919). Henry Joel Cadbury, *The Style and Literary Method of Luke. II,* HTS 6 (Cambridge: Harvard University Press, 1920). It was Cadbury who coined the hyphenated term: "Luke-Acts." He studied Luke's vocabulary, investigated the medical language of Luke and arrived at the conclusion that "the so called medical language could not be used as evidence to prove that Luke is a physician." Cadbury, *Style and Literary Method: I,* 51. Thus, he challenged the notion advocated by William Kirk Hobart that the medical language proved Luke was a medical doctor, William Kirk Hobart, *The Medical Language of St. Luke; A Proof from Internal Evidence that "The Gospel according to St. Luke" and "The Acts of the Apostles" Were Written by the Same Person, and That the Writer Was a Medical Man,* Dublin University Press Series (Dublin: Hodges, 1882). However, he overlooked the "heaven" language. It seems that redaction criticism is not sufficient in the study of Luke-Acts. Other methods should be taken into consideration.

25. Matthew Sleeman, *Geography and the Ascension Narrative in Acts,* SNTSMS 146 (New York: Cambridge University Press, 2009); Steve Walton, "'The Heavens Opened': Cosmological and Theological Transformation in Luke and Acts," in *Cosmology and New Testament Theology* ed. Jonathan T. Pennington and Sean M. McDonough, LNTS 355 (London: T&T Clark, 2008), 60–73; Pennington, *Heaven and Earth in Matthew.* Michael Theobald, "Ich sah den Satan aus dem Himmel stürzen . . . ": Überlieferungskritische Beobachtungen zu Lk 10, 18–20," *BZ* 49 (2005): 174–90; Heinrich Baarlink, "Friede im Himmel: die lukanische Redaktion von Lk 19:38 und ihre Deutung," *ZNW* 76 (1985): 170–186.

26. Sleeman examined the heaven language in Acts 1:1–11:18. See Sleeman, *Geography and the Ascension Narrative,* 61–264.

27. Sleeman earned his first PhD from Cambridge University in 1996. His dissertation is entitled "The Geography of Citizenship Strategies in a Rural South Australian Aboriginal Community, 1940–1993."

After explaining Soja's three-space theory and exploring earlier research on the geography of Acts, especially the role of the ascension in Acts,[28] he applied the theory to the exegesis of Acts 1:1—11:18. He argued that the third spatial effect of 1:9–11 established "Jesus as the central character in the unfolding plot."[29] The ascension space, as the third-space, enables the mission and the growth of the early Christian movement. The third-space pervades all these chapters. Sleeman argued for an active role for the "absent Christ," labeling this a "post-Conzelmann reading of Acts." He did provide a "spatial" interpretation of Acts with many exegetical insights, the foremost of which was to view heaven as a space. He offered a suggestive way of reading the book of Acts. However, several weaknesses should be noted.

One major weakness is that Sleeman overlooks the conceptualization of space by the first audience. While solely drawing on a postmodern geographical theory that focuses on the third-space, Sleeman neglects the space categories of the first-century audience. Did ancient listeners/readers have any idea of the third-space theory of the twenty-first century? What was the ancient concept of geography? How did the Old Testament (such as the books of Genesis and Daniel) and the Second Temple literature (e.g. the book of *Jubilees*) view geography? Sleeman seems to have isolated the biblical text from its literary context (i.e. the Old Testament and the Second Temple literature) and placed the Sojan theory upon the text, thus offering this "spacial reading" of Acts. One asks how the examination of the perception of heaven in the Old Testament and in Second Temple Jewish literature will affect Sleeman's special reading of Acts.

Second, it seems that his spatialized ascension of Christ is the sole driving force of the evangelization and the growth of the church. One wonders where the role of the Holy Spirit in the mission of the apostles is. Time and again the Holy Spirit came upon the apostles and enabled them to do their mission. For instance, the Spirit took Philip away and placed him at Azotus, where Philip preached the gospel (Acts 8:39). The initiation of the Holy Spirit is also seen in the Apostle Paul's first mission trip with Barnabas (Acts 13:2). The Holy Spirit forbade Paul from preaching the word of God

---

28. Sleeman, *Geography and the Ascension Narrative*, 3–56.
29. Ibid., 67.

in the province of Asia (Acts 16:6). While emphasizing the importance of the ascension of Jesus, one should not overlook the role of the Holy Spirit as Sleeman does.

Third, Sleeman desired to present a post-Conzelmann reading of Acts. One wonders how Sleeman could offer a "post-Conzelmann reading of Acts" by focusing on a conception of geography that is external to the Book of Acts. It is well acknowledged that Conzelmann's comment on geography was based on his analysis of the Gospel of Luke. And there are more occurrences of heaven language in Luke's gospel than in Acts. One wonders how the result of the perception of heaven in Luke's gospel will affect Sleeman's understanding of the geography of Acts. Thus, it seems hard for him to provide a post-Conzelmann reading of Acts by ignoring the study of the Third gospel.

Another recent collection of essays that deals more with heaven language was edited by Jonathan T. Pennington and Sean M. McDonough.[30] The contributors of this book attempted to discern the cosmology for each book of the New Testament beginning with the cosmology of the Greco-Roman and ancient Jewish periods and proceeding through the Gospels, Paul's epistles, and the remaining New Testament books. Steve Walton provided a survey of cosmological terms in his essay on Luke-Acts.[31] Three aspects explored by Walton were the birth of Jesus, his baptism, and the ascension of Jesus. Then, he examined the word pair "heaven and earth." He viewed heaven as God's throne and the earth as inferior. Heaven is in contrast with the earth.[32] Walton went on to examine the unique passages that narrate the ascension of Jesus (Luke 24:50–53 and Acts 1:6–11). Generally speaking, this essay was a survey of the usage of "heaven" from the perspective of cosmology. It has been intriguing for readers to ponder the importance of heaven language in relation to Jesus and the Holy Spirit, etc., and thus this has stimulated further research in this area.[33]

---

30. Jonathan T. Pennington and Sean M. McDonough, eds., *Cosmology and New Testament Theology*, LNTS 355 (London: T&T Clark, 2008).

31. Walton, "The Heavens Opened," 60–73.

32. Ibid., 63.

33. Jonathan T. Pennington and Sean M. McDonough, "Introduction," ibid., 4.

The third work that deserves discussion was written by Jonathan T. Pennington, who was among the first to perform a thorough study of heaven language in the Gospel of Matthew, although not in Luke.[34] He challenged the long-assumed view that Matthew's expression "the kingdom of heaven" is nothing more than a circumlocution for the word God. Pennington's thesis is that Matthew uses the heaven and earth theme to highlight the tension between heaven/God and earth/humanity in his community and to seek an eschatological resolution.[35] He concluded that Matthew uses the heaven and earth theme "to emphasize the universality of God's dominion . . . to strengthen the Christological claims of the Gospel . . . to undergird the radical nature of the ethics and teachings of Jesus . . . and to encourage readers that they are the true people of God."[36] Pennington provided many insights and showed the significance of the heaven language in Matthew. Most importantly, Pennington addressed the neglected topic of the "heaven and earth" motif in the long history of Matthean scholarship. Nevertheless, this work has several weaknesses.

First, it seems that Pennington hastily jumped to the conclusion that the use of heaven is rhetorical rather referential when he surveyed the literature. For instance, the referential circumlocution was found not only in the Old Testament, such as in Daniel 4:23, but also in apocryphal books like 1 Maccabees, where "heaven" appears repeatedly in place of "God" or "Lord." The fact is that the OT and apocryphal literature have more influence on the New Testament writer (here Matthew) than rabbinic traditions and may be expected to influence at least some of the references in the Gospels. Therefore, the meaning of "heaven" in Matthew is probably a "both/and," reflecting both the referential and the rhetorical meanings of heaven (i.e. a reverence for God and a highlighting of God's universal dominion).

Another weakness of Pennington is that, time and again, one gets the impression that Pennington intentionally ignores the parallel passages in Synoptics, while emphasizing the distinctiveness of the "heaven" usage in Matthew. For instance, in his study of the "heaven and earth" pair, he

---

34. Pennington provided statistical data of the references to heaven. Pennington, *Heaven and Earth in Matthew*, 2, 123–124, 349–351.

35. Ibid., x.

36. Ibid., 343–348.

observed three occurrences of "the Lord of heaven and earth" in Matthew (5:18; 11:25; 24:35). He commented that this expression was common in the Second Temple literature, and that God was rarely referred to in this way in the NT (cf. Acts 17:24).[37] In actuality, each of these three occurrences in Matthew has a parallel in Luke (16:17; 10:21; 21:33). One wonders whether these parallels were not addressed because they might discredit the notion that Matthew's usage was distinctive.

This literature review shows that redaction studies that focus on the editorial process have not detected the Lukan significance of heaven language, though they should have. Sleeman's study focuses only on the first part of Acts. He ignores both the rest of the Lukan writings and the literary milieu of the biblical text. Walton merely surveys the "heaven" words in Luke-Acts from the perspective of cosmology. The heaven motif in Luke-Acts, therefore, remains neglected.

Thesis Statement

The introduction to this project shows that the heaven motif appears in significant narratives in Luke-Acts and is threaded through the whole fabric of Luke-Acts. The literature review demonstrates that the study of the heaven motif has long been a neglected topic. In recent Lukan scholarship, a few works focus on geography in the Book of Acts (Sleeman) or on cosmology in Luke-Acts (Walton) and have some discussion of heaven language, though their contribution to scholarship is limited since they seemed to ignore the heaven motif itself. By overlooking this motif, scholarship will be partially impoverished in its understanding of Luke-Acts, especially in Luke's presentation of salvation history.

Is heaven simply a place where God is? Is it the symbol of God's power? The answer to both questions is probably "no," since heaven in Luke-Acts is dynamic and not a static place. Heaven language points to the unfolding of cosmic warfare, the effects of which are to be well felt on earth. Heaven points to the arrival of God's eschatological kingdom on earth.

---

37. Ibid., 194.

Methodology

In order to pursue this topic, narrative criticism will be used primarily.[38] A narrative approach focuses on how biblical literature functions as literature by which the author (narrator) communicates messages. By careful study of the literature in terms of its internal elements (genre, structure, content, style) and its external elements (historical and social settings), one can ascertain its message.[39]

In addition to narrative criticism, redaction criticism of Luke's gospel will also be used.[40] Redaction criticism originated in the 1950s.[41] This approach has been found to be as a useful tool in the study of the Synoptic Gospels, the goals of which "are to understand why the items from the tradition were modified and connected as they were, to identify the theological motifs that were at work in composing a finished Gospel, and to elucidate the theological point of view which is expressed in and through the composition."[42] The approach of redaction criticism has been attested and used in the study of Synoptics.[43] By combining these two methods, we

---

38. We are fully aware of the weaknesses of narrative criticism. See Grant R. Osborne, *The Hermeneutical Spiral: A Comprehensive Introduction to Biblical Interpretation* (Downers Grove: IVP, 1991), 164–168.

39. Aune defines "narrative criticism" as "the interpretation and evaluation of a literary work through the careful examination and analysis of the work itself on the basis of both internal factors (e.g. genre, structure, content, style, source) and external factors (e.g. historical setting, social setting, biographical data, psychological information)." David E. Aune, *The New Testament in Its Literary Environment*, LEC (Philadelphia: Westminster, 1987), 19.

40. We are fully aware the weaknesses of redaction criticism. See Grant R. Osborne, "Redaction Criticism," in *New Testament Criticism & Interpretation*, eds. David Alan Black and David S. Dockery (Grand Rapids: Zondervan, 1991), 213–215; Stephen S. Smalley, "Redaction Criticism," in *New Testament Interpretation*, ed. I. Howard Marshall (Exeter, England: Paternoster, 1977), 191–192.

41. Hans Conzelmann was considered to be the pioneer who applied this method to study Luke-Acts though the term *Redaktionsgeschichte* (redaction criticism) did not appear in his work published in 1954: *Die Mitte der Zeit* (*The Theology of St. Luke*). Later Willi Marxsen applied this approach to study Mark's gospel. Willi Marxsen, *Der Evangelist Markus; Studien zur Redaktionsgeschichte des Evangeliums* (Göttingen: Vandenhoeck & Ruprecht, 1956). English Edition: Willi Marxsen, *Mark the Evangelist; Studies on the Redaction History of the Gospel*, trans. D. Juel J. Boyce, W. Poehlmann, and R. A. Harrisville (Nashville: Abingdon, 1969).

42. Perrin, *Redaction Criticism*, vi–vii.

43. F. Gerald Downing, "Redaction Criticism: Josephus' Antiquities and the Synoptic Gospels, pt 1," *JSNT* (1980): 46–65; F. Gerald Downing, "Redaction Criticism: Josephus' Antiquities and the Synoptic Gospels, pt 2," *JSNT* (1980): 29–48; Grant R. Osborne,

could discern the theological concerns of the author (narrator/redactor). In order to further our understanding of the passages in view, we will study each passage in its Old Testament, Second Temple literature and Greco-Roman world background if necessary. Examining each area against the backdrop of this literature will help explain the passages under consideration. The primary aim is not a source-critical study of the texts; rather, it is to see the continuity and discontinuity in the use of heaven language between the Old Testament and Second Temple literature, on the one hand, and Luke-Acts, on the other hand.[44] In the following, we will briefly discuss some of the previous narrative approaches to Luke-Acts and point out their strengths and weaknesses.

The narrative critical approach, which is one of the different approaches that have been applied to the study of Luke-Acts (historical,[45] theological,[46] and socio-historical[47]), has brought many insights to the discussion. Narrative

---

"Redaction Criticism and the Great Commission: A Case Study toward A Biblical Understanding of Inerrancy," *JETS* 19 (1976): 73–85.

44. Some call this a study of intertextuality. Julia Kristeva coined this term and defined it as the "transposition of one (or several) sign system(s) in to another." She says, "[t]exte se construit somme mosaique de citations, tout texte est aborption et transformation d'un autre texts." ("text is constructed mosaic amount of citations , every text is absorption and transformation of another text") (translation mine). Julia Kristeva, *Sēmelōtikē: Recherches pour une sémanalyse* (Paris: Éditions du Seuil, 1969), 146. See Jean Delorme, "Intertextualities about Mark," in *Intertextuality in Biblical writings* (Kampen, Netherlands: J. H. Kok, 1989), 35–42. See also Richard B. Hays, *Echoes of Scripture in the Letters of Paul* (New Haven: Yale University Press, 1993).

45. Gregory E. Sterling, *Historiography and Self-definition: Josephus, Luke-Acts and Apologetic Historiography*, SNT, 5 vols. (Leiden: E. J. Brill, 1992); Bruce W. Winter, ed., *The Book of Acts in Its First Century Setting*, 5 vols. (Grand Rapids: Eerdmans, 1993–96); Héctor Sánchez, *Das lukanische Geschichtswerk im Spiegel Heilsgeschichtlicher Übergänge* (Paderborn; Zürich: Schöningh, 2001); Alexander Mittelstaedt, *Lukas als Historiker: zur Datierung des lukanischen Doppelwerkes*, Texte und Arbeiten zum Neutestamentlichen Zeitalter 43 (Tübingen: Francke, 2005).

46. Joel B. Green, *The Theology of the Gospel of Luke* (New York: Cambridge University Press, 1995); Jacob Jervell, *The Theology of the Acts of the Apostles* (New York: Cambridge University Press, 1996); I. Howard Marshall and David Peterson, *Witness to the Gospel: The Theology of Acts* (Grand Rapids: Eerdmans, 1998); I. Howard Marshall, *Luke: Historian and Theologian* (Grand Rapids: Eerdmans, 1971); François Bovon, *Luke the Theologian: Fifty-five Years of Research (1950–2005)* (Waco, TX: Baylor University Press, 2006).

47. Jerome H. Neyrey, *The Social World of Luke-Acts: Models for Interpretation* (Peabody: Hendrickson, 1991); Ben Witherington, *The Acts of the Apostles: A Socio-Rhetorical Commentary* (Grand Rapids: Eerdmans, 1998); Bruce J. Malina and John J. Pilch, *Social-Science Commentary on the Book of Acts* (Minneapolis: Fortress, 2008); Jonathan Marshall,

criticism has not only been applied to the biblical text in general,[48] but also to Luke-Acts in particular.[49] Inquiries into the narrative of Luke-Acts trace back to Charles H. Talbert and Norman Petersen in the 1970s. Talbert's work examined Luke's patterning techniques by blending architectural analysis with narrative analysis.[50] Talbert argued that Luke-Acts was connected by structural patterns (parallelism, chiastic arrangement) and other devices. Talbert's work was a harbinger of literary approaches to the New Testament up to the present date.[51] Along this line, N. R. Petersen approached the narrative of Luke-Acts from the perspective of its poetic function, using the work of Roman Jakobson as his methodological basis. He focused on how the linear elements and repetitive cycles constitute the narrative's plot. In his pioneering work, *Literary Criticism for New Testament Critics*,[52] he pointed out some weaknesses of historical criticism. He stated that "the text itself must be comprehended in its own terms before we can ask of what it is evident, whether in relation to the times of writing or in relation to the events referred to in it."[53] The Biblical text as a literary document was no exception.

Jesus, Patrons, and Benefactors: Roman Palestine and the Gospel of Luke, WUNT 259 (Tübingen: Mohr Siebeck, 2009).

48. Robert Alter, *The Art of Biblical Narrative* (New York: Basic, 1981).

49. Charles H. Talbert, *Literary Patterns, Theological Themes, and the Genre of Luke-Acts* (Missoula: Society of Bibical Literature-Scholars, 1974); Robert C. Tannehill, *The Narrative Unity of Luke-Acts: A Literary Interpretation, Vol. 2* (Minneapolis: Augsburg Fortress, 1990); Luke Timothy Johnson, *The Literary Function of Possessions in Luke-Acts*, SBLDS 39 (Scholars, 1977); C. M. Tuckett, ed., *Luke's Literary Achievement: Collected Essays*, JSNTSup 116 (Sheffield: Sheffield Academic, 1995); Richard I. Pervo, *Profit with Delight: The Literary Genre of the Acts of the Apostles* (Philadelphia: Fortress, 1987); Daniel Marguerat, *The First Christian Historian: Writing the 'Acts of the Apostles'*, SNTSMS 121 (Cambridge: Cambridge University Press, 2002); David W. Pao, *Acts and the Isaianic New Exodus*, WUNT 2.130 (Tübingen: Mohr Siebeck, 2000); Alan J. Thompson, *One Lord, One People: The Unity of the Church in Acts in Its Literary Setting*, LNTS 359 (London: T&T Clark, 2008); Osvaldo Padilla, *The Speeches of Outsiders in Acts: Poetics, Theology and Historiography*, SNTSMS 144 (Cambridge: Cambridge University Press, 2008); David W. Pao, "Waiters or Preachers: Acts 6:1–7 and the Lukan Table Fellowship Motif," *SBL* 130 (2011): 127–144; Kazuhiko Yamazaki-Ransom, *The Roman Empire in Luke's Narrative* (New York: T&T Clark, 2010).

50. Talbert, *Literary Patterns*.

51. Tannehill, *The Narrative Unity of Luke-Acts*; Luke Timothy Johnson, *The Acts of the Apostles* (Collegeville: Liturgical, 2006); F. Scott Spencer, *Journeying through Acts: A Literary Cultural Reading* (Peabody: Hendrickson, 2004); F. Scott Spencer, *The Gospel of Luke and Acts of the Apostles*, Interpreting Biblical Texts Series (Nashville: Abingdon, 2008).

52. Norman R. Petersen, *Literary Criticism for New Testament Critics* (Minneapolis: Fortress, 1978).

53. Ibid., 20.

Starting with Robert C. Tannehill, scholarship began to move towards a more encompassing methodology called narrative criticism.[54] With a combination of historical criticism and narrative criticism, Swiss scholar Daniel Marguerat investigated various aspects of the narrative of Luke-Acts.[55] His study illustrated both the detail and the overall impact of Luke's narrative. Marguerat presented a thorough and convincing literary investigation of Luke-Acts; however, his study fell short on the following points. First, he did not seem to consider the narrative of the gospel, even though the title of his book indicated its inclusion; rather, he focused on select sections that were mostly from Acts. More importantly, as a narrative reading of Luke-Acts, Marguerat neglected the wider literary environments of Luke-Acts (the Old Testament and Second Temple Jewish literature). A consideration of the larger literary environments is essential to enriching the understanding of the narrative of Luke-Acts.

Scott Spencer also applied the narrative approach and used the first-century culture as the backdrop to provide a nuanced reading of Acts.[56] Spencer did offer an insightful narrative reading of Acts while not ignoring the theological importance of Acts, he did not explore theological issues at length.[57] A significant weakness of Spencer is that he clearly interacted little with the Second Temple literature.[58] While providing many insights, Spencer's insufficient interaction with the text's literary environment (i.e. the Old Testament and the Second Temple literature) undermines his understanding of the Book of Acts.

The above discussion shows that the narrative-critical approach is an indispensable tool in the reading of Luke-Acts. Scholars using this approach

---

54. Tannehill, *The Narrative Unity of Luke-Acts*.

55. Marguerat, *The First Christian Historian*.

56. Spencer, *Journeying through Acts*.

57. Ibid., 26–27.

58. Spencer stated in the introduction, "I partially make up for the lack of theological analysis by consistent attention to intertextual links with other portions of the biblical canon, especially the Old Testament, the Gospel of Luke, and the letters of Paul." See ibid., 27. One wonders why Spencer interacts little with the Second Temple literature. The Index of References at the end of the book shows this clearly. The book that Spencer cited the most was Josephus's *Antiquity*. For Philo's extensive writings, only a couple of references from *Aet. Mund.* are cited. And only seven books (*3 Macc.*; *Jub.*; *Ps-Philo*; *Pss. Sol.*; *T. Jud*; *T. Levi*; *T. Reub.*) are sporadically cited. Most books of the Jewish Pseudepigrapha were neglected by Spencer. As for the Qumran literature, only three verses from *1QS* were used. See ibid., 26–27.

have paid more attention to the biblical text than those who rely solely on the historical method. However, narrative scholars to date have either done insufficient studies on the wider literary environments of Luke-Acts or overlooked the literary milieu of the text. Therefore, studies on Luke-Acts should combine narrative analysis and redaction critical methods that focus on Luke's writings for their own sake with an analysis of Jewish background material informing the significance of Luke's heaven motif.

This first chapter has provided an analysis of the heaven motif, a literature review, a thesis statement and methodology of this study. Each of the following chapters will focus on one programmatic passage in which the heaven motif occurs. Chapter 2 will examine the heavenly hymn of Luke 2:14. Chapter 3 will study the fall of Satan in Luke 10:18. Chapter 4 will focus on the ascension narratives (Luke 24:50–53 and Acts 1:9–11). Chapter 5 will examine another programmatic passage, Acts 3:21. Each of these chapters will also study other related passages that make references to heaven. Chapter 6 will summarize the findings and provide the implications and areas for further research.

CHAPTER 2

The Invasion of the Heavenly Glory on Earth

Luke 2:14

Introduction

In chapter 1, we demonstrated that the heaven motif is a significant one that pervades Luke-Acts. This motif is first introduced by the heavenly hymn of Luke 2:14. The heavenly hymn is not simply a wish. It is an acclamation from heaven. Its significance is highlighted not only in the early chapters in the Gospel of Luke. The importance also extends to the rest of Lukan writings. This chapter will argue that Luke 2:14 is programmatic in Luke's presentation of salvation history. First, we will show through our analysis of the structure of the birth episode in Luke 2:8–20 that Luke 2:14 is particularly highlighted, suggesting that the glory of God in heaven has invaded earth by the birth of Jesus. Second, we will study the heaven motif in the heavenly hymn (Luke 2:14). We will show that there are two interrelated motifs in Luke 2:14: the heaven motif and the peace motif. These motifs are closely connected in Luke's gospel (Luke 1:78–79; 2:29–32 and 19:38). Last, this heavenly glory is manifested on earth through the outworking of the peace motif in Luke-Acts: (1) the heavenly glory has been manifested by peace in the ministries of Jesus (7:50; 8:48); (2) the heavenly glory is expressed in the mission of the disciples of Jesus (10:5–6); and (3) the heavenly glory is revealed by the peace manifested at an ecclesial level in Acts 9:31 and 10:36 where Jews and Gentiles have become one.

Narrative Analysis of the Infancy Narrative

In the Synoptic Gospels, Luke provides the most detailed account of the birth of Jesus: the foretelling of the birth of Jesus (Luke 1:26–38); Mary's song of praise (Luke 1:46–56); Zechariah's prophecy (Luke 1:67–79) and the birth of Jesus (Luke 2:4–21).[1] It is well-acknowledged that the infancy narrative contains important theological themes in Luke-Acts.[2] While Conzelmann overlooked the significance of the infancy narrative in his seminal work, *The Theology of St. Luke*,[3] Brown takes the view that Luke 1–2 is a prime expression of the evangelist's own perspective.[4] Luke as an inspired theologian and a reliable historian who "has carefully investigated everything from the beginning" (παρηκολουθηκότι ἄνωθεν πᾶσιν ἀκριβῶς) provides two chapters for the infancy narrative in his "orderly account" (καθεξῆς διήγησις) for his theological concerns.[5] Robert Tannehill rightly states that the infancy narrative introduces major themes to be developed as the story progresses.[6] The Lukan infancy narrative does have theological concerns that should not be overlooked. One of the concerns is the heaven

---

1. Matthew gives only eight verses (Matt 1:18–25) for the birth of Jesus. Comparatively, Matthew's infancy account is much briefer than Luke's. Mark totally omits it. For a discussion of the source of the infancy narrative, see Raymond Edward Brown, *The Birth of the Messiah: A Commentary on the Infancy Narratives in the Gospels of Matthew and Luke* (New York: Doubleday, 1993), 25, 32–33.

The story of the birth of Jesus has evoked much discussion among scholars. H. Gressmann proposes that it is based on a pre-Christian legend. R. Bultmann criticizes this view and argues that the birth story is from Hellenistic Christianity. See Rudolf Karl Bultmann, *The History of the Synoptic Tradition* (New York: Harper & Row, 1963), 297–299. I. H. Marshall argues that the story comes from Christian circles like the story of the John the Baptist in Luke 1. See I. Howard Marshall, *The Gospel of Luke: A Commentary on the Greek Text,* NIGTC eds. I. Howard Marshall and W. Ward Gasque (Grand Rapids: Eerdmans, 1978), 97.

2. Brown, *The Birth of the Messiah*, 25.

3. Conzelmann starts his work by "the significance of John the Baptist." He leaves the birth narratives unexamined. See Conzelmann, *Theology*, 18.

4. Brown, *The Birth of the Messiah*, 239–252.

5. Unless otherwise noted, Scripture quotations are from the NIV (1984); Greek text is from NA[27].

6. Robert C. Tannehill, *The Narrative Unity of Luke-Acts: A Literary Interpretation, Vol. 1: The Gospel according to Luke* (Philadelphia: Fortress, 1986), 15–44.

motif introduced by the heavenly hymn in Luke 2:14. First we will study the narrative accounts of the birth of John the Baptist and the birth of Jesus to show the significance of the heavenly hymn (Luke 2:14).

Following Luke's "orderly account" (καθεξῆς διήγησις), we will analyze the infancy narrative in order to see the importance of the heavenly hymn (Luke 2:14). The comparison of the two birth accounts in the Lukan infancy narrative demonstrates the significance of the heavenly hymn (Luke 2:14).

It is well acknowledged that Luke is fond of using two-by-two parallels in his two-volume narrative.[7] The first two-by-two parallel appears in the infancy narrative. The account of the birth of John the Baptist and that of the birth of Jesus share the following pattern: (1) the heavenly figure/angel announces the birth (1:13; 1:31); (2) the intervention of heaven into the inability of the woman to conceive (Luke 1:18; 1:26–27); (3) the woman's response to conception (Luke 1:24–25; 1:46–55); (4) the response to the birth (1:68–79; 2:10–14).[8]

While the two accounts share the same pattern, one finds an increasing force in the narrative of the birth of Jesus compared to that of John the Baptist. First, the announcement shows an increased force. While both John and Jesus will be great in the sight of the Lord (ἔσται γὰρ μέγας ἐνώπιον [τοῦ] κυρίου), only Jesus is called the Son of the Most High (οὗτος ἔσται μέγας καὶ υἱὸς ὑψίστου κληθήσεται) (1:15; 32).

Second, one finds increasing difficulty in the conception. It is harder for a virgin (παρθένος) who has no knowledge of a man (ἄνδρα οὐ γινώσκω) to conceive than for an old married woman who lives with her husband (ἐγὼ γάρ εἰμι πρεσβύτης καὶ ἡ γυνή μου προβεβηκυῖα ἐν ταῖς ἡμέραις αὐτῆς) (Luke 1:18).

---

7. Helmut Flender, *St Luke: Theologian of Redemptive History* (London: SPCK, 1967), 8; Giancarlo Biguzzi, "Witnessing Two by Two in the Acts of the Apostles," *Bib* 92 (2011): 1–20. Elsewhere one can find the two mission narrations (Luke 9 and 10) and the two ascension accounts (Luke 24 and Acts 1). One also finds the parallel structure of Jesus and Paul. Murphy-O'Conner convincingly presents six areas with the parallel: (1) the same age; (2) ripped from their roots; (3) adapting to an alien environment; (4) temporary vocations as prophet and Pharisee; (5) a second conversion; and (6) execution by the Romans; see J. Murphy-O'Connor, *Jesus and Paul: Parallel Lives* (Collegeville: Liturgical Press, 2007), 1–104; Andrew Jacob Mattill, "Jesus-Paul Parallels and the Purpose of Luke-Acts: H H Evans Reconsidered," *NovT* 17 (1975): 15–46.

8. Joel B. Green, *The Gospel of Luke*, NICNT ed. Gordon D. Fee (Grand Rapids: Eerdmans, 1997), 50.

Third, there are more people responding to the conception of Jesus than to that of John the Baptist. For the conception of John the Baptist, only Elizabeth responded (Luke 1:25); for that of Jesus there was Mary, Elizabeth, and the baby John the Baptist (1:46–55, 42–45).

Fourth, only an earthly figure, Zechariah, responded to the birth of John the Baptist (1:76–77), but to the birth of Jesus both earthly and heavenly beings responded. Zechariah, as the earthly figure, responded to John's birth but also prophesied the birth of Jesus (1:68–75, 78–79), which was also announced by a heavenly being, the angel in Luke 2:9–12.

Fifth, of special importance is what is missing in the narrative of the birth of John compared to the narrative of the birth of Jesus. When Jesus was born there was a heavenly announcement and a heavenly response, which do not appear in the birth of John the Baptist. Heaven is involved in the announcement of the birth of Jesus: the heavenly figure/angel and the glory of the Lord came onto the earth to announce the birth of Jesus (ἄγγελος κυρίου ἐπέστη αὐτοῖς καὶ δόξα κυρίου περιέλαμψεν αὐτούς) (Luke 2:9). The heavenly host also came to the earth (ἐξαίφνης ἐγένετο σὺν τῷ ἀγγέλῳ πλῆθος στρατιᾶς οὐρανίου αἰνούντων τὸν θεὸν) (Luke 2:13) to sing a heavenly hymn on account of the birth of Jesus: "Glory in the highest to God and peace on earth to men with whom He is pleased (δόξα ἐν ὑψίστοις θεῷ καὶ ἐπὶ γῆς εἰρήνη ἐν ἀνθρώποις εὐδοκίας) (Luke 2:14). It is the heavenly hymn (Luke 2:14) that brings forth the significance of the birth of Jesus and culminates the infancy narrative.

Therefore, we can see that Luke purposely provides a lengthy infancy narrative at the beginning of his orderly account. We also find that there is an increased force to the birth of Jesus compared to that of John the Baptist. The increased force reaches its peak in the response of heavenly beings that is absent in the narrative of John the Baptist. This increased force demonstrates the significance of the birth of Jesus. Next, we will show that the heavenly response (Luke 2:14) is the central point in the structure of the birth of Jesus (Luke 2:8–20).

Structural Analysis of Luke 2:8–20

The importance of chiastic structures in ancient literature has long been noticed by scholars. This method has also been applied to the analysis of biblical literature.[9] In what follows we will examine the structure of the birth narrative of Jesus (2:8–20). We will demonstrate that there is a chiastic structure within this passage. At the center of this chiasmus lies the hymn of the heavenly host (2:14). It is this hymn that Luke highlights in his account of the birth of Jesus. This paragraph could be broken down as follows.[10]

---

9. Chiastic writing uses words, phrases and ideas from the first half of the passage in reverse order in the second half. At the center of the chiastic structure is the focus of the author. John Breck, "Chiasmus as a Key to Biblical Interpretation," *St Vladimir's Theological Quarterly* 43 (1999): 249–267. See also Victor Rhee, "The Role of Chiasm for Understanding Christology in Hebrews 1:1–14," *JBL* 131 (2012): 341–362. Niles Wilhelm Lund shows the chiasmus from the OT to the NT. See Nils W. Lund, *Chiasmus in the New Testament: A Study in the Form and Function of Chiastic Structures* (Peabody, MA: Hendrickson Pubs, 1991), 139–411. This use can hardly be denied in the Gospels. C. Clifton Black outlined in *The Rhetoric of the Gospel* (2001) the craft of a literate minority, and noted the "miniature rhetorical masterpiece" in the thirteenth chapter of Mark. See C. Clifton Black, *The Rhetoric of the Gospel: Theological Artistry in the Gospels and Acts* (St Louis: Chalice, 2001), 47–70. Despite some grammatical roughness in that chapter, "audience contact is maintained by chiastic, coherent, and climactic narration," Black wrote. "If moderns have lost their appreciation for chiasmus it is because they have been educated in a vastly different way," said Augustine Stock in writing about elaborate memorization regimens of Greco-Roman education. "Chiasmus afforded a seriously needed element of internal organization in ancient writings, which did not make use of paragraphs, punctuation, capitalization and other such synthetic devices to communicate the conclusion of one idea and the commencement of the next." See Augustine Stock, "Chiastic Awareness and Education in Antiquity," *BTB* 14 (1984): 23–27. Wolfe even found a big chiastic structure in Luke-Acts. See Kenneth R. Wolfe, "The Chiastic Structure of Luke-Acts and Some Implications for Worship," *SwJT* 22 (1980): 60–71. Robert Stephen Reid found many chiastic structures in Mark's gospel. See Robert Stephen Reid, *Preaching Mark* (St Louis: Chalice, 1999), 18, 23–25, 50–51, 75–76, 100–103, 113–114, 140–142.

10. John Dart provides a chiastic structure of Luke 2:8–20. John Dart, "Scriptural Schemes: The ABCBAs of Biblical Writing," *ChrCent* 121 (2004): 22–25. Dart's version is indeed helpful; however, our analysis differs from Dart's in a couple of ways. First, his structure is based in the NRSV and lacks further analysis. This analysis is based on Greek text (NA[27]) and we provide an analysis on each parallel. Second, based on the NRSV, Dart divides verse fourteen into three parts: 14a, "Glory to God in the highest"; 14b, "and on earth peace"; 14c, "among people he favors." Thus he casts 14a and 14c as parallel and leaves 14b at the center of this chiastic pattern. This seems arbitrary because one cannot find any other equivalent parts in 14a and 14c except "God" versus "he." And, the idea of "Glory to God in the highest" does not parallel "among people he favors." Further, the prepositional phrase ἐν ἀνθρώποις εὐδοκίας could hardly be considered as equivalent to a noun with the prepositional phrase δόξα ἐν ὑψίστοις θεῷ. It is more likely that one should take verse fourteen (δόξα ἐν ὑψίστοις θεῷ ἐπὶ γῆς εἰρήνη ἐν ἀνθρώποις εὐδοκίας) as a whole.

Bovon finds a parallel structure in verse 14. He takes glory (A) as parallel to peace (A'); highest (B) as parallel to earth (B'). This analysis shows the beauty of the heavenly hymn. However, he does not provide the whole structure of the birth episode (Luke 2:8–20). François Bovon, *Luke 1, A Commentary on the Gospel of Luke 1:1–9:50*, trans. Christine M. Thomas (Minneapolis: Fortress, 2002), 90–91.

A ⁸Καὶ <u>ποιμένες</u> ἦσαν ἐν τῇ χώρᾳ τῇ αὐτῇ ἀγραυλοῦντες καὶ φυλάσσοντες φυλακὰς τῆς νυκτὸς ἐπὶ τὴν ποίμνην αὐτῶν. ⁹ καὶ ἄγγελος κυρίου ἐπέστη αὐτοῖς καὶ <u>δόξα</u> κυρίου περιέλαμψεν αὐτούς, καὶ ἐφοβήθησαν φόβον μέγαν. ¹⁰ καὶ εἶπεν αὐτοῖς ὁ ἄγγελος· μὴ φοβεῖσθε, ἰδοὺ γὰρ εὐαγγελίζομαι ὑμῖν χαρὰν μεγάλην ἥτις ἔσται παντὶ τῷ λαῷ,

B ¹¹ ὅτι <u>ἐτέχθη</u> ὑμῖν σήμερον σωτὴρ ὅς ἐστιν <u>χριστὸς κύριος ἐν πόλει Δαυίδ</u>. ¹² καὶ τοῦτο ὑμῖν τὸ σημεῖον, <u>εὑρήσετε βρέφος</u> ἐσπαργανωμένον καὶ <u>κείμενον ἐν φάτνῃ</u>.

C ¹³ καὶ ἐξαίφνης <u>ἐγένετο</u> σὺν <u>τῷ ἀγγέλῳ</u> πλῆθος στρατιᾶς <u>οὐρανίου</u> αἰνούντων τὸν θεὸν καὶ λεγόντων·

D ¹⁴ <u>δόξα ἐν ὑψίστοις θεῷ</u> καὶ <u>ἐπὶ γῆς εἰρήνη ἐν ἀνθρώποις</u> εὐδοκίας.

C' ¹⁵ᵃ Καὶ <u>ἐγένετο</u> ὡς ἀπῆλθον ἀπ' αὐτῶν εἰς τὸν <u>οὐρανὸν οἱ ἄγγελοι</u>, οἱ ποιμένες ἐλάλουν πρὸς ἀλλήλους·

B' ¹⁵ᵇ διέλθωμεν δὴ ἕως <u>Βηθλέεμ</u> καὶ ἴδωμεν τὸ ῥῆμα τοῦτο τὸ <u>γεγονὸς ὃ ὁ κύριος</u> ἐγνώρισεν ἡμῖν. ¹⁶ καὶ ἦλθαν σπεύσαντες καὶ <u>ἀνεῦραν</u> τήν τε Μαριὰμ καὶ τὸν Ἰωσὴφ καὶ <u>τὸ βρέφος κείμενον ἐν τῇ φάτνῃ</u>·

A' ¹⁷ <u>ἰδόντες</u> δὲ ἐγνώρισαν περὶ τοῦ ῥήματος τοῦ λαληθέντος αὐτοῖς περὶ τοῦ παιδίου τούτου. ¹⁸ καὶ πάντες οἱ ἀκούσαντες <u>ἐθαύμασαν</u> περὶ τῶν λαληθέντων ὑπὸ τῶν <u>ποιμένων</u> πρὸς αὐτούς. ¹⁹ ἡ δὲ Μαριὰμ πάντα συνετήρει τὰ ῥήματα ταῦτα συμβάλλουσα ἐν τῇ καρδίᾳ αὐτῆς. ²⁰ καὶ ὑπέστρεψαν <u>οἱ ποιμένες δοξάζοντες</u> καὶ αἰνοῦντες τὸν θεὸν ἐπὶ πᾶσιν οἷς ἤκουσαν καὶ εἶδον καθὼς ἐλαλήθη πρὸς αὐτούς.

The first parallel is between verse 13 and verse 15a, which share the following words: "angel" (ἄγγελος), "to be" (γίνομαι), and "heaven" (οὐρανός)/"heavenly" (οὐράνιος). In verse 13 the angels come down from heaven; in verse 15a the angels go back to heaven.

The second parallel is between verses 11–12 and verses 15b–16, with their references to "the city of David" (ἐν πόλει Δαυίδ) and to "Bethlehem" (Βηθλέεμ). Both passages speak of "the child lying in the manger" (τὸ βρέφος κείμενον ἐν τῇ φάτνῃ) and use the word "find" (ἀνευρίσκω). The pronoun "you" (ὑμῖν) in verse 12 parallels the word "shepherds" (οἱ ποιμένες) in verse 15b. Verses 11–12 relate the report of the angel to the shepherds concerning who and where Jesus is; verses 15b–16 narrate the shepherds trying to see the reality of what the angel tells them.

The third parallel stands between verses 8–10 and 17–20. Similar words occur in these verses: "the shepherds" (οἱ ποιμένες); "glory" (δόξα)/"glorify" (δοξάζω); and "to say" (λέγω)/"to speak" (λαλέω). In verses 8–10 the angel heralds the birth of Jesus to the shepherds, leading to a response of fear; in verses 17–20 the shepherds continue to respond when they see that things happened as the angel told them, which leads to a response of praise by Mary.

This structural analysis shows that there is a chiastic pattern in the narrative of the birth of Jesus. At the center of the structure stands the hymn of the heavenly host (2:14): "Glory to God in the highest, and on earth peace to men on whom his favor rests" (δόξα ἐν ὑψίστοις θεῷ καὶ ἐπὶ γῆς εἰρήνη ἐν ἀνθρώποις εὐδοκίας). According to the purpose of the chiastic structure, the center is the focus of the episode. Thus, we see Luke carefully arranges the structure of the birth of Jesus to single out the significance of the heavenly hymn (2:14).

The narrative analysis and the structural study show the importance of the heavenly hymn (Luke 2:14) at the beginning of the Lukan narrative (διήγησις) (Luke 1–3). The heavenly hymn of Luke 2:14 is the climax of Luke 1–3. It also functions as the programmatic passage for the rest of the Lukan writings to which we will reserve the discussion later in this chapter.

The study so far only provides a gleam of the importance of the heavenly hymn. The full picture of the significance of the heavenly hymn (2:14) could be seen in the rest narrative of Luke-Acts. Failing to recognize the programmatic significance of the heavenly hymn (Luke 2:14) in the Lukan writings one could not properly appreciate how Luke presents salvation history by employing the heaven motif in Luke-Acts. In the following we will demonstrate that Luke 2:14 is programmatic in Luke-Acts by analyzing the motifs in the heavenly hymn and by examining how these motifs work out in the entire Lukan program.

The Heavenly Hymn: Luke 2:14

In the following, we will study Luke 2:14 with regard to a textual issue, the term "highest" (ὕψιστος), the concept of heavenly glory, and the relationship between heaven and peace. First, we will examine the textual issue.

Textual Issue

The narrative analysis and chiastic structure show that the climax of the narrative of the birth of Jesus is the heavenly hymn (Luke 2:14). The heavenly hymn has evoked much discussion. It is described as "cryptic in the extreme, using neither definite article nor verbs to control the syntax."[11] Debates focus on the issue of the case of the noun εὐδοκία – nominative or genitive (εὐδοκία or εὐδοκίας). Evidences show that the genitive case outweighs the normative case.[12] Thus there is a bicolon structure: "glory" vs. "peace;" "the highest" (the abode of God-heaven) vs. "earth" (the inhabitance of men); "God" vs. "people." God gets glory in the highest since he gives peace to men.[13]

A Study of "Highest" (ὕψιστος)

Before proceeding to study the heaven motif and the peace motif in Luke 2:14, it would be helpful to study the plural form of the word ὕψιστος since

---

11. John Nolland, *Luke 1–9:20*, WBC 35A (Dallas: Word, 1989), 108.

12. This issue is well-discussed. In some ancient manuscripts (Y Q ¥ Û X) it is the nominative case, thus reading as follows: "Glory to God in the highest/ and on earth peace/ good will towards men." In some manuscripts, including A B, D, W, the word is in the genitive case. NA[27] prefers the latter. NA[28] is the same. The internal evidence also supports the latter reading. Glory in the highest heaven to God; and on earth peace for people whom he favors since the genitive case has the better internal and external support. Thus, εὐδοκίας should be accepted as the original reading. And the reading "glory in the highest to God, and on earth peace for people whom God's favors" fits well with Lukan theology in that it is God's free will to choose those whom he wills to favor and save. The old translation "men of good will" (CCD – Confraternity of Christian Doctrine) lacks theological support, because it suggests a human merit. Second, in the Dead Sea Scrolls, we find the equivalent genitive use both in Hebrew (1QH 4:32–33; 9:9: "children of His good will") and in Aramaic (4Q, 18: "a man of His good will). Third, the bicolon in Luke 19:38 "peace in heaven and glory in the highest heaven" also supports the bicolon reading of Luke 2:14. See Joseph A. Fitzmyer, *The Gospel According to Luke 1–9*, AB 28 (New York: Doubleday, 1981), 410–412; Nolland, *Luke 1–9*, 108–109; Brown, *The Birth of the Messiah*, 403–405. See also Albert M. Wolters, "Anthrōpoi Eudokias (Luke 2:14) and 'Nšy Rswn (4Q416)," *JBL* 113 (1994): 291–292. Thus the genitive case εὐδοκίας gains more support than the nominative case, and the bicolon structure of verse 14 could be established. Also see Metzger, *Textual Commentary*, 133.

13. B. E. Reid, "Puzzling Passages: Luke 2:14," *TBT* 32 (1994): 369.

some may claim that the notion of heaven is absent in this hymn. The following study will demonstrate that the word ὑψίστοις refers to "the highest heaven." This hymn does contain the notion of heaven.

First, the word ὑψίστοις in the LXX refers exclusively to the highest heaven where God abides.[14] Several examples will suffice. In Psalm 71:19 (LXX 70:19), the righteousness of God (אֱלֹהִים) reaches the high heavens (ἕως ὑψίστων) (עַד־מָרוֹם). Psalm 148:1 says "praise the Lord (יְהוָה) in the high heavens (ἐν τοῖς ὑψίστοις) (בַּמְּרוֹמִים)." Job 16:19 tells us that God dwells in the high heaven: "my Witness is in heaven, and He that testifies of me is in the high heavens (ὁ δὲ συνίστωρ μου ἐν ὑψίστοις)." The context indicates that Job's witness is God who lives in heaven (ἐν ὑψίστοις). This same God who testifies of him is in high heaven. This could also be found in Job 31:2: "For what would be the portion of God (אֱלוֹהַּ) from above, and the heritage of the Almighty from on high (שַׁדַּי מִמְּרֹמִים)." The LXX translation is ἐξ ὑψίστων.[15] One can find a pattern that the word ὕψιστος is used with prepositions like ἐν, ἐκ or ἕως. One also finds that in places where the plural form occurs with God/Lord, it refers to the high/highest heaven where God dwells.

Second, in the OT Apocrypha, one finds that all the occurrences of the plural form with prepositions (ἀπό, ἐν) refer to the highest heaven. For instance, in Wis 9:17, God sent you the Holy Spirit from the highest heaven (ἔπεμψας τὸ ἅγιόν σου πνεῦμα ἀπὸ ὑψίστων). Two cases are found in Sir 26:16 and 43:9. In Sir 26:16, "the sun arises in the high heaven of the Lord (ἥλιος ἀνατέλλων ἐν ὑψίστοις κυρίου)." In Sir 43:9, the glory of the stars

---

14. In Homer's *Il.* 5:756 and *Od.* 1:45, Zeus was called ὕπατος. The word (ὕψιστος) in the Hellenistic age, as it is known, has two root origins. One is the Greek word for Zeus. In classical Greek, this word is used to express the highest degree possible of perfection. The Hebrew word עֶלְיוֹן is exclusively rendered ὕψιστος in the LXX whenever it designates the name of God. Philo's use of ὕψιστος also demonstrates this point (see the following footnote). See G. Bertram, "ὕψιστος," *TDNT* 8: 615. In the LXX, the singular form (ὕψιστος) is almost exclusively used as a synonym for God except for a few passages where it is used as high heaven (Job 25:2 and Micah 6:6). In all the OT passages in which the word עֶלְיוֹן is used as the divine title, it is translated as ὕψιστος. Other Hebrew words are also translated as ὕψιστος such as מָרוֹם, שְׁמַיָּא מָעַל. Josephus seldom used this word (only in *Ant.* 16:163) and likewise Philo used it only a few times (as the Most High or of the Most High God, see *Leg.* 3:24, 3:82[3x]; *Post.* 1:89; *Plant.* 1:59; *Ebr.* 105; *Congr.* 58; *Mut.* 202; *Flacc.* 46; *Legat.* 157; 278 and 317.

15. All the plural forms of ὕψιστος in the LXX are the translation of the Hebrew word מָרוֹם.

makes the beauty of the sky, a brilliant adornment of the high heaven of the Lord (κάλλος οὐρανοῦ δόξα ἄστρων κόσμος φωτίζων ἐν ὑψίστοις κυρίου). Thus, we find the same usage that when the plural form appears with God or with the word Lord it means high heaven.

Third, the same usage also appears in OT Pseudepigrapha. The only appearance of ὕψιστος is in Psalms of Solomon 18:10. The word ὕψιστος denotes the highest heaven – "Great is our God and glorious, living in the highest heaven" (Μέγας ἡμῶν ὁ θεὸς καὶ ἔνδοξος ἐν ὑψίστοις κατοικῶν).[16]

Finally, an analysis of the Lukan use of the word ὕψιστος also helps us to understand its meaning. Luke is fond of the word "highest" (ὕψιστος). There are a total of thirteen occurrences of the term (ὑψίστος) in the New Testament; nine are in Luke-Acts.[17] The majority of the occurrences are in uniquely Lukan passages (1:32, 35, 76; 2:14; 6:35).[18] There are four occurrences in the infancy narrative (1:32, 35, 76; 2:14). The first two occurrences appear in the conception of the Jesus. The son born to Mary will be named Jesus, who will be great and called the Son of the Most High (οὗτος ἔσται μέγας καὶ υἱὸς ὑψίστου κληθήσεται) (1:32). The power of the Most High will overshadow Mary (δύναμις ὑψίστου ἐπισκιάσει) (1:35). The third occurrence appears in Zechariah's prophecy (1:76). John the Baptist will be called the prophet of the Most High (προφήτης ὑψίστου κληθήσῃ). Luke employs the absolute use of the word ὕψιστος as a synonym for God (Luke 1:32, 35; 6:35; Acts 7:48).[19] Luke is the only writer of the New Testament

---

16. Philo of Alexandra uses ὕψιστος only thirteen times. In most cases (nine out of thirteen) this term occurs with God, referring to "God the most high." In the other four instances, it occurs by itself, referring to "the Most High." Philo uses this word for his apologetic purpose in *Leg.* 3:82. "For he (Melchizedek) is the priest of the Most High God' [Gen 14:18]. Not that there is any other God who is not the most high; for God being one, is in the heaven above, and in the earth beneath, and there is no other besides him" (τοῦ γὰρ ὑψίστου ἐστὶν ἱερεύς, οὐχ ὅτι ἐστί τις ἄλλος οὐχ ὕψιστος ὁ γὰρ θεὸς εἷς ὢν "ἐν τῷ οὐρανῷ ἄνω ἐστὶ καὶ ἐπὶ τῆς γῆς κάτω, καὶ οὐκ ἔστιν ἔτι πλὴν αὐτοῦ).

17. Matt 21:19; Mark 5:7; 11:10; Luke 1:32, 35, 76; 2:14; 6:35; 8:28; 19:38; Acts 7:48; 16:17; Heb 7:1. Four times are in the plural form (Matt 21:19; Mark 11:10; Luke 2:14; 19:38); the rest are singular.

18. The word in Luke 8:28 finds its parallel in Mark 5:7, a parallel which Matthew omits. Another occurrence in Luke 19:38 has its parallels in Mark 11:10 and Matt 21:9. Both Luke and Matthew are based on Mark's account of Jesus's entry into Jerusalem (11:1–11).

19. In Mark 5:7, the demon possessed man called: "Jesus, Son of the Most High God" (Ἰησοῦ υἱὲ τοῦ θεοῦ τοῦ ὑψίστου). The genitive (τοῦ ὑψίστου) stands in apposition with God (τοῦ θεοῦ).

who uses the word ὕψιστος as a synonym for God.²⁰ The Lukan usage of the singular word ὕψιστος as a synonym for God indicates that he uses the plural form ὑψίστοις as the dwelling place (the high heaven) of the "highest God."²¹

The study of the word ὕψιστος in Second Temple literature shows that the plural form preceded by a preposition or an adverb refers to the highest heaven. The study of Luke's use of the singular form of the word ὕψιστος supports that the plural form, ὑψίστοις, is the highest heaven where God dwells.²² The study shows that there is the notion of heaven in Luke 2:14. Having studied the word ὑψίστοις we will study who is the heavenly glory before we proceed to examine motifs in the heavenly hymn (Luke 2:14).

Who/What Is This Heavenly Glory?

In the following, we will examine three passages (Luke 1:78–79; 2:29–32; and 3:4–6) to demonstrate that Jesus is the heavenly glory. Our attention will first turn to Luke 1:78–79.

---

20. In Luke 6:35, he uses "the sons of the Most High" instead of "the sons of the Father in heaven" (cf. Matt 5:45). The word ὑψηλο,ς occurs eleven times in the NT. It means "high place" ("mountain") (Matt 4:8; 17:1; Mark 9:2). In Heb 1:3 the plural form also denotes the high heaven (ἐν ὑψηλοῖς): "He is the radiance of the glory of God and the exact imprint of his nature, and he upholds the universe by the word of his power. After making purification for sins, he sat down at the right hand of the Majesty on high." The verb (ὑψόω) occurs twenty times in the NT. Nine are in Luke-Acts. The theologically important passages are in Acts 2:33 and 5:31, which denote the exaltation of Jesus (also see John 3:14; 8:28; 12:32, 34). In Luke 10:5, Jesus asks if Capernaum will be exalted to heaven and claims instead that it shall be brought down to Hades. In Luke 1:52; 13:11; and 18:14, the term refers to self-exaltation. The term ὑψηλοφρονέω in 1 Tim 6:17 means, "to be proud," or, "to think highly." Another cognate word, ὕψωμα, occurs twice in the NT. It means "height" in Rom 8:39 or "high things" in 2 Cor 10:5. Heb 7:26 says, "Τοιοῦτος γὰρ ἡμῖν καὶ ἔπρεπεν ἀρχιερεύς, ὅσιος ἄκακος ἀμίαντος, κεχωρισμένος ἀπὸ τῶν ἁμαρτωλῶν καὶ ὑψηλότερος τῶν οὐρανῶν γενόμενος." The comparative form ὑψηλότερος means "higher heaven" ("high heaven").

21. The other three references to the plural form in Matt 21:9, Mark 11:10 and Luke 19:38 refer to the highest heaven. Luke omits the definite article (τοῖς). "Hosanna in the highest" (ὡσαννὰ ἐν τοῖς ὑψίστοις) (Matt 21:9 and Mark 11:10).

22. Luke is fond of the word ὕψιστος. Nine of the thirteen occurrences of this word in the NT are found in Luke-Acts. Luke also uses the word ὕψος twice (Luke 1:78 and 24:49). In both cases, this word has a spatial reference referring to the height of heaven in which God dwells (also see Eph 4:8). The plural form of ὕψος is found in Heb 1:3 (ἐν ὑψηλοῖς). There it also means "heaven" or "high heaven." The context shows that this is the highest heaven where God dwells.

Luke 1:78–79

We will first show that the word ἀνατολή not only refers to the imagery of light but also refers metaphorically to Jesus Christ who is the glory/light from heaven. We will argue first that the word ἀνατολή denotes the imagery of light. Then we will demonstrate that the word ἀνατολή refers to the Messianic figure, Jesus Christ. Last, the phrase ἀνατολὴ ἐξ ὕψους in the context of Luke 1:78–79 refers to Jesus who comes from heaven. Jesus is the heavenly glory.

Ἀνατολή – The image of light

The word ἀνατολή refers to the imagery of light. First, this reading is found in the Old Testament. This word means "light" or "brightness" in Isaiah 60:19. In addition, this usage is also evidenced in Second Temple literature. The word ἀνατολή and the phrase ἡ ἀνατολὴ τοῦ ἡλίου are frequently used to refer to the "sunrise."[23] Josephus uses this word in reference to the rising of the sun in *Ant.* 9:39 (ἀνατολὴν ἡλίου).[24] Last, the theme of "light and darkness" in the immediate context and the appearance of the verb "to shine" (ἐπιφᾶναι) also favor this reading. Thus, the word ἀνατολή refers to the imagery of light.

Ἀνατολή – A metaphor of the messiah

This light imagery is a metaphor that denotes the Messiah, Jesus Christ.[25] Several points illustrate this view. First, this light or sunrise that denotes the eschatological Messiah could be found in the Old Testament. The eschatological figure is Jesus Christ. This could be evidenced again in the book of Isaiah (LXX). It has been noticed that the verb (ἀνατέλλω) repeatedly occurs in the context of God's eschatological restoration of Israel (Isa 42:9; 43:19; 44:4, 26; 45:8; 60:1; 61:11; 66:14). Further examination of these texts shows that the means God uses for the restoration of Israel is the Messiah (Isa 42:1–9) – the new thing is the appearance of the Messianic figure – Jesus

---

23. See Judg 5:31; 2 Macc 10:28; Wis 16:28; *Sib.* 2:329 and 8:427; *T. Job* 37:8; and 3 Macc 4:15.

24. In Philo, one finds the similar usage of this word: "The rising of the whole universe in *Mut.* 1:264 (ἀνατολὴ τῶν ὅλων)." In *Sep.* 3:187, planets rising and setting (ἀνατολαῖς καὶ δύσεσιν).

25. For a good study of Luke 78–79, see S. Gathercole, "The Heavenly Anatole (Luke 1:78–9)," *JTS* 56 (2005): 471–488.

Christ. Isaiah 45:8 is the springing up of salvation. In Isaiah 61:11, this refers to the messianic figure (cf. 61:1–3). In Zechariah 3:8, Ἀνατολήν (τὸν δοῦλόν μου Ἀνατολήν) refers to the Messiah of God. It is the translation of the Hebrew word (צֶמַח). One can also find the same usage in Zechariah 6:12 and Jeremiah 23:5.

Second, Philo comments on Zech 6:12: ("whose name is the East") in *Conf.* 62 (ἰδοὺ ἄνθρωπος ᾧ ὄνομα ἀνατολή). The following verse (*Conf.* 63) shows that this figure is the Son of God: "For the Father of the universe has caused him to spring up as the eldest son, whom, in another passage, he calls the firstborn; and he who is thus born, imitating the ways of his father" (τοῦτον μὲν γὰρ πρεσβύτατον υἱὸν ὁ τῶν ὅλων ἀνέτειλε πατήρ, ὃν ἑτέρωθι πρωτόγονον ὠνόμασε, καὶ ὁ γεννηθεὶς μέντοι, μιμούμενος τὰς τοῦ πατρὸς ὁδούς).[26]

Last, the verb "guide" (κατευθύνω) also favors this reading. This verb occurs only three times in the New Testament.[27] In Philo, *Decal.* 1:60, God "directs" (κατευθύνει). The contrast of "shadow of death" (σκιᾷ θανάτου) to the "way of peace" (ὁδὸν εἰρήνης) also indicates that ἀνατολὴ ἐξ ὕψους is a person who could direct those who sit in the shadow of death to the way of peace (life).

The above study shows that the word ἀνατολή conveys the image of light and metaphorically refers to the eschatological figure, Jesus Christ.

Ἀνατολὴ ἐξ ὕψους

A study of ἀνατολὴ ἐξ ὕψους shows that Jesus, the Messiah, the light/glory, is from heaven. First, Luke uses the noun ὕψος twice in his gospel (1:78 and 24:49), both referring to "heaven, where God stays." Second, Luke's usage of the cognate word ὕψιστος also supports that the word ὕψος refers to heaven/highest heaven. Luke's absolute usage of the word ὕψιστος (Luke 1:32, 35, 76; 6:35; Acts 7:48) as a synonym for God or in apposition to the name of God (Luke 8:28; and Acts 16:17) also supports that ὕψους refers

---

26. The plural form can refer to people of the East ("... that is respected by all the East and by all the west) (εἰς ὃν ἀνατολαὶ καὶ δύσεις ἀποβλέπουσιν) (*Legat.* 191).

27. In the other occurrences, it is used to refer to God or the Lord directing. In 1 Thess 3:11, Paul wishes that "the Lord Jesus would direct our way to you" (ὁ κύριος ἡμῶν Ἰησοῦς κατευθύναι τὴν ὁδὸν ἡμῶν πρὸς ὑμᾶς). In 2 Thess 3:5, he wishes that "the Lord would direct your hearts" (Ὁ δὲ κύριος κατευθύναι ὑμῶν τὰς καρδίας).

to heaven where God dwells. Last, the similar phrase, ἐξ ὕψους δύναμιν in 24:49 supports this reading. In 24:49, Luke relates that the power (the Holy Spirit) comes from on high (ἐξ ὕψους δύναμιν).[28] This study of the phrase ἀνατολὴ ἐξ ὕψους shows that Jesus is the glory from heaven.

In sum, the above study shows first that the word ἀνατολή conveys the image of light. Second, the word also metaphorically refers to the Messianic figure, Jesus Christ. Third, the phrase ἀνατολὴ ἐξ ὕψους and its context (1:78–79) show that Jesus Christ is the heavenly glory/light, who came down from heaven. Thus, we can see that the light/sunrise from on high refers to Jesus, the Messiah, the heavenly glory. We now turn our attention to the next passage.

Luke 2:29–32

The second passage (Luke 2:29–32) also shows that Jesus is the glory from heaven. The *Nunc Dimittis* is the response of Simeon when he saw baby Jesus in the temple. Two points in 2:29–32 need to be noted. First is about Simeon himself who says "dismiss your servant in peace" (ἀπολύεις τὸν δοῦλόν σου . . . ἐν εἰρήνῃ). This point relates closely to the word peace that we will reserve to later discussions. The second point is about the person of Jesus, who is "salvation . . . a light for revelation to the Gentiles and glory to your people Israel" (2:30–32). In the following we will focus on the second point to show that Jesus is the heavenly glory.

Φῶς εἰς ἀποκάλυψιν ἐθνῶν

We will show that the phrase "light for revelation to the Gentiles" (φῶς εἰς ἀποκάλυψιν ἐθνῶν) refers to Jesus who is the glory from heaven. The context tells us that "light" here stands in apposition to "salvation" (τὸ σωτήριόν). Here again we see the light image. The idea of light and salvation (φῶς/τὸ σωτήριόν) echoes Isaiah 49:6; 42:6; and 60:3 (LXX). The Servant of YHWH has been described as light and salvation in the book of Isaiah (Isa 42:1–9; 49:1–6). Jesus is the light. The adverbial phrase εἰς ἀποκάλυψιν further defines the "light" (φῶς). The word ἀποκάλυψις often relates to God who

---

28. Paul talked about the resurrected Jesus who ascended on high (Eph 4:8). This word occurs six times in the NT. Paul uses it twice (Eph 3:18; 4:8); James and John use it once (Jas 1:9 and Rev 21:16). Another cognate word (ὕψωμα) occurs twice in the NT. It means "height" in Rom 8:39 or "high things" in 2 Cor 10:5.

dwells in heaven. Jesus is the light sent from God who dwells in heaven. So he is called the light for revelation to the Gentiles. Therefore, Jesus is the glory from heaven.

Furthermore, this passage emphasizes the inclusion of Gentiles in God's salvific work. Luke 2:29–32 is an allusion to Isaiah 42:6 (cf. Isa 49:6), which relates the work of the suffering servant (i.e. Jesus). The phrases "a light for revelation to the Gentiles" (φῶς εἰς ἀποκάλυψιν ἐθνῶν) and "in the sight of all people" (κατὰ πρόσωπον πάντων τῶν λαῶν) that appear at the very beginning of the Lukan writing anticipate the arrival of salvation to all human beings.[29] Salvation to the Gentiles in particular is emphasized, as the book of Acts demonstrates.

Δόξαν λαοῦ σου Ἰσραήλ

A study of the phrase "glory to your people Israel" also shows that Jesus is the heavenly glory. The glory of the Lord (δόξα Κυρίου) that filled the tabernacle (ἐνέπλησε τὴν σκηνήν) in the book of Exodus is considered as the divine presence of YHWH.[30] The concept of "glory to the people of Israel" (δόξαν λαοῦ σου Ἰσραήλ) finds its parallel in Isaiah 60:1–2: "Shine, shine, O Jerusalem, for your light has come, and the glory of the Lord has risen upon you . . . the Lord will appear over you and his glory will be seen over you" (φωτίζου φωτίζου Ιερουσαλημ ἥκει γάρ σου τὸ φῶς καὶ ἡ δόξα κυρίου ἐπὶ σὲ ἀνατέταλκεν . . . φανήσεται κύριος καὶ ἡ δόξα αὐτοῦ ἐπὶ σὲ ὀφθήσεται).[31] The context of this passage is about the eschatological ingathering of the people of Israel. The idea of the bestowal of the heavenly glory to the covenant people survives in Bar 4:24: "So shall they see shortly salvation from your God which shall come upon you with great glory and brightness of the Everlasting" (οὕτως ὄψονται ἐν τάχει τὴν παρὰ τοῦ θεοῦ ὑμῶν σωτηρίαν ἣ ἐπελεύσεται ὑμῖν μετὰ δόξης μεγάλης καὶ λαμπρότητος τοῦ αἰωνίου). Further, the combination of the appearance of glory and salvation occurs in Isaiah 46:13: "I bring near my righteousness, and the salvation that comes from me shall not tarry; and I have placed salvation in Zion

---

29. Pao, *Isaianic New Exodus*, 228.

30. James K. Bruckner, *Exodus* (Peabody: Hendrickson, 2008), 330; Thomas B. Dozeman, *Exodus* (Grand Rapids: Eerdmans, 2009), 764.

31. Translation mine.

for Israel for my glory" (ἤγγισα τὴν δικαιοσύνην μου καὶ τὴν σωτηρίαν τὴν παρ' ἐμοῦ οὐ βραδυνῶ δέδωκα ἐν Σιων σωτηρίαν τῷ Ισραηλ εἰς δόξασμα).[32] Thus we can see Jesus, who is salvation, is the heavenly glory that appears to the people of Israel.

In light of the above study, light and glory are closely related to salvation. The context of this passage also suggests that light and glory stand in apposition to salvation (2:29–32).[33] The word "light" is in apposition to the word "glory." Jesus, the divine glory became the glory to the people of Israel and the glory/light of the nations. Jesus is the heavenly glory. Next, we will examine Luke 3:4–6 to show that Jesus is the heavenly glory.

Luke 3:4–6

That Jesus is the heavenly glory could also be demonstrated in the third passage (Luke 3:4–6). Luke 3:4–6 is an explicit quotation of Isaiah 40:3–5. This quotation is anticipated by Luke 2:30 (εἶδον οἱ ὀφθαλμοί μου τὸ σωτήριόν σου) since the singular neuter form of salvation (τὸ σωτήριόν) recurs in 3:6. In 3:4–6, Luke follows Isaiah 40:3–5 (LXX) with almost the same wording except for an omission and some minor changes.[34] Luke omits, "And the glory of the LORD shall be revealed" (καὶ ὀφθήσεται ἡ δόξα κυρίου). Isaiah 40:5 LXX reads καὶ ὀφθήσεται ἡ δόξα κυρίου καὶ ὄψεται πᾶσα σὰρξ τὸ σωτήριον τοῦ θεοῦ ὅτι κύριος ἐλάλησεν (MT: וְנִגְלָה כְּבוֹד יְהוָה וְרָאוּ כָל־בָּשָׂר יַחְדָּו כִּי פִּי יְהוָה דִּבֵּר). Luke's omission is probably "due to the presence of a similar phrase that contains a central idea in Luke's writings."[35] Marshall argues that the reason for the omission is that "perhaps Luke did not regard it as being fulfilled in the earthly ministry of Jesus (24:26; Acts 3:13)."[36] This seems unlikely. First, it is true that it is suffering that brought Jesus into his glory. However, this does not necessarily mean that the glory of the Lord does not appear in the ministry of Jesus. For example, Jesus's raising of the

---

32. Translation mine.

33. John J. Kilgallen, "Jesus, Savior, the Glory of Your People Israel," *Bib* 75 (1994): 305–28; Bovon, *Luke 1:1–9:50*, 103.

34. For a helpful discussion of these changes, Marshall, *Luke*, 136–37. Also see David W. Pao and Eckhard J. Schnabel, *Luke* in Gregory K. Beale and Donald A. Carson, eds., *Commentary on the New Testament Use of the Old Testament* (Grand Rapids, MI; Nottingham: Baker; Apollos, 2007), 277.

35. Pao and Schnabel, *Luke*, 277.

36. Marshall, *Luke*, 137.

widow's son at Nain is described as the visitation of God on his people (i.e. the presence of God/the glory of God appearing [7:16]). Later, we will show that the glory of heaven did appear in the ministry of Jesus (7:50; 8:48). Second, the context of Isaiah 40:5 is more likely construed that "the glory of the Lord" stands in the apposition to salvation: "And the glory of the LORD shall be revealed, and all flesh shall see it together." Here salvation is equated with the glory of the Lord. Thus, Jesus is the glory of Lord (i.e. the glory of heaven).[37]

Therefore, based on the study of three passages (Luke 1:78–79; 2:29–32 and 3:4–6) one will see that Jesus is the heavenly glory.

In sum, our study shows that there is the notion of heaven in the heavenly hymn (Luke 2:14) and that Jesus is the heavenly glory. Bearing this in mind we will study the motifs in the heavenly hymn.

Heaven and Peace in Luke 2:14

The eleven-word heavenly hymn: "Glory to God in the highest, and on earth peace to men on whom his favor rests" (δόξα ἐν ὑψίστοις θεῷ καὶ ἐπὶ γῆς εἰρήνη ἐν ἀνθρώποις εὐδοκίας) – parallels "glory in heaven" and "peace on earth" as well as "God" and "human beings." Two motifs could be identified in this heavenly hymn: the heavenly glory motif (about God) and the earthly peace motif (about human beings). The proclamation of divine glory in heaven (δόξα ἐν ὑψίστοις θεῷ) is paralleled by the declaration of the divine peace on earth (ἐπὶ γῆς εἰρήνη ἐν ἀνθρώποις εὐδοκίας).

Summary

The heavenly hymn should not simply be viewed as a praise or exaltation; it is also an acclamation, "ein Hymnus im akklamatorischen Stil."[38] The heavenly host proclaimed God's work done through the birth of Jesus. This is the heavenly response to the birth of Jesus. The heavenly hymn contains two motifs: the heaven motif and the peace motif. These two motifs encompass "the glory in heaven and the peace on earth." Its cosmic dimension

---

37. Another passage from the book of Isaiah also supports the notion that Jesus is the glory of heaven. Isaiah 60:1 is the ingathering of Israel by the appearance of the glory of the God (the messianic figure, Jesus Christ).

38. B. Olsson, "The Canticle of the Heavenly Host (Luke 2:14) in History and Culture," *NTS* 50 (2004): 147–166; Erik Peterson, *Theologische Traktate* (Munich: Kösel, 1951), 317.

includes both the divine God and human beings. In the following section we will demonstrate the relationship between the heaven motif and the peace motif. We will also demonstrate that the heaven motif is actually expressed in the peace motif. We will first study the relationship between the heaven motif and the peace motif.

The Heaven Motif and the Peace Motif

We will first provide a survey of the study of the peace motif in recent Lukan scholarship to show the need for our study of the peace motif and the heaven motif. Second, we will investigate the term "peace" in Luke-Acts to demonstrate that Luke is purposely using the term "peace" for his theological concerns. Third, we will study the term "peace" in the heavenly hymn (Luke 2:14) to show that "peace" primarily refers not to a good relationship among human beings, but to the eschatological peace (i.e. salvation). Fourth, we will examine the relationship between the two motifs to show that they are closely connected. This relationship has first been prophesied in the *Benedictus* (1:78–79). This relationship has also been materialized in the *Nunc Dimittis* (2:29–32). The relationship between the two motifs has finally been confirmed by human acclamation (19:38), since a similar phrase (δόξα ἐν ὑψίστοις θεῷ καὶ εἰρήνη) recurs in Luke 19:38. Those who reject this "glory" are therefore rejecting this "peace" (Luke 19:38) and as such will be judged. In demonstrating this, we will show that the heaven motif has been expressed in the peace motif. The "peace" motif in Luke-Acts is actually the outworking of this important programmatic passage (Luke 2:14). The heaven motif has been made manifest by the peace motif.

Peace Motif in Recent Lukan Scholarship

Scholars have acknowledged the importance of the term "peace" in Luke-Acts.[39] Guy D. Nave noticed the importance of peace in Luke-Acts and

---

39. Willard M. Swartley, "Politics and Peace (Eirēnē) in Luke's Gospel," in *Political Issues in Luke-Acts* (Maryknoll: Orbis Books, 1983), 18–37; William Klassen, "A Child of Peace" (Luke 10:6) in First Century Context," *NTS* 27 (1981); ibid., 488–506; Willard M. Swartley, *Covenant of Peace: the Missing Peace in New Testament Theology and Ethics* (Grand Rapids: Eerdmans, 2006), 121–176.

studied the word peace in a political sense.[40] Pieter G. R. De Williers studied the term "peace" particularly in biblical spirituality. His article discussed how Luke-Acts provided material that illuminated the role and function of peace in the spiritual life of the early Christian community.[41] John J. Kilgallen focused on the way of peace according to Luke. He viewed that by and large peace was esteemed as a gift by which God put an end to various types of strife and confusion.[42] J. Grassi, in his book, *Peace on Earth: Roots and Practice*, took his starting point from the angelic proclamation of "peace on earth" at Jesus's birth (Luke 2:14). He focused on social justice, traced the theme of peace through Luke's gospel with a special emphasis on the very practical means that Jesus suggested to make it a reality.[43] A. Lindemann studied peace in the entire New Testament. He started from Luke 2:14 and provided a survey of NT perspectives on peace.[44]

Of special mention is the study of Willard M. Swartley. Swartley noticed the importance of the term "peace" in Luke.[45] He studied each individual occurrence of the term "peace."[46] He emphasized peace politically and in relation to justice.[47] He studied peace from the viewpoint of ethics. In a similar manner, he treated the peace occurrences in Acts. He grouped ecclesial occurrences of peace (7:26; 9:31; 10:36; 15:33).[48] He also related peace to the world of *Pax Romana* (12:20; 16:36; 24:2).[49] Then he related

---

40. Guy D. Nave, Jr., "No Pax Romana: A Lukan Rejection of Imperial Peace," *Theologies and Cultures* 2 (2005): 56–72.

41. Pieter G. R. De Villiers, "Peace in Luke and Acts: A Perspective on Biblical Spirituality," *Acta Patristica et Byzantina* 19 (2008): 110–134.

42. John J. Kilgallen, ""Peace" in the Gospel of Luke and Acts of Apostles," *Studia Missionalia* 38 (1989): 55–79.

43. Joseph A. Grassi, *Peace on Earth: Roots and Practices from Luke's Gospel* (Collegeville, MN: Liturgical Press, 2004), 1–168; Joseph A. Grassi, *Jesus Is Shalom: A Vision of Peace from the Gospels* (New York: Paulist, 2006), 92–129.

44. A. Lindemann, "'. . . und auf Erden Frieden.' (Lk 2, 14): Zum Friedensverständnis im Neuen Testament," *BK* 61 (2006): 138–143.

45. Swartley, *Covenant of Peace*, 121–151.

46. Ibid., 123–128.

47. Ibid., 133–144.

48. Ibid., 155.

49. Ibid., 164.

peace to justice.⁵⁰ Swartley concluded that Luke takes the peace motif as anti-imperial propaganda.

Likewise, Yamazaki-Ransom Kazuhiko argued that Luke purposefully employed Roman imperial ideology to criticize the Roman emperors.⁵¹ Roman emperors promised to bring peace (εἰρήνη) to the whole world. The phrase *Pax Romana* ("Roman peace") was widely used in Roman propaganda. Inscriptions of Augustus show that he was considered to be Rome's "savior" (σωτήρ) who would bring "peace" (εἰρήνη) to the world. This indicates that, for Luke, Jesus, not Augustus, is the true Savior and he alone can bring real peace to the world.⁵² Certainly, Luke employs the peace motif to bring out an anti-imperial aspect (Acts 12:20; 16:36; 24:2). Other peace occurrences in Luke (1:79; 2:29; 7:50; 8:48; 10:5, 6; 19:38) and Acts (Acts 7:26; 9:31; 10:36; 15:33) indicate that Luke has a larger agenda in that the peace motif relates to the eschatological kingdom of God regarding which we will provide full discussion in due course.

These scholars have indeed contributed to Lukan scholarship in terms of peace from various perspectives. However, a study of the inter-relationship between the peace occurrences in Luke-Acts is still lacking, and the relationship between the peace motif and the heaven motif remains unexamined. The fact that the word peace (εἰρήνη) in the heavenly hymn (Luke 2:14) introduces a significant motif that goes through Luke-Acts remains untouched. The failure to apprehend the peace motif in the Lukan writings and its connection with the heaven motif will inevitably impoverish our understanding of Luke's theological concerns in presenting salvation history. With these concerns we will first study the peace occurrences in Luke-Acts.

The Term Peace (εἰρήνη) in Luke-Acts

Among Synoptic writers, Luke employs the term "peace" most frequently.⁵³ He uses it fourteen times in his gospel and nine times in Acts. Mark uses

---

50. Ibid., 171–173.

51. Yamazaki-Ransom, *The Roman Empire in Luke's Narrative*, 82–85.

52. Ibid., 83.

53. The usage of the term of peace in NT is as follows: (1) the general sense is the normal state of all things (1 Cor 14:33, "For God is a God not of disorder but of peace"); (2) the eschatological salvation of the whole man (this is the usage that Lukan emphasizes); (3) the peace relationship with God (Eph 2:14–17); (4) the relationship among people (Rom 14:17, "The kingdom of God is not food and drink but righteousness and peace and joy in

it only once (5:34) and Matthew four times (Matt 10:13 [2x], 34 [2x]).[54] Out of the fourteen occurrences in Luke-Acts, ten are in uniquely Lukan passages (1:79; 2:14, 29; 7:50; 10:5, 6 [2x]; 14:32; 19:42 and 24:36).[55] Two occurrences in Luke have synoptic parallels: Luke 11:21 (Mark 3:27 and Matt 12:29) and 19:38 (Mark 11:10 and Matt 21:9). The other two appearances in Luke 8:48 and 12:51 find their parallels to Mark 5:34 and Matthew 10:34 respectively.[56] Luke's unique usage and redaction emphasis of the term "peace" in his gospel reveals his theological concerns.

"Peace" (εἰρήνη) in Luke 2:14

In this section, we will first summarize Lukan scholarship on the word "peace" in Luke 2:14. Then we will argue that the concept of peace in the heavenly hymn (Luke 2:14) is primarily not an ordinary interpersonal relationship but is the eschatological peace (i.e. salvation). This notion is well-rooted in the Old Testament and is evidenced in Second Temple literature as well as in Luke's gospel (in the *Benedictus*).

---

the Holy Spirit." See also 1 Cor 7:15; Jas 3:18); and (5) peace of soul (Rom 15:13, "May the God of hope fill you with all joy and peace in believing"). The verb (εἰρηνεύω) means "to keep peace" and only occurs in Mark 9:50; Rom 12:18; 2 Cor 13:11 and 1 Thess 5:13). The word (εἰρηνικός) occurs twice in NT and means "peaceful" or "peaceable" (Heb 12:11 and Jas 3:17). The adjective (εἰρηνοποιός) only appears in Matt 5:9 and means "peacemaker." The verb (εἰρηνοποιέω) occurs only in Col 1:20, and it means "make peace" on a cosmic scope related to salvation.

54. Luke also uses this term seven times in Acts two which we will discuss later. The statistic shows that Luke ranks number one among NT writers in using the term "peace." The word peace occurs eighty-nine times in NT. In the Gospel of John six times; Romans ten; 1 Corinthians four; 2 Corinthians two, Galatians three; Ephesians eight; Philippians three; Colossians two; 1 Thessalonians three; 2 Thessalonians three; Titus one; Philemon one; Hebrews four; James three; 1 Peter three; 2 Peter two; 2 John one; 3 John one; Jude one; and Revelation two times.

55. One may say that Luke 10:1–16 has a parallel with Matt 10:5–16. The comparison of these two passages and the existence of Luke 9:1–6 show that the charge of the seventy(-two) is a different episode that is uniquely to Luke. See William Hendriksen, *The Gospel of Luke* (NTC: Baker, 1978), 573.

56. Luke 11:21 the parable of Jesus and Beelzebul – the basic Greek meaning is "a state of peace," "safe," "security." In Luke 12:51; Acts 7:26 and Acts 12:20, Luke here uses the developed meaning of peace as "relationship between people." See *T. Gad* 6:3. Philo uses it as "Peaceful relationship between Abraham and Lot." In Luke 14:32, peace denotes unconditional submission. See 1 Sam 30:21; 2 Sam 8:10; 1 Chr 18:10; Ps 121:6). Peace means "political peace," "free from war." See LXX Prov 17:1; Isa 14:30. Luke 24:36; Acts 15:33 and 16:36; Jesus greets his disciples with "peace to you." This is the greeting used for coming and going (cf. Gen 29:6; Exod 18:7). In Acts 24:2, it may denote a "state of rest and free from war."

A Survey of the Study of "Peace" in Luke 2:14

The word "peace" in Luke 2:14 (ἐπὶ γῆς εἰρήνη ἐν ἀνθρώποις εὐδοκίας) has received much discussion. Brown provided a two-page footnote analyzing the structure of Luke 2:14 with a focus on the discussion of the word εὐδοκίας. This is helpful for the understanding of 2:14; however, he missed the point of this verse by overlooking the importance of the word peace (εἰρήνη).[57] Some scholars view that the peace is the manifestation of God's peace with humans.[58] E. Earle Ellis comments that this peace is that "the redemption has arrived."[59] Fred B. Craddock takes this peace as "the eschatological hope" in the Old Testament (Isa 9:6; Zech 9:9–10) that "will be fulfilled in Jesus."[60] Green views this peace as "salvation"/"good news."[61] Nolland points out that this peace is "especially linked to the coming messianic salvation."[62] Marshall even states more clearly that "the peace is tantamount to σωτηρι,α."[63] The above survey shows that some scholars have noticed that the peace here relates to God's redemptive work. Others have correctly pinpointed that the peace here is the eschatological peace/salvation. However, substantial evidence to support that the peace in Luke 2:14 refers to eschatological salvation seems still lacking. In the following we will show that the notion of eschatological peace is well-rooted in the Old Testament, survives in Second Temple literature and is evidenced in Lukan writings.

Eschatological Peace in the Old Testament

The concept of the Hebrew word שָׁלוֹם is not limited to interpersonal relationships. It conveys the idea of eschatological peace. This can be seen in many Old Testament books, especially in the book of Isaiah.[64] First, Isaiah

---

57. Brown, *The Birth of the Messiah*, 403–405.
58. Bovon, *Luke 1:1–9:50*, 90; Fitzmyer, *Luke 1–9*, 379; Darrell L. Bock, *Luke 1:1–9:50*, BECNT (Grand Rapids: Baker, 1994), 220; Reid, "Puzzling Passages," 369. See also H. Beck and C. Brown, "Peace," in "NIDNTT,": 2:781.
59. E. Earle Ellis, *The Gospel of Luke* (Marshall, Morgan & Scott, 1981), 80–82.
60. Fred B. Craddock, *Luke,* IBC (Louisville: Westminster, 1990), 36.
61. Green, *The Gospel of Luke*, 137. See also William Klassen, "Peace," in David Noel Freedman, "The Anchor Bible Dictionary," 5: 209.
62. Nolland, *Luke 1–9*, 108.
63. Marshall, *Luke*, 112.
64. Bart J. Koet, "Isaiah in Luke-Acts," in *Isaiah in the New Testament* (London: T&T Clark, 2005), 79–100; James A. Sanders, "Isaiah in Luke," *Int* 36 (1982): 144–155; Peter

9:6–7 speaks of the coming of the Messiah who is described as the prince of peace who will establish the eschatological peace in his kingdom. With the coming of the Messiah, the eschatological peace of God's reign will be realized (Isa 32:17–18).⁶⁵ The eschatological peace is depicted as salvation to Zion announced by a divine messenger (Isa 52:7): "How beautiful upon the mountains are the feet of him who brings good news, who publishes peace, who brings good news of happiness, who publishes salvation, who says to Zion, 'Your God reigns'" (ὡς ὥρα ἐπὶ τῶν ὀρέων ὡς πόδες εὐαγγελιζομένου ἀκοὴν εἰρήνης ὡς εὐαγγελιζόμενος ἀγαθά ὅτι ἀκουστὴν ποιήσω τὴν σωτηρίαν σου λέγων Σιων βασιλεύσει σου ὁ θεός). The herald defines the good news as the coming of God (40:9), the salvific reign of God in peace and justice.⁶⁶ The everlasting peace that is salvation was promised metaphorically to the people of Israel who were barren and desolate (Isa 54:10).⁶⁷ A promise of help and healing is peace from the Lord (57:19). For the unjust and oppressors, there is no peace, but rather punishment (Isa 59:8). Peace as salvation will be provided at the ingathering of the dispersed Israel (Isa 60:17). One can see that the eschatological peace has been well-expressed in the Book of Isaiah.

Second, this idea is also found in the Book of Ezekiel. The covenant of peace will be present at the coming of the Messianic age (34:25; 37:26). In the Book of Zechariah, one finds everlasting peace in the eschatological era.

Therefore, that the Hebrew word שָׁלוֹם has the concept of eschatological peace is well-attested in the Old Testament. The concept of eschatological peace also appears in Second Temple literature. To this we now turn.

Eschatological Peace in Second Temple Literature

In what follows, we will study the term "peace" in Second Temple literature. First, eschatological peace (i.e. salvation) is found in Bar 3:13.⁶⁸ The context reveals that Israel was in the land of their enemies (3:10–12), but if they

---

Mallen, *The Reading and Transformation of Isaiah in Luke-Acts,* LNTS (London: T&T Clark, 2007), 105–113.

65. J. A. Motyer, *Isaiah,* TOTC 20 (Downers Grove: InterVarsity, 1999), 228–229.

66. Paul D. Hanson, *Isaiah 40–66,* IBC (Louisville: Westminster John Knox, 1996), 148–149.

67. Ibid., 169–170.

68. Bruce Manning Metzger, *Introduction to the Apocrypha* (New York: Oxford University Press, 1957), 87–94.

listened to God they would have eternal peace: "Had you walked in the way of God, you would be living in peace forever" (τῇ ὁδῷ τοῦ θεοῦ εἰ ἐπορεύθης κατῴκεις ἂν ἐν εἰρήνῃ τὸν αἰῶνα).

Second, this idea of eschatological peace also appears in the *Sibylline Oracles*. Eschatological peace will be established when time reaches its consummation: *Sib. Or.* 3:741–755, "For there will be great peace throughout the whole earth." In 3:780, all peace will come upon the land of the good.

Third, the concept of eschatological peace occurs repeatedly in the *Testament of the Twelve Patriarchs*. "My kingdom will be brought to an end among foreigners, until the salvation of Israel comes, until the coming of the God of righteousness, and until Jacob and all the nations come to rest in peace" (*T. Jud* 22:2). The Messianic figure will come in with peace. In *T. Jud* 24:1, it says, "And after these things a star will arise to you from Jacob in peace, and a man will arise from my seed, like the sun of righteousness, coming along with the sons of men in gentleness and righteousness, and no sin will be found in him." *Testament of Levi* 18:4 refers to "[t]he eschatological peace brought by the new priest-king." In *T. Dan* 5:9–10 it says, "Therefore when you turn back to the Lord, you will receive mercy, and he will lead you into his holy place, proclaiming peace to you. And there shall arise for you from the tribe of Judah and the tribe of Levi the Lord's salvation." The eternal peace will be granted to those who call on his name (5:11). Those people will rejoice in the New Jerusalem and will glorify God forever (5:12).[69]

Thus, one can see that the notion of eschatological peace has been well-preserved in the Second Temple period. Next, we will examine this notion in the Dead Sea Scrolls.

Eschatological Peace in the Dead Sea Scrolls

The concept of eschatological peace also appears in the Dead Sea Scrolls. The War Scroll, at Col. 17, refers to peace and blessing for the lot of God at the final battle. In Col. 19, in the thanksgiving for the final victory, the

---

69. Philo uses the term "peace" in contrast to war in most cases. In his commentary on Dreams, he considers that for God who is trustworthy and truthful, he alone is peace (ἴσθι δή, ὦ γενναῖε, ὅτι θεὸς μόνος ἡ ἀψευδεστάτη καὶ πρὸς ἀλήθειάν ἐστιν εἰρήνη). In *Decal.* 1:178, God is the prince of peace (ὁ μὲν θεὸς πρύτανις εἰρήνης). Josephus also uses the term "peace" in contrast to war.

King of Glory is with us and the host of his spirits is with our steps. This battle is the eschatological one.[70]

Eschatological Peace in the Benedictus

Eschatological peace is also predicted in the Benedictus. This eschatological peace has been prophesied by Zechariah in Luke 1:79. The first part of 1:79 ("who sit in darkness and in the shadow of death") is an echo of Psalm 107:10, 14 (LXX 106:10, 14) where God delivered those who sit in darkness and in the shadow of death (καθημένους ἐν σκότει καὶ σκιᾷ θανάτου) (καὶ ἐξήγαγεν αὐτοὺς ἐκ σκότους καὶ σκιᾶς θανάτου καὶ τοὺς δεσμοὺς αὐτῶν διέρρηξεν) (106:10, 14). The second part of 1:79 finds a parallel in Isaiah 42:6–7: "I have made you . . . a light to the nations, to open the eyes that are blind, to bring out . . . persons who sit in darkness." In terms of the context, this verse also has another parallel to Isaiah 9:2b (LXX 9:1b): "the people who walked in darkness have seen a great light; those who lived in a land of deep darkness – on them light has shined (ὁ λαὸς ὁ πορευόμενος ἐν σκότει ἴδετε φῶς μέγα οἱ κατοικοῦντες ἐν χώρᾳ καὶ σκιᾷ θανάτου φῶς λάμψει ἐφ' ὑμᾶς)." "The way of peace" (ὁδὸν εἰρήνης) echoes Isaiah 59:8 (cf. Rom 3:17). Here one finds a pattern: in Isaiah 9:1–7, the great light (the Prince of Peace) shines his light to the people who sit in darkness and in the shadow of death. He will establish endless peace, justice and righteousness. This is exactly the same pattern in Luke 1:79: light from heaven will shine to those who sit in darkness and in the shadow of death and will guide their feet onto the way of peace.

Therefore, one can see that the notion of eschatological peace stems from the OT and that the Hebrew word שָׁלוֹם conveys the notion of eschatological peace. This concept also survived in the Second Temple period. And the idea of eschatological peace is predicted in the earlier text of Luke 1:79. Peace in Luke 2:14 is not merely good interpersonal relationships; rather, it is the eschatological peace, salvation.[71] It is the term "peace" that introduces the significant peace motif in Luke-Acts.

---

70. Peter W. Flint et al., eds., *Celebrating the Dead Sea Scrolls: A Canadian Collection*, vol. 30 (Atlanta: SBL, 2011), 359.

71. Certainly, the eschatological peace includes interpersonal relationship. It does include peace between God and man and between man and man.

The Relationship between the Heaven Motif and the Peace Motif

Having studied the word "peace" in Luke 2:14, we must now investigate the relationship between the heaven motif and the peace motif. In this section, we will demonstrate that the heaven motif and the peace motif are closely connected in that the heavenly glory motif has been worked out by the peace motif. This relationship has not only been anticipated in the infancy narrative (Luke 1:78–79; 2:29–32) but also realized in the Gospel of Luke (19:38) and in the book of Acts. Our attention will focus on Luke 1:78–79 to investigate the relationship between the two motifs.

Luke 1:78–79

The heaven motif and the peace motif in Luke 2:14 have been anticipated at the end of the *Benedictus* (Luke 1:78–79). Earlier study has shown that "the sunrise from on high" (ἀνατολὴ ἐξ ὕψους) is the glory from heaven. We have also argued that "the glory from heaven" refers to Jesus. The purpose of the visiting (ἐπισκέπτομαι) of the heavenly glory is expressed by the following two infinitive clauses: "to shine those who sit in darkness and in the shadow of death" (ἐπιφᾶναι τοῖς ἐν σκότει καὶ σκιᾷ θανάτου καθημένοις) and "to guide our feet into the way of peace" (τοῦ κατευθῦναι τοὺς πόδας ἡμῶν εἰς ὁδὸν εἰρήνης). Grammatically, the two infinitive clauses function as the purpose of the main verb, "visit" (ἐπισκέψεται). The second infinitive clause further explains the first as "epexegetic."[72] As Bovon comments, when people who sat in the darkness see the life-giving light, their steps are being guided to the way of life.[73] Thematically, "peace" stands in contrast to "darkness" and "the shadow of death." As argued this peace is the eschatological peace. The word κατευθύνω is elsewhere used of Jesus or the Lord who directs.[74] Thus the purpose of the visit of the heavenly glory (Jesus) is to guide people who sat in darkness and the shadow of death to the way of eschatological peace. Therefore, the heaven (glory) motif is expressed by

---

72. Heinz Schürmann, *Das Lukasevangelium, vol. 1: Komentar zu Kap 1:1–9:50*, HTKNT (Freiburg im Br: Herder, 1969), 92.

73. Bovon, *Luke 1:1–9:50*, 76.

74. 1 Thess 3:11 says, "Jesus directs our way" (Ἰησοῦς κατευθύναι τὴν ὁδὸν ἡμῶν). Another occasion is in 2 Thess 3:5: "The Lord directs our hearts to the love of God" (Ὁ δὲ κύριος κατευθύναι ὑμῶν τὰς καρδίας εἰς τὴν ἀγάπην τοῦ θεοῦ).

the peace motif. Next, we will examine another passage to demonstrate the relationship between the two motifs.

Luke 2:29–32
Another passage that contains the glory and peace references is Luke 2:29–32. We will show that the heavenly glory motif is again expressed by the peace motif. First, we will argue that the meaning of peace is not a customary one. It is the eschatological peace. Second, we will demonstrate that the heavenly glory has been manifested by peace.

First, in the *Nunc Dimittis*, Simeon said that he could die in peace since his eyes have seen God's salvation (νῦν ἀπολύεις τὸν δοῦλόν σου, δέσποτα, κατὰ τὸ ῥῆμά σου ἐν εἰρήνῃ ὅτι εἶδον οἱ ὀφθαλμοί μου τὸ σωτήριόν σου). The word ἀπολύω has been demonstrated to be a euphemistic reference to death (e.g. Gen 15:2; Num 20:29; Tob 3:6, 13; 2 Mac 7:9.SB II, 138f). The best parallel is Genesis 15:15 (LXX) "As for yourself, you shall go to your fathers in peace; you shall be buried in a good old age" (σὺ δὲ ἀπελεύσῃ πρὸς τοὺς πατέρας σου μετ' εἰρήνης ταφεὶς ἐν γήρει καλῷ). Here the word ἀπελεύσῃ refers to the death of Abraham. One finds a similar usage in Numbers 20:29, when the entire congregation saw that Aaron was dead (καὶ εἶδεν πᾶσα ἡ συναγωγὴ ὅτι ἀπελύθη Ααρων). Why did Simeon say he could die in peace (ἀπολύεις . . . ἐν εἰρήνῃ)? The following text tells the reason. Because Simeon's eyes saw God's salvation (ὅτι εἶδον οἱ ὀφθαλμοί μου τὸ σωτήριόν σου) he could die in peace. The similar phrase, "depart/go in peace" (πορεύου εἰς εἰρήνην), recurs in the healing accounts of Jesus's ministries (7:50; 8:48), in which we will argue that the peace referred to is also the eschatological peace, salvation. Thus, peace here is the eschatological peace.

Second, when Simeon saw the heavenly glory that is the light to the nations (φῶς εἰς ἀποκάλυψιν ἐθνῶν) and the glory for your people Israel (δόξαν λαοῦ σου Ἰσραήλ) he was sure that he could receive the eschatological peace. The appearance of the heavenly glory/salvation (Jesus) brings peace to a pious Jew, Simeon.

Therefore, our study shows that the peace in Luke 2:29–32 is the eschatological peace (i.e. salvation). This eschatological peace has also been materialized in Simeon who has been looking for the consolation of Israel (2:29–32). This shows that the heaven motif has first been realized by the peace motif on a personal level. The study of another passage will reveal that this relationship occurs also on a grand level, peoples in Jerusalem. To this we now turn.

Luke 19:38

The relationship between the heaven motif and the peace motif could be further demonstrated in Luke 19:38, which is worded similarly to Luke 2:14. We will argue that the rejection of this heavenly glory (i.e. Jesus) is the rejection of peace. In what follows we will first show that "the visitation" (τῆς ἐπισκοπῆς) in Luke 19:44 refers to Jesus. Second, we will argue that to reject Jesus is to reject the peace. Third, this study will show that the purpose of the visitation is to bring peace. Last, we will show that to reject peace is to rejection the heavenly glory, Jesus. Thus judgment follows.

First, a word study of ἐπισκοπή will show that "the visitation" is Jesus Christ, the heavenly glory. The noun ἐπισκοπή occurs only once in Luke's gospel.[75] The verb ἐπισκέπτομαι occurs three times in Luke. The first occurrence is in Luke 1:68 (Εὐλογητὸς κύριος ὁ θεὸς τοῦ Ἰσραήλ, ὅτι ἐπεσκέψατο καὶ ἐποίησεν λύτρωσιν τῷ λαῷ αὐτοῦ). The Lord God visited them and gave redemption to his people. The following verses explain how God visited them and gave this redemption. God visited his people by rising up a horn of salvation in the house of David (ἤγειρεν κέρας σωτηρίας ἡμῖν ἐν οἴκῳ Δαυὶδ παιδὸς αὐτοῦ) (Luke 1:69). It is clear that the horn of salvation refers to Jesus who will be born soon. Verses 70–75 explain that God uses Jesus to save his people from its enemies. The second occurrence is in Luke 1:78 (ἐπισκέψεται ἡμᾶς ἀνατολὴ ἐξ ὕψους). Here again by God's tender mercy the sunrise from heaven will visit us. Based on the study earlier, this is the heavenly glory that visits the people. The third occurrence is in Luke 7:16 (ἐπεσκέψατο ὁ θεὸς τὸν λαὸν αὐτοῦ). Here, God visiting his people is conducted by means of the presence of Jesus (προφήτης μέγας ἠγέρθη ἐν ἡμῖν) who has raised a dead person (ἀνεκάθισεν ὁ νεκρὸς καὶ ἤρξατο λαλεῖν), though the people have not yet fully apprehended who Jesus was at that moment. Therefore, our word study of ἐπισκοπή indicates that the visitation is the presence of the heavenly glory, Jesus Christ.

---

75. This noun occurs four times in the NT. One is in Luke 19:44. Another occurrence in the Lukan writings is in Acts 1:20, where it means the "overseeing office" which Judah lost. The other occurrences are in 1 Tim 3:1 and 1 Pet 2:12. In 1 Tim 3:1, it means the "office of the overseer." In 1 Pet 2:12 this word means "visitation."

Second, the context will show that the rejection of the visitation is the rejection of Jesus, the heavenly glory. The rejection of Jesus in Luke 19:39 indicates that this opinion of the Pharisees is prevailing. The rejection of Jesus could be seen in Luke 23:13, 18, 21, 23, where the chief priests and the leaders, together with the people of Jerusalem, asked Pilate to crucify Jesus. Unfortunately, the people in the city of Jerusalem did not perceive the time of God's visitation.

Third, what is the purpose of this visit of the heavenly glory? Luke 19:42 provides the answer. The purpose of this invitation is to bring peace. Luke 19:42 and 44 have something in common. First, they have the same subject, "you" (σύ), which refers to Jerusalem. Second, they both have the same verb, "to recognize" (γινώσκω). Third, they share a similar temporal phrase – "this day" (ἐν τῇ ἡμέρᾳ ταύτῃ) and "the time" (τὸν καιρὸν). The former temporal phrase functions as a temporal preposition, the latter a temporal object. These points show that verse 44 echoes verse 42. The difference is that verse 42 emphasizes the things for peace while verse 44 focuses on the time of visitation (i.e. Jesus, the heavenly glory). The "things" (τὰ) are the visitation and teachings of Jesus. Thus, we see that the purpose of the visitation is to bring peace to Jerusalem. This visitation and peace relationship has been illustrated in our earlier study of Luke 1:78–79, where the visitation of the heavenly glory (which is Jesus as we have argued) is to bring peace to people who do not have peace (κατευθῦναι τοὺς πόδας ἡμῶν εἰς ὁδὸν εἰρήνης).[76] Thus, the visitation of Jesus is to bring peace to people in Jerusalem.

Finally, rejection of peace is rejection of the heavenly glory. The similar phrase, "peace in heaven and glory in the highest" (ἐν οὐρανῷ εἰρήνη καὶ δόξα ἐν ὑψίστοις), in Luke 19:38 echoes the phrase, "Glory to God in the highest, and on earth peace" (δόξα ἐν ὑψίστοις θεῷ καὶ ἐπὶ γῆς εἰρήνη), in Luke 2:14. Comparing the phrase in Luke 19:38 to the one in 2:14, there are two major differences. One is that in 19:38, Luke omits the recipients of glory and peace. Another is that 19:38 says "peace in heaven" (ἐν οὐρανῷ εἰρήνη) instead of "peace on earth" (ἐπὶ γῆς εἰρήνη). Glory in the highest heaven remains the same (δόξα ἐν ὑψίστοις) in both verses. Two reasons

---

76. The parallel passage in Luke 13:34–35 describes the visitation of Jesus. And the purpose of the visitation is to gather the people of Israel and provide protection (peace) for them.

may explain the omissions. One is that there is no need to mention the recipients of peace in heaven since the inhabitants in heaven have already enjoyed peace. Second, in line with the first point, the omission of "to God" (θεῷ) subsequently brings the result of keeping the poetic symmetry: peace in heaven and glory in the highest.

Why does Luke make the second difference "peace in heaven"? Scholars have offered various opinions.[77] It is true that this peace does come from heaven. However, this seems to miss the point in which Luke bears his theological concern. It is highly likely that because Jerusalem rejects the heavenly glory/Jesus this peace returns to heaven.

Thus we see that the visitation is Jesus, the heavenly glory. To reject Jesus is to reject the peace. This study will show that the purpose of the visitation is to bring peace. The rejection of peace is the rejection the heavenly glory, Jesus. Thus judgment follows. Therefore we can see that the heaven motif and the peace motif are closely connected. The heaven motif is expressed by the peace motif.

Summary

The foregoing study shows first that the relationship between heaven and peace in the heavenly hymn (2:14) has been anticipated in Luke 1:78–79 in that the heaven motif is expressed by the peace motif. Second, this relationship is demonstrated in Luke 2:29–32, in which the heavenly glory is manifested on a personal level. Third, that the heaven motif is manifested by the peace motif is further evidenced in Luke 19:38 on a larger scale – to the people in Jerusalem. Therefore, one can see that the heaven motif has been carried out by the peace motif. In the following, we will show that the heaven motif is expressed by the peace motif in a grand way in Luke-Acts. The heavenly glory has been manifested by peace in the ministry of Jesus (7:50; 8:48), is expressed by peace in the mission of the disciples of Jesus (10:5–6), and has been worked out by peace on an ecclesial level in Acts (9:31; 10:36). To these considerations we now turn.

---

77. Heaven is the source of this peace. See Joseph A. Fitzmyer, *The Gospel according to Luke 10–24*, AB 28A (New York: Doubleday, 1985), 1251. Peace refers to "the divine intention." Green, *The Gospel of Luke*. Peace is removed to heaven since the Jewish people rejected Jesus. John Nolland, *Luke 18:35–24:53*, WBC 35c, ed. Lynn Allan Losie Ralph P. Martin (Dallas: Word, 1993), 927.

The Outworking of the Heaven Motif by the Peace Motif in Luke-Acts

The glory of God in heaven is manifested on earth by peace in various ways. First, the heavenly glory is manifested by "peace" in the ministries of Jesus (7:50; 8:48), thus signifying the presence of the heavenly glory on earth. Second, the heavenly glory is materialized by peace in the mission of the seventy(-two) (10:5–6), indicating the progression of the realization of the heavenly glory on earth. Finally, the heavenly glory is presented by peace at the ecclesial level in Acts 9:31 and 10:36 highlighting that the Jews and Gentiles have become one. We will begin our study from the first point.

Heavenly Glory Manifested by Peace in the Ministry of Jesus

The above study shows that the heavenly glory motif is expressed by the peace motif. In what follows, we will demonstrate that heavenly glory is made manifest by peace in the ministry of Jesus in Luke 7:50 and 8:48. The "peace" in these passages is the eschatological peace proclaimed by the angels in the heavenly hymn (Luke 2:14). The heavenly glory has been manifested by peace on earth in the ministries of Jesus. First we will study Luke 7:50.

Luke 7:50

Some scholars take the phrase "go in peace" (πορεύου εἰς εἰρήνην) as a customary farewell that echoes an Old Testament dismissal formula (1 Sam 1:17; 20:42; 29:7).[78] Others, like Green, argue that "peace" is the full restoration of her social status.[79] Still others noted that the phrase "go in peace" has a deeper meaning that indicates the divine salvation or eschatological peace upon this forgiven woman.[80] These views are indeed helpful by relating the word peace to the divine salvation, but to study the term "peace" in Luke 7:50 in an isolated way will miss its theological significance. Some scholars like Bock, Nolland, and Foerster have noticed that the word peace

---

78. Fitzmyer, *Luke 1–9*, 692; Nolland, *Luke 1–9*. See also R. C. H. Lenski, *The Interpretation of St. Luke's Gospel*, 437.

79. Green, *The Gospel of Luke*, 314.

80. Bovon, *Luke 1:1–9:50*, 298; Marshall, *Luke*, 314; Nolland, *Luke 1–9*, 390; Bock, *Luke 1:1–9:50*, 707–708.

links Luke 7:50 with Luke 2:14. This is insightful enough. However, to simply link the term "peace" to Luke 2:14 while ignoring the peace motif in the wider narrative framework of the Lukan writings will downplay its theological importance. In the following study we will demonstrate that the peace here is the eschatological peace (i.e. salvation). Luke carefully pens the term "peace" here to show the manifestation of the heavenly glory in the ministry of Jesus.

"Peace" in *Luke 7:50*

The term "peace" first appears in the ministry of Jesus in Luke 7:50. We will demonstrate that this peace is the eschatological peace/salvation. First, the forgiveness of sins links this peace to salvation. Jesus said to her: "Your sins are forgiven" (ἀφέωνταί σου αἱ ἁμαρτίαι) (7:48). This echoes Luke 1:77: "To give knowledge of salvation unto his people in the remission of their sins" (τοῦ δοῦναι γνῶσιν σωτηρίας τῷ λαῷ αὐτοῦ ἐν ἀφέσει ἁμαρτιῶν αὐτῶν). We see that the forgiveness of sin leads one to salvation. This idea can also be found in Luke 24:47: "and that repentance for forgiveness of sins should be proclaimed in His name to all the nations, beginning from Jerusalem" (καὶ κηρυχθῆναι ἐπὶ τῷ ὀνόματι αὐτοῦ μετάνοιαν εἰς ἄφεσιν ἁμαρτιῶν εἰς πάντα τὰ ἔθνη. ἀρξάμενοι ἀπὸ Ἰερουσαλὴμ). The concept of the remission of sins to salvation is well-demonstrated in the book of Acts. Acts 2:38 says, "Repent and be baptized, every one of you, in the name of Jesus Christ for the forgiveness of sins and receive the gift of the Holy Spirit" (μετανοήσατε, [φησίν,] καὶ βαπτισθήτω ἕκαστος ὑμῶν ἐπὶ τῷ ὀνόματι Ἰησοῦ Χριστοῦ εἰς ἄφεσιν τῶν ἁμαρτιῶν ὑμῶν καὶ λήμψεσθε τὴν δωρεὰν τοῦ ἁγίου πνεύματος). Acts 3:19 says, "Repent, then, and turn, so that your sins may be wiped out, that times of refreshing may come from the Lord" (μετανοήσατε οὖν καὶ ἐπιστρέψατε εἰς τὸ ἐξαλειφθῆναι ὑμῶν τὰς ἁμαρτίας). In Acts 5:31, it says, "God exalted him to his own right hand as Prince and Savior that he might give repentance and forgiveness of sins to Israel" (τοῦτον ὁ θεὸς ἀρχηγὸν καὶ σωτῆρα ὕψωσεν τῇ δεξιᾷ αὐτοῦ [τοῦ] δοῦναι μετάνοιαν τῷ Ἰσραὴλ καὶ ἄφεσιν ἁμαρτιῶν). Acts 10:43 says, "Of Him all the prophets bear witness that through His name everyone who believes in Him receives forgiveness of sins" (τούτῳ πάντες οἱ προφῆται μαρτυροῦσιν ἄφεσιν ἁμαρτιῶν λαβεῖν διὰ τοῦ ὀνόματος αὐτοῦ πάντα τὸν πιστεύοντα εἰς αὐτόν). A similar idea appears in Acts 22:16 and 26:18. Therefore, the forgiveness of sins links peace and salvation.

Second, a study of the sentence "your faith has saved you" (Luke 7:50), also supports that the peace is salvation. The sentence, ἡ πίστις σου σέσωκέν σε, is uniquely Lukan.[81] The faith of this woman has been stressed in this account (Luke 7:36–50). On the one hand, the sinful woman shows her faith in Jesus by her loving actions: washing his feet with her tears, drying them up with her hair, kissing his feet, and anointing his feet with ointment. On the other hand, this woman's faith is demonstrated by contrasting it to that of Simon (Luke 7:44–46). Simon did not give Jesus any water for his feet, but the woman wet Jesus's feet with her tears and wiped them with her hair. Simon did not give Jesus a kiss, but this woman, from the time Jesus entered, has not stopped kissing his feet. Simon did not put oil on Jesus's head, but she has poured perfume on his feet. Thus, the faith of the woman has been highly emphasized. Faith in Jesus leads her to salvation.

Third, the peace here echoes the peace in Luke 1:79. Jesus said: "Your faith has saved you, go in peace" (ἡ πίστις σου σέσωκέν σε· πορεύου εἰς εἰρήνην). The phrase "in peace" (εἰς εἰρήνην) occurs only four times in the New Testament (Mark 5:34; Luke 7:50; 8:48 and Acts 7:26). "Go in peace" (πορεύου εἰς εἰρήνην) parallels "to guide . . . on the way of peace" (τοῦ κατευθῦναι . . . τοὺς πόδας ἡμῶν εἰς ὁδὸν εἰρήνης) in Luke 1:79. This is an individual materialization of the eschatological peace on earth (1:79; 2:14).[82]

Therefore, the phrase "go in peace" (πορεύου εἰς εἰρήνην) is not a customary farewell. This is the eschatological peace/salvation obtained by the sinful woman who believes in Jesus and has been forgiven of her sins.

The significance of the occurrences of "peace"

Having studied the meaning of the term "peace" in Luke 7:50, in what follows, it will be demonstrated that Luke purposely puts the term "peace" here to show that the heavenly glory has been made manifest in the early ministries of Jesus.

---

81. This phrase occurs seven times in the NT (Matt 9:22; Mark 5:34; 10:52; Luke 7:50; 8:48; 17:19; 18:42).

82. Nolland, *Luke 1–9*, 360.

There is no consensus on whether the episode (Luke 7:36–50) is the same event as the one in Matthew 26:6–13 and Mark 14:3–9.[83] It is more likely that it was the same event but in various forms passed by the oral tradition.[84] What is clear is that Luke places this episode that contains the term "peace" in the early ministry of Jesus to show that the heavenly glory has been materialized on earth.

The above study demonstrates that the meaning of the term "peace" in Luke 7:50 is not a customary farewell; rather, it is the eschatological peace (i.e. salvation). Luke purposely locates the term "peace" at the early stage of Jesus's ministry to show that the heavenly glory has been made manifest on earth. A study of another passage will also illustrate this point.

Luke 8:48

Another peace occurrence appears in the ministry of Jesus in Luke 8:48. We will argue that the word "peace" refers to the eschatological peace/salvation. The meaning of this peace includes more than physical healing.

This account differs from that of "the sinful woman" episode in that this account does not deal with the forgiveness of sins. But one theme is in common: when one has faith in Jesus, salvation follows. "Daughter, your faith has saved you, go in peace" (θυγάτηρ, ἡ πίστις σου σέσωκέν σε· πορεύου εἰς εἰρήνην).[85] In this account, the woman's faith is highly stressed. First the woman was so courageous that she pressed in and came up to Jesus, took the action of touching him, and a miracle immediately happened (προσελθοῦσα ὄπισθεν ἥψατο τοῦ κρασπέδου τοῦ ἱματίου αὐτοῦ καὶ παραχρῆμα ἔστη ἡ ῥύσις τοῦ αἵματος αὐτῆς). Second, the following context tells us the importance of faith/believing because the request of Jesus is: "do not fear, only, believe, and she will be saved" (μὴ φοβοῦ, μόνον πίστευσον, καὶ σωθήσεται).

---

83. They have much similarity and also much difference. For discussions, see Bock, *Luke 1:1–9:50*, 689–691.

84. Fitzmyer, *Luke 1–9*, 686.

85. In Mark 5:34, there is the phrase "Go in peace" (ὕπαγε εἰς εἰρήνην). In Matt 9:22, there is no "Go in peace." Luke follows Mark with this regard. But Matthew does not. In Luke 17:11–19, a Samaritan leper was healed and gave praise to God. Jesus said to him, "Get up and go on your way; you faith has saved you (ἀναστὰς πορεύου ἡ πίστις σου σέσωκέν σε)." In Luke 18:35–43, Jesus heals a blind beggar near Jericho. Jesus said to him, "Receive sight, your faith has saved you" (ἀνάβλεψον· ἡ πίστις σου σέσωκέν σε). Why is there no "in peace" in these two accounts? These narratives probably indicate the meaning of "in peace." The term "peace" in Luke 7:50 and 8:48 stresses the relationship between peace/salvation and faith.

This is exactly what the woman did. Third, the unbelief of the crowd is so enormous. When Jesus said to the crowd "do not weep, for she is not dead but sleeping," they even laughed at him (κατεγέλων αὐτοῦ). This casts such a clear contrast to the faith of the woman. Thus, it is her faith that leads her to salvation and subsequently obtains the healing. Therefore the peace is the eschatological peace, salvation.[86]

Summary

In sum, our study of the term "peace" in Luke 7:50 and 8:48 demonstrates that the peace formula is not a conventional farewell; it is the eschatological peace, salvation. Luke uses the word "peace" twice in the ministry of Jesus to express that the heavenly glory has been carried out by peace. The heavenly glory has been materialized by peace on earth. Our next study will demonstrate that the heavenly glory has also been presented by peace in the mission of Jesus's disciples.

Heavenly Glory Presented by Peace in the Mission of the Disciples

Heavenly glory has been materialized not only by peace in the ministry of Jesus but also by peace in the mission of the disciples of Jesus (Luke 10:5–6). This episode is unique to Luke for he is the only evangelist who recorded it (cf. Mark 6:7–12).[87] In this section we will first argue that the reference to peace is not primarily a customary greeting; rather, it is a reference to the gift of salvation either received or lost.[88] Second, we will argue that the mission of Jesus's disciples is to preach this eschatological peace.

---

86. Our study of the term "peace" in Luke 7:50 and 8:48 shows that this peace is not a customary farewell. However, this does not necessarily mean that "peace" always has this meaning. One may find that the term "peace" in the same phrase, "Go in peace" (πορεύεσθε ἐν εἰρήνῃ) does mean farewell. For instance, Acts 16:36 says, "The jailer told Paul and Silas, "Now you can leave. Go in peace" (νῦν οὖν ἐξελθόντες πορεύεσθε ἐν εἰρήνῃ).

87. Luke probably composed this account based on Mark and the "Q." There is also a possibility that Luke used the "Q" here and Mark in Luke 9. Matthew conflated materials from Mark and the "Q" (Matt 10:5–16).

88. Marshall, *Luke*, 419.

Luke 10:5–6

"Peace" in *Luke 10:5–6*

Green took the phrase "peace to this house" (εἰρήνη τῷ οἴκῳ τούτῳ) as the marker of identification of the followers of Jesus.[89] Bock viewed this as a wish; goodwill from God reflects the Hebrew concept of שָׁלוֹם.[90] Nolland considered the peace as "the bestowal of the blessing of God (cf. Acts 10:36 and 2:14).[91] Fitzmyer argued that the peace is brought by salvation.[92] One can see that there is no consensus on the meaning of the term "peace" here. This is due probably to the lack of the consideration of the term "peace" in the wider literary context. A study of this "special greeting" in the OT and Second Temple literature will be helpful for the understanding of the term peace. In this section we will first argue that the "peace" in the saying, "peace to this house" (εἰρήνη τῷ οἴκῳ τούτῳ), is not a customary greeting. Second, we will examine the content of "the greeting" to demonstrate that this is the eschatological peace (i.e. salvation) preached to the household.

The greeting, "peace to this house," should not be taken merely as a customary greeting. First, the context (10:1, 5) indicates that the house they will enter is foreign to them. Usually, greetings happen between people who know each other. This is evidenced in the Old Testament. For example, in Exodus 18:7, this verb, "to greet" (ἀσπάζομαι), is used of Moses greeting his father-in-law with a concern for his welfare. In Judges (A) 18:15, five men who knew Micah (Judge 18:3–6) greeted Micah and "asked him for peace" (ἠρώτησαν αὐτὸν εἰς εἰρήνην). In Esther 5:2, the king greets Esther (ἠσπάσατο αὐτὴν). Second, a similar situation could be found in Tob 5:10; 9:6; 10:11, where Tobit greeted his brother (καὶ ἐκάλεσεν αὐτόν καὶ εἰσῆλθεν καὶ ἠσπάσαντο ἀλλήλους).[93] Third, one finds that greetings occur among people who are familiar with each other in Luke-Acts. The verb (ἀσπάζομαι)

---

89. Green, *The Gospel of Luke*, 414.

90. Darrell L. Bock, *Luke 9:51–24:53*, BECNT (Grand Rapids: Baker, 1996), 997. Also see Garland, *Luke*, 426.

91. Nolland, *Luke 9:21–18:34*, 552.

92. Fitzmyer, *Luke 10–24*, 847.

93. Only in 1 and 3 Maccabees do people do those with whom they were not acquainted (1 Macc 7:29, 33; 11:6; 12:17). The Jewish leaders greet the foreign king Antiochus (3 Macc 1:8). In these cases, the term "greeting" functioned in a diplomatic manner. Philo and Josephus seldom employ this term.

occurs twice in the Gospel of Luke (1:40 and 10:4) and five times in the Book of Acts (18:22; 20:1; 21:7, 19; 25:13). In Luke 1:40, Mary greets her relative Elizabeth. In Acts 18: 22; 20:1; 21:7, 19, the apostle Paul greets Christians. In Acts 25:13, King Agrippa II greets Festus whom he probably knew quite well.[94] Finally, the "do not greet anyone on the road" (καὶ μηδένα κατὰ τὴν ὁδὸν ἀσπάσησθε) (10:4) also suggests that "peace to this house" is not an ordinary one. The above study shows that greeting strangers is unconventional. Next, we will examine the content of "peace" to demonstrate that the peace is salvation.

Having shown that this is not a customary greeting, it will be demonstrated that the peace is salvation. (1) The "eating and drinking (ἐσθίοντες καὶ πίνοντες)" at a house indicates that what the disciples did warrants their eating and drinking at that house. Eating and drinking are the daily needs of that time. The disciples deserve to get their daily needs met for sharing the eschatological gospel/salvation with that house. The eating and drinking are their wages in a sense.[95] (2) The phrase "peace to this house" (εἰρήνη τῷ οἴκῳ τούτῳ) is similar to the phrase, "salvation to this house" (σωτηρία τῷ οἴκῳ τούτῳ), in Luke 19:9. One point needs to be noted. The house in this phrase (τῷ οἴκῳ τούτῳ) refers to the people who live in it. Luke 19:9 makes this point clear. Zaccheus believes in Jesus and receives salvation. This point is further supported by Acts 16:31, 34 and 18:8. In Acts 16:31, Paul says, "Believe in Jesus, and you and your household will be saved" (σωθήσῃ σὺ καὶ ὁ οἶκός σου). Acts 16:34 makes clear that "this house" refers to "the household." Acts 18:8, says Crispus "believed in the Lord along with his entire household" (ἐπίστευσεν τῷ κυρίῳ σὺν ὅλῳ τῷ οἴκῳ αὐτου). "Peace to this house" means peace to the people in the house. (3) "Son of peace" (υἱὸς

---

94. According to Josephus, Agrippa II was brought up in Rome with Claudius Caesar. When King Agrippa I died, Claudius appointed the younger Agrippa to succeed his father (*Ant.* 19:360–362). Later Nero sent Festus as the procurator of Judea (*Ant* 20:182). They probably knew each other quite well and have had a very good relationship (*Ant.* 20:189–196).

95. That the laborer deserves his wages (ἄξιος γὰρ ὁ ἐργάτης τοῦ μισθοῦ αὐτου) finds its support in Paul's defense to himself in 1 Cor 9:4–14. Paul says, "Do we not have the right to our food and drink?" (μὴ οὐκ ἔχομεν ἐξουσίαν φαγεῖν καὶ πεῖν). Paul employs the metaphors of soldiers serving in the military, farmers working on plants, shepherds tending a flock, and priests working at temple to show repeatedly that evangelists are like soldiers, farmers, shepherds, and temple workers and that Paul and Barnabas should get their daily needs by sharing the gospel with others.

εἰρήνης) should be considered as "a man worthy of, or destined for peace."⁹⁶ William Klassen argues that peace was an identity marker for the disciples. God has reconciled mankind to himself. The arrival of the kingdom in the person of Jesus was for the early Christians an integral part of their experience of all dimensions of peace. Child of peace means "those who carried on his work as the 'children of peace' described by Jesus." Jews and Greeks in the first century often viewed peace as one of the most important pillars of human existence.⁹⁷ Klassen's argument is helpful for us to understand the importance of the peace in "son of peace." He singles out that peace is an outstanding outcome of the gospel. We would say that the term "peace" here refers to salvation. The "son of peace" recalls the expression, "on earth peace to man on whom God's favor rests," in the heavenly hymn (Luke 2:14). This peace rests on whom God wills. (4) That peace is salvation (i.e. the kingdom of God) is further indicated in the context. The peace to a household and the kingdom of God to a city parallel each other. This parallel is hinted in 10:1, where "Jesus sent seventy(-two) ahead of him two by two to every town and place where he himself was about to go." After giving the general instruction to his disciples, in verses 5–6 the disciples enter an individual house. In verses 8–12 the disciples enter a larger place, a town. Within each episode, there is a pattern: the saying/preaching; the stay of eating and drinking; the receiving and rejecting sayings. We found that the sayings "peace to this house" and "the kingdom of God has come near to the city" are counterparts. The contents of these sayings actually have the same meaning. The peace is the eschatological peace (salvation), which was brought to earth by the birth of Jesus, the heavenly glory. The kingdom of God here means the salvation brought by Jesus. It is not the glorious kingdom that Jesus brings in his second coming as Conzelmann argues.⁹⁸ Thus the peace is the eschatological peace (i.e. salvation).⁹⁹

---

96. Other uses include "sons of hell" and "sons of the resurrection" in Luke 20:36 and 16:8.

97. Klassen, "Son of Peace," 488–506.

98. Conzelmann, *Theology*, 98, 104–111.

99. In the parallel passage (Matt 10:7–16), the missional peace is personified. If a house accepts the peace of God then the gospel will come to it. Otherwise, the house will be under the judgment of God. See Grant R. Osborne, *Matthew* (Grand Rapids: Zondervan, 2010), 380.

The above study demonstrates that the saying "peace to this house" is not merely a conventional greeting. The peace represents salvation. Peace to this house means salvation to the household. What the disciples did is preach the gospel to each house. We will discuss this last point more in the next section.

Peace and the mission of the disciples

We will demonstrate that the mission of the disciples is to bring this peace/salvation to others. First, the context of Luke 10:2 refrains us from taking the word θερισμο,ς according to the literal meaning of a harvest of a crop.[100] "The harvest is plentiful, but the laborers are few. Therefore pray earnestly to the Lord of the harvest to send out laborers into his harvest" (ὁ μὲν θερισμὸς πολύς, οἱ δὲ ἐργάται ὀλίγοι· δεήθητε οὖν τοῦ κυρίου τοῦ θερισμοῦ ὅπως ἐργάτας ἐκβάλῃ εἰς τὸν θερισμὸν αὐτοῦ). Arthur A. Just argued that this metaphor recalled the parable of the sower (8:4–8). The disciples (workers) work is twofold: first, they sow the seed, and second, they bring believers into the church.[101] This is highly unlikely because the text says clearly that "the harvest is (already) plenty and the workers are few" (ὁ μὲν θερισμὸς πολύς, οἱ δὲ ἐργάται ὀλίγοι). Just probably read the meaning of the parable of the sower into this text. Osborne rightly commented that here the workers are soul harvesters who brings the harvest.[102] In other words, these harvests are evangelists who bring salvation/the gospel to people. Meanwhile, one cannot deny that there exists an eschatological overtone since this also links to the eschatological harvest according to the judgment described in verses 12–15.

Second, the following verses (vv. 8–11) show that the peace is salvation. Luke 10:8 further speaks of the salvific work of curing the sick done by the

---

100. In the OT, most cases of this term (θερισμο,ς) refer literally to the harvest of crops (Genesis, Leviticus, Joshua, Ruth, 1, and 2 Samuel, Isaiah and Jeremiah refer to crop harvest). In Exod 23:16, the term is used to refer to the Feast of Harvest. In Job 14:9; 18:16; and 29:19, it refers to branch of a tree. But in Isa 27: 11–12, in the eschatological context, it refers to judgment. God rejects the nations as chaff and gathers Israel as valuable wheat. Also see Joel 3:13 (LXX 4:13), where it is the harvest of a vintage (τρύγητος).

This term in the Pseudepigrapha was used mostly for the harvest of crops (Jdt 2:27; 8:2 wheat harvest; Sir 24:26, time of harvest.) However, in *4 Ezra* 4:28, the harvest (end time) of evil has not yet come (9:17, 31). Philo uses the word eight times *in De somniis*, each time in reference to a harvest of crops.

101. Arthur A. Just, Jr., *Luke 9:51–24:53: A Theological Exposition of Sacred Scripture* (St. Louis, MO: Concordia, 1997), 436.

102. Osborne, *Matthew*, 365–66.

disciples and the preaching of the kingdom of God. Verse 10 again mentions the disciples' declaration of the kingdom of God to those who rejected the good tidings. We see that the mission of the disciples is to preach the kingdom of God. This supports our understanding that the peace is salvation.[103]

Third, the parallel account, Luke 9:1–6, also supports that the disciples' mission is to preach the gospel to others. The sending of the seventy(-two) in Luke 10:1–12 has its parallel to the sending of the twelve in Luke 9:1–6. One finds the following parallels. (1) the calling (συγκαλέω) of the twelve (9:1) and the appointing (ἀναδείκνυμι) of the seventy(-two) (10:1); (2) the similar instructions about the journey (9:3; 10:4); (3) the likely manner towards those who refuse to receive them (9:5; 10:10). The purpose of sending the twelve is to proclaim the kingdom of God; the purpose of appointing the seventy(-two) is to bring peace (i.e. to preach the gospel). Within this parallel Luke makes a change in the first part (10:1–7) by using the word "peace" instead of "the kingdom of God" (i.e. salvation), thus bearing his theological concern.[104] Therefore, the mission of the disciples is to bring peace to others.

Summary

In sum, the above study demonstrates that "peace to this house" is not merely a customary greeting. The peace is the eschatological peace/salvation. Jesus's disciples enter each house to bring this eschatological peace/salvation to the household if there is one whom God favors (Luke 2:14). Otherwise this peace/salvation still belongs to the disciples. The studies of the context and of the parallel, Luke 9:1–5, show that the mission of the disciples is to preach peace to others. This eschatological peace has been manifested in the mission of Jesus's disciples. Thus, one can see that the heavenly glory has been made manifest by peace in the mission of the disciples. In next section we will show that this eschatological peace/salvation has been further evidenced at an ecclesial level.

---

103. Of course, we cannot say that the kingdom of God is totally equal with salvation. The former emphasizes the sovereignty of God, the latter the content.

104. The number seventy in Genesis 10 MT and seventy(-two) in Genesis 10 LXX denotes all the nations of the world. See James M. Scott, *Geography in Early Judaism and Christianity*, SNTSMS 146 (Cambridge; New York: Cambridge University Press, 2002), 24–39, 51–55. Also see Flender, *Theologian of Redemptive History*, 20–23.

Heavenly Glory Manifested in the Ecclesial Dimension
The glory of heaven is also manifested by peace in an ecclesial dimension in that Jews and Gentiles became one (Acts 9:31 and 10:36). We will first pay attention to Acts 9:31.

Acts 9:31
This section will demonstrate that the term "peace" is not a state of being free from persecution but is the eschatological peace among the people in the church.

Peace in *Acts 9:31*
This is the first time the term "peace" (εἰρήνη) occurs with the term "church" (ἐκκλησία) (Acts 9:31). The term "peace" in Acts 9:31 (Ἡ μὲν οὖν ἐκκλησία καθ' ὅλης τῆς Ἰουδαίας καὶ Γαλιλαίας καὶ Σαμαρείας εἶχεν εἰρήνην) has often been taken as freedom from persecution.[105] It is not simply that the peace is in contrast to the external disturbance as many scholars comment.

In what follows, we will demonstrate that the peace here is not freedom from persecution, but eschatological peace. First, there is no evidence in the context that there is persecution of the church. The basic assumption of the view that the church is free from persecution is due to Saul's conversion.[106] The fact is that Paul's conversion does not necessarily mean the persecution has downgraded or ceased. Paul's conversion means that Paul himself did not do any more harm to the church. The assumption that the conversion of Saul ceases the persecution seems unlikely in light of the time consideration. Acts 9:23 says, "After the conversion of Paul, there were many days passed" (Ὡς δὲ ἐπληροῦντο ἡμέραι ἱκαναί). "These many days" include the days of Saul's evangelizing in Damascus (9:22) and his stay in Arabia. According

---

105. Eckhard J. Schnabel, *Acts*, ZECNT 5, ed. Clinton E. Arnold (Grand Rapids: Zondervan, 2012), 466–467. Schnabel says that "Peace refers to the combination of political peace and personal contentment in the land of promise."Ibid., 466. Pervo comments that because persecution has subsided, the church gains peace. See Richard I. Pervo, *Acts: A Commentary*, Hermeneia (Minneapolis: Fortress, 2009), 248. Fitzmyer has the similar opinion that the peace is "in contrast to the reaction of Jerusalem Jews to Paul." See Joseph A. Fitzmyer, *The Acts of the Apostles*, AB 31 (New York: Doubleday, 1998), 441. Peterson also takes this view. See David Peterson, *The Acts of the Apostles*, PNTC (Nottingham: Apollos, 2009), 318. Williams lists factors that contribute to the external peace besides the conversion of Paul. See David J. Williams, *Acts*, NICNT (Peabody: Hendrickson, 1990), 177–178.

106. Schnabel, *Acts*, 466.

to Galatians 1:18, there are about two to three years between Paul's conversion and his visit to Jerusalem (also see Acts 20:31), depending on how one reckons it.[107] But, one thing is certain, that there are at least two years between the conversion of Saul and his coming up to Jerusalem. Further, the conclusion (Acts 9:31) of the narrative episode (6:8–9:30) happened later than the event of Paul's going up to Jerusalem. That is to say that there was even a longer period of time (more than two years) between Paul's conversion and the time of the peace of the church than there is between Paul's conversion and his going up to Jerusalem. In other words, the date that the church enjoyed peace came long after the date of Saul's conversion. Ignoring the gap between the date of Paul's conversion and the date that the church enjoyed peace hinders one from understanding the meaning of peace in Acts 9:31. Therefore, one can see that the view that the peace of the church is freedom from persecution based on Saul's conversion is unconvincing.

Second, the immediate context shows that persecution was still there or probably even more intense. First, the context repeatedly indicates the existence of persecution. In Damascus, Jews (οἱ Ἰουδαῖοι) plotted to kill Paul (συνεβουλεύσαντο οἱ Ἰουδαῖοι ἀνελεῖν αὐτόν) (9:23–25; cf. 2 Cor 11:32–33). So he had to be lowered down in a basket through an opening in the wall of Damascus (9:25). Second, in Jerusalem, two years later, the Greek speaking Jews (Ἑλληνιστής; cf. Acts 6:1 and 11:20) also wanted to kill Paul (οἱ δὲ ἐπεχείρουν ἀνελεῖν αὐτόν) (9:29). Thus, Paul was forced to withdraw from Jerusalem and had to be brought to Tarsus (9:29). This again is not in favor the view that there is no persecution of the church; rather, it shows that the persecution was still ongoing. And Paul's conversion probably provoked a more intense persecution of the church.[108]

Therefore, we may conclude that the conversion of Paul did not stop or mitigate persecution against the church. After his conversion, Paul's powerful

---

107. F. F. Bruce, *The Book of the Acts,* NICNT (Grand Rapids: Eerdmans, 1988), 241; Donald A. Carson and Douglas J. Moo, *An Introduction to the New Testament* (Leicester: Apollos, 2006), 224–226. See Schnabel, *Acts,* 454.

108. John Calvin rightly points out that Paul's presence after his conversion "greatly provoked" the enemies and made them "furious"; however, he still takes the view that the peace is a sort of freedom from persecution. He comments that the peace is "when he [God] appeases or mitigates the winds and storms of persecutions." See John Calvin, *Acts of the Apostles, 1–13* (Edinburgh: Oliver & Boyd, 1965), 392–393.

preaching of this gospel at Damascus and in Jerusalem probably provoked a more intense persecution against the church. The peace for the church is not freedom from persecution. Next, we will show that the peace is the eschatological peace in the church.

Ἐκκλησία in Acts 9:31

Bock insightfully pointed out the existence of the pressure from persecution on the church; however, he seems to ignore the importance of the peace occurrence in relation to other peace references.[109] The significance of the term "peace" occurring together with the term church would not be properly appropriated without studying the term church in Acts 9:31.

In order to perceive the importance of the term church in Acts 9:31 ("So the church throughout all Judea and Galilee and Samaria enjoyed peace," Ἡ μὲν οὖν ἐκκλησία καθ᾽ ὅλης τῆς Ἰουδαίας καὶ Γαλιλαίας καὶ Σαμαρείας εἶχεν εἰρήνην), three points need to be noted. First is the exceptional use of the singular form of "church." Second is the appearance of the term "church" with the term "peace." Last is the effect of the eschatological peace.

First, why does Luke use the term church in the singular form for different church locales? The term "church" (ἐκκλησία) does not appear in Luke's gospel at all. He uses the term exclusively in the book of Acts, twenty-three times.[110] This term first appears in Acts 5:11 and then in Acts 8:1, 3 where it refers to the church in Jerusalem. This singular form also occurs in Stephen's speech (7:38) where it refers to "the congregation." Other singular form occurrences refer either to the church as a whole (Acts 5:11: "Great fear came upon the whole church [ὅλην τὴν ἐκκλησίαν]") or to a specific local church: the church in Jerusalem (Acts 8:1, 3; 11:22; 15:4; 15:22; and probably 12:1 and 12:5, though these references are not certain), the church in Antioch (11:26; 13:1; 14:27; 15:3), every church (14:23), the church in Caesarea (18:22), the church in Ephesus (20:17, 28).

On the other hand, when Luke describes churches in multiple locales, he employs the plural form (Acts 15:41; 16:5). Thus, we can see that Luke's

---

109. Darrell L. Bock, *Acts*, BECNT (Grand Rapids: Baker, 2007), 372–373.

110. Out of the twenty-three occurrences, twenty-one are in singular form and two are plural. One occurrence in 7:38 refers to the gathering of the people of Israel in the wilderness. Three occurrences in singular form (Acts 19:32, 39, 40) are translated "the assembly," because they are not in a Christian context.

use of the singular form of "church" for three different locales in Acts 9:31 reflects his theological purpose. He employs the singular form of "church" instead of the plural to denote the unity of the believers. The singular form is an exception in referring to three regional churches (the whole land of Israel).

Second, of particular importance is the first appearance of the term "church" together with "Samaria."[111] That the Samaritans received Jesus Christ has been considered something new because of the historical background. First, Samaria was used to designate the territory of the northern kingdom of ancient Israel. Since it was captured by Assyria and the Jews had mingled marriage with Assyrians, the Samaritans were viewed as semi-Jews. The Samaritans were even considered outcasts.[112] Second, the response of the apostles to the Samaritans' reception of the gospel also supports this point. Earlier narrative describes the existence of the believers in Samaria (8:4–25). In Acts 8:5, Philip went to the city of Samaria to preach the Messiah. When the apostles at Jerusalem heard that Samaria had accepted the word of God (8:14) they sent Peter and John to verify this new situation (Acts 8:15–17). A similar response is found when the Gentiles received salvation; the church in Jerusalem sent Barabbas to Antioch in Syria (Acts 11:22). Third, the Great Commission of the risen Lord also shows that the preaching of the gospel to the Samaritans is a necessary further step that the disciples will take. Samaria is one of the areas that the disciples must preach the gospel.[113] That the Samaritans shared the gospel with Jews was foreign for the apostles. The church that encompasses Judea, Galilee and Samaria signifies the reunion of Jews with the semi-Jews. Theologically, the church that unites those three areas also indicates the restoration of ancient Israel. Geographically, the gospel so far is still confined to the territory of ancient Israel.[114]

---

111. This is also the first time Luke mentions the church in Galilee. Since Jesus did his mission in Galilee in his early stage, it might be that there were not many Christians there. The woes to the towns in Galilee illustrate this point (Luke 10:13–15).

112. Johnson, *The Acts of the Apostles*, 151.

113. One may notice that the term "Galilee" is omitted. This is due probably to the fact that the gospel had already been preached in the area of Galilee during the early stage of Jesus's ministries. Since people in Galilee were Jews like those in Judea, ethnically, the term Judea in 1:8 may be considered to include Galilee.

114. Bruce, *Acts*, 245–246.

Finally, the effect of the eschatological peace is well-expressed in Acts 9:31. As we have argued, the peace in 9:31 is the eschatological peace. It is this peace that united believing Jews and believing Samaritans into one church body. The heavenly glory has been manifested by peace in the church. That the effect of the term "peace" occurs in the context of the church can be seen in the second half of verse 31. The first effect is the internal outcome expressed by the first two participial clauses. The church had peace so that it was built up. The first participle, οἰκοδομουμένη should be taken as the result of the main sentence (ἐκκλησία καθ' ὅλης τῆς Ἰουδαίας καὶ Γαλιλαίας καὶ Σαμαρείας εἶχεν εἰρήνην). This is a temple-building metaphor (cf. 1 Pet 2:5). The divine passive indicates that it is God who builds up the church. The church was strengthened in the faith, and they increased in number. Peace and the walking in the fear of the Lord are the results of the eschatological peace they have. The Lord, in the backdrop of this chapter, is the risen Jesus, the glorified Jesus (Acts 9:5, 10–17, 27, 35, 42). The foregoing text and the text that follows tell us that the Lord is the risen Jesus. Thus one may see that in 9:31, the Lord is the glorified Jesus. The peace they have is due to the relationship of the believers with the glorified Jesus, the Lord. The second participle (πορευομένη) is also the result of the main clause (εἶχεν εἰρήνην).[115] It is the eschatological peace/salvation that brings the result of the relationship of the believers with the Lord so that they can walk in the fear of the Lord (τῷ φόβῳ τοῦ κυρίου) (objective genitive). Peace and comfort are given by the Holy Spirit (τῇ παρακλήσει τοῦ ἁγίου πνεύματος) (subjective genitive). The third phrase "in the encouragement/comfort of the Holy Spirit (τῇ παρακλήσει τοῦ ἁγίου πνεύματος) likewise is another subsequent result of the main clause (εἶχεν εἰρήνην) because the church had salvation so that the Christians could obtain the relationship with the Holy Spirit and thus could be encouraged/comforted by the Holy Spirit.

Another main sentence, "it [the church] grew in number" (ἐπληθύνετο) further describes the situation of the church in that more people have shared the eschatological peace (salvation). The passive verb indicates that the agent is again God himself (cf. the first participle). The two main sentences are closely linked. The growth of the church stands in line with the obtaining of

---

115. Grammatically, the two participles could also be modifying "grew in number." But syntactically, this seems unlikely.

eschatological peace. That people share the peace echoes Luke 2:14, "peace on earth to those whom God favors."

This study of the term "peace" in 9:31 demonstrates first that the peace is the eschatological peace in the church. Second it demonstrates that it is this peace that united Samaritans, the semi-Jewish people, as a whole to one church body. Third, the reunion of those people indicates the restoration of Israel. The heavenly glory has been manifested in the church through peace. As having noted, this eschatological peace has still been confined to the land of ancient Israel. This peace continues to be manifest at an ecclesial level for an even wider range of people. To this we now turn.

Acts 10:36

Another occasion of the term "peace" appearing in the second volume of the Lukan writings is found in Acts 10:36 (εὐαγγελιζόμενος εἰρήνην διὰ Ἰησοῦ Χριστοῦ, οὗτός ἐστιν πάντων κύριος). We will show that the term "peace" here is the eschatological peace (i.e. salvation through Jesus Christ). The eschatological peace has been evidenced in an even wider capacity at an ecclesial level in that the Gentiles have come in and enjoyed this peace. The heavenly glory thus has been manifested on earth among Gentiles.

"Peace" in Acts 10:36

The importance of the term "peace" in Acts 10:36 has been noticed by Swartley. He viewed this peace as the unity between Jews and Gentiles in an ecclesial sense.[116] He also grouped the "peace" appearances in Acts at an ecclesiological level (Acts 7:26; 9:31; 10:36 and 15:33), which is very helpful for our understanding of the term "peace."[117] However, he seems to overlook the interrelationship between this appearance of peace and other peace references, such as the one in Luke 2:14. Therefore, it seems hard for him to fully comprehend the importance of the term "peace" in Luke-Acts. In this section we will first study the meaning of the term "peace." Second, we will examine why the Lukan Peter phrases his message as "peace through Jesus Christ." Third, we will consider the relationship between the term "peace" in Acts 10:36 and that in Luke 2:14.

---

116. Swartley, *Covenant of Peace*, 155–163. He also relates the peace occurrences in 7:26; 9:31 and 15:33 to the church context in Acts.

117. Ibid., 155–164.

First, let us consider the meaning of the term "peace" in Acts 10:36. The context of 10:36 is the preaching of Peter to the people at Cornelius' house (10:34–48). At the beginning of the preaching at Cornelius' house (10:34–43), Peter says in his introduction (34–35) that "God is not partial" (οὐκ ἔστιν προσωπολήμπτης ὁ θεός). Then, he addresses the message of the proclamation of Jesus (vv. 36–41). Peter concludes the preaching by offering salvation (vv. 42–43). At the central part (vv. 36–41) Peter first of all declares that his message is "peace through Jesus Christ" (εἰρήνην διὰ Ἰησοῦ Χριστοῦ). Preaching peace echoes Isaiah 52:7 (LXX). Other citations of Isaiah (Isa 42:6 in Luke 2:32; Isa 40:3–5 in Luke 3:4–6; and Isa 61:1–3 in Luke 4:16–30) favor this allusion.[118] What does this peace mean? It means the gospel/salvation. The word "peace" (εἰρήνην) stands in apposition to the word "Word" (λόγον).

"The Word" in this context is the gospel. This is evidenced by the Lukan use of this term. In Acts 6:2, the apostles' priority is to preach the Word of God (τὸν λόγον τοῦ θεοῦ). In Acts 6:4, the apostles carried out the ministry of the Word of God. In Acts 8:4, the scattered Christians were "preaching the word" (εὐαγγελιζόμενοι τὸν λόγον). In Acts 8:14, the Samaritans received the Word. In Acts 10:44, when Peter was still saying these things, the Holy Spirit fell upon whose who were hearing the Word (ἐπέπεσεν τὸ πνεῦμα τὸ ἅγιον ἐπὶ πάντας τοὺς ἀκούοντας τὸν λόγον), and in 11:1 it summarizes this event saying that "the Gentiles received the Word of God" (τὰ ἔθνη ἐδέξαντο τὸν λόγον τοῦ θεοῦ). In Acts 13:5, Paul and Barnabas proclaimed the Word of God to Jews (κατήγγελλον τὸν λόγον τοῦ θεοῦ ἐν ταῖς συναγωγαῖς τῶν Ἰουδαίων), and in Acts 13:26, they said, "to us has been sent the word of this salvation" (ἡμῖν ὁ λόγος τῆς σωτηρίας ταύτης ἐξαπεστάλη). In Acts 13:46, Paul and Barnabas explained the meaning of the Word of God that is "for eternal life" (τῆς αἰωνίου ζωῆς) (i.e., salvation). In Acts 13:49, the Word of the Lord was spreading (διεφέρετο δὲ ὁ λόγος τοῦ κυρίου δι' ὅλης τῆς χώρας). In Acts 15:7, Peter says that God chose that the Gentiles would hear the word of the gospel through his mouth (ἀκοῦσαι τὰ ἔθνη τὸν λόγον τοῦ εὐαγγελίου καὶ πιστεῦσαι). In Acts 16:6, Paul was kept from "speaking

---

118. Pao's argument also strengthens this view. See Pao, *Isaianic New Exodus*, 160.

the word in Asia."[119] Peace is the gospel, the eschatological peace. The word λόγος is used in other senses in Acts, but so often it is used to reference the "gospel," which is likely the case here, and because "peace" stands in apposition to "the Word," then the peace spoken of in Acts 10:36 is likely the gospel itself, the eschatological peace.[120]

Second, why does Peter phrase his message as "preaching peace"? Having discussed the meaning of "peace," we now proceed to study why Luke uses this term. The term "peace" appears in a crucial juncture of Acts. As noticed earlier, geographically speaking, so far we see that the peace/salvation was still in the territory of ancient Israel. Ethnically, peace has been preached to Jews (Acts 1–7) and has reached out to Samaritan-Jewish people (Acts 8–9). From Acts 10 onward, the narrative focuses on salvation to the Gentiles. The incorporation of Gentiles into this eschatological peace in the new community is central to the rest of the narrative in Acts. Acts 10 is the watershed of the Lukan narrative. It is at this juncture that the Lukan Peter relates the gospel, phrased in the language of peace (εὐαγγελιζόμενος εἰρήνην). Luke purposely chose the term "peace" (εἰρήνη) as a synonym for the gospel for his theological concerns. It is the very gospel preached to "the sons of Israel" that is also preached to the Gentiles. The following text confirms that the Gentiles indeed accepted this gospel. The relationship between the Gentiles and salvation is confirmed in Acts 10:45. Besides, the phrase "the Lord of all" (πάντων κύριος) (10:36b) indicates the reaching out of the eschatological peace to Gentiles. This is a religious phrase.[121] This idea survives in Second Temple Judaism (e.g. Wis 7:7; 8:3: "for he who is Lord over all," ὁ πάντων δεσπότης). That this peace rests upon the Gentiles was an astounding event for the Jews (Acts 10:44–46). The peace here denotes the Messianic salvation. Jesus is the messiah (Ἰησοῦς Χριστός; 10:36, 38). He is Lord of all (οὗτός ἐστιν πάντων κύριος). The plural adjective, πάντων, can be either neuter (referring to the whole creation) or masculine (referring to all the people).

---

119. The Word of God is also personified in Acts (Acts 6:7; 12:24; 19:20). Pao argues convincingly that the word of God is the central character in Acts to accomplish the Isaianic new exodus. Ibid., 150–156.

120. Thus said, we acknowledge that the word (λόγος) does not always refer to the gospel in Acts, such as in Acts 1:1; 2:22, 40; 5:5, 24; 6:5, etc.

121. See Pindar, *Isthm* ("Zeus, the Lord of All.") and Plutarch, *Is. Os* 355e ("The Lord of all advances to the light").

Third, it should be noted that the peace among Gentiles echoes Luke 2:14 "peace on earth among those whom he favors." Taking the *Nunc Dimittis* (Luke 2:29–32) into consideration, the peace among the Gentiles is the realization of the heavenly light to the Gentiles.

Thus, the term "peace" in Acts 10:36 is the gospel. It is once again the eschatological peace (i.e. salvation). The term "peace" at this crucial point shows that Jews and Gentiles have become one. The heavenly glory has been presented on earth among Gentiles.

Summary

Therefore, the peace occurrences in Acts 9:31 and 10:36 highlight the ecclesiological implications. The Jews and semi-Jews (Samaritans) were united into one. The Jews and Gentiles became one. The heavenly glory has been manifested on earth by the peace between Jews and semi-Jews and between Jews and Gentiles.

Conclusion

This chapter demonstrates the significance of the heavenly hymn (Luke 2:14). First, the analysis of the infancy narrative shows the importance of the birth of Jesus. It is this heavenly response (Luke 2:14) that singles out the significance of the birth of Jesus over that of John the Baptist.

Second, the structural study demonstrates that there is a chiastic structure in the birth account of Jesus (Luke 2:8–20). At the center of the structure stands the heavenly hymn (Luke 2:14). Thus the significance of the heavenly hymn has been highlighted.

Third, we have studied the heavenly hymn of Luke 2:14. (1) The textual study shows that there is a bi-colon structure in this hymn in that the phrase "glory in the highest" parallels the phrase "peace on earth" and the word "God" parallels the word "men." (2) The word study of "highest" (ὕψιστος) in the LXX and in the OT Apocrypha and Pseudepigrapha shows that this word refers to the "highest heaven." The heavenly hymn thus conveys the notion of heaven. (3) Studies of three passages (1:78–79; 2:29–32; and 3:4–6) reveal that the heavenly glory is Jesus the Christ. (4) The study of the heavenly hymn itself shows that there are two motifs in this hymn: the heaven motif and the peace motif.

Fourth, the study of "peace" occurrences in Luke-Acts shows that Luke is fond of using the word "peace." He employs it for his theological purposes. The scrutiny of the word "peace" in the heavenly hymn (Luke 2:14) demonstrates that the term "peace" refers to the eschatological peace. It is salvation. One can see that the notion of eschatological peace stems from the OT. That the Hebrew word שָׁלוֹם has the notion of eschatological peace has been well-attested in the Old Testament. This concept also survived in the Second Temple period. And the idea of eschatological peace is predicted in the earlier text of Luke 1:79. Peace in Luke 2:14 is not merely positive interpersonal relationships; rather, it is the eschatological peace, salvation. It is the term "peace" that introduces a significant peace motif in Luke-Acts. Our study of the relationship between the heaven motif and peace motif in three passages (1:78–79; 2:29–32; and 19:38) demonstrates that these two motifs are closely connected. The heaven motif has been expressed by the peace motif. This point has been anticipated in Luke 1:78–79 and has been further made clear in Luke 2:29–32 and 19:38. This study shows that the heaven motif has been outworked by the peace motif.

Fifth, the heavenly glory has been manifested by peace in various means. First, the heavenly glory has been manifested by peace in the ministry of Jesus (7:50; 8:48). Our studies show that the phrase "go in peace" in both verses is not an ordinary farewell. The peace is the eschatological peace (i.e. salvation). It is the eschatological peace proclaimed by the angels in the heavenly hymn (Luke 2:14). This peace/salvation could only be obtained by faith. The heavenly glory has been made manifest by peace on earth in the ministries of Jesus, thus signifying the presence of the heavenly glory on earth. Second, the heavenly glory has also been expressed by peace in the mission of the disciples (Luke 10:5–6). Our study shows that the saying, "peace to this house," is not a customary greeting; rather, it is the eschatological peace/salvation. The mission of Jesus's disciples is to preach salvation to others. This eschatological peace has been preached in the mission of Jesus's disciples. Thus, one can see that the heavenly glory has been presented by peace in the mission of the disciples. Third, the ecclesiological implications of the heavenly glory have also been revealed in an ecclesial dimension (Acts 9:31 and 10:36). Our study of the term "peace" in Acts 9:31 demonstrates that the peace is the eschatological peace in the church that united Jews and

Samaritans in one whole church body. This reunion indicates the restoration of Israel. The term "peace" in Acts 10:36 refers to the gospel. It is once again the eschatological peace (i.e. salvation). The term "peace" at this crucial point shows that Jews and Gentiles have become one. The heavenly glory has been manifested at a church level through peace.

Therefore, one can see that the peace motif in Luke-Acts is actually the outworking of this important programmatic passage, Luke 2:14. The heaven motif is expressed by the peace motif. The glory of the highest heaven has been manifested on earth by peace.

CHAPTER 3

The Victory of God in Heaven and Its Impact on Earth

The Fall of Satan From Heaven in Luke 10:18

Introduction

In chapter 2, our study of the first programmatic passage, Luke 2:14, demonstrated that the glory of God in heaven has been manifested on earth by the eschatological peace (salvation). Heaven has brought salvation down to earth. Luke 10:18 serves as another programmatic passage since the reference to heaven here points to the victory of God in heaven, and its impact on earth is well documented by Luke.

The vision of the fall of Satan from heaven in Luke 10:18 has received much attention. Some took a redaction critical approach to the vision.[1] Others focused on source criticism.[2] Still others studied this passage against the backdrop of a missional context.[3] These studies indeed contributed to the understanding of the vision in Lukan scholarship. However, there is still a great need for a thorough examination of the passage on Satan's fall against

---

1. M. Theobald, "'Ich sah den Satan aus dem Himmel stürzen.' Überlieferungskritische Beobachtungen zu Lk 10, 18–20," *BZ* 49 (2005): 174–190.

2. A. Hultgard, "La chute de Satan: L'arrière-plan iranien d'un logion de Jésus (Luc 10,18)," 80 (2000): 69–77; D. Rusam, "Sah Jesus wirklich den Satan vom Himmel fallen (Lk 10.18)? Auf der Suche nach einem neuen Differenzkriterium," *NTS* 50 (2004): 87–105.

3. Bock, *Luke 9:51–24:53*, 1007; William Manson, *The Gospel of Luke* (New York: Richard R Smith, 1930), 126.

the background of its contextual passages (Luke 10:1–12; 10:12–15; 10:21–24). Also needed is a study of the relationship between this event and the exorcism stories. Lastly, there is a great need for a study of the relationship between heaven and earth in Luke 10:18. Without a thorough contextual study of the vision of Satan's fall, one falls short of capturing the full meaning of this vision. By neglecting the relationship of the vision of the fall of Satan to other Lukan exorcism narratives, one may miss the significance of the vision. By overlooking the connection between heaven and earth in the vision, one probably loses Luke's theological concern for the impact of heaven upon earth. Therefore, it seems necessary to study the vision of the fall of Satan in its context, its relationship to the exorcism narratives, and the connection between heaven and earth in this passage.

There are two sections in this chapter. In the first section we will focus on the vision of Satan's fall from heaven (Luke 10:18). We will demonstrate that this vision is a real event and that Jesus watched Satan falling down from heaven when the seventy(-two) were performing exorcisms in their mission trip. Satan's fall from heaven symbolizes the victory of God in heaven over Satan's forces. God uses Jesus and the disciples of Jesus to execute his victory over Satan. The impact of the victory of God over Satan is to bring forth the eschatological kingdom (i.e. salvation on earth).

In the second section of this chapter, we will first provide a brief study of the exorcisms in Luke-Acts to show Luke's unique concerns for exorcisms. Second, we will examine the theological significance of exorcisms to reveal that exorcisms connect closely to the vision of Satan's fall. Last, we will investigate some individual exorcisms to show that exorcisms are the impact of the victory of God in heaven over Satan on earth.

By investigating the passage on Satan's fall, its contextual passages, and the exorcism stories, we will show that the victory of God over Satan's forces in heaven makes its impact on earth by the realization of the eschatological kingdom of God on earth. Heaven here points to the arrival of God's eschatological kingdom on earth.

The Fall of Satan in Luke 10:18

In this section, we will first consider several views proposed on the vision of Satan's fall (Luke 10:18). We will argue that this vision represents Jesus's witness of an actual occurrence of Satan's fall when the seventy(-two) were performing exorcisms. Second, we will demonstrate the symbolic understanding of the vision of Satan's fall from heaven. Third, we will examine Luke 10:18 within its literary context to show that it refers to the victory of God in heaven over Satan. Fourth, we will argue that the agent/agents of the victory of God in heaven are Jesus and his disciples. Finally, we will examine the literary context of Luke 10:18 and will demonstrate that the main theme of the contextual passages (Luke 10:17–20; 10:1–12; 10:13–16; and 10:21–24) is the salvation/eschatological kingdom of God. The victory of God in heaven over Satan's forces brings forth the eschatological kingdom of God on earth.

Views on the Vision of Satan's Fall

Luke 10:18 has been depicted as "the most intriguing logion" of Jesus.[4] This logion is uniquely Lukan and is thus attributed to the Lukan source "L."[5] Luke 10:18 fits Lukan theology exactly.[6] This verse has received much

---

4. Julian Victor Hills, "Luke 10:18 – Who Saw Satan Fall," *JSNT* (1992): 25–40. There are a number of interpretive issues here. Hills argued that the subject of this verse is not Jesus, but the demons. Grammatically, this is possible since the neuter plural takes the singular form. However, the context does not favor this reading.

Another issue is the position of the phrase ἐκ τοῦ οὐρανοῦ. There are three textual variations, which are due probably to the ambiguity of the relation of the phrase "from heaven" as to whether it modifies "Satan" or "lightening." First, ms. B and Origen took the phrase ἐκ τοῦ οὐρανοῦ as ἐκ τοῦ οὐρανοῦ ὡς ἀστραπὴν πεσόντα. Second, the P[75] and Epiphanius viewed the phrase at the end of the sentence, thus read ὡς ἀστραπὴν πεσόντα ἐκ τοῦ οὐρανοῦ. This reading finds it similar structure in Acts 11:5: εἶδον ἐν ἐκστάσει ὅραμα, καταβαῖνον σκεῦός τι ὡς ὀθόνην μεγάλην τέσσαρσιν ἀρχαῖς καθιεμένην ἐκ τοῦ οὐρανοῦ ("I saw something . . . coming down like . . . lowered down by four corners from heaven). It is probably that the scribe removed the ambiguity by placing the phrase ἐκ τοῦ οὐρανοῦ at the end of the sentence. Thus it makes this reading least probable according to the principle of textual criticism. Third, the NA[27] takes the phrase ἐκ τοῦ οὐρανοῦ at the middle thus makes the word order as ὡς ἀστραπὴν ἐκ τοῦ οὐρανοῦ πεσόντα. Since Greek word order usually does not constrain the meaning of a sentence, two translations could be drawn; one being, "I saw Satan fall like lightening from heaven," in which the case the preposition phrase ἐκ τοῦ οὐρανοῦ functions as a descriptive modifier of lightening and takes τοῦ οὐρανοῦ as the source from which the lightening comes; another being, "I saw Satan fall from heaven like lightening," in which case, the preposition phrase ἐκ τοῦ οὐρανοῦ modifies the participial πεσόντα and takes τοῦ οὐρανοῦ as the place from which Satan has fallen. The latter is more likely.

5. Nolland, *Luke 9:21–18:34*, 562–563; Fitzmyer, *Luke 10–24*, 859; Michael F. Bird, "Mission as An Apocalyptic Event: Reflections on Luke 10:18 and Mark 13:10," *EvQ* 76 (2004): 120.

6. Rusam, "Sah Jesus wirklich den Satan vom Himmel fallen," 87–105.

discussion.[7] The debate surrounding the interpretation of this vision largely concerns the moment at which the fall of Satan occurs. Three principle interpretations of the vision of Satan's fall have been proposed. Did the event occur in a primeval past? Or did it happen in the recent past (at a certain event in the life of Jesus or at the exorcising of the seventy(-two)? Or will it occur in the future (futuristic/prophetic/eschatological)? We will examine each view and will argue that (1) Satan did fall in the primeval past, but this is the first fall, not the one in Luke 10:18; (2) the fall of Satan in Luke 10:18 is the second fall; and (3) this fall of Satan occurs when the seventy(-two) perform exorcisms.

The Primeval View

The primeval view entails the pre-existence of Jesus. Jesus saw the fall of Satan in the distant past.[8] In the following, we will examine this view and demonstrate that the primeval fall of Satan (first fall) is not supported by strong canonical evidence, though one cannot deny the first fall of Satan. Either way, we will show that it is unlikely that Luke 10:18 refers to the primeval fall of Satan.

The primeval view could be traced back to the interpretations embedded in *2 En.* (first century BCE) and in *Life of Adam and Eve* (first century BCE). This view has also been held by some early Church Fathers.

Second Enoch

An argument for this view is the idea that Satan's fall occurred on the second day when God created the world:

> [God said] "And from the rock I cut off a great fire, and from the fire I created the rank and their clothes are burning flames.

---

7. Helmut Merklein, *Jesu Botschaft von der Gottesherrschaft: Eine Skizze* (Stuttgart: Katholisches Bibelwerk, 1983), 60–62; Joseph A. Fitzmyer, *Luke the Theologian: Aspects of His Teaching* (London: Geoffrey Chapman, 1989), 164–169; Edith M. Humphrey, "'I Saw Satan Fall . . . ' The Rhetoric of Vision," *ARC* 21 (1993): 75–88; A. M. Sweet, "The Fall of the Angels," *BibT* 32 (1994): 15–20; Joel Marcus, "Jesus' Baptismal Vision," *NTS* 41 (1995): 512–521; Sydney H. T. Page, *Powers of Evil: A Biblical Study of Satan and Demons* (Grand Rapids: Baker, 1995); Hills, "Who Saw Satan Fall," 25–40; Anders Hultgård, "La chute de Satan: L'arrière-plan iranien d'un logion de Jésus (Luc 10, 18)," *RHPR* 80 (2000): 69–77; Simon J. Gathercole, "Jesus' Eschatological Vision of the Fall of Satan: Luke 10, 18 Reconsidered," *ZNW* 94 (2003): 143–163.

8. Fitzmyer, *Luke the Theologian*, 167; Green, *The Gospel of Luke*, 419.

And I gave orders that each should stand in his own rank. But one from the order of the archangels deviated, together with the division that was under his authority. He thought up the impossible idea, that he might place his throne higher than the clouds which are above the earth, and that he might become equal to my power. And I hurled him out from the height, together with his angels. And he was flying around in the air, ceaselessly, above the Bottomless. And thus I created the entire heavens. And the third day came." (*2 En.* 29:3–6)

The late first-century Slavonic Apocalypse (*2 En.*) is an amplification of Genesis 5:21–32.[9] The idea of the fall of Satan is thought to have been derived from Isaiah 14.[10] First, the same catchwords occur in both passages. Terms like "throne," "clouds/heaven," and "to elevate" appear in both accounts. Second, both passages focus on Satan's pride, complete with references to "elevating one's position" and being "equal to the Most High." Third, both passages mention that the consequence of that pride is Satan's being cast out from a high position to a low one. Therefore this interpretation of Satan's fall is based on Isaiah 14:12–15.

Life of Adam and Eve
This view could also be found in the *Life of Adam and Eve*. On the sixth day of Creation, Satan fell because he refused to worship Adam who was made in the image of God:

> And Michael went out and called all the angels, saying, 'worship the image of the Lord God, as the Lord God has instructed.' And Michael himself worships first, and called me and said, 'Worship the image of God, Yahweh.' And I answered, 'I do not worship Adam.' And when Michael kept forcing me to worship, I said to him, why do you compel me? I will not worship one inferior and subsequent to me. I am prior to him in creation; before he was made, I was already made. He ought to worship me. When they heard this, other angels who were under me

---

9. James H. Charlesworth, ed., *The Old Testament Pseudepigrapha. Vol. 1, Apocalyptic Literature and Testaments* (Garden City: Doubleday, 1983), 91.
10. See Pao, *Lujia Fuyin, vol.* 1, 479.

refused to worship him. And Michael asserted, 'Worship the image of God. But if now you will not worship, the Lord God will be wrathful with you.' And I said, 'If he be wrathful with me, I will set my throne above the stars of heaven and will be like the Most High.' And the Lord God was angry with me and sent me with my angels out from our glory; and because of you, we were expelled into this world from our dwellings and have been cast onto the earth. And immediately we were made to grieve, since we had been deprived of so great glory. (*Life of Adam and Eve* 14:1–16:2)[11]

This passage, *L.A.E.* 14:1–16:2, has some similarities to Isaiah 14. First, some terms resemble Isaiah 14: "the throne," "heaven," "the Most High," and "expel." Second, "the prideful notion" appears in both passages. Finally, the same result of the prideful one is indicated in both passages. Thus, one finds that the interpretation of Satan's fall in the *Life of Adam and Eve* is based on Isaiah 14:12–15.

Two major problems have been lingering with regard to the view that Satan fell during the week of creation. One is that there are no canonical texts that explicitly support this view. As we can see there is no scriptural evidence in Genesis 1–2 to back up this view. Another problem is the equation between Satan and the one who fell in Isaiah 14:12.[12] With the development of the historical criticism, scholars have reached a consensus in understanding Isaiah 14:12–15 as an oracle of the downfall of the king of Babylon.[13]

New Testament passages

Revelation 12:7–9. Some scholars hold that Revelation 12:7–9 describes the primeval fall of Satan.[14] Aune argues that the fall of Satan in Revelation 12:7–9 "is narrated as an *eschatological* event in 12:9 (as it is in Luke 10:18; cf. the language of John 12:31), but as an exclusively *primordial* or

---

11. This text is from James H. Charlesworth, *The Old Testament Pseudepigrapha. Vol. 2, Expansions of the "Old Testament" and Legends* (London: Darton, 1985), 262.

12. One can see the KJV translation of "Lucifer," the "common" synonym of Satan.

13. Having said so, this does not mean that Luke does not take Isa 14:12 as an allusion in his depict of the fall of Satan. We will reserve this issue for later discussion.

14. Grant R. Osborne, *Revelation,* BECNT (Grand Rapids: Baker, 2002), 468–471; David E. Aune, *Revelation 6–16,* WBC 52B (Dallas: Word, 1998), 695.

protological event in early Jewish and Islamic literature, a motif based on Isaiah 14:12–15."[15] In other words, Aune argues that the fall of Satan is actually a primeval fall, though it narrates as an eschatological event. He also equates the fall of Satan here to that in Luke 10:18. Osborne argues that the fall of Satan in Revelation 12:7–9 is the original expulsion of Satan from heaven in light of "the OT teaching of the defeat of Leviathan/the serpent at creation and the Jewish tradition of an original expulsion in keeping with the Genesis 6:1–4 incident."[16] Likewise, Luke 10:18, with its past-referring verb, ἐθεώρουν, speaks of this original fall.[17] Two questions need to be raised: Is the fall of Satan in Revelation 12:7–9 the original fall? And is the fall of Satan in Luke 10:18 the same fall as the one in Revelation 12:7–9?

Regarding the first question, there is much debate on the vision of the fall of Satan in Revelation 12:7–9. We will argue that the fall of Satan here occurs after the resurrection and ascension of Jesus. First, the context of Revelation 12:7–9 supports this understanding. Revelation 12:5 provides the background of this vision. This verse describes the birth, resurrection, and ascension/exaltation of Jesus. "And her child was snatched up to God and to his throne (καὶ ἡρπάσθη τὸ τέκνον αὐτῆς πρὸς τὸν θεὸν καὶ πρὸς τὸν θρόνον αὐτοῦ). The ascension and exaltation of Jesus are highlighted here. His ministry, death and resurrection are also included, though not explicitly narrated. This verse provides the background for the vision in verses 7–9.[18] The patterning interpretation in verses 10–11 further confirms that the victory in heaven over Satan and his followers are due to the Christ event, namely, the death, resurrection and ascension/exaltation of Jesus.[19] The fall of Satan and his followers is caused by the Christ event. Second, it is unlikely that the primeval fall of Satan is based on Isaiah 14:12–15, as we showed earlier. Isaiah 14:12–15 actually describes the downfall of the king of Babylon. Third, the original fall of Satan based on Genesis 6:1–4 also seems unconvincing. Our following section will demonstrate this point. Therefore,

---

15. Aune, *Revelation*, 695. Italics original.

16. Osborne, *Revelation*, 470–471.

17. Ibid., 468, 471.

18. Gregory K. Beale, *The Book of Revelation: A Commentary on the Greek Text* (Grand Rapids: Eerdmans, 1999), 658–660; Robert H. Mounce, *The Book of Revelation*, NICNT (Grand Rapids: Eerdmans, 1998), 234.

19. Beale, *Revelation*, 656–657.

our study demonstrates that the fall of Satan in Revelation 12:7–9 is due to the Christ event and occurs after the resurrection and ascension/exaltation of Jesus. The primeval fall of Satan based on Isaiah 14:12–15 and Genesis 6:1–4 is unconvincing.

As for the second question, the fall of Satan in Luke 10:18 is not to be equated with that in Revelation 12:7–9. This is simply because Jesus's vision of "Satan falling from heaven" occurs before his death, resurrection and ascension/exaltation. A detailed study of the fall of Satan in Luke 10:18 will be presented in its due course.

Besides Revelation 12:7–9, other passages in the NT may relate to the fall of Satan and his followers. One is in 2 Peter and the other is in Jude.

Second 2 Peter. 2 Peter 2:4 relates the angelic falling when Peter warns the false prophets. It says, "For if God did not spare angels when they sinned, but sent them to hell, putting them into gloomy dungeons to be held for judgment" (Εἰ γὰρ ὁ θεὸς ἀγγέλων ἁμαρτησάντων οὐκ ἐφείσατο ἀλλὰ σειραῖς ζόφου ταρταρώσας παρέδωκεν εἰς κρίσιν τηρουμένους). A traditional understanding of the fall of angles is based on Genesis 6:1–4,[20] though this opinion is still debated.[21] This interpretation is found in *1 En.* 6–12, known the story of the "Watchers." *1 En.* 6:1–2 says, "In those days, when the children of man had multiplied, it happened that there were born unto them handsome and beautiful daughters. And the angels, the children of heaven, saw them and desired them; and they said to one another, 'Come, let us choose wives of ourselves from among the daughters of man and beget us children.'"[22] And they did what they wanted (*1 En.* 7). Granted this interpretation, the fall of these angels occurred before the flood happened (*1 En.* 10), thus sometime before two thousand BCE.[23] The context of 2 Peter 2:4 also indicates that the angelic fall happened in the distant past. Peter illustrates God's punishment upon the unrighteous in time past in 2:4–7. God punished the ungodly by the flood (2:5); he judged Sodom and Gomorrah with fire (2:6–7). Though the fall of angels did happen in the distant past, it is hard to identify this fall

---

20. Ruth A. Reese, *2 Peter and Jude* (Grand Rapids: Eerdmans, 2007), 150; Steven J. Kraftchick, *Jude, 2 Peter,* ANTC (Nashville: Abingdon, 2002), 126.

21. Gene L. Green, *Jude and 2 Peter,* BECNT (Grand Rapids: Baker, 2008), 66.

22. Charlesworth ed., *Pseudepigrapha,* 15.

23. John H. Walton, *Genesis* (Grand Rapids: Zondervan, 2001), 48.

as the primeval fall of Satan. The principal reason is that the term "Satan" does not appear in the text. Thus it is unlikely that 2 Peter 2:4 describes the primeval fall of Satan.

Does this fall of angels equate with the one in Revelation 12:7–9? The answer is probably no. One reason is that the fall of angels in 2 Peter 2:4 occurred in the distant past, while the fall in Revelation 12:7–9 happened at the Christ event, as we demonstrated earlier. Another reason is that the number of the fallen angels in 2 Peter 2:4 is about two hundred. *1 En.* 6:6 says, "And they were altogether two hundred; and they descended into Ardos." The number of the fallen angels in Revelation 12:7–9 is not indicated but is probably much more than two hundred.[24]

Jude 6. A similar angelic fall (cf. 2 Pet 2:4) appears in Jude 6, where it says, "And the angels who did not keep their positions of authority but abandoned their own home – these he has kept in darkness, bound with everlasting chains for judgment on the great Day" (ἀγγέλους τε τοὺς μὴ τηρήσαντας τὴν ἑαυτῶν ἀρχὴν ἀλλὰ ἀπολιπόντας τὸ ἴδιον οἰκητήριον εἰς κρίσιν μεγάλης ἡμέρας δεσμοῖς ἀϊδίοις ὑπὸ ζόφον τετήρηκεν). Compared to 2 Peter 2:4, Jude 6 provides more information on the angels' fall from heaven. Jude focuses on the angelic apostasy that they refused to maintain the divine order. Thus the divine judgment fell upon them inevitably. Similar reasons could apply here that this angelic fall (Jude 6 and 2 Pet 2:4) is different from the one in Revelation 12:7–9.

Early church fathers

The view that Satan's fall happened in the primeval past is also held by some early Church Fathers. Tertullian (160–225 CE), the father of Latin Christianity, takes Genesis 6:1–4 as descriptive of the fall of Satan: "as for the details of how some of the angels, of their own accord, were perverted and then constituted the source of the even more corrupt race of devils, a race and him whom we have mentioned as their leader, the account is found in the Sacred Scripture."[25] Critics of this view assert that the text does not show evidence of the fall of Satan. The term "Satan" is absent in the text. This

---

24. Lewis Sperry Chafer, "Angelology," *BSas* 98 (1941): 404–405.
25. Tertullian, et al., *Tertullian's Apologetical Works and the Octavius of Minucius Felix* (New York: Fathers of the Church, Inc), 68.

account has been widely interpreted as the fall of angels as we demonstrated earlier. This text is also considered as an account of the fall of the Nephilim.[26]

Origen (184–253 CE), the early Christian theologian, interprets Ezekiel 28:11–19 as a reference to the primeval fall of Satan. He said that given such exalted terms, this prince should not be the king of Tyre, but rather the prince of evil.[27] Later, he cites Isaiah 14:12–15 to confirm that Isaiah predicted the same figure, Lucifer, falling from heaven. He says, "Most evidently by these words is he who formerly was Lucifer, who used to arise in the morning, and is shown to have fallen from heaven."[28] He interprets this Isaianic passage as describing Lucifer, the Daystar, the son of Dawn, falling from heaven. Origen's interpretations of Ezekiel 28:11–19 and Isaiah 14:12–15 are due probably to his principal of interpreting Scripture allegorically. With the rise of historical criticism, the allegorical method faded. Now scholars agree that Ezekiel 28:11–19 is an oracle against the king of Tyre and Isaiah 14:12–15 is a prophecy against the king of Babylon.

Summary

Our study has shown that early efforts to discover a primeval fall of Satan based on Isaiah 14 (*2 En., Life of Adam and Eve*, Origen) or Genesis 6:1–4 (Tertullian) are unconvincing. Second, the assumption that Isaiah 14:12–15 or Ezekiel 28:11–19 refers to Satan's fall is problematic. Third, a major critique of this view is that there is no explicit canonical evidence to support the fall of Satan as having occurred in the primeval past.[29] The fall of Satan described in Revelation 12:7–9 occurred when the Christ event happened. It is not the primeval fall of Satan. The angelic fall narrated in 2 Peter 2:4 and Jude 6 did occur in time past and does not equate to the fall of angels in Revelation 12:7–9. While the primeval view of Satan's fall lacks scriptural evidence, this criticism is insufficient to rule out the idea of a primeval fall of Satan. The question of at what exact time Satan fell from heaven remains unanswered. Scholars have concluded that Satan fell from the presence of

---

26. S. Gathercole, "Jesus' Eschatological Vision of the Fall of Satan: Luke 10, 18 Reconsidered," *ZNW* 94 (2003): 145.

27. Origen, *De Principiis*. I, 5, 4.

28. Origen, *De Principiis*. I, 5, 5.

29. Michi Miyoshi, *Der Anfang des Reiseberichts, Lk 9, 51–10, 24* (Rome: Biblical Institute Press, 1974), 100–101; Nolland, *Luke 9:21–18:34*, 563.

God sometime in the distant past. This is the first fall of Satan who made his own decision.

But that Luke 10:18 refers to a primeval fall occurring in Creation is unlikely. First, theologically, this is unlikely as Fitzymer asserts strongly, "Luke never reckons with the pre-existence of Jesus (unlike the Fourth Evangelist)."[30] Besides, from a narrative point of view, the location of the description of the fall of Satan in Luke 10:18 does not favor this view. Luke could have put this episode elsewhere, but he did not. He locates the narrative of the fall of Satan right after the performing of exorcisms by the seventy(-two). In due course, we will argue that Luke 10:18 refers not to the primeval fall of Satan but to another fall of Satan who has been defeated by the power of God.[31] Next, we will examine the futuristic/prophetic/eschatological view of Satan's fall.

A Futuristic/Prophetic/Eschatological View

Compared to the primeval view, the view of the vision as a future event attracts more scholars. The main arguments for this view could be summarized as follows. The content of the vision has not yet occurred. It will be materialized in the future since Satan is still active in many ways at the time of Jesus and even after the resurrection of Jesus. For instance, Green argues that in Luke-Acts Satan was still working to bring about the death of Jesus (Luke 22:3; 23:44). Furthermore, Satan continues his activity in Acts (13:4–12; 26:18).[32] Nolland and Gathercole also hold this view while arguing on a slightly different line than that of Green.[33] Conzelmann takes a further step to argue that Luke 10:18 is an eschatological event (i.e. it could only occur at the Eschaton).[34]

---

30. Fitzmyer, *Luke the Theologian*, 167.

31. There are three major falls of Satan. Osborne describes the three falls of Satan as three "bindings" (Osborne, *Revelation*, 469. The primeval fall happened in the distant past, though there is no explicit canonical text to support it. The second major fall(s) of Satan occurred at the ministry (Luke 10:18) and death of Jesus (Rev 12:7–9). The final fall of Satan will happen at the eschaton. We will argue that the fall of Satan in Luke 10:18 occurred at the ministry of Jesus and more importantly that it has a symbolic meaning.

32. Green, *The Gospel of Luke*, 418–419.

33. Gathercole, "Eschatological Vision," 153; Nolland, *Luke 9:21–18:34*.

34. Conzelmann, *Theology*, 107–108.

The "present-active role" of Satan

In response to this view on the present-active role of Satan, we will argue that the seemingly active Satan actually plays an instrumental role in the hand of God. A couple of examples will suffice. First is Luke 22:3, which says, "Then Satan entered Judas, called Iscariot, one of the Twelve." The Lukan contexts provide the answer. In Luke 22:22, it says, "The Son of Man will go as it has been decreed, but woe to that man who betrays him." Luke uses the word ὁρίζω to show that this is predestined. Elsewhere, this word almost exclusively refers to the predestination of God (cf. Acts 2:23; 10:42; 17:26, 31). Another explicit passage in support of this point is Acts 1:16–20 where Peter relates the betrayal of the Son of Man by Judas as having long been prophesied by the Psalter (Ps 69:26; 109:8). Therefore, we can see that God permits Satan to enter Judas' heart in order to fulfill his salvation plan. The betrayal of Jesus by Judas was predetermined by God according to his own will. Satan is only an instrument in God's hand.

Second, God allows the temporary apparent victory of Satan in the crucifixion of Jesus. Luke 23:44, which says, "It was now about the sixth hour, and darkness came over the whole land until the ninth hour" (cf. Luke 22:53) alludes to Amos 8:9 (cf. Joel 2:10, 30–31; 3:15; Zeph 1:15) which says, "In that day, declares the Sovereign LORD, 'I will make the sun go down at noon and darken the earth in broad daylight.'" The darkness of the earth prophesied by Amos has now been realized. In these hours of darkness God is still in control and allows Satan and his followers to crucify Jesus in order to fulfill his salvific plan.

Third, Satan appears to be in control at the beginning of the early Christian movement, such as in Acts 5:1–11. But those whom Satan filled were defeated by the apostle Peter. Satan seems to be triumphant in filling the heart of Ananias (5:3) in order to lie to God at the beginning of the church. But the power of the apostle Peter from God overcame Satan. The attempt of Satan to use Ananias to lie to the Holy Spirit was thwarted by the death of Ananias and Sapphira (5:5, 10). Thus, one can see that God's power overcame Satan and that Satan was controlled by God.

The above study shows first that though Satan still has an active role on earth, he plays only an instrumental role in the hand of God. Our study also demonstrates that Satan tried to fight against God, but God's power overcame him. Satan is a defeated enemy of God. Thus, the view that Satan is still actively opposing God in battle seems unconvincing. This is a basic criticism of the prophetic/eschatological view. Next, we will dialogue with scholars in this camp who emphasize different aspects of the futuristic view.

Scholars in this camp argue for an unrealized event of the fall of Satan in Luke 10:18 from various angles. Nolland and Gathercole argue from the prophetic aspect. Conzelmann argues from an eschatological viewpoint. In what follows, we will have a dialogue with these scholars to argue that the futuristic view (the prophetic/eschatological) is unconvincing.

The prophetic view

Nolland and others argue that the vision is prophetic.[35] For instance, Nolland takes the vision as "an actual visionary experience of Jesus" proposing that the vision is similar to that of some OT prophets (Amos 8:1–2; Jer 1:13–19; Ezek 2:9–10; and Isa 6:1–13).[36] For Nolland, this vision is "[n]ot what is, or what has now happened in heaven, but what is to be."[37] Nolland applies the visionary experiences of the prophets in the Old Testament to the vision Jesus had in Luke 10:18. In visions the prophets (Amos; Jeremiah; Ezekiel; and Isaiah) spoke of what God showed them and found their own roles in relation to the visions given. Nolland's view is that this vision is real and that Jesus's role is similar to that of the prophets.

Nolland's view that the vision of Jesus is likened to that of the prophets is problematic. First, the OT prophets were mere seers and proclaimers of visions. They did not act as agents in materializing their visions. For instance, Amos was only involved in seeing his visions (Amos 8:1–2) without playing the agent role of executing the contents of his visions. Likewise, Ezekiel saw the vision and was requested to proclaim what God had revealed to him (Ezek 2:9–10). He, like Amos, was not involved in realizing his vision, nor were Jeremiah or Isaiah (Jer 1:13–19; Isa 6:1–13). These prophets did not get involved in making what they had seen happen.[38] The relationship of Jesus to the vision does not mirror that of the prophets. Jesus not only saw the

---

35. Green, *The Gospel of Luke*, 418–19; Nolland, *Luke 9:21–18:34*, 565.
36. Nolland, *Luke 9:21–18:34*, 565.
37. Ibid., 564.
38. Ibid.

vision, but more importantly, he brought about the fall of Satan.[39] Nolland admits this point, saying, "Jesus saw that God intended to cause the downfall of Satan and that it was his task to achieve this in God's name . . . [T]hrough exorcism, healing, and proclaiming of the kingdom of God, Jesus's vision becomes tangible reality upon the earth."[40] Thus, one can see that Nolland's equating the vision of Jesus with visions of the prophets is problematic.

Second, Nolland seems to contradict himself in his argument about the temporal point of view. On the one hand, he insists that this vision is prophetic, namely, that the vision will happen in the future. On the other hand, he admits that the vision of the fall of Satan has become a reality in Jesus's own ministry of exorcism, healing, and proclaiming the kingdom of God.[41] This means that the execution of the fall of Satan has been conducted by Jesus's exorcising of demons. The fact is that by the time Jesus utters this vision (Luke 10:18), there have already been at least four exorcisms performed by Jesus in Luke (Luke 4:31–37; 4:41; 8:26–39; and 9:37–43). These exorcism stories indicate that by the time of the vision, the contents of the vision of "Satan falling from heaven" have indeed occurred. One cannot help but ask, "How could this vision be prophetic?" The prophetic visions of Amos, Jeremiah, Ezekiel, and Isaiah, to which Nolland appeals have exclusively materialized in the future. Thus, we can see that the vision of Jesus does not mirror the visions of the prophets. Next, we will examine a prophetic view, but with its emphasis being on the eschatological future.

Prophetic vision of the eschatological future

Like Nolland, Gathercole also holds that the vision is prophetic. But he takes a step further to argue that the prophetic vision points to the eschatological future.[42] Based on his prophetic understanding of the vision, he concludes that "Jesus's vision is of the eschatological fall of Satan to wreak havoc on the earth prior to his final destruction."[43] In what follows we will

---

39. Later our study will show that the event of the fall of Satan happens when his disciples are performing exorcisms.
40. Nolland, *Luke 9:21–18:34*, 566.
41. Ibid.
42. Gathercole, "Eschatological Vision," 154–163.
43. Ibid., 163.

argue that Gathercole's argument for the "eschatological featured prophetic vision" is insufficient.

First, Gathercole's argument for the prophetic vision as based on the verb θεωρέω is unconvincing. Two points need to be noted. For one, Gathercole views that this verb is used in "an explicitly futuristic context."[44] He lists verses in the Book of Daniel to show that the verb ἐθεώρουν is used to describe a vision that takes place in the future.[45] One finds that Gathercole relies too much on the use of this verb in Daniel, overlooking the usage of the verb in its immediate Lukan context, on the one hand, and in its wider literary milieu in the Second Temple period, on the other hand. The fact is that Luke uses the same verb θεωρέω to describe visions that already took place. For instance, at the end of Stephen's speech, "he said, 'behold, I see heaven opened'" (εἶπεν· ἰδοὺ θεωρῶ τοὺς οὐρανοὺς διηνοιγμένους) (Acts 7:56). It is hard to say that the vision Stephen saw is futuristic. The fact is that the "opening of heaven" has already happened. Another example is Peter's vision at Joppa. "He [Peter] saw the heaven opened (θεωρεῖ τὸν οὐρανὸν ἀνεῳγμένον) and something like a large sheet being let down to earth by its four corners (Acts 10:11)." The fact is that the vision Peter saw really occurred. Heaven has been opened, and a large sheet has come down to earth before him. The only difference is that Luke chooses the present tense in Acts 7:56 and 10:11, and the imperfect tense in Luke 10:18. The imperfect tense describes the fall of Satan as being like lightening (ingressive imperfect) when the seventy(-two) did the exorcisms, which we will discuss in due course.[46]

But the same verb in exactly the same tense (ἐθεώρουν) is used elsewhere to describe a vision that is not future-oriented. In Judges (A) 13:20 (LXX), Samson's parents saw a vision that really happened. It says: "As the flame blazed up from the altar toward heaven, the angel of the LORD ascended in the flame. Seeing this, Manoah and his wife fell with their faces to the ground" (καὶ ἐγένετο ἐν τῷ ἀναβῆναι τὴν φλόγα ἐπάνωθεν τοῦ θυσιαστηρίου

---

44. S. Gathercole, "Jesus' Eschatological Vision of the Fall of Satan : Luke 10, 18 Reconsidered," 94 (2003): 146–163.

45. Dan 4:13; 7:2; 4, 6, 7, 9, 11, 13, 21; and 8:15.

46. Buist M. Fanning, *Verbal Aspect in New Testament Greek* (Oxford: Clarendon, 1990), 241.

εἰς τὸν οὐρανὸν καὶ ἀνέβη ὁ ἄγγελος κυρίου ἐν τῇ φλογί καὶ Μανωε καὶ ἡ γυνὴ αὐτοῦ ἐθεώρουν καὶ ἔπεσον ἐπὶ πρόσωπον αὐτῶν ἐπὶ τὴν γῆν).

Here one finds exactly the same verb with the same tense to describe a vision of a past event. Thus, Gathercole's argument based on the usage of the verb "to watch" (θεωρέω) as introducing a futuristic vision is untenable.

Further, Gathercole's attempt to build his argument on Daniel 7 is also not compelling. Gathercole seems to ignore the context of Luke 10:18. It is clear that Daniel 7 is in a prophetic context (chs. 7–8). Daniel 7:2–14 describes the visions, with Daniel 7:15–27 giving the interpretation of the visions that will be fulfilled in the future. In the same pattern, Daniel 8:1–14 is another vision, and Daniel 8:15–25 is its interpretation that regards the future. However, the context of Luke 10:18 does not share the prophetic backdrop of Daniel 7. The background of Luke 10:18 is the narrative of the mission trip of Jesus's disciples. Luke 10:17 narrates the return of the disciples and the report to Jesus. "Lord, in your name even the demons submit to us." Luke 10:18 is Jesus's response to the report (10:17), where he says he "saw Satan fall from heaven like a lightening" (10:18). The following verse is the statement that further explains the fall of Satan from heaven (Luke 10:19). The Greek verb δίδωμι in the indicative mood and perfect tense (δέδωκα) has the basic force that the action of the passing of authority to the disciples was "completed in the past."[47] And Luke purposely chooses the perfect tense to emphasize the present state produced by the past action.[48] The narrative context of Luke 10:18 does not favor the prophetic view.

Therefore, Gathercole's conclusion, based on the verb θεωρέω as used in Daniel, is unlikely. The context of Luke 10:18 is not like that of Daniel 7 and thus is not in favor of the futuristic view. One finds that Gathercole's eschatological-prophetic view has no basis on which to stand. It is Hans

---

47. Daniel B. Wallace, *Greek Grammar beyond the Basics: An Exegetical Syntax of the New Testament* (Grand Rapids: Zondervan, 1996), 573. Stanley E. Porter understands "the Perfect [tense] is used to grammaticalize a state of affair." See Stanley E. Porter, *Verbal Aspect in the Greek of the New Testament, with Reference to Tense and Mood* (Frankfurt am Main: Peter Lang, 1989), 258.

48. The use of the perfect tense of a verb is often with deliberate choice. James Hope Moulton, *A Grammar of New Testament Greek. vol. 1, Prolegomena* (Edinburgh: T&T Clark, 1908), 140. The perfect tense should be taken as "intensive perfect or called resultative perfect." Wallace, *Greek Grammar* 574.

Conzelmann who abandons the prophetic aspect of this vision and argues solely for an eschatological vision. To this we now turn.

The eschatological view

Under the umbrella of the futuristic view, Hans Conzelmann argues for a purely eschatological realization of Satan's fall (Luke 10:18), (i.e. Satan's fall happens at the Parousia). He asserts that the vision of Jesus "is only an image of it (the kingdom)" which can be realized at the Parousia.[49] He interprets this vision as a picture yet to materialize because of Luke 10:20. He remarks, "Why should they not rejoice at this? Is it so that they should not think this is the end of the struggle, in other words, that they are not to mistake this event for the End?"[50] For Conzelmann, the reason why Jesus's disciples should not rejoice in the victory over demons is because there is much distress and struggle ahead that they must undergo. The disciples have to be prepared for these struggles during the interval (i.e. between the time of Jesus and the Eschaton).[51] Conzelmann's argument based on the interpretation of verse 18 is less convincing for the following reasons.

First, the saying, "do not rejoice at this," in Luke 10:20 does not necessarily mean that there should be no joy at all about the submission of the demons. Rather, it more likely means "do not rejoice primarily that the demons submit to you, but rather that your names have been written in heaven."[52] In other words, the disciples should rejoice more at the inscription of their names in heaven (i.e. their salvation), than at the submission of the demons.[53] This kind of comparison could be evidenced elsewhere in Luke's gospel. For instance, Luke 12:4–5 reads, "I tell you, my friends, do not be afraid of those who kill the body and after that can do no more. But I will warn you whom to fear: fear the One who after He has killed has authority to cast into hell; yes, I tell you, fear Him!" Obviously, this does not mean there is no fear at all for those who can kill the body. Rather, one should fear the latter more than the former. Another example is Luke 23:28 in which

---

49. Conzelmann, *Theology*, 107.
50. Ibid., 107–108.
51. Ibid.
52. Marshall, *Luke*, 430.
53. Conzelmann also admits that the names written in heaven refer to salvation. Conzelmann, *Theology*, 107.

Jesus turned and said to onlookers, "Daughters of Jerusalem, do not weep for me; weep for yourselves and for your children." Likewise, it means they should weep more for themselves than for Jesus. The last example is from Luke 10:38–42, where Luke uses the same pattern. Which is more important: Martha's generous hospitality towards Jesus (10:38) or sitting at the feet of Jesus to hear his word (10:39)? Jesus singles out the most important thing in Luke 10:42, saying, "But only one thing is needed. Mary has chosen what is better, and it will not be taken away from her." Serving the Lord with many tasks is not unimportant; however, compared to listening to the word of Jesus, it becomes less important. Thus, one can see that not to rejoice "that the spirits submit to you, but that your names are written in heaven," more likely means that there should be more rejoicing over their salvation than over their success over demons. Garrett comments well in this regard, saying, "The reason Jesus tells the disciples not to rejoice is not that their authority over spirits is 'bad,' but that it pales in comparison to the wonder of their protection against post-resurrection satanic activity."[54] Therefore, Conzelmann's argument that disciples should not rejoice at this, since they are not to mistake this event (Satan's fall) for the end, is unconvincing.

Second, Conzelmann's view that the vision is only an image is unconvincing. He comments about the vision that "it is not until the Parousia that the Kingdom itself will come; what is seen now is only an image of it."[55] One can see that for Conzelmann, the vision of Satan's fall witnessed by Jesus is only an image of what will happen in the Parousia.[56] A few lines earlier, he comments on why the Lukan Jesus says he saw this vision, saying, "[I]t is clear that this is a traditional eschatological saying. But what is its meaning in Luke's context? It adds support of course to the statement in verse 17, and makes possible the bestowal of authority in verse 19."[57] One can see that

---

54. Susan R. Garrett, *The Demise of the Devil: Magic and the Demonic in Luke's Writings* (Minneapolis: Augsburg Fortress, 1989), 57.

55. Conzelmann, *Theology*, 107.

56. We see that Conzelmann has a narrow understanding of the kingdom of God. He equates the kingdom of God with the Parousia. He denies salvation on earth as the realization of God's eschatological kingdom. As he says later on in his comments on Luke 10:18, "The context from v. 16 to v. 20, and also vv. 21 f. and 23 f., presents a picture of the salvation that has been manifested in Jesus." This is only a picture, not a material one. Ibid.

57. Ibid.

in Conzelmann's view verse 18 has a crucial significance for verses 17 and 19. Luke 10:18 not only gives support to the submission of the demons, but also provides the foundation for the distribution of authority. So far we see Conzelmann's understanding of verse 18 as Jesus borrowing the "yet to happen" image of Satan's fall to "add support to" the submission of the demons and to "make possible the bestowal of authority in verse 19." One wonders how a yet-to-be realized image of Satan's fall helps to support the already-happened fact of the submission of demons. It is more likely that this image has really happened when the disciples were expelling demons. One also wonders how a yet-to-be realized image of Satan's fall makes possible the already-realized situation of the passing on of the authority of Jesus to his disciples (as we have studied the verb with the perfect tense). Only a vision of an already-occurred event (Satan's fall) can provide the basis for the bestowal of authority to the disciples. One can see the flaw of the temporal logic in Conzelmann's argument. Thus, we see that Conzelmann's eschatological understanding of the vision of Satan's fall is problematic.

One more point on Conzelmann's comment on the vision of the fall of Satan needs to be noted. Conzelmann states that "in the interval the disciples represent their Master, as we see in Acts, and here they are being prepared.[58] One can see that Conzelmann views the vision of Satan's fall as preparing the disciples for their coming struggles during the time when Luke wrote his gospel and leading up to the Parousia. For Conzelmann this saying of Jesus (Luke 10:18) has a hortatory purpose. This seems to downplay the importance of Luke 10:18, the significance of which we will demonstrate later.

Gathercole stands in line with Conzelmann on the pastoral understanding of Luke 10:18, but he further develops this thought. First, he connects the fall of Satan to the preservation of the elect during the final woes. He takes Luke 21 as the context for an outbreak of these woes in the time before the coming of the Son of Man. This means that Jesus's exhortation to the disciples is focused on their perseverance during these woes, a perseverance which is dependent not primarily upon their authority over the evil spirits, but on God's election. Second, he views that Luke 10:21–24 is to reinforce

---

58. Ibid., 107–108.

this hortative function.⁵⁹ Third, Gathercole views the vision as eschatological. He appeals to Revelation 12:10–11 to show that the fall of Satan will take place at the final time of havoc that is the eschatological defeat of Satan and the final victory of the elect.⁶⁰ For Gathercole, Luke 21 envisages turmoil that requires believers to persevere. Luke 10:18 then means that "it is not this exorcistic power which would ultimately preserve them; that preservation is only guaranteed by the inscription of their names in the heavenly book of life."⁶¹ He says, "Their confidence during the final tribulation should rest in the fact that they belong to God's elect, that their names are written in the heavenly book of life."⁶²

Gathercole seems to follow Conzelmann's eschatological view of the vision of Satan's fall. His appeal to Luke 21 in support of his pastoral understanding of Luke 10:18 is forced, and his interpretation of Luke 10:20 is problematic for the reasons we considered above.

Therefore, we see Conzelmann's eschatological understanding of the vision of Satan's fall based on Luke 10:19–20 is problematic. Conzelmann and Gathercole's hortatory understanding of the fall of Satan downplays its significance.

Summary

In summary, the futuristic view argues that Satan is active during the time of Jesus's ministry and at the time of the early church, but we have shown that Satan plays only an instrumental role in the hand of God. Our study also shows that the prophetic view represented by Nolland and Gathercole is problematic, as is the eschatological view represented by Conzelmann. Thus the futuristic/prophetic/eschatological view of the vision of Satan's fall is unlikely. Space does not permit a consideration of the other scholars who hold this view, but similar responses could be given to their arguments. Instead we turn now to the view that the event happened in the recent past.

---

59. Gathercole, "Eschatological Vision," 163.
60. Ibid., 157.
61. Ibid., 161.
62. Ibid., 162.

An Event in the Recent Past
Scholars have advocated different occasions in which the event of the fall of Satan took place. In the following we will examine proposals of the recent past.

At the incarnation of Jesus
Some scholars hold that the fall of Satan occurred at the incarnation of Jesus.[63] In general, it is true that the incarnation of Jesus plays a foundational role in the defeat of Satan and the evil forces. However, to juxtapose the event of the fall of Satan from heaven (Luke 10:18) and the incarnation of Jesus seems speculative. The principle critique against this view is that one cannot find explicit biblical support for the connection between the incarnation of Jesus and the fall of Satan. Thus, this view is unlikely.

At the temptation of Jesus
Some have argued that Satan fell from heaven at the temptation of Jesus.[64] The temptation account (Luke 4:1–13) does indeed show the victory of Jesus in resisting the temptations of Satan. However, to equate that event with the fall of Satan from heaven in Luke 10:18 is problematic. First, the key terms in Luke 10:18 do not appear in the temptation account. Terms like "heaven" (οὐρανός) and "to fall" (πίπτω) are absent in Luke 4:1–13. Another point is that the narrative at the end of the temptation episode does not favor this view. It says, "When the devil had finished all this tempting, he left him until an opportune time" (Luke 4:13). This may indicate rather a different picture.[65] Therefore, it is hard to equate the event of the temptation with the event of Satan's fall from heaven in Luke 10:18.

At the baptism of Jesus
Joel Marcus associates the fall of Satan with the Jesus's baptism.[66] Marcus argues that "Jesus's baptism was a formative experience in his life, and this

---

63. Alfred Plummer, *A Critical and Exegetical Commentary on the Gospel according to St Luke*, ICC (New York: Charles Scribner's Sons, 1896), 278.
64. Page, *Powers of Evil*, 111; Norval Geldenhuys, *Commentary on the Gospel of Luke* (Grand Rapids: Eerdmans, 1951), 302.
65. Gathercole, "Eschatological Vision," 152.
66. Marcus, "Jesus' Baptismal Vision," 516.

may suggest that it had a visionary element."[67] He goes further to link the two events and argues for the coherence of the two events. Marcus proposes that the fall of Satan originates from the baptismal event. He attempts to make connections between both visions, such as, "I saw Satan like lightning from heaven falling and the Spirit like a dove from heaven descending."[68] As Marcus himself says, "why not link the vision that lacks a setting (Luke 10:18) with the visionary setting that lacks a plausible vision."[69] It is true that the coming of the Holy Spirit upon Jesus empowers Jesus in his ministries. But to juxtapose the two events seems overly imaginative.

At the resurrection/ascension

Other scholars have indentified the fall of Satan in Luke 10:18 with Jesus's resurrection/ascension.[70] Garrett builds her argument on a Qumran document that is especially important for her. She argues that Satan's fall happens at the resurrection/ascension of Jesus. In 11QMelch, at the year of Jubilee, the release of captives is proclaimed (Isa 61:1; Lev 25:10; cf. Luke 4:18–19). Following the command of God, Melchizedek will be enthroned in the heights, above all the heavenly beings. It is true that there is a similar concept to the Gospel of Luke where Jesus was anointed to set captives free in the year of Lord's favor (Luke 4:18–19). However, one needs to be aware that there is a significant dissimilarity between these two passages. In 11QMelch, there is a scene in which the Spirit-anointed redeemer ascends to his throne.[71] However, in Luke 10:17–20, there are no explicit or implicit references to the enthronement of Jesus. The fact is that the enthronement of Jesus occurs after the crucifixion and resurrection events (Luke 24:51–52; Acts 1:6–11).

---

67. Ibid., 513.

68. Ibid., 519.

69. Ibid., 516.

70. Garrett, *Demise of the Devil*, 51; Beale, *Revelation*, 660. In his study of the vision of the fall of Satan (Rev 12:7–12), G. K. Beale links the fall of Satan in Luke 10:18 to the one in Rev 12:7–9. We agree with his view that the fall of Satan and his followers in Rev 12:7–9 happens right after Jesus's death, resurrection, and ascension. But one needs to be aware of the sequence of the events of the fall of Satan. Satan's fall in Luke 10:18 occurs when the disciples are executing exorcisms, as we will demonstrate later, i.e. before the suffering of Jesus, while the one in Rev 12:7–9 occurs after the suffering of Jesus.

71. Martin Abegg Jr. Michael Wise, and Edward Cook, *The Dead Sea Scrolls: A New Translation*, trans. Martin G. Abegg, et al. (Rydalmere, NSW: Harper SanFrancisco; Hodder Headline, 1996), 592.

Garrett appears to simply suppose that Luke 10:17–20 contains a picture of the enthronement of a savor.[72] It seems that Garrett read the exaltation/enthronement of Jesus into the present text (Luke 10:18) without sufficient exegetical basis.

So far we have examined proposals that Satan's fall occurred at a certain event in the life Jesus. Besides the argument we have offered, a principle criticism of these views is again that there is no direct textual link between the fall of Satan (Luke 10:18) and those events (baptism, temptation, exaltation/resurrection). In what follows we will examine the vision of Satan's fall (Luke 10:18) and its context to demonstrate that there is a direct link to the mission of the seventy(two). The fall of Satan occurred when the disciples performed exorcisms on their mission trip.

At the mission of the seventy(-two)

Some scholars have pointed out that the event of Satan's fall occurred during the mission of the seventy(-two).[73] However, they do not provide sufficient evidence to support this view. In the following section, we will first explore the context of the vision of the fall of Satan in order to find the direct link between this vision and the exorcisms performed by the seventy(-two). Second, we will demonstrate that the vision has actually occurred. Jesus watched Satan falling when his disciples expulsed demons.

The major issue for those who equate the fall of Satan with key events in the life of Jesus is the lack of explicit canonical connections. What is needed is a direct link between a certain event and this vision (Luke 10:18). A good way to find such a link is to consider the context of the vision (Luke 10:17–20; 1–16; 21–24). To this we now turn.

The following study of the context of Luke 10:18 shows that a direct canonical link exists between the exorcising activity of the seventy(-two) and the fall of Satan. Texts preceding the vision of Satan's fall (Luke 10:18) are crucial for understanding the vision.

First, linguistic connections are presented in verses 17 and 18. One finds that demonic terminology appears in both passages. Demons (τὰ δαιμόνια)

---

72. Garrett, *Demise of the Devil*, 53.
73. Manson, *The Gospel of Luke*, 126; Frederick W. Danker, *Jesus and the New Age: A Commentary on St Luke's Gospel* (Philadelphia: Fortress, 1988), 217; Bock, *Luke 9:51–24:53*, 1007.

and Satan (Σατανᾶς) appear in verses 17 and 18, respectively. The term Satan is a Hellenized form of a Hebrew or Aramaic term for an adversary.[74] Satan is regarded as the chief of demons. References to Jesus also appear in both verses. The term "Lord" (κύριε) occurs in verse 17 and the phrase "in your name" (ἐν τῷ ὀνόματί σου) also indicates the person of Jesus, the Lord. The subject of both εἶπεν and ἐθεώρουν in verse 18 is likewise Jesus. Furthermore, the term "us" (ἡμῖν) in verse 17 and the term "them" (αὐτοῖς) in verse 18 both refer to the seventy(-two) disciples (cf. Luke 10:1, 17).

Second, the same notion of submission of demons appears in both passages. The concept of subjection has been brought forth by the verbs, "to submit" (ὑποτάσσω) (Luke 10:17) and "to fall" (πίπτω) (Luke 10:18). The submission of the demons is closely related to the fall of Satan.

Third, the narrative flow also connects these two verses. Hearing the report of the seventy(-two), Jesus responded by saying "I watched Satan fall from heaven." Verse 18 is a natural response to verse 17. One cannot deny the coherent narrative flow of the two verses.

Finally, verse 17 directly relates to the mission of the seventy(-two) (Luke 10:1–12). This relation is obvious. First, verse 1 is the sending of the seventy(-two). Verse 17 is their return. Second, verse 9 relates the mission of the seventy(-two) to the curing of the sick while proclaiming the kingdom of God. For Luke, the curing/healing of the sick often relates to the casting out of unclean spirits.[75] Verse 17 is the report of the seventy(-two) on their exorcising events.

---

74. Nolland, *Luke 9:21–18:34*, 563.

75. For instance, Luke chooses the term "to heal" (θεραπεύω) in the ministry of Jesus (Luke 7:21): "Jesus cured many who had diseases, sicknesses and evil spirits, and gave sight to many who were blind" (ἐθεράπευσεν πολλοὺς ἀπὸ νόσων καὶ μαστίγων καὶ πνευμάτων πονηρῶν καὶ τυφλοῖς πολλοῖς ἐχαρίσατο βλέπειν). In Luke 8:2, it says, "Some women who had been cured of evil spirits and diseases" (γυναῖκές τινες αἳ ἦσαν τεθεραπευμέναι ἀπὸ πνευμάτων πονηρῶν καὶ ἀσθενειῶν). Luke also uses the term "to heal" to describe people tormented by demons (Acts 5:16). Luke also uses the similar term "to heal" (ἰάομαι). One can find another case in Luke 9:37–43 in which Jesus healed a boy with a demon. Sickness often includes demon possession. As in Luke 10:9, Jesus told his disciples: "Heal the sick who are there and tell them, 'The kingdom of God is near you." In Luke 13:10–17, the bent over woman is described by Luke as having an ailment caused by Satan. The close relationship or overlap of the casting out of demons and the curing of the sick could be defended based on Luke 13:32. Jesus said, "Go tell that fox, 'I will drive out demons and heal people today and tomorrow, and on the third day I will reach my goal" (Καὶ εἶπεν αὐτοῖς, Πορευθέντες

Thus the study of the key terms in these two passages shows the linguistic connection between the exorcism mission of the seventy(-two) and the vision of Satan's fall. The concept of submission occurring in both passages further demonstrates the close connection between the two events. This contextual study reveals a direct link between the vision of Satan's fall and the exorcising activity of the seventy(-two). Therefore, we have found that the vision has a context.[76] The vision of Satan's fall happened in the context of the mission of the seventy(-two). By detecting the direct link between the vision of Satan's fall and the mission of the seventy(-two), one finds the time at which this vision occurred. Thus, we can say that the fall of Satan occurred when the seventy(-two) were expelling demons. The vision depicts a recent past event. The following study also supports this view.

Other pieces of evidence also support this view. First, the use of the verb "to watch" indicates that the event was happening. The verb "to watch" (θεωρέω) is used here in the imperfect tense, ἐθεώρουν. The imperfect tense in the narrative context displays the internal aspect. This imperfect could best be understood as "an ingressive imperfect," emphasizing the beginning of the fall of Satan, with implications that continue for some time.[77]

Second, contextually, the text that follows supports the fall of Satan. When the disciples reported that the demons submitted to them in the name of Jesus (Luke 10:17), Jesus said that he saw Satan fall from heaven like lightning (10:18). Naturally, this means that Jesus saw Satan fall from heaven while they were exorcising demons. This provides the foundation for the bestowal of authority on the disciples. Satan's fall demonstrates the victory of God in heaven.[78] Based on this victory, Jesus grants his authority to the disciples so that they can tread on snakes and scorpions and over all the power of the enemy, and nothing will hurt them (Luke 10:19).

Further, Satan's fall from heaven is connected to the inscription of the disciples' names in heaven (Luke 10:20). That names are inscribed in heaven

---

εἴπατε τῇ ἀλώπεκι ταύτῃ, Ἰδού, ἐκβάλλω δαιμόνια καὶ ἰάσεις ἐπιτελῶ σήμερον καὶ αὔριον, καὶ τῇ τρίτῃ τελειοῦμαι).

76. Here, one can see that Luke 10:18 does have a setting. It is not like what Marcus states that there is no setting of the fall of Satan in 10:18. See Marcus, "Jesus' Baptismal Vision," 516.

77. Wallace, *Greek Grammar* 544.

78. We will discuss this point in a greater detail below.

indicates the realization of the salvific plan of God. God expelling Satan from heaven signifies the victory of God in heaven and thus ensures the upcoming citizenships of the disciples in heaven. Therefore, the study of the verb ἐθεώρουν and the examination of the context demonstrate that the vision of the fall of Satan indeed occurred.

The contextual study demonstrates that the vision has a direct link to the exorcising activity of the seventy(-two). The fact of this link cannot be denied. The primeval and prophetic views ignore this direct link. Such a close connection between verses 17 and 18 indicates that Satan's fall is related to the exorcising activity of the seventy(-two). Jesus saw Satan fall from heaven when the seventy(-two) were exorcising demons in their mission.

Having argued that the event of the fall of Satan occurred when the seventy(-two) were exorcising demons, we will next examine the significance of the fall of Satan.

The Symbolic View

With regard to the significance of the fall of Satan, Fitzmyer and others propose a symbolic understanding of Satan's fall.[79] Fitzmyer and Marshall assert that the fall of Satan symbolically summarizes the effect of the mission of the seventy(-two), but the content of the vision did not actually take place. Jesus says Satan fell simply to sum up (Fitzmyer) or explain (Marshall) symbolically the significance of the exorcising activity of the seventy(-two).[80] For Fitzmyer, "the fall of Satan" is a "contemplation" of Jesus. The purpose of this "contemplation" is to show "how their [disciples'] activity [exorcism] expressed victory over Satan's power or influence. The evil that Satan symbolizes has met with ignominious defeat, and he has been dethroned from his prosecutor's role in the heavenly court."[81] For Fitzmyer, this saying of Jesus does not concern an actual event.[82] He simply states that Satan's fall

---

79. Fitzmyer, *Luke 10–24*, 860; Robert H. Stein, *Luke,* NAC (Nashville: Broadman, 1992), 209; Marshall, *Luke*, 428.

80. Marshall, *Luke*, 428–429; Josef Schmid, *Das Evangelium nach Lukas,* RNT (Regensburg, Germany: Friedrich Pustet, 1960), 187; Fitzmyer, *Luke 10–24*, 860.

81. Fitzmyer, *Luke 10–24*, 860.

82. Ibid.

is only a contemplation of Jesus without providing substantial support for his understanding of the vision.[83]

We agree with Fitzmyer that the fall of Satan symbolizes the victory of God in heaven over Satan's forces, but to deny the fall of Satan as an actual event is problematic. Given Fitzmyer's "contemplation" understanding of this vision, can we say the vision of Stephen in Acts 7:56 is his "contemplation"? Or shall we understand the vision of Peter (Acts 10:11) as his "contemplation"? Or consider the visions of Paul (Acts 9:3–6 and 16:9–10). Are these contemplations or even imaginations?[84] Or the vision of Cornelius (Acts 10:3–6) must likewise be a "contemplation" of Cornelius and so on. The fact is that the visions of Stephen, Peter, Paul, and Cornelius are described as events that took place in history. There are no narrative clues that support Fitzmyer's "contemplation" view of the fall of Satan.[85]

With regard to the symbolic view, both Fitzmyer and Marshall barely provide evidence to support this view.[86] The vision concerns a real event that occurred in the past as we have studied earlier. It also has a symbolic meaning to show the significance of the exorcisms done by the seventy(-two). In what follows, we will argue that the real content of the vision symbolically demonstrates the victory of God in heaven.

---

83. Ibid., 860–862. Fitzmyer's comment on the verb ἐθεώρουν seems incorrect. He says, "I recognize that this Greek vb. is used only in the pres. and impf." The fact is that a tense like aorist could be found not only in LXX, but also in Second Temple literature and even in Lukan writings. The aorist tense is found in Ps 67:25, which reads, "Your procession has come into view, O God, the procession of my God and King into the sanctuary" (ἐθεωρήθησαν αἱ πορεῖαί σου ὁ θεός αἱ πορεῖαι τοῦ θεοῦ μου τοῦ βασιλέως τοῦ ἐν τῷ ἁγίῳ"). The aorist also appears in Prov 31:16 and Sir 42:22. In Luke 23:48, one finds the aorist tense. Luke 23:48 says, "When all the people who had gathered to witness this sight saw what took place, they beat their breasts and went away" (καὶ πάντες οἱ συμπαραγενόμενοι ὄχλοι ἐπὶ τὴν θεωρίαν ταύτην, θεωρήσαντες τὰ γενόμενα, τύπτοντες τὰ στήθη ὑπέστρεφον). Marshall prefers this view. However, he does not to provide evidence to support this view. Marshall, *Luke*, 428.

84. One may also wonder that visions of John in the book of Revelation are his "contemplations."

85. Marshall prefers to the symbolic understanding of Luke 10:18. He, likewise, does not provide any argument to support this reading. See Marshall, *Luke*, 428.

86. Fitzmyer, *Luke 10–24*, 860; Marshall, *Luke*, 428.

The mission context (*Luke 10:1–12*)

The context of Luke 10:18 supports a symbolic meaning behind the actual event. We will study the context of Luke 10:18. Several points contribute to this reading.

The number seventy(-two) suggests that there is a symbolic significance for the vision of Satan's fall. This symbolism could be adduced in the Lukan use of this number as well as its use in the OT, in Second Temple literature, and in the Greco-Roman context.

The study of the number seventy(-two) in the Lukan writings supports the symbolic significance of the vision of Satan's fall. First, Luke uniquely narrates two mission accounts. One is the sending of the twelve (Luke 9:1–6) and the other is the sending of the seventy(-two) (Luke 10:1–12).[87] As seen earlier, Luke is fond of using narrative doublets to bring forth his theological concerns. The two mission accounts (Luke 9:1–6 and 10:1–12) is another case that shows a theological emphasis.[88] The two mission narratives share the same theme: Jesus sent his disciples to proclaim the kingdom of God (9:1–2; 10:1, 9). A major difference is the number of the disciples Jesus sent. In the first passage it is the twelve (9:1). In the latter it is the seventy(-two). It is this difference that brings forth the Lukan theological concern.

Second, the number seventy(-two) shows the symbolic meaning of the mission. The number seventy(-two) in the mission is hardly arbitrary. It is well acknowledged that the twelve apostles represent the twelve tribes of Israel and thus the number twelve represents the nation of Israel.[89] This point is also evidenced elsewhere in the Lukan writings.[90] One finds the

---

87. For the discussion of the Lukan source see, Sidney Jellicoe, "St Luke and the "Seventy(-two)"," *NTS* 6 (1960): 319–321. For textual criticism see Bruce Manning Metzger and Bart D. Ehrman, *The Text of the New Testament: Its Transmission, Corruption, and Restoration* (New York: Oxford University Press, 2005), 299–306. It seems, according to Metzger, both readings almost contain the same weight. That which one is the original remains unknown.

88. Both Matthew and Mark present only one mission account (Matt 10:5–15; Mark 6:7–17) that is, the sending of the Twelve.

89. "The chosen of Matthias" indicates the restoration of the twelve apostles. Thus, they represent the nation of Israel (Acts 1:12–26).

90. Luke 22:30 reads, "So that you may eat and drink at my table in my kingdom and sit on thrones, judging the twelve tribes of Israel." In Acts 7:8, it says, "Then he gave Abraham the covenant of circumcision. And Abraham became the father of Isaac and circumcised him eight days after his birth. Later Isaac became the father of Jacob, and Jacob became the father

number twelve representing the nation of Israel. The mission of the Twelve denotes the preaching of the gospel to Israel. Thus, the sending of the twelve apostles symbolizes the eschatological regathering of the twelve tribes of Israel.[91] While the number twelve denotes the nation of Israel,[92] the number seventy(-two) symbolizes all the nations of the world. The seventy in Genesis 10 in the MT or the seventy(-two) in the LXX denotes all the nations of the world.[93]

Third, the seventy(-two) in the Lukan genealogy supports a symbolic meaning. Luke first presents this idea in the genealogy (Luke 3:23–38). Luke presents the genealogy of Jesus in a different way from Matthew. Luke lists seventy-two (or seventy-seven) generations while Matthew has only forty-two (3x14). Textual criticism shows that scribes probably added some names to bring the number up to seventy-seven in order to show the ultimate significance of Jesus since the number seventy-seven was regarded as perfect.[94] One principal of textual criticism is that the shorter reading is more likely the original.[95] Thus, the seventy-two generations is preferred. The seventy(-two) is in line with the nations in Genesis 10. The seventy-two generations in the Lukan genealogy indicates all the nations of the world.

---

of the twelve patriarchs." We see the number twelve denotes the nation of the twelve tribes. The number twelve in Rev 21 also supports this point. Rev 21:12 reads, "It had a great, high wall with twelve gates and with twelve angels at the gates. On the gates were written the names of the twelve tribes of Israel." Another passage says, "The wall of the city had twelve foundations, and on them were the names of the twelve apostles of the Lamb (Rev 21:14)." Rev 21:21 reads, "The twelve gates were twelve pearls, each gate made of a single pearl. The great street of the city was of pure gold, like transparent glass."

91. Scot McKnight, "Jesus and the Twelve," *BBR* 11 (2001): 203–231.

92. The number twelve in OT and NT is often associated with the nation of Israel. This is evidenced in Luke-Acts.

93. Flender, *Theologian of Redemptive History*, 23; Scott, *Geography*, 51–55. It is unlikely that the seventy/seventy-two refers to the seventy elders who were appointed by Moses to share his responsibility (Num 11:16–25). Garrett argues that the number seventy(-two) refers to Num 11 where Moses appointed seventy(-two) helpers and here Jesus did likewise. See Garrett, *Demise of the Devil*, 47–48. This is plausible, but most likely it is that this number denotes to the whole world as it is in Gen 10 in MT and in LXX. For more discussion, see Scott, *Geography*, 51–55.

94. Cf. Gen 4:24 says, "If Cain is avenged seven times, then Lamech seventy-seven times." Matt 18:21–22 says, "Then Peter came to Jesus and asked, 'Lord, how many times shall I forgive my brother when he sins against me?' Up to seven times? Jesus answered, 'I tell you, not seven times, but seventy-seven times.'" Scott, *Geography*, 49.

95. Metzger and Ehrman, *Text of the New Testament*, 303.

Another point in the Lukan genealogy needs to be noted. Unlike Matthew who starts the genealogy of Jesus with Abraham, Luke traces Jesus's genealogy back far beyond Abraham to the first man, Adam, and then to God (Luke 3:23–38). The Lukan version of the genealogy stresses the theological concern that Jesus has universal significance for the entire humanity.[96] His ministries are not limited to the single nation of Israel, but rather, to all created human beings.[97] The relation of Jesus to all humanity also supports the universalism indicated by the number seventy(-two).

Therefore, we see that the number seventy(-two) in the Lukan writings denotes all the nations of the world. This notion also appears in Greco-Roman literature.

The number seventy(-two) has a universal notion in the Greco-Roman world. *Hieroglyphica* 1:14 says, "There are seventy-two ancient countries in the inhabited world" (ἑβδομήκοντα δύο χώρας τὰς ἀρχαίας φασὶ τῆς οἰκουμένης εἶναι). Other evidence could be found in Greek literature and in astrological tradition.[98] Thus, one finds that the number seventy(two) also denotes universalism in the Greco-Roman world.

Some terms and phrases Luke uses point to a universal notion. First is the word "every" (πᾶς) in verse 1. Jesus sent the seventy(-two) to every town and place (πᾶσαν πόλιν καὶ τόπον) where he is about to go. The term "every" (πᾶσαν) shows the inclusiveness. Second, the use of the phrase "every town" in the OT supports this point (Deut 2:34; 3:6; 2 Kgs 3:19; Jer 31:8). The uniquely Lukan phrase "every town and place" has the connotation of the wholeness of the world. Third, the term "plentiful" (πολύς) in "plentiful harvest" (θερισμὸς πολύς) (Luke 10:2) indicates the innumerable size of the people in the world.

Therefore, the above study of the number seventy(-two) in the Lukan writings and in Greco-Roman literature shows that the number seventy(-two), like the number twelve, has a symbolic meaning. Some terms and phrases in the mission narrative (Luke 10:1–12) also support the notion

---

96. Green, *The Gospel of Luke*, 189; Craddock, *Luke*, 53; Marshall, *Luke*, 161. Also see Irenaeus, 3.22.3. James R. Payton, Jr., *Irenaeus on the Christian Faith: A Condensation of Against Heresies* (Eugene, OR: Pickwick, 2011), 80.

97. Bock, *Luke 1:1–9:50*, 360.

98. Scott, *Geography*, 53.

that the mission of the seventy(-two) is to all the people of the world. The number, seventy(-two), symbolizes all the nations of the world. The mission of the seventy(-two) symbolizes the mission to the whole wide world. Next, we will provide more evidence to show that the mission of the seventy(-two) indicates a universal mission.

The parallel of the two mission narratives
Scholars have acknowledged that Luke is fond of using parallelism in Luke-Acts in order to bring forth the force of the comparison.[99] It is Flender who gives an excellent commentary on the two mission narratives (Luke 9:1–6 and 10:1–12). Flender observes the difference in the dimensions of the two mission accounts. He persuasively points out the parallels in Luke-Acts, which represent typical Lukan style in his narrative.[100] One of these patterns is climactic parallelism.[101] The two mission accounts (Luke 9:1–6 and 10:1–12) fit in the pattern of the climactic parallelism.[102] The mission of the twelve "remains earth-bound and preliminary."[103] The mission of the seventy(-two) is cosmological because "[i]t deals with peace on earth (in Luke 10:5ff, the term "peace" appears three times: cf. Luke 2:14) or the last judgment, which is on a cosmic scale (10:15). The precondition for this is the fall of Satan from heaven (10:18) . . . What happens on the celestial plane is decisive (10:20). The mission of the seventy(-two) becomes the sign of the consummation in heaven."[104]

Flender's cosmological understanding of the mission of the seventy(-two) is to be affirmed, but one point needs to be noted. Flender takes the fall of Satan from heaven (Luke 10:18) as the precondition of the mission of the seventy(-two). He probably holds that Satan's fall occurred before the mission of the seventy(-two). As our earlier studies have demonstrated, the fall of Satan happened at the time that the seventy(-two) were exorcising demons. It is the mission of the seventy(-two) that caused Satan to fall from heaven. Thus, this mission is cosmological.

---

99. Flender, *Theologian of Redemptive History*, 8.
100. Ibid., 8–27.
101. Ibid., 20–21.
102. Ibid., 22–23.
103. Ibid., 23.
104. Ibid.

Therefore, our study of the number seventy(-two) in its mission context (Luke 10:1–12), in the OT and Greco-Roman litierature, and an examination of the two mission narratives (Luke 9:1–6; 10:1–12) demonstrated that the vision of the fall of Satan in Luke 10:18 has a symbolic meaning.

Summary

The preceding study of the views on the vision of Satan's fall demonstrated that there is no direct link between the fall of Satan in Luke 10:18 and the primeval fall of Satan. The fall of Satan here connects to the exorcisms of the disciples of Jesus. Satan fell when the seventy(-two) performed exorcisms. The fall of Satan is an actual event. Exorcisms performed by the seventy(-two) symbolize the universality of the exorcisms of the disciples. This is an attack on Satan and his followers. The submission of demons to the seventy(-two) disciples symbolizes the defeat of all the evil forces of Satan. This indicates the victory of God in heaven. Next, we will show how Satan's fall denotes the victory of God in heaven.

The Victory of God in Heaven

The defeat of Satan and the victory of God in heaven could be evidenced by the following studies. First, we will study the Isaianic allusion. Second, we will examine the Lukan use of the term "Satan." Third, we will study the judgment narrative (Luke 11:13–15). Fourth, we will investigate Luke 10:19. Last, we will study the four heaven references (Luke 10:13, 18; 20, 21).

Allusion to Isaiah 14:12

Our study of the Isaianic passage will demonstrate the victory of God in heaven. The statement "the victory of God in heaven" does not suggest that Satan has been completely defeated. We are aware that the climax of the victory of God is of course on the cross and in the resurrection of Jesus, and the final consummation lies in the Parousia.

The Lukan reinterpretation of Isaiah 14 brings forth the victory of God in heaven. In what follows we will demonstrate that Luke applies this Isaianic passage to the fall of Satan in order to bring forth the victory of God in heaven. To say that Luke 10:18 is an allusion to Isaiah 14:12 does not necessarily mean that Luke equates Isaiah 14:12 with the fall of Satan in Luke

10:18, but rather that the allusion is Luke's way to reinterpret the Isaianic passage for his theological concerns.

It is certain that the vision of Satan's fall in Luke 10:18 is an allusion to Isa 14:12.[105] One can observe that Luke carefully follows the logic of Isaiah 14.[106] First, Luke follows the Isaianic context. Isaiah 14:1–2 is a prophecy of the restoration of Judah and the joining in of the Gentiles/nations. Prior to these events, God will defeat their enemy, the king of Babylon (Isa 14:3–22), who wanted to ascend to the tops of the clouds and to make himself like the Most High (Isa 14:14).[107] But God threw him down because of his prideful thoughts. God's victory over the enemy ensures the restoration of Judah and the joining in of the Gentiles. In Luke's logic, the devil (ὁ διάβολος) similarly wanted to obtain divine glory by asking Jesus to worship him (Luke 4:7).[108] The devil also wanted to be equal to the Most High. This has been made obvious by Jesus's reply that God is the only one to be worshiped (Luke 4:8).[109] That Satan previously resided in heaven has been evidenced in the OT (Job 1:6–12; 2:1–7; Zech 3:1–2), in Second Temple literature (Ascen. Isa 7:9; Philo, *On the Giants* 6), and also in the NT (Eph 2:2). Satan similarly had prideful thoughts. Then God cast him down from heaven.

The victory of God in heaven ensures the coming of the kingdom of God among Israel and the Gentiles through the missions of the twelve (9:1–6) and the seventy(-two) (10:1–12). One finds that the occasion for the fall of Satan in Luke 10 parallels the occasion for the fall of the king of

---

105. Isaiah probably used the myth of the Ancient Near East to depict the fall of Satan. See A. Marx, A. Marx, "La chute de 'Lucifer' (Esaïe 14, 12–15; Luc 10, 18): Préhistoire d'un mythe," *RHPR* 80 (2000): 171–185.

106. Garrett, *Demise of the Devil*, 50–51.

107. Clouds usually indicate the glory of God in both OT and NT.

108. Garrett, *Demise of the Devil*, 50.

109. Similarly, demons were cast out of heaven because of their wickedness. Here is the Testament of Solomon (first to third Century BCE) from 20:14–17: "I [Solomon] asked him [Ornias], 'Tell me, then, how you, being demons, are able to ascend into heaven.' He replied, 'Whatever things are accomplished in heaven in the same way also on earth; for the principalities and authorities and powers above fly around and are considered worthy of entering heaven. But we who are demons are exhausted from not having a way station from which to ascend or on which to rest; so we fell down like leaves from the trees and the men who are watching thought that stars were falling from heaven. That is not true, King; rather, we fell because of our weakness and, since there is nothing on which to hold, we were dropped like flashes of lighting to the earth.'"

Babylon in Isaiah 14.[110] Therefore, Luke follows the logic of Isaiah 14:1–22 to bring forth the victory of God over Satan's forces and the realization of the kingdom of God on earth. The term "Satan" also shows the victory of God over Satan.

The Term "Satan"

The victory of God over Satan's forces is also indicated by the occurrence of the term Satan. Prior to the narrative of the fall of Satan (Luke 10:18), Luke prefers the term "the devil" (ὁ διάβολος) instead of "Satan" (Luke 4:2, 3, 6, 13; 8:12). The term "Satan" (Σατανᾶς) in Luke 10:18 is the first occurrence in Gospel of Luke. Satan is the enemy of God. Satan is also the prince of evil spirits. Here Luke purposely makes the change by using the term Satan instead of the devil to signify that the head of evil has been defeated. Satan has fallen from heaven. God has won the victory over Satan in heaven. Next, we will examine the judgment narrative to demonstrate the victory of God in heaven.

The Judgment Narrative (Luke 10:13–15)

The judgment narrative (10:13–15) also shows the victory of God in heaven. In light of the mission of the seventy(-two) (Luke 10:1–12), Luke 10:13–15 narrates the consequence of the people who failed to respond well to the gospel message.[111] Luke 10:16 stresses the "rejection aspect" since the term ἀθετέω occurs repeatedly (four times). Extending the serious consequence of the rejection by the town (πόλις) (10:11–12), Luke 10:13–15 singles out specific towns that failed to repent at the message of Jesus. Those towns were near Capernaum. The towns represent the citizens who live in them. In early Jewish and Christian apocalyptic literature, people used cities to denote an evil generation.[112] The fate of people who did not respond well to the gospel message would be worse off than those who failed to respond well to the

---

110. Marx, "La chute de 'Lucifer'," 171–185. Marx also takes that Luke 10:18 is the reinterpretation of Isa 14:12. He considers Luke's implicit reference to Isa 14:12, in which the king of Babylon is interpreted as having "fallen from heaven," and the application of this passage to Satan. Garrett, *Demise of the Devil*, 51.

111. Matthew puts this episode in a different setting (Matt 10:20–24).

112. Richard Bauckham, *The Climax of Prophecy: Studies on the Book of Revelation* (Edinburgh: T&T Clark, 1993), 338–383.

prophetic messages in Tyre and Sidon (Jer 25:22; 47:4; Ezek 26:1—28:24).[113] The point is that the refusal of the gospel message is dead serious. Why would Capernaum be thrown into hell? The reason is that Capernaum had been considered as the hub of Jesus's early ministry. People in Capernaum had witnessed more of Jesus's healing ministries and other mighty deeds (Luke 4:23, 31–37; 7:1–10; cf. Mark 1:21–3:6; 9:33–37) than those in other cities. The judgment of the cities shows the authority of God on earth. This is the impact of the victory of God in heaven on earth. Jesus evokes this imagery to point to the eschatological judgment, and at the same time, shows that he is in the midst of a battle against evil forces (Satan).[114]

The Authority over Every/All the Power of the Enemy (Luke 10:19)

Luke 10:19 shows the impact on earth of the victory of God in heaven over Satan. Luke 10:19 reads, "I have given you authority to trample on snakes and scorpions and to overcome all the power of the enemy; nothing will harm you." This is an allusion to Psalm 91:13 (LXX 90:13), which probably has its background in Deuteronomy 8. Both of these OT texts appear in the temptation account in Luke 4:1–13. Psalm 91 is also related to exorcism in Second Temple literature. The Qumran text of 11QPsAp^a groups three non-canonical apotropaic psalms with Psalm 91.[115] Thus, we see that Luke alludes to Psalm 91 here to demonstrate the triumph of God in heaven and its impact on earth, namely that the disciples of Jesus receive authority to overcome all the power of enemy, including that of evil spirits. The combination of the strong negative words "nothing" (οὐδὲν) and "not" (οὐ μὴ) emphasizes the secure protection by the mighty power of God over his enemy, Satan. Therefore, the bestowal of the authority of Jesus upon his disciples is the earth's realization of the victory of God in heaven.

---

113. In the OT, the enemy of God refused to listen to God and was thus punished. Now, the people of God are like those enemies who refused to listen to God. Their fate is thus serious judgment.

114. David W. Pao, *Lujia Fuyin, vol. 1*, 476.

115. Michael Wise, *Dead Sea Scrolls*, 376–377; David C. Mitchell, *The Message of the Psalter: An Eschatological Programme in the Book of Psalms*, JSOTSup 252 (Sheffield: Sheffield Academic, 1997), 279–281. Pao, *Lujia Fuyin, vol. 2*, 211.

The Four Heaven References (Luke 10:16, 18, 20, 21)

The four heaven references are hardly accidental. First, they show the victory of God in heaven. The first reference to heaven appears in Luke 10:16. Capernaum may think it will be raised up into heaven (ἕως οὐρανοῦ ὑψωθήσῃ) since it has witnessed so many mighty works of Jesus, as Luke 10:13 indicates. The fact is that the city indeed had witnessed more mighty works of Jesus than other cities had (Luke 4:31–41). Capernaum is of unique importance because it is so closely associated with Jesus and his mission. Luke locates the "woe to Capernaum" phrase here for two reasons. One is to show that the judgment upon that city is worse than that upon Chorazin and Bethsaida (cf. Luke 6:17). The second is to show that God has sovereignty in heaven. Heaven is not a place that one could enter apart from accepting the message of Jesus. Otherwise one would definitely be thrown down into Hades (ἕως τοῦ ᾅδου καταβήσῃ).

The second reference to heaven is in verse 18, where Satan falls from heaven (ἐκ τοῦ οὐρανοῦ πεσόντα). This shows that Satan had lost his heavenly status. God's expulsion of Satan from heaven shows God's power and authority in heaven. Heaven will no longer be a place for Satan and his followers.

The third reference to heaven is in verse 20, where Jesus says the disciples' names are written in heaven (τὰ ὀνόματα ὑμῶν ἐγγέγραπται ἐν τοῖς οὐρανοῖς). This means that those disciples have been granted citizenship in heaven and have thus received their heavenly status. The divine passive verb, ἐγγέγραπται, shows that it is God who granted their heavenly status.

The last reference to heaven appears in Luke 10:21. God is addressed as the Lord of heaven and earth (κύριε τοῦ οὐρανοῦ καὶ τῆς γῆς) by Jesus. The word κύριε shows his sovereignty. The phrase "heaven and earth" (τοῦ οὐρανοῦ καὶ τῆς γῆς) also shows his dominion. The sovereignty of the Lord God is over heaven and earth. The heaven reference here asserts the sovereignty of God over heaven and earth. Thus, it confirms the victory of God in heaven.

The four references to heaven show the dynamics of God in heaven. Capernaum wants to be elevated into heaven, but it will be thrown down. Satan once lived in heaven, but he has fallen down from heaven. The earth-dwelling disciples have gained citizenship in heaven. These things have occurred because God is the Lord of heaven and earth. Heaven is not a static place; it points to heavenly battles, but God has won the battle over Satan in heaven.

Summary

Therefore, the study of Luke's allusion to Isaiah 14 shows that Luke reinterprets the Isaianic passage to highlight the victory of God in heaven. The study of the unique appearance of the term Satan (Luke 10:18) shows the defeat of Satan by God. The examination of the judgment narrative (Luke 10:13–16) demonstrates the authority of God and thus stresses the victory of God. The study of the bestowal of the authority of Jesus upon his disciples (Luke 10:19) shows the victory of God in heaven and its impact on earth. The scrutiny of the four references of heaven (Luke 10:16, 18, 20, 21) confirms the victory of God in heaven. Satan was expelled from heaven. God has won the battle in heaven. Next, we will explore the agent of the victory of God.

The Agent of the Victory of God

In this section, we will argue that God uses Jesus and his followers as the agents to defeat Satan. With regard to the agents of the victory of God, scholars have different views. Müller argues that the defeat of Satan is simply an act of God that has nothing to do with Jesus and his disciples.[116] He makes a clear distinction between the defeat of Satan in heaven and the ministry of Jesus and his disciples.[117] For Müller, God simply shows his power by casting out Satan from heaven, thus providing the foundation for the materialization of the eschatological kingdom (i.e. salvation).[118] It is true that exorcism is the work of God. However, to separate the salvific work of God from Jesus, his ministry, and the ministry of his disciples is problematic. In the following, we will argue that God's defeat of Satan is by the agent Jesus and also by his disciples. First, we will show that Jesus is the agent of God in defeating Satan. Then we will demonstrate that the disciples of Jesus are also agents in defeating Satan.

---

116. Ulrich B. Müller, "Vision und Botschaft: Erwägungen zur prophetischen Struktur der Verkündigung Jesu," *ZTK* 74 (1977): 418.

117. Ibid.

118. Ibid., 422.

Jesus as the Agent of God

We will argue that Jesus is the agent of God in defeating Satan. This is evidenced in the New Testament as well as in Second Temple literature.

Evidence from the NT

First, repeatedly Luke closely relates Jesus and God in regard to the work of salvation.[119] A few examples will suffice. In Luke 1:47 and 2:11 respectively, God and Jesus are both called "Savior." Second, in Luke 8:39 ("Return home and tell how much God has done for you") and 9:43 ("And they were all amazed at the greatness of God"), the name "God" is probably applied to Jesus.[120] Third, the father-son relationship in Luke 10:16–17 and 21–24 shows that the Son (Jesus) is closely related to the Father (God). Fourth, Luke 11:20 implies that Jesus's acts are the acts of God himself: "But if I drive out demons by the finger of God, then the kingdom of God has come to you."

Second, there is evidence that God's plan to defeat the evil forces is initiated in Jesus. In the Benedictus, Zechariah prophesies that God has raised a mighty savior (Jesus) to save the people of Israel from their enemies (1:68–73). Here the enemies include Satan and his evil forces. Verses 78–79 read, "because of the tender mercy of our God, by which the rising sun will come to us from heaven to shine on those living in darkness and in the shadow of death, to guide our feet into the path of peace." Here the "darkness" (σκότος) and "the shadow of death" (σκιᾷ θανάτου) metaphorically refer to the evil forces. As we have already demonstrated, the ἀνατολὴ ἐξ ὕψους refers to Jesus, the Messiah. We can see that God the Father, who has tender mercy, rescued his people by his agent, Jesus.

Third, Luke 4:18–19 also supports this notion. This passage is an allusion to Isaiah 61:1–2 (cf. 58:6). God the Father conducts his salvific work through Jesus to bring good news to the poor, to proclaim release to the captives and to let the oppressed go free. While one cannot deny the literary meaning of the captives and the oppressed, these terms also refer to people

---

119. Luke, in some places, does show the difference between God the Father and God the Son. In Luke 23:46, Jesus commends his spirit to the Father. In Acts 1:6–7, God the Father has the authority to set times or periods to restore the kingdom to Israel, etc.

120. John T. Carroll, *Luke: A Commentary*, NTL (Louisville, KY: Westminster, 2012), 12.

who were captive and oppressed by Satan. It is Jesus who will rescue his people from Satan.

Thus Luke closely relates Jesus to God in the work of salvation. God initiates the salvific plan and Jesus executes the plan.

Evidence in the Second Temple literature
Other evidence shows that the fall of Satan will take place when the Messiah comes. When the Messiah comes he will defeat the evil one. This notion exists in the Second Temple period, evidence of which is found in the Pseudepigrapha (*Testaments of the Twelve Patriarchs*). Showing the general conception that when the Messiah comes he will defeat Satan, *T. Levi* reads, "And then the Lord will raise up a new priest to whom all the words of the Lord will be revealed . . . And Beliar shall be bound by him. And he shall grant to his children the authority to trample on wicked spirits" (18:2, 12). One can see that the new priest is the priestly Messiah, who will defeat the evil one and bestow authority to trample on evil spirits to his children. We can see the astonishing parallels between this passage and Luke 10:17–20.

Likewise, *T. Sim.* 6:5–6 reads, "Then Shem shall be glorified; because God the Lord, the Great One in Israel, will be manifest upon the earth [as a man]. He himself will save Adam. Then all the spirits of error shall be given over to being trampled underfoot. And men will have mastery over the evil spirits. Then I shall arise in gladness and I shall bless the Most High for his marvels, [because God has taken a body, eats with human beings, and saves human beings]."

Therefore, one cannot separate the work of God from Jesus in the defeat of Satan. God the Father uses his Son, Jesus, to destroy Satan and his forces.

The Disciples as Representatives of Jesus
That the disciples are representatives of Jesus has been made clear in Luke 10:16: "He who listens to you listens to me; he who rejects you rejects me; but he who rejects me rejects him who sent me." This connection between the disciples and Jesus has been shown in two ways. Positively, those who listen to the disciples listen to Jesus. This connection is also stated negatively, thus reconfirming this relationship: those who reject the disciples reject Jesus. The two-way connection between the disciples and Jesus shows that the disciples are representatives of Jesus. Further, Jesus even links the disciples

to God the Father. Those who reject Jesus reject the Father. Consequently, those who reject the disciples reject the Father.

The exorcisms performed by the disciples in the name of Jesus also show that the disciples are the representatives of Jesus (Luke 10:17). Jesus's bestowal of authority upon the disciples (Luke 10:19) again demonstrates the connection between the disciples and Jesus. Thus, the disciples have been identified as representatives of Jesus. The disciples stand along with Jesus as agents executing the victory of God over Satan and his followers.

Summary

Therefore, our study shows that one cannot separate the act of God from Jesus who is the agent by which God gains the victory in heaven over Satan. And the disciples as the representatives of Jesus also join as agents to gain the victory of God.

The Victory of God over Satan in Heaven and Its Impact on Earth

In this section, we will demonstrate that the victory of God over Satan in heaven impacts earth in that the eschatological kingdom of God (salvation) has been made manifest on earth. This is evidenced by the kingdom concern in Luke 10:17–20 and also in a wider context (Luke 10:1–24).

Luke 10:17–20

First, the report of the seventy(-two) about their exorcisms shows the kingdom concern of this passage. Unlike the mission of the twelve, Luke especially narrates the exorcism report in the mission of the seventy(-two). The significance of the exorcism has been made clear in Luke 11:20 which says, "But if I drive out demons by the finger of God, then the kingdom of God has come to you." Marshall provides an excellent comment on the phrase "the kingdom of God has come to you" (ἔφθασεν ἐφ' ὑμᾶς ἡ βασιλεία τοῦ θεοῦ). In his response to Clark who argues that "the the verb (ἔφθασεν) means 'to draw near, even to the very point of contact' but no more."[121] Marshall comments that "it is, however, splitting hairs to take this to mean that the kingdom has not arrived. What is of significance is surely

---

121. Kenneth Willis Clark, "Realized Eschatology," *JBL* 59 (1940): 367–383.

the addition ἐφ' ὑμᾶς; the point is that the kingly and saving power of God has drawn near to the hearers and is there for them to grasp; the proof that it is near to them is that its power has been evidenced in the lives of other people, namely in the exorcisms."[122] Jesus illustrates why he exorcises and brings out the virtue of the exorcism in Luke 11:14–23. He talks about two kingdoms: the kingdom of God and the kingdom of Satan. He also shows two powers: the power of God and the power of Satan. "But if it is by the finger of God that I cast out demons, then the kingdom of God has come to you" (11:20). When the stronger man attacks the strong one, he (Jesus) overpowers him (Satan) and takes away his armor in which he trusted and divides his plunder. Jesus as the agent of God attacks Satan and overpowers the kingdom of Satan. The notion that by doing exorcisms the kingdom of God has been manifested is also noted.[123] The dominion of the evil one has been broken. The reign of the sovereign God has come.

Second, the fall of Satan from heaven (Luke 10:18) concerns the kingdom of God. As mentioned, the fall of Satan from heaven happened when the seventy(-two) performed exorcisms in their mission trip (Luke 10:1–12). The expelling of demons indicates the presence of the kingdom of God on earth. Satan's fall from heaven shows the victory of God in heaven. Its impact is the materialization of the eschatological kingdom of God on earth.

Third, in Luke 10:19, the bestowal of authority over all the power of the enemies on the one hand shows the victory of God over Satan. On the other hand, it shows the sovereignty of God. This indicates that the kingdom of God has overcome the kingdom of Satan.

Finally, Luke 10:20 has a kingdom concern. The names of the disciples "having been inscribed in heaven" (ἐγγέγραπται ἐν τοῖς οὐρανοῖς) shows the citizenship of the disciples. The disciples have already gotten salvation. That their names are written in heaven indicates that the disciples are citizens of heaven. These disciples belong to the heavenly kingdom. The notion of the book of life is prevalent in the Old Testament (Exod 32:32–33; Pss 69:28; 56:9; 87:6; Isa 4:3; 34:16; Dan 21:1; Mal 3:16–17) and also in the New Testament (Phil 4:3; Heb 12:23; Rev 3:5; 13:8). And evidence could also

---

122. Marshall, *Luke*, 476.
123. Graham Twelftree, *In the Name of Jesus: Exorcism among Early Christians* (Grand Rapids: Baker, 2007), 134.

be found in Second Temple literature (*Jub.* 30:19–23; *1 En.* 47:3; 104:1, 7; 108:3, 7; 1 QM 12:2; 4Q180 1:3). The verb ἐγγράφω only occurs here and in 2 Corinthians 3:2, 3. In all three occurrences the verb is passive, because the action is done by God. That names having been written in heaven signifies that the names remain engraved in heaven forever.

Thus, the exorcism report (Luke 10:17), the fall of Satan from heaven (Luke 10:18), the bestowal of the authority of Jesus to his disciples (Luke 10:19), and the names of the disciples written in heaven (Luke 10:20) demonstrate that the main concern of this passage is the kingdom of God. Next, we will examine the mission narrative (Luke 10:1–12) to show that its main theme is the kingdom of God.

Luke 10:1–12

A couple of points will show that the main theme of the mission of the seventy(-two) is the kingdom of God. First is the unique greeting "peace to this house" (10:5), meaning to bring salvation to the house, as was observed earlier. The phrase "peace to this house" (εἰρήνη τῷ οἴκῳ τούτῳ) is not merely a customary greeting, as our earlier studies demonstrate. The term "peace" is the eschatological peace (i.e. salvation).

Besides, curing the sick is one of the means of the preaching of the kingdom of God. The following text shows this point. Luke 10:9 says, "Heal the sick who are there and tell them the kingdom of God is near you." This point is also apparent in Acts 4:29–30 where curing of the sick accompanies preaching the word of God. "Now, Lord, consider their threats and enable your servants to speak your word with great boldness. Stretch out your hand to heal and perform miraculous signs and wonders through the name of your holy servant Jesus (Acts 4:29–30)."

In addition, Luke intends to blur the demarcations of healing the sick and exorcisms. He often makes healing stories into exorcisms and vice versa.[124] For instance, in the account of Jesus healing Peter's mother-in-law (Luke 4:38–41), Luke chooses the term "rebuke" (ἐπιτιμάω) which is a typical term in Luke's exorcism stories (Luke 4:35, 41; 9:42). In Luke 13:10–17, where there was "a woman who had a spirit of weakness for eighteen years" (ἰδοὺ γυνὴ πνεῦμα ἔχουσα ἀσθενείας ἔτη δεκαοκτώ), Luke uses the term

---

124. Ibid., 132.

"to heal" (θεραπεύω) (Luke 13:14). Last, the most explicit passage is the commission of Jesus to his disciples. They should declare that "the kingdom of God has come upon you (ἤγγικεν ἐφ' ὑμᾶς ἡ βασιλεία τοῦ θεου)." The similar sentence of preaching of the kingdom of God recurs in verse 11 to emphasizing this commission. As we see in Luke 10:11, "the kingdom of God has come near (ἤγγικεν ἡ βασιλεία τοῦ θεοῦ) (Luke 10:11)."

Thus one finds that a major concern of the mission is to bring salvation/the eschatological kingdom to people. Bird comments rightly that mission is viewed as "the mechanism of God's eschatological salvation."[125] While the mission narrative is the preaching of the kingdom of God, the following judgment account also concerns the kingdom of God.

Luke 10:13–16

The judgment in Luke 10:13–16 depicts salvation/the kingdom of God from another angle. The consequence of rejecting the kingdom message is dead serious. Luke 10:13–15 describes the consequence for those who reject the kingdom message (i.e. salvation). Unlike Matthew, Luke puts this episode right after the account of the mission of the seventy(-two).[126] The rejection of the kingdom message has been foreshadowed in the mission account (Luke 10:10–11). The wiping off of the dust of the town that does not receive the messengers and their message suggests separation from a town that will be punished.[127] Luke 10:16 stresses the "reject" aspect since the term ἀθετέω occurs four times. The word ἀθετέω is very strong language, meaning "despise." The judgment of those who reject the kingdom message extends the consequence of the rejection of the town (πόλις) (10:11–12). It is their refusal of the coming kingdom that brings judgment upon them. The judgment narrative tells of the serious consequences for those who reject the kingdom message. Therefore, we see that the main concern of the judgment episode is salvation/the kingdom of God. In what follows, our study will examine another contextual passage (Luke 10:21–24) to show that its main theme is again the kingdom of God.

---

125. Bird, "Mission as an Apocalyptic Event," 133.
126. Matthew locates this episode in a different setting (Matt 10:20–24).
127. Nolland, *Luke 1–9*, 428.

Luke 10:21–24

What Jesus's rejoiced at is the realization of the kingdom on earth. First, the expression, "Lord of heaven and earth" indicates that God is the one who conducts the eschatological salvation.[128] In prophetic tradition, "the Lord who made the heaven and earth, the sea and everything in them" (δέσποτα, σὺ ὁ ποιήσας τὸν οὐρανὸν καὶ τὴν γῆν καὶ τὴν θάλασσαν καὶ πάντα τὰ ἐν αὐτοῖς) is the Lord who has power and is able to rescue his people (Isa 40:28; 43:15; 45:18; 65:17–18). Second, the phrase, "for such is your gracious will," is about salvation/the kingdom of God. The only two occurrences of the word (εὐδοκία) in Lukan writings are hardly accidental (cf. Luke 2:14). As we have seen, the "peace on earth to men on whom his favor rests," this is the eschatological peace (i.e. salvation). In the Book of Psalms (LXX 18:15; 50:20; 68:14; 88:18; 105:4; 140:5) the Lord's "favor" refers to his salvation plan. This idea also survives in the Second Temple period. *Psalms of Solomon* (1st century BCE) 8:33 reads, "May (you) be pleased with us and our children forever; Lord, our savor, we will not be troubled at the end of time" (ἡμῖν καὶ τοῖς τέκνοις ἡμῶν ἡ εὐδοκία εἰς τὸν αἰῶνα κύριε σωτὴρ ἡμῶν οὐ σαλευθησόμεθα ἔτι τὸν αἰῶνα χρόνον). Therefore, the main concern of this passage is the kingdom of God.

Luke 10:25–37 in which the lawyer asks he must do to inherit eternal life (Luke 10:25) also supports this reading. In Luke 10:38–42, Jesus emphasizes the importance of the word of God, which is the only thing people need that can bring eternal life.[129]

Summary

Therefore, our study of this passage (Luke 10:17–20) shows that the main concern of the fall of Satan is the kingdom of God. Our studies of the mission narrative (Luke 10:1–12), the judgment account (Luke 10:13–16), and the rejoicing of Jesus episode (Luke 10:21–24) demonstrate that the concern is consistently the kingdom of God. Even such passages as Luke 10:25–37 and 38–42 are in favor of this point. Therefore, we see that the theme of the kingdom of God/salvation is prevalent through all these passages.

---

128. Pao, *Lujia Fuyin*, vol. 1, 483.
129. Marshall, *Luke*, 440.

Summary

In this section, the following have been demonstrated. First, we have investigated views on the vision of Satan's fall (Luke 10:18). The primeval view on this vision based on Isaiah 14 is problematic. While Satan first fell at some time in the distant past, this is not what Jesus is seeing in Luke 10:18. The prophetic view of this vision is also unconvincing. The vision of Jesus does not mirror that of the prophets, in that Jesus not only sees the vision (in a way the prophets did) but also acts as the agent executing Satan's fall. The vision of the fall of Satan is not purely futuristic as in the Prophets. So too is the eschatological view of Satan's fall problematic, since the content of the vision of Satan's fall has already occurred. Our study of the passage on the vision of Satan's fall (Luke 10:18) shows that the vision is a real experience of Jesus. Our studies of its immediate context (Luke 10:17–20) and its larger context (Luke 10:1–24) reveal that the vision refers directly to the exorcising activity of the seventy(-two). The vision occurred when the seventy(-two) performed exorcisms. Jesus watched as Satan was falling from heaven while the disciples were expelling demons.

Second, our study of the mission context (Luke 10:1–12) reveals that the fall of Satan from heaven has a symbolic meaning. The mission of the seventy(-two) symbolizes the universal mission of the kingdom of God. The exorcisms by the seventy(-two) symbolize grand attacks on Satan's forces. The content of the vision is real and it symbolizes the victory of God in heaven over Satan.

Third, our study demonstrates the victory of God in heaven over Satan. (1) Our study of Luke's allusion to Isaiah 14:12 shows the victory of God in heaven over Satan as similar to the victory of God over the king of Babylon. (2) Our study of the term "Satan" (Luke 10:18) supports God's power over Satan's forces. (3) Our examination of the judgment narrative (Luke 10:13–16) demonstrates the authority of God over Satan. Our examination of the bestowal of the authority of Jesus upon his disciples (Luke 10:19) shows the victory of God in heaven and its impact on earth. Our scrutiny of the four references to heaven (Luke 10:15, 18, 20, 21) confirms the victory of God in heaven.

Fourth, our study shows that the agents of the victory of God are Jesus and his disciples. God gains the victory in heaven over Satan by his Son, and the disciples are representatives of Jesus and therefore are also agents of the victory of God.

Finally, our studies of Luke 10 reveal that its main concern is the kingdom of God. The eschatological kingdom of God is the main concern of (1) the fall of Satan from heaven in Luke 10:18; (2) the mission of the seventy(-two) in Luke 10:1–12; (3) the judgment narrative in Luke 10:13–16; and (4) the rejoicing of Jesus in Luke 10:21–24.

Therefore, one finds that the fall of Satan from heaven is the victory of God in heaven. The impact of the victory of God in heaven has been made manifest in the eschatological kingdom on earth. Next, we will study exorcisms in Luke to demonstrate the impact of the victory of God in heaven on earth.

Exorcisms in Luke

Having studied the fall of Satan from heaven, in this section we will examine other references to exorcism in Luke. First, we will study exorcisms in the Gospel of Luke more broadly. Second, we will demonstrate the theological significance of exorcisms by investigating Jesus's comment on the exorcisms in Luke 11:14–23. We will argue that Luke intentionally modifies his source to show the close connection of this passage to the passage on Satan's fall (Luke 10:18). Luke views the exorcism as a sign from heaven. We will also demonstrate that this passage stresses the victory of God in heaven over Satan's forces. Its impact on earth is the manifestation of the eschatological kingdom of God upon earth. Third, we will study some individual exorcism narratives (Luke 4:31–37; 8:26–39; and 9:37–43a). We will show that each exorcism story shows the victory of Jesus/God over Satan and his followers in general and each of them stresses a specific aspect of the kingdom of God in particular.

Exorcisms

The importance of the exorcisms of Jesus has been noted by scholars. Luke, the Evangelist, especially stresses the significance of the exorcisms in the following ways.¹³⁰ First, Luke considers some healing stories as exorcisms (e.g. Luke 13:10–17 and 4:38–41). Second, in the response of Jesus to the request of the disciples of John the Baptist (Luke 7:20), Luke, unlike Matthew, begins with, "At that very time Jesus cured many who had diseases, sicknesses and evil spirits, and gave sight to many who were blind" (Luke 7:21; cf. Matt 11:2–6). Third, the importance of exorcisms in the ministry of Jesus is evident in an occasion of his indirect response to King Herod (Luke 13:32). Jesus said: "Go tell that fox, 'I will drive out demons and heal people today and tomorrow, and on the third day I will reach my goal.'" One finds the significance of the exorcisms in the ministry of Jesus.¹³¹ Last but not least, the significance of exorcism has also been stressed in the Book of Acts. Exorcisms play an important role in the ministries of Philip the Evangelist (Acts 8:4–8) and the apostle Paul (Acts 19:11–12).¹³²

The Theological Significance of Exorcisms: *Luke 11:14–23*

In this section, we will study the comment of Jesus on exorcisms (Luke 11:14–23). First, we will show that exorcism ties closely to the vision of the fall of Satan (Luke 10:18). Second, we will demonstrate that this passage clearly depicts a battle aired to show the victory of God over Satan. Third, we will argue that the main concern of exorcisms is to materialize the eschatological kingdom of God on earth.

Exorcisms (Luke 11:14–23) and the Fall of Satan (Luke 10:18)

Exorcisms on earth are the effect of the victory of God in heaven. The most explicit passage explaining Jesus's views on the significance of exorcism is Luke 11:14–23. The power of God overcomes the power of Satan. The victory of God brings the presence of the kingdom of God. We will first argue that Luke modifies his source to bring force to the connection between exorcisms and the passage on Satan's fall (Luke 10:18). Second, he displays the battle scene of this account and thus shows the victory of God over Satan's forces.

---

130. Exorcisms in Luke occur in the following passages: 4:33–37; 4:40–41; 8:26–39; 9:37–43; 9:1–2; 10:17–20; 11:14–23; and 13:31–33. Exorcisms in the Book of Acts occur in the following passages: 8:4–8; 10:36–43; 16:16–18; 19:8–12; and 19:13–20.

131. Twelftree, *In the Name of Jesus*, 131–133.

132. Ibid., 134.

The close connection between this passage (Luke 11:14–23) and the fall of Satan from heaven (Luke 10:18) will be established by the following study. This episode stands in line with the passage on Satan's fall and indicates the effect on earth of the victory of God in heaven.

Linguistic markers

First, the linguistic markers show the close connection between this passage and the fall of Satan (Luke 10:18). A couple of terms Luke edits from his source show this connection. First is the verb "to fall" (πίπτω) (Luke 10:17). Differing from Mark, Luke edits his source by using the verb "to fall" (πίπτω) instead of "to stand" (ἵστημι). In Mark 3:25, it says: "If a house is divided against itself, that house cannot stand (καὶ ἐὰν οἰκία ἐφ' ἑαυτὴν μερισθῇ, οὐ δυνήσεται ἡ οἰκία ἐκείνη σταθῆναι)." Luke, however, modifies Mark's wording to "a house divided against itself will fall (οἶκος ἐπὶ οἶκον πίπτει) (Luke 11:17)."[133] The verb "to fall" (πίπτω) echoes "the fall of Satan from heaven τὸν σατανᾶν . . . ἐκ τοῦ οὐρανοῦ πεσόντα).

The second is the demonic terms like "Satan" (Σατανᾶς) and "the demons" (τὰ δαιμόνια). Luke uses the term Σατανᾶς in 11:18, recalling Luke 10:18. The repeated occurrences of the word demon (δαιμόνιον) in Luke 11:14, 15, 17, 18 also refer back to Luke 10:17. Those linguistic markers show the close connection between these two passages.

Third, the name of Beelzebul also indicates the close connection between this passage and the fall of Satan. The word (Βεελζεβούλ) occurs only in the Synoptic Gospels (Mark 3:22; Matt 10:25; 12:24, 27 and Luke 11:15, 18–19). It is found in most manuscripts. It has two parts: *Beel* and *zᵉ bul*. The former means "Baal, the Prince" and the later refers to "the exalted abode" (i.e. the heavens).[134] Luke provides the meaning of Beelzebul as the "prince of demons." Given the exorcism occasion, this name indicates that this prince once dwelled in the heavens but now has his abode on earth by possessing human bodies. Even though Satan fell from heaven and abides in humans, Jesus, the stronger man, drove him out of human beings. Thus,

---

133. Matthew follows Mark with this regard. Matt 12:25 reads, ". . . and every city or household divided against itself will not stand" (καὶ πᾶσα πόλις ἢ οἰκία μερισθεῖσα καθ' ἑαυτῆς οὐ σταθήσεται).

134. Fitzmyer, *Luke 10–24*, 920; William Ewart Maurice Aitken, "Beelzebul," *JBL* 31 (1912): 34–53.

the term Beelzebul contains the notion of heaven and earth. Satan formerly dwelled in heaven and now is on earth. In other words, Satan has fallen from heaven to earth. We see the connection between this passage and the fall of Satan from heaven.

Luke 11:16

First, an examination of Luke 11:16 and its context shows that Luke intentionally locates this verse here to make a linguistic connection between this passage and that of the fall of Satan through the word "heaven" (οὐρανός). With regard to verse 16, Marshall states that "Luke intends the verse to prepare for his later saying (i.e. Luke 11:29–32) and he may have meant to suggest that the exorcisms performed by Jesus made a sign from heaven unnecessary."[135] That Marshall's comment on Luke 11:16 is "to prepare for his later saying (Luke 11:29–32)" seems likely. But why does Luke put this verse before the explanation of exorcisms (Luke 11:17–23)? Why does he not place this verse right before verse 29 to make a better coherence of both texts (Luke 11:16 and 29–32) as Matthew does (Matt 12:38)? One can observe that between Luke 11:16 and Luke 11:29–32 there exist first the "the explanation of the exorcism account" (Luke 11:17–23); second, the "return of the unclean spirit" narrative (Luke 11:24–26); and third, "the saying of Jesus on the true blessedness" (Luke 11:27–28). One may wonder why Luke places the request (Luke 11:16) in thirteen verses that contain three different accounts ahead of the response (Luke 11:29–32)? Indeed, there are some reasons for Luke putting the request here. The first is the appearance of the term heaven (οὐρανός) (Luke 11:16). Matthew modifies the Markan source to present the request as "a sign from Jesus" (Matt 12:38–42). Luke, however, follows his Markan source to present the request as "a sign from heaven" (σημεῖον ἐξ οὐρανοῦ). Luke modifies his source by placing verse 16 within Luke 11:14–23. This verse contains the term heaven: "Others tested him by asking for a sign from heaven" (ἕτεροι δὲ πειράζοντες σημεῖον ἐξ οὐρανοῦ ἐζήτουν παρ' αὐτοῦ).[136]

---

135. Nolland, *Luke 9:21–18:34*, 637; Marshall, *Luke*, 473.

136. Matthew puts this verse in Matt 12:38. The Matthean Jesus rightly provides the answer by referencing the sign of Jonah (12:39–41). At another occasion, Matthew again reiterates the request (Matt 16:1) and he again immediately gives the response (Matt 16:2–4). Mark locates it in 8:11. Markan Jesus also gave them the reply (8:12–13).

Second, by positioning the request here, Luke probably wants to indicate that the exorcism is a sign from heaven. Marshall rightly comments that Luke may suggest that "the exorcisms performed by Jesus made a sign from heaven unnecessary."[137] But he does not explain "how" exorcisms made the request of a sign from heaven unnecessary. We will show that the allusion of the phrase "the finger of God" to Exodus 8:15 (LXX) suggests that the exorcism is a sign from God/heaven. In Exodus, God commanded Moses and Aaron to use their staffs to perform signs (καὶ τὴν ῥάβδον ταύτην τὴν στραφεῖσαν εἰς ὄφιν λήμψῃ ἐν τῇ χειρί σου ἐν ᾗ ποιήσεις ἐν αὐτῇ τὰ σημεῖα) (Exod 4:17). And they did just as God told them (Exod 7:9; 7:19; 8:1; 8:12; etc.).[138] In this context, the third plague is interpreted by the magicians as "the finger of God." This means that the sign is performed by the finger of God; it is a sign from God. Luke indicates explicitly that by God's finger Jesus performs the exorcisms to show that the exorcism is a sign from God/heaven. Jesus's explanation of the exorcism indicates that it is a sign from heaven. Thus, it makes the request of a sign from heaven unnecessary.

This study of the heaven reference and the phrase "the finger of God" shows that Luke intentionally locates the request of "a sign from heaven" right before the explanation of the exorcism, which shows his concern for the connection between exorcisms and the event of Satan's fall.

Theme of exorcism

Thematically, the most obvious evidence is the exorcism act. The theme in Luke 11:14–23 is the exorcism. In the exorcism, Jesus as the stronger man (ὁ ἰσχυρότερος) conquers the strong man (ὁ ἰσχυρός). This echoes back to the authority and power of the name of Jesus over demons (Luke 10:17). Luke 11:20 describes the relationship between the exorcism and the kingdom of God. By executing exorcisms, the kingdom of God is realized. As shown in our earlier study, Luke 10:17–20 contains the theme of the kingdom of God. Luke 11:14–23 brings out the significance of the exorcisms in that the casting out of demons signals God's kingdom coming upon the earth.

Luke locates this verse (Luke 11:16) here to show the connection between this episode and the passage on Satan's fall and, at the same time, to indicate

---

137. Marshall, *Luke*, 473.
138. Further discussion will be reserved for a later section.

that the exorcism is a sign from heaven in that the kingdom of God has been made manifest on earth (11:20).

In sum, our linguistic study first shows that Luke modifies his source to make a connection between the exorcism and the fall of Satan. Second, Luke locates the request (Luke 11:16) here to make a connection between the exorcism passage and the fall of Satan (Luke 10:18). Luke views the exorcism as a sign from heaven. Last, the theme of Luke 11:14–23 echoes that of Luke 10:18. Thus, one finds a close connection between these passages. The victory of God in heaven impacts earth by the exorcising events. Next, we will demonstrate that the victory of God has been well documented in Lukan exorcism stories.

The Battle Scene and the Victory of God over Satan (Luke 11:14–23)

The battle scene

In the Lukan version, the Jesus and Beelzebul controversy is described as a battle scene rather than a burglary as in Matthew and Mark (Luke 11:21–22; cf. Matt 18:29; Mark 3:27).[139] Terms like "a strong man" (ὁ ἰσχυρὸς), "fully armed" (καθοπλίζω), "to guard" (φυλάσσω), "a stronger man" (ὁ ἰσχυρότερος), "to attack" (ἐπέρχομαι), "to conquer" (νικάω), "the full armor" (πανοπλία), "to distribute" (διαδίδωμι), and "the plunder" (τὰ σκῦλα) are typical battle terms, giving Luke 11:21–22 a strong military sense and a picture of warfare.

Other terms also depict a battle. Unlike Mark and Matthew, Luke employs the word καθοπλίζω ("to arm fully" or "to equip") in this passage to emphasize the context of battle. This word is uniquely Lukan since it occurs only here in the New Testament. The only occurrence in the OT describes the men of Cush and Put who are fully armed. Jeremiah 26:9 (LXX) says, "Charge, O horses! Drive furiously, O charioteers! March on, O warriors – men of Cush and Put who carry shields, men of Lydia who draw the bow" (ἐπίβητε ἐπὶ τοὺς ἵππους παρασκευάσατε τὰ ἅρματα ἐξέλθατε οἱ μαχηταὶ Αἰθιόπων καὶ Λίβυες καθωπλισμένοι ὅπλοις καὶ Λυδοί ἀνάβητε ἐντείνατε

---

139. Martin Emmrich, "The Lucan Account of the Beelzebul Controversy," *WTJ* 62 (2000): 267–279.

τόξον). In Second Temple literature, most occurrences are found in 2, 3 and 4 Maccabees. In most cases, this term is used of soldiers fully equipped. In 2 Macc 4:40, Lysimachus armed three thousand men and launched an unjust attack (καθοπλίσας ὁ Λυσίμαχος πρὸς τρισχιλίους κατήρξατο χειρῶν ἀδίκων). In 2 Macc 15:11, Maccabeus armed each of them (ἕκαστον δὲ αὐτῶν καθοπλίσας). In 3 Macc 5:38, the king summoned Hermon and ordered him "to fully arm tomorrow to vanquish the Jews" (καὶ νῦν καθόπλισον εἰς τὴν αὔριον ἐπὶ τὸν τῶν Ἰουδαίων ἀφανισμόν). In 4 Macc 3:12, there are "two young soldiers fully armed" (δύο νεανίσκοι στρατιῶται καρτεροὶ καταιδεσθέντες). In 4 Macc 4:10, the word is used of "armed soldiers" (καθωπλισμένης τῆς στρατιᾶς). Thus, Luke picks up a typical military term to depict the exorcism event.

Further, differing from Mark and Matthew, Luke chooses the term "to attack" (ἐπέρχομαι) to show how the battle unfolds.[140] This usage is uniquely Lukan. Literally it means "having come upon." Here it has a hostile sense and means "coming against."[141] Luke employs the word "palace" (αὐλή) instead of the term "house" (οἰκία) to indicate a grand palace in which the prince lives. All the Synoptic writers use this term to describe the grand palace in which the high priest lived (Mark 14:54, 66; 15:16; Matt 26:3, 58, 69; Luke 22:55). Both Mark and Matthew chose the word "house" (οἰκία) here; but Luke picks up the word "palace" (αὐλή). Last but not least, Luke modifies his Markan source (3:27) by changing the verb "to conquer" (νικάω) instead of "to bind" (δέω) to bring force to the military flavor.[142] Therefore, one finds that Luke chooses military terms to show the battle aspect of the exorcism.

The victory of God

The victory of God has been stressed in this account. Several points contribute to this notion. First, the unique terms Luke chooses support this point. The term "to conquer" (νικάω) is a very strong military term to show victory.[143] Luke modifies his source of Mark 3:27 by using the word "to

---

140. Both Mark and Matthew use the term "enter" (εἰσέρχομαι) (Mark 3:27; Matt 12:29).

141. Fitzmyer, *Luke 10–24*, 923.

142. Matthew follows Mark with this regard. See Matt 12:29.

143. John, the writer of Revelation, uses seventeen times (seventeen out of twenty-eight) to describe the victory of Jesus and his followers over evil forces.

conquer" (νικάω) instead of "bind" (δέω). This word suggests superiority over an opposing force.[144] It occurs most frequently in 2, 3 and especially 4 Maccabees. It is exclusively used in reference to victory in a battle: in 2 Macc 13:15, he gave his men the watchword "the victory of God" (ἀναδοὺς δὲ τοῖς περὶ αὐτὸν σύνθημα θεοῦ νίκην). In 2 Macc 10:38, the Lord gives Israel the victory (καὶ ἐξομολογήσεων εὐλόγουν τῷ κυρίῳ τῷ μεγάλως εὐεργετοῦντι τὸν Ισραηλ καὶ τὸ νῖκος αὐτοῖς διδόντι).[145] Luke chooses this term to bring out the victory of God over Satan.

Second, the word "to cast out" (ἐκβάλλω) has military connotations of one person overcoming another. In the LXX this word is often used when God casts out an enemy of his people (Exod 23:30 and Deut 33:27). Exodus 23:30 reads, "Little by little I will drive them out before you, until you have increased enough to take possession of the land" (κατὰ μικρὸν μικρὸν ἐκβαλῶ αὐτοὺς ἀπὸ σοῦ ἕως ἂν αὐξηθῇς καὶ κληρονομήσῃς τὴν γῆν). Similarly, Deuteronomy 33:27–28 says, "The eternal God is your refuge, and underneath are the everlasting arms. He will drive out your enemy before you, saying, 'Destroy him!'" (καὶ σκέπασις θεοῦ ἀρχῆς καὶ ὑπὸ ἰσχὺν βραχιόνων ἀενάων καὶ ἐκβαλεῖ ἀπὸ προσώπου σου ἐχθρὸν λέγων ἀπόλοιο).

Third, the battle between God and Satan has been clearly expressed in the narrative of the stronger man attacking the strong one. The "stronger man" (ἰσχυρότερος) indicates Jesus, the Messiah (the Son of the Most High). The comparative form of the word ἰσχυρότερος occurs only four times in the New Testament (Matt 3:11; Mark 1:7; Luke 3:16 and 11:22) and twice in the Old Testament (Num 13:18 and Prov 30:30). This term "stronger/more powerful one" appears in all the synoptic gospels (Matt 3:11; Mark 1:7 and Luke 3:16) where it refers to Jesus. Only Luke uses this word twice, here and in Luke 3:16. Here it echoes to Luke 3:16 where it explicitly refers to Jesus. That Luke edits his source of Mark 3:27 by adding this term is hardly

---

144. Bauernfeind, "νικάω," *TDNT*, 4:942.

145. This term is used on a personal level (2 Macc 3:5), military level (3 Macc 1:4), and religious level, where good things overcome bad things (4 Macc 1:4; 3:17; 6:33; 7:4; 9:30; 11:20; 13:2;16:4; 17:15; also see Prov 6:5). The term is also used to refer to national battle overcoming a tyrant (4 Macc 1:11; 17:24); personal bravery overcoming torture (4 Macc 6:10); and Aaron overcoming the fiery angel (4 Macc 7:11). In 1 Esd 3:12, the power of truth is victor over all things (ὑπὲρ δὲ πάντα νικᾷ ἡ ἀλήθεια). Military victory in 1 Esd 4:5 shows that the king is strong to conquer.

accidental. Luke intentionally tells his reader that the "stronger one" is Jesus. The strong man (ὁ ἰσχυρὸς) obviously refers to Satan.

Therefore, Luke 11:14–23, expresses the victory of God in heaven and its impact on earth.

Kingdom concern

The kingdom concern has been expressed in this passage. A study of the phrase "the finger of God" shows the kingdom concern of this passage (Luke 11:14–23). First, we will argue that the phrase "the finger of God" is an allusion to Exodus 8:15. Then, we will argue that this allusion to Exodus 8:15 introduces the new exodus motif.

Allusion to *Exodus 8:15*

Luke intentionally chooses the phrase "the finger of God" (ἐκβάλλω τὰ δαιμόνια) to depict a kingdom concern.[146] It might be that Luke uses the term "spirit" and "hand/finger" interchangeably in the Gospel of Luke, such as in Luke 1:15, "and he will be filled with the Holy Spirit even from birth," (καὶ πνεύματος ἁγίου πλησθήσεται ἔτι ἐκ κοιλίας μητρὸς αὐτοῦ) and 1:66, "the Lord's hand was with him," (καὶ γὰρ χεὶρ κυρίου ἦν μετ' αὐτοῦ). Twelftree notices that "spirit" and "hand" are used synonymously in Ezekiel (8:1). He then argues that the "spirit" and "the finger of God" contain the same idea.[147] Some scholars identified the phrase "the finger of God" as an allusion to Deuteronomy 9:10 and then argue for God's written law at Sinai.[148] There might be some similarities on themes and linguistic data between Luke 9:51–19:10 and Deuteronomy 1–26. However, to link "the finger of God" to the written law in Sinai is too hasty and seems arbitrary. The context of the phrase "the finger of God" in Luke 11:14–23 is considerably different from that of Deut 9. Luke 11:14–23 deals with the issue of exorcisms while Deuteronomy 9 deals with the rebelling of Israel. These are different issues. Along this line, Robert W. Wall agrees that the phrase "the finger of God"

---

146. Matthew says, "by spirit." For more discussion, see Twelftree, *In the Name of Jesus*, 89–92.

147. Ibid., 91.

148. Craig A. Evans, *Luke,* NIBC, ed. W. Ward Gasque (Peabody: Hendrickson, 1990), 186; Robert W. Wall, "The Finger of God: Deuteronomy 9:10 and Luke 11:20," *NTS* 33 (1987): 144–150; C. F. Evans, *Saint Luke* (London: SCM, 1990), 44.

is the allusion to Deuteronomy 9:10. He argues that Luke uses this phrase to introduce the theme of rejection. Thus the old theme of rejection came alive at the time of Jesus. In Deuteronomy, the "old" Israel rejected Moses. Now the people of Israel likewise reject Jesus, the new Moses. While one cannot deny that there is a theme of rejection in Luke, especially in Luke 4:16–30, to argue for this theme on the basis of the phrase "the finger of God" in Luke 11 seems like a council of despair. Wall even goes so far as to identify the strong man as "Israel" and the stronger man as "Satan." He says that the battle is not between Jesus/God and Satan but between Satan and Israel.[149] This sort of allegorical reading is rather unconvincing. Wall seems to ignore the exorcism context in Luke 11. Instead the phrase "the finger of God" should be seen as an allusion to Exodus 8:19 (LXX 8:15).

First, the context of this phrase in Exodus 8:19 is similar to the context of this phrase in Luke 11. Both passages deal with a stand against the enemies of God. In Luke 11, the enemy is Satan, the prince of demons. In Exodus 8, the enemy is Pharaoh, the king of Egypt. Scholars also provide convincing evidence to support this view.[150]

Second, this phrase in the OT points to the power of God. Psalm 8:4 (LXX) depicts the power of God, reading, "When I consider your heavens, the work of your fingers, the moon and the stars, which you have set in place" (ὅτι ὄψομαι τοὺς οὐρανούς ἔργα τῶν δακτύλων σου σελήνην καὶ ἀστέρας ἃ σὺ ἐθεμελίωσας). This is also seen in Deuteronomy 9:10 where "The LORD gave me two stone tablets inscribed by the finger of God" (καὶ ἔδωκεν κύριος ἐμοὶ τὰς δύο πλάκας τὰς λιθίνας γεγραμμένας ἐν τῷ δακτύλῳ τοῦ θεοῦ). We see that "the finger of God" has the power to create the heavens. It also has the power to write on stone.

Third, the term "finger" (δάκτυλος) contains the idea of fighting. Psalm 143:1 says, "Praise is to the LORD my Rock, who trains my hands for war, my fingers for battle" (τῷ Δαυιδ πρὸς τὸν Γολιαδ εὐλογητὸς κύριος ὁ θεός μου ὁ διδάσκων τὰς χεῖράς μου εἰς παράταξιν τοὺς δακτύλους μου εἰς πόλεμον). This notion is in favor of the battle scene in both passages. In Luke 11:20,

---

149. Wall, "The Finger of God," 147.
150. Green, *The Gospel of Luke*, 456; Fitzmyer, *Luke 10–24*, 922.

Jesus uses the "finger of God" to cast out demons. In Exodus 8:15 (19), the finger of God is considered to fight against Pharaoh and his magicians.

Therefore, the above study of the context and the meanings of the phrase show that the phrase "the finger of God" is an allusion to Exodus 8:19 (LXX 8:15). Next, we will argue that Luke appeals to this allusion of the "the finger of God" for a wider theological concern.

New Exodus motif

With regard to Luke's change of "the spirit of God" to "the finger of God," Marshall states that "there is no good reason for a change by Luke can be found."[151] However, we will argue that the allusion to Exodus 8:19 (LXX 8:15) does provide a good reason for this change. Luke carefully chooses the phrase "the finger of God" (δάκτυλος θεοῦ) to bring out the new exodus motif.

First, the exodus motif exists behind Exodus 8:19 (LXX 8:15). God uses the ten plagues to punish and defeat Pharaoh (Exod 7–11) in order to free his people and lead them into the Promised Land. The third plague (Exod 8:16–19) is one that shows the power of God overcoming magicians, who said "to Pharaoh, 'this is the finger of God.'" Here Luke wants to show that Jesus is the new Moses who is to lead Israel on the new exodus. This is exactly the same motif/theme that exists in the Lukan writings. By the finger of God in Luke 11:20, Jesus casts out demons to set God's people free from the bondage of Satan. Here again it echoes the Nazareth synagogue sermon of Jesus (Luke 4:18–19) where it says, "let the oppressed go free" (ἀποστεῖλαι τεθραυσμένους ἐν ἀφέσει). As Twelftree rightly comments: "it may be that in using 'finger' Luke wanted to bring out a parallel between the miracles by which God released Israel from bondage and the miracle by which God, in Jesus, also released Israel from the bondage of Satan."[152]

Second, Luke, familiar with the LXX, uses of the verb "to cast out' (ἐκβάλλω) in the account of the Beelzebul controversy to show the same motif. This can be seen in the following examples. Exodus 23:30 says, "Little by little I will drive them out before you, until you have increased enough to take possession of the land" (κατὰ μικρὸν μικρὸν ἐκβαλῶ αὐτοὺς ἀπὸ σοῦ

---

151. Marshall, *Luke*, 476.
152. Twelftree, *In the Name of Jesus*, 135.

ἕως ἂν αὐξηθῇς καὶ κληρονομήσῃς τὴν γῆν). Another case is in Deuteronomy 33:27–28; "The eternal God is your refuge, and underneath are the everlasting arms. He will drive out your enemy before you, saying, 'Destroy him'" (καὶ σκέπασις θεοῦ ἀρχῆς καὶ ὑπὸ ἰσχὺν βραχιόνων ἀενάων καὶ ἐκβαλεῖ ἀπὸ προσώπου σου ἐχθρὸν λέγων ἀπόλοιο). One can see the same pattern in both passages: the driving out of the enemy of God and then the possessing of the enemy's land by the people of God. God drove out the enemy and then his people could possess the land. This is what Luke intends to express: the casting out of demons and then the presence of the kingdom of God.

Another exorcism/healing account would illustrate this point. Luke 13:10–17. A woman had a spirit of infirmity (γυνὴ πνεῦμα ἔχουσα ἀσθενείας). Jesus called her and said to her "you are set free from your infirmity" (ἀπολέλυσαι τῆς ἀσθενείας σου). Jesus further in verse 16 argues, "Then should not this woman, a daughter of Abraham, whom Satan has kept bound for eighteen long years, be set free on the Sabbath day from what bound her?" (ταύτην δὲ θυγατέρα Ἀβραὰμ οὖσαν, ἣν ἔδησεν ὁ σατανᾶς ἰδοὺ δέκα καὶ ὀκτὼ ἔτη, οὐκ ἔδει λυθῆναι ἀπὸ τοῦ δεσμοῦ τούτου τῇ ἡμέρᾳ τοῦ σαββάτου;). The comment, "and immediately she straightened up and praised God," shows that the woman gains a new life. We see that Jesus set the woman free from the bondage of Satan and gave her a new life.

Finally, the Lukan text also points to the relationship between exorcisms and the kingdom of God. "If I cast out of demons by the finger of God, then the kingdom of God has come to you" (εἰ δὲ ἐν δακτύλῳ θεοῦ [ἐγὼ] ἐκβάλλω τὰ δαιμόνια, ἄρα ἔφθασεν ἐφ' ὑμᾶς ἡ βασιλεία τοῦ θεοῦ). The word "come to" (ἔφθασεν) has a range meaning, its aorist tense emphasizing the already realized circumstance.[153]

One can see that there is similar pattern in both passages: driving out the enemy of God and then the possessing the land of the enemy by God's people. God drove out the enemy and then his people could possess the land. The only difference is that in Exodus, God led his people to the earthly land after defeating his enemy, while in Luke 11:14–23, God defeated Satan and brings the eschatological kingdom to his people. As Eric Sorensen concludes, "the New Testament also made use of exorcism as a means of visualizing

---

153. Osborne, *Matthew*, 475.

its eschatological message of the Kingdom of God overcoming the power of Satan."[154]

Summary

Therefore, our study shows first that the phrase "the finger of God" is an allusion to Exodus 8:15 (LXX). Second, the allusion brings forth the new exodus motif that shows the victory of God that brings the salvation to people from the bounds of Satan. The victory of God in heaven has its impact on earth – the kingdom is realized on earth. Next, we will study individual exorcism narratives to reveal that these exorcising accounts show the power of God over satanic forces in general and emphasize various aspects of the impact of the kingdom on earth (eschatological salvation) in particular.

Individual Exorcism Narrative

A study of the individual exorcisms will reveal the theme of the authority and victory of God. Space does not allow an investigation of every exorcism account. Among many exorcism accounts, Luke provides three detailed ones: Luke 4:33–37; 8:26–39 and 9:37–43.[155]

The New Testament exorcism stories individualize the warfare between the divine and the devil so that the body of the possessed person is a battleground within which the demonic and divine forces engage one another.[156] In the Synoptic Gospels, the exorcistic work of Jesus is interpreted as the sign of God's overthrowing of Satan (Mark 3:22–27; Matt 12:22–29 and Luke 11:14–22).

Luke 4:31–37

Luke 4:31–37 is the first exorcism account Luke presents in his two-volume work. This episode occurs immediately after the teaching of Jesus in the synagogue in Nazareth (4:16–30).[157] One can see first the victory of Jesus over the demon. Second, one can see the dominion of God over Satan.

---

154. Eric Sorensen, *Possession and Exorcism in the New Testament and Early Christianity*, WUNT 157 (Tübingen: Mohr Siebeck, 2002), 128–129, 166.

155. Elsewhere Luke mentions the exorcisms: Luke 4:41; 7:21; 8:2; 9:1–2; 10:17; 13:32.

156. Sorensen, *Possession and Exorcism*, 129.

157. Mark puts this exorcism rightly after the call of the first disciples (Mark 1:23–37).

Victory of Jesus over demons

The notion of the victory of God over demons is clearly expressed in this exorcism story. First, the word ἀπόλλυμι means, "to destroy or kill."[158] In the Old Testament, this word was frequently used to refer to God destroying Sodom (e.g. Gen 18:28), Moab (e.g. Num 21:29), and the nations in Canaan (e.g. Deut 8:20). This idea also emerges in Second Temple literature. God killed his enemy (2 Macc 3:39).[159] Luke takes this meaning here to show the victory of God over Satan. The saying of the evil spirit, "Have you come to destroy us?" describes exactly what Jesus is going to do.

Second, the terms used by Jesus reveal the authority of Jesus. The verb "to rebuke" (ἐπιτιμάω) (4:35) refers in the LXX to a higher ranked authority rebuking the lower ones (e.g. Gen 37:10). God rebuked nations and the wicked (Ps 9:6), the beasts (Ps 67:31), the Red Sea (Ps 105:9), and the arrogant (Ps 118:21). The most explicit passage is when God rebuked Satan in Zechariah 3:2: "The LORD said to Satan, 'The LORD rebukes you, Satan'" (καὶ εἶπεν κύριος πρὸς τὸν διάβολον ἐπιτιμήσαι κύριος ἐν σοί διάβολε καὶ ἐπιτιμῆσαι κύριος). This usage could also be found in 3 Macc 2:24 where God warned and punished Ptolemy. Thus, we see that the term "to rebuke" shows the authority of Jesus over the evil spirits.

Third, the term "to command" (ἐπιτάσσω) also shows the authority of Jesus. In the Old Testament, this word is used for a father commanding his sons (Gen 49:33). It is used for a king commanding his people (Esth 8:11). This usage also appears in Daniel 2:2; 3:19, 20. This idea even survived in the Second Temple literature. First Maccabees 5:49 reads, "Judas commanded his proclamation to be made to the army" (ἐπέταξεν Ιουδας κηρύξαι ἐν τῇ παρεμβολῇ τοῦ παρεμβαλεῖν ἕκαστον ἐν ᾧ ἐστιν τόπῳ) (cf. Dan 9:54; 10:81; 12:27, 43). We see that this word has been used for people who had a higher rank giving orders to the ones who had lower ranks.

Fourth, the term "power" (δύναμις) also shows the authority of Jesus over the evil forces. Generally, Luke follows Mark in this account (Mark 1:23–28). But he made some changes,[160] one of which is that he adds the

---

158. Oepke, "ἀποκατάστασις," *TDNT*, 1:394.

159. Antiochus destroyed the people of Israel (1 Macc 1:30). The killing actions are also recorded (1 Macc 2:37).

160. Fitzmyer, *Luke 1–9*, 542.

term "power" (δυνάμει) in verse 36 "With authority and power he gives orders to evil spirits and they come out" (ἐν ἐξουσίᾳ καὶ δυνάμει ἐπιτάσσει τοῖς ἀκαθάρτοις πνεύμασιν καὶ ἐξέρχονται).

Besides these terms, the Lukan redaction of his Markan source shows the authority and power of Jesus over evil spirits. Luke follows Mark with regard to the command of Jesus, "Be silent, and come out of him," (Φιμώθητι, καὶ ἔξελθε ἐξ αὐτοῦ), in Luke 4:35 (cf. Mark 1:25). Then Luke edits Mark's "he cried with a loud voice and came out of him" (φωνῆσαν φωνῇ μεγάλῃ ἐξῆλθεν ἐξ αὐτοῦ) by omitting "he cried with a loud voice" (φωνῆσαν φωνῇ μεγάλῃ). Hearing the command of Jesus, the unclean spirit followed just what Jesus commanded him: he came out of the man without making any sound of crying. The redaction of Luke stresses the authority of Jesus over demons.

The terms "to destroy" (ἀπόλλυμι), "to rebuke" (ἐπιτιμάω), "to command" (ἐπιτάσσω), and "power" (δύναμις) as well as Luke's redaction of his Markan source demonstrate the authority of Jesus over evil forces. The victory of God over demons is emphasized.

Uniqueness of this exorcism story

The uniqueness of using the plural pronoun "us" (ἡμῖν) brings forth the victory of God over satanic forces. The dominion of God overtook the dominion of Satan. The kingdom of God was made manifest on earth.

A point should be noted about the plural pronoun "us" (ἡμῖν). Luke 4:34 reads, "What do you want with us, Jesus of Nazareth? Have you come to destroy us?" (τί ἡμῖν καὶ σοί, Ἰησοῦ Ναζαρηνέ; ἦλθες ἀπολέσαι ἡμᾶς). Luke follows Mark 1:24 in using the plural pronoun for his theological concern. Danker views the pronoun "us" as referring to the unclean spirit and the man.[161] This seems unlikely. First, Luke's modification of the Markan wording does not favor Danker's reading. Luke adds that the demon left the man without doing any harm to him (ἐξῆλθεν ἀπ' αὐτοῦ μηδὲν βλάψαν αὐτόν) (Luke 4:35; cf. Mark 1:26). Second, theologically speaking, this view is problematic because the common understanding is that the coming of Jesus is to save rather than to destroy people. All the exorcisms tell this fact that Jesus never harms demon-possessed people (e.g. Luke 4:31–37; 8:26–39; 9:37–3);

---

161. Danker, *Jesus and the New Age*, 111.

rather, he saves them. On the contrary, it is Satan and demons that hurt men and women. Last but not least, the context is against Danker's reading in that the response of the by-standers shows that the plural pronoun refers to "demons." In Luke 4:36, it says, "for Jesus with authority and power he commands unclean spirits and they came out" (ὅτι ἐν ἐξουσίᾳ καὶ δυνάμει ἐπιτάσσει τοῖς ἀκαθάρτοις πνεύμασιν, καὶ ἐξέρχονται). It is explicit that there are "many unclean spirits" (τοῖς ἀκαθάρτοις πνεύμασιν). It is more likely that the plural pronoun represents all the demons. Fitzmyer and others note this, but they somehow did not provide a substantial argument that a singular evil spirit uses the plural "us" to represent all the evil spirits. Jesus's power is over all the evil spirits.[162] A single demon uttering with the first person plural pronoun, "us," instead of singular pronoun, "me," indicates that he is representing the whole demonic realm. The subduing of an unclean spirit represents the submission of all evil spirits.

Here the submission of all the demons (us) foreshadows the fall of Satan from heaven (τὸν σατανᾶν ὡς ἀστραπὴν ἐκ τοῦ οὐρανοῦ πεσόντα) (Luke 10:18) and Jesus's power is "to overcome all the power of the enemy; nothing will harm you" (ἐπὶ πᾶσαν τὴν δύναμιν τοῦ ἐχθροῦ, καὶ οὐδὲν ὑμᾶς οὐ μὴ ἀδικήσῃ) (Luke 10:19). Demons of course are major enemies of God. The subjection of all the demons has also been explained in Luke 11:19–21 in that the kingdom of God has been made manifest.

Based on the study above, we see that the plural pronoun represents all demons. The term "destroy" shows that God's power is bringing satanic forces to an end. The dominion of God is overtaking the dominion of Satan. The eschatological kingdom has been realized on earth. The first exorcism account indicates the authority of Jesus. He will destroy the dominion of the evil one. Its significance is far beyond this single exorcism. It anticipates the victory of God over Satan (Luke 10:18). God's kingdom (here represented by Jesus and later by his disciples) will overcome the kingdom of Satan. This notion has clearly been illustrated in Luke 11:14–23.

Therefore, the exorcism story in Luke 4:31–37 demonstrates the authority of Jesus over evil spirits. It also anticipates the victory of God over all

---

162. Fitzmyer, *Luke 1–9*, 545.

evil spirits. In other words, the kingdom of God takes over the dominion of Satan.

Luke 8:26–39
Another detailed exorcism story is found in Luke 8:26–39.[163] This exorcism story shows first the power of Jesus over demons (the victory of God) and second the presence of the salvation/eschatological kingdom.

The victory of God over Satan
As noted by scholars, Luke does not make extensive alterations to his source.[164] However, he does make some changes in order to bring out Luke's theological concerns. Several points need to be noted.

The first point is the Lukan modification of his source that shows the victory of God. Luke uniquely uses the word "abyss" (ἄβυσσος) (Luke 8:31). Mark 5:10 reads, "And he begged Jesus again and again not to send them out of the area" (καὶ παρεκάλει αὐτὸν πολλὰ ἵνα μὴ αὐτὰ ἀποστείλῃ ἔξω τῆς χώρας). Matthew omits this verse. This Lukan redaction indicates two points of Luke's theological concern. One is that Luke emphasizes the defeat of Satan and the victory of God. The abyss is considered as the prison of evil spirits in the New Testament era. This is evidenced by Revelation 9:1 and 20:1, 3, where Satan is defeated by God.[165] In the Old Testament, the plural form of the word is used in reference to the realm of the dead. The Psalter asks the Lord to revive him "from the depths of the earth" (ἐκ τῶν ἀβύσσων τῆς γῆς) (Ps 70:20). The appeal of the demon "not to order them to go into the abyss" (μὴ ἐπιτάξῃ αὐτοῖς εἰς τὴν ἄβυσσον ἀπελθεῖν) shows the defeat of Satan and the victory of God.

The second point is that this redaction brings out the cosmic dimension of the victory of God in heaven over satanic forces. First, the abyss (ἄβυσσος) is viewed as the opposite of heaven(s). This notion can be found in Second Temple literature. In Sir 1:13, heaven is contrasted to abyss: "the height of heaven and the . . . abyss, who can search them out" (ὕψος οὐρανοῦ καὶ πλάτος γῆς καὶ ἄβυσσον καὶ σοφίαν τίς ἐξιχνιάσει). The same contrast can

---

163. This exorcism account appears in all the synoptic gospels (Matt 8:28–34; Mark 5:1–20).

164. Marshall, *Luke*, 335.

165. Joachim Jeremias, "ἄβυσσος," *TDNT*, 1:9–10.

be seen in Sir 16:18: "Behold, heaven and the highest heaven, the abyss and the earth will tremble at his visitation" (ἰδοὺ ὁ οὐρανὸς καὶ ὁ οὐρανὸς τοῦ οὐρανοῦ ἄβυσσος καὶ γῆ ἐν τῇ ἐπισκοπῇ αὐτοῦ σαλευθήσονται). Again one finds this notion in Sir 24:5: "alone I have made the circuit of the vault of heaven and have walked in the depths of the abyss" (γῦρον οὐρανοῦ ἐκύκλωσα μόνη καὶ ἐν βάθει ἀβύσσων περιεπάτησα). Second, the addressing of God as "the Most High" (Ἰησοῦ υἱὲ τοῦ θεοῦ τοῦ ὑψίστου) plays on this contrast between the highest heaven and the abyss.[166] Third, as shown earlier, Beelzebul once dwelled in heaven, but now will be cast into the abyss. This term recalls Satan's fall from heaven. God's victory in heaven has been manifested on earth.

Finally, a study of the term "legion" (λεγιών) also supports this reading. There are only four occurrences of this term in the NT. Three relate to the demon-possessed man (Mark 5:9, 15 and Luke 8:30). Another occurrence is in Matthew 26:53. This term refers exclusively to supernatural beings, either angels or demons.[167] The supernatural power of demons is indicated. The power of demons was indicated by the breaking of "chains" and "fetters" (ἁλύσεσιν καὶ πέδαις). And the demons even broke them many times (πολλοῖς γὰρ χρόνοις). Here, in the exorcism story, this term shows the power of Jesus. It shows the victory of God over demonic forces, even as they gather together as legions.

The exorcism story emphasizes the realization of salvation

This exorcism story emphasizes the coming of salvation/the eschatological kingdom. Luke alters his source by adding the term "to save" (σῴζω) in verse 36: "Those who had seen it told the people how the demon-possessed man had been saved" (ἀπήγγειλαν δὲ αὐτοῖς οἱ ἰδόντες πῶς ἐσώθη ὁ δαιμονισθείς).[168] In Mark, the response of the by-standers is, "Those who had seen it told the people what had happened to the demon-possessed man – and told about the pigs as well (Mark 5:16)." Mark mentions nothing about the situation of the free demon-possession man. But Luke edits the Markan source by

---

166. Luke follows Mark to address God as "the Most High" (cf. Mark 5:7). Matthew uses the term God (Matt 8:29).

167. Preisker, "λεγιών," *TDNT*, 4:68–69.

168. Translation mine.

adding how the demon possessed man was saved. This verb, "ἐσώθη," means much more than "to heal" as most translators render it.[169] It refers to the salvific work that God has performed on him by freeing this man from the bondage of Satan.[170] The following saying of Jesus (v. 39) shows that this is salvation. When the man wants to follow Jesus, Jesus says to him: "Return home and tell how much God has done for you." So the man went away and told all over town how much Jesus had done for him" (ὑπόστρεφε εἰς τὸν οἶκόν σου καὶ διηγοῦ ὅσα σοι ἐποίησεν ὁ θεός. καὶ ἀπῆλθεν καθ' ὅλην τὴν πόλιν κηρύσσων ὅσα ἐποίησεν αὐτῷ ὁ Ἰησοῦς). The phrase "how much God has done" (ὅσα ἐποίησεν ὁ θεός) elsewhere in Lukan writings refers exclusively to salvation (Acts 14:27; 15:4, 12). Acts 14:27 says, "On arriving there, they gathered the church together and reported all that God had done through them and how he had opened the door of faith to the Gentiles" (ὅσα ἐποίησεν ὁ θεὸς μετ' αὐτῶν καὶ ὅτι ἤνοιξεν τοῖς ἔθνεσιν θύραν πίστεως). In Acts 15:4, Paul and Barnabas report to the apostles and elders in Jerusalem "everything God had done through them" (ὅσα ὁ θεὸς ἐποίησεν μετ' αὐτῶν). It is obvious that the main point here is the salvation of the Gentiles. Again, in Acts 15:12, it is more explicit, being "about the miraculous signs and wonders God had done among the Gentiles through them" (ὅσα ἐποίησεν ὁ θεὸς σημεῖα καὶ τέρατα ἐν τοῖς ἔθνεσιν δι' αὐτῶν). The salvific significance is further confirmed by Luke 11:20: the casting out of demons indicates that the kingdom of God has come.

Our study of this exorcism narrative demonstrates first the victory of God/Jesus. Second, the Lukan alteration of the term "abyss" brings forth the cosmological dimension of the victory of God/Jesus over satanic forces. Last, our study shows that the exorcising of demons brings the eschatological salvation to man.

Luke 9:37–43a

Another exorcism account in Luke 9:37–43a stresses the victory of God over Satan and the salvific work of God on earth.

---

169. See KJV, NAS, NIV, ESV, etc.

170. The unique title of Jesus "Son of the Most High God" (υἱὲ τοῦ θεοῦ τοῦ ὑψίστου) probably implies the messianic status of Jesus, thus indicating the coming of salvation. See Amanda Witmer, *Jesus, the Galilean Exorcist: His Exorcisms in Social and Political Context*, LNTS 10 (New York: T&T Clark, 2012), 180.

The victory of God over demons

This exorcism story, similarly to the others, shows the victory of God over the demon. The typical term for exorcising reappears: Jesus rebuked (ἐπετίμησεν) the unclean spirit. The casting out of the demon is indicated in the healing of this boy. Jesus "healed the boy" (ἰάσατο τὸν παῖδα) and gave him back to his father (Luke 9:42). In Acts 10:38, Luke uses the same verb "to heal" (ἰάομαι) to express the exorcising events: Jesus went around doing good deeds and "healing all who were under the power of the devil" (ἰώμενος πάντας τοὺς καταδυναστευομένους ὑπὸ τοῦ διαβόλου). Thus, one finds the victory of God over evil forces in this exorcism.

Kingdom concern

Luke, to a certain degree, abbreviates the Markan narrative.[171] There are two redactional changes that need to be noted. One is the omission of the dialogue between the disciples and Jesus. The disciples asked why they could not cast it out. Jesus answered that only by prayer could they drive out the demon (Mark 9:28–29).[172] Luke probably wants to minimize the failure of the disciples.[173] Another point is that Luke adds the response of those watching: "All the people were astounded at the greatness of God (μεγαλειότης) (9:43)." This verse is considered a typical Lukan reaction to miracles, which does not appear in Mark and Matthew. Luke even further modifies his typical response to the exorcism. In addition to giving a typical reaction of those watching (cf. 4:32; 8:25), Luke here adds the words "at the greatness of God" to bring out the saving power of God.[174] Luke uses the cognate μεγαλεῖος ("greatness") to show the saving power of God. For example, in Luke 1:49, "the Mighty One has done great things for me" (ἐποίησέν μοι μεγάλα ὁ δυνατός). The great things include giving her "a child who will be the Savior."[175] Mary's use of the title "my Savior" also supports this notion. Another example is in Acts 2:11, where the disciples declared "the wonders of God" (τὰ μεγαλεῖα τοῦ θεοῦ) at the Pentecost event. The

---

171. Marshall, *Luke*, 390.
172. Luke moves this part to 17:6 to increase the faith of his disciples.
173. Fitzmyer, *Luke 1–9*, 810.
174. Marshall, *Luke*, 392. Luke uses this word twice. The other occurrence is in Acts 19:27, which describes the greatness of the goddess Artemis.
175. Fitzmyer, *Luke 1–9*, 367.

expression "wonders of God" refers to the redemptive work of God.[176] In both instances, the cognate word indicates the saving deeds of God.

Therefore, our examination of this exorcism shows once again the victory of God over satanic forces. It also singles out the presence of the eschatological salvation in this exorcising story.[177]

Summary

In this section, our study demonstrates the following. First, for Luke, exorcisms play an important role in the ministry of Jesus. Second, the explanation for the exorcisms by Jesus (Luke 11:14–23) demonstrates: (1) Luke 11:14–23 is closely connected to the fall of Satan (Luke 10:18). The modification of the Markan source; and the same exorcism theme demonstrate the connection of this passage to the passage on Satan's fall. (2) Luke even considers the exorcism as a sign from heaven. (3) The uniquely Lukan use of battle terms stress the victory of God. (4) The phrase "the finger of God" contains an allusion to Exodus 8:15, and this allusion brings forth the new exodus motif and the victory of God. (5) The main concern of Luke 11:14–23 is the kingdom of God.

Third, our study of the individual exorcism stories shows the victory of God in general, and each of them stresses a specific aspect of the kingdom of God/salvation. (1) Luke 4:33–37 shows the victory of Jesus over the demon. It emphasizes the kingdom (dominion) of God over the dominion of Satan. (2) Luke 8:26–39 shows the power of Jesus over many demons. This exorcism story singles out the realization of the eschatological kingdom of God. (3) Luke 9:37–43a once again stresses the victory of God over satanic forces and shows that the exorcisms are the salvific work of God on earth. The victory of God in heaven impacts earth in the exorcising events.

---

176. C. K. Barrett, *The Acts of the Apostles: A Shorter Commentary* (London: T&T Clark, 2002), 20.

177. For the importance of the exorcism in the ministry of Jesus, two passages especially single out the significance of the exorcism: Luke 18–23 and 13:31–33. In Luke 13:32, which describes the ministry of Jesus (Luke 13:32), he replied, "Go tell that fox, 'I will drive out demons and heal people today and tomorrow, and on the third day I will reach my goal.'" This shows the ministry of Jesus and the exorcism.

Conclusion

In the first section of this chapter, we examined a number of views of the vision of Satan's fall (Luke 10:18). Our study demonstrates the following. (1) The primeval view has no canonical basis to support it. (2) The prophetic view is unconvincing. The vision of Jesus does not mirror the prophetic visions of the OT prophets. The eschatological view is also problematic. The content of the vision has already occurred. (3) Each of the views that locate Satan's fall at a key event in Jesus's life (his incarnation, baptism, temptation, or resurrection/ascension) lacks canonical support and is thus unconvincing. (4) Satan's fall is a real experience of Jesus that happened in the recent past. Jesus saw the fall of Satan from heaven when the seventy(-two) disciples were doing exorcisms in their mission.

Second, the context of the vision shows the symbolic meaning of the vision of Satan's fall. It symbolizes the victory of God in heaven over Satan. This is well evidenced by the context of Luke 10:18 and the allusion to the Isaianic passage (Isa 14:12), understood within its original context (Isa 14).

Third, we showed the victory of God in heaven over Satan and his forces. This is evidenced by an examination of Luke's allusion to Isaiah 14:12, the term "Satan," the judgment narrative (Luke 10:13–15), the bestowal of authority of Jesus to his disciples (Luke 10:19), and the four heaven references (Luke 10:15, 18, 20, 21).

Fourth, this section demonstrated that Jesus is the agent for the victory of God in heaven over Satan. This is supported in the NT as well as in Second Temple literature. The disciples, as representatives of Jesus, are also agents for the victory of God.

Finally, this section revealed that the main concern of the vision of Satan's fall is the kingdom of God/eschatological salvation. The kingdom concern is also the major concern of the whole chapter of Luke 10. The victory of God in heaven by defeating Satan has brought forth the eschatological kingdom on earth. The impact of the victory of God in heaven can also be evidenced in the exorcisms.

In the second section of this chapter, our study of exorcisms demonstrated first that exorcisms are crucial for Luke in the ministry of Jesus and his disciples in materializing the kingdom of God.

Second, the passage where Jesus explains the exorcisms (Luke 11:14–23) connects closely to the vision of Satan's fall (Luke 10:18). Luke probably considers the exorcism as a sign from heaven. The exorcisms are the impact of the victory of God in heaven. Our study further showed that Luke 11:14–23 stresses the victory of God over Satan and the realization of the eschatological kingdom on earth. Our study also evidenced that the phrase "the finger of God" is an allusion to Exodus 8:15 (LXX). This allusion suggests a new exodus motif that reveals the victory of God over Satan by setting his people free from the bondage of Satan and bringing them the eschatological kingdom of God. The victory of God in heaven has its impact on earth by materializing the kingdom of God on earth.

Third, the examination of each individual exorcism narrative reveals that these exorcising accounts show the power of God over satanic forces in general and emphasize various aspects of the eschatological salvation on earth in particular. The exorcism story in Luke 4:33–37 indicates the coming victory of God over all the evil spirits and that the kingdom of God will take over the dominion of Satan. The exorcism account in Luke 8:26–39 shows again the victory of God over Satan and also demonstrates the presence of the eschatological kingdom on earth. The exorcism narrative in Luke 9:37–43a reveals once again the victory of God over Satan and demonstrates especially that the exorcising act is a salvific work of God by which he brings the presence of the eschatological kingdom on earth.

The victory of God over Satan and his forces does not mean that this is the final defeat of Satan. The climax of the victory of God over Satan is of course at the cross, the resurrection, and the ascension. To this we will turn in chapter 4.

CHAPTER 4

The Ascension of Jesus
Luke 24:50–53 and Acts 1:9–11

Introduction

Our study of the reference to heaven in Luke 2:14 demonstrated that the heavenly glory has been made manifest on earth by bringing the eschatological peace down to earth (ch. 2). Our examination of the reference to heaven in Luke 10:18 demonstrated that the victory of God in heaven over satanic forces impacts earth by materializing the eschatological kingdom on earth (ch. 3). The effects of this are well documented in Acts. It is interesting that at critical junctures in the Lukan writings, one finds references to heaven (Luke 24:50–53 and Acts 1:9–11). Luke 24:50–53 and Acts 1:9–11 serve as the third programmatic statements, pointing to yet another stage in Luke's narrative. Heaven would point to the exaltation of the cosmic Lord (e.g. Acts 7:49). Inclusion of the Gentiles will be discussed here (Acts 10–11) especially when Paul's call to the Gentiles is described as a vision from heaven (Acts 9, 22, 26). Anti-idol polemic plays a part here (Acts 14:8–18; 17:22–31; 19:23–41) since this unique lordship of Christ cannot be challenged, not even by idols of various nations. The critique of idols then becomes the affirmation of the cosmic lordship of Yahweh. Interestingly, the fall of Artemis is depicted as a fall from heaven (Acts 19:35). This further affirms the cosmic lordship of God.

In this chapter, we will first provide a review of Lukan scholarship on the ascension narrative and show that the heaven references in the ascension narratives have often been overlooked. The relationship of the heaven references in the ascension narratives to other heaven references in Luke-Acts remains neglected. This makes our study of the ascension of Jesus necessary. Second, we will study the ascension of Jesus and demonstrate its literary and theological concerns. Third, it will be argued that the ascension leads to the exaltation of Jesus. Finally we will demonstrate that the exalted Jesus becomes the cosmic Lord. The cosmic Lord challenges the earthly obstacles from heaven. The heavenly-exalted Jesus also critiques the idols of the nations. The cosmic lordship cannot be challenged. The anti-idol polemic affirms the cosmic lordship of Yahweh. First, we will study the ascension of Jesus.

The Ascension of Jesus

In what follows, we will first review Lukan scholarship on the ascension of Jesus and will show that the study of the heaven references in the ascension narrative has been either overlooked or insufficiently treated. Second, it will be demonstrated that the two ascension narratives are actually depicting one event – the ascension of Jesus. Third, we will demonstrate that the two accounts of the ascension of Jesus have a literary function for Luke's two-volume work. Fourth, we will examine the relationship between the ascension and the resurrection of Jesus. Finally, we will bring forth the theological significance of the ascension of Jesus.

Scholarship on the Ascension of Jesus

Among gospel writers, Luke alone narrates the ascension of Jesus and he does it twice (Luke 24:50–53 and Acts 1:9–11). The importance of the ascension of Jesus has been well acknowledged by scholars. James D. G. Dunn asserts, "The ascension of Jesus is potentially one of the most important episodes in the NT story of Jesus."[1]

Some major works have been done on the ascension of Jesus. G. Lohfink applies the *traditionsgeschichtlich* approach to the study of the ascension

---

1. James D. G. Dunn, "The Ascension of Jesus: A Test Case for Hermeneutics," in *Auferstehung*, ed. Hermann Lichtenberger Friedrich Avenaris (Tübingen: Mohr Siebeck, 2001), 301.

narratives (Luke 24:36–53 and Acts 1:1–12). After comparing the ascension narrative to Greco-Roman and Jewish literature, Lohfink concludes that "for Luke, the Ascension of Jesus is a rapture" (*Die Himmelfahrt Jesu bei Lukas ist eine Entrückung*).[2] He asserts that Luke has historicized the earlier tradition of the invisible ascension of Jesus into a visible one.[3] Lohfink views the ascension of Jesus as a purely Lukan composition. Lohfink's study of the ascension narrative has indeed contributed to Lukan scholarship from a historical-traditional point of view. However, Lohfink fails to provide the theological significance of the ascension narratives in Luke-Acts.[4] This is due probably to his overlooking of the heaven references in the ascension narratives that contribute to the heaven motif that goes through Luke-Acts.

Similar to Lohfink, A. W. Zwiep asserts that the ascension event is a rapture story. Unlike Lohfink, Zwiep applies the form-critical method to the study of the ascension story. He devotes his study especially to the Jewish ascension stories such as the ascensions of Enoch (Gen 5:21–24) and Elijah (2 Kgs 2:9–14). He claims that the tradition of the Jewish rapture stories stands behind the ascension of Jesus.[5] He asserts that whereas the raptures of Enoch and Elijah were originally seen merely as "a crown to their career," over time they came to be "seen as a precursory event which set temporarily aside as it were for a future task in the eschaton."[6] For Zwiep, the Jewish "rapture-preservation scheme,"[7] sheds so much light on the ascension of Jesus so that he concludes, "Jesus, after a period of forty days of final instruction (Acts 1:3) is taken up into heaven, where he is kept until the end of times (Acts 3:21) to make his appearance again at the Parousia (Acts 1:11; 3:20–21)."[8]

---

2. Gerhard Lohfink, *Die Himmelfahrt Jesu; Untersuchungen zu den Himmelfahrts- und Erhöhungstexten bei Lukas,* SANT (München: Kösel, 1971), 75.

3. Ibid.

4. D. Minguez comments on the work of Lohfink: "After so laborious an analysis, what remains in our hands" is only that the account of the ascension is a pure Lucan composition. But have we really understood the text? Here lies the foundational limitation of reducing everything to a "Traditionsgeschichte." See the review of Gehard Lohfink, D. Minguez, "Die Himmelfahrt Jesu: Untersuchungen zu den Himmelfahrts-und Erhöhunngstexten bei Lukas," *CBQ* 35 (1973): 399–400.

5. Arie W. Zwiep, *The Ascension of the Messiah in Lukan Christology,* NovTSup 87 (Leiden: Brill, 1997), 37–76.

6. Ibid., 78. Italics original.

7. Ibid., 79.

8. Ibid.

For Zwiep, the *Sitz im Leben* of Luke's Christology is the problem of the delay of the Parousia.[9] This opinion seems to be influenced by Conzelmann's rigid periodization of Lukan salvation history.[10] Unlike Conzelmann, Zwiep addresses the delay of the Parousia from a rapture point of view. He asserts, "the ascension marks the transition point at which the Jesus event continued to be effective along two separate lines, i.e. ἐν οὐρανῷ (where the risen Lord is being kept in preservation) καὶ ἐπὶ γῆς (through the Spirit working in the Church)."[11] Zwiep provides a reading of the ascension through the eyes of first-century Christians who have had the background of Jewish tradition. While recognizing the heaven references in the ascension narratives, he relies so heavily on the Jewish ascension material that he concludes that "the ascension of Jesus is reserved for a future reentry, namely the eschaton."[12] Zwiep's narrowly focused study of the ascension of Jesus makes him overlook the theological significance of the ascension of Jesus. For Zwiep Jesus's ascent to heaven means Jesus is "temporarily on a sidetrack, waiting for the Parousia."[13] The ascension functions as "a confirmation of the certainty of the promise of the Parousia."[14] Heaven for Zwiep is merely a waiting room for the second coming of Jesus. That Zwiep notices the relationship of the ascension to salvation history is promising; however, his Conzelmannian view of salvation-history prevents him from exploring salvation from the heaven references in the ascension narrative.[15] The significance of the four heaven references in the ascension accounts has largely been reduced by his "delay of the Parousia" reading. And this reading further hinders him from exploring the connection between the heaven references in the ascension narratives and the other heaven references in the Lukan corpus.

M. C. Parsons applies multiple methods to studying the double ascension narratives in his monograph, *The Departure of Jesus in Luke-Acts*. After reviewing previous studies (ch. 1), he examines Luke 24:50–53 in its

---

9. Ibid., 177–180, 197.
10. Ibid., 175–181.
11. Ibid., 185.
12. Ibid., 63, 79.
13. Ibid., 164.
14. Ibid., 169.
15. Ibid., 196.

historical (diachronic analysis) and narrative contexts (synchronic analysis) respectively (chs. 2 and 3). And he does the same with Acts 1:1–11 (chs. 4 and 5). Unlike Lohfink, he does not adopt higher-critical methods (redaction studies, narrative criticism and structuralism).[16] Differing from Zwiep, who devotes much attention to the ascension in its Jewish milieu, Parsons devotes his study to probing the literary significance by applying the literary techniques of secular works.[17] He uses these literary techniques to analysis the ascension narratives.[18] He concludes that Luke employs various literary devices (redundancy, repetition, variation) for a literary purpose.[19] From the literary perspective, Parsons' study of the ascension narrative is excellent and drives home Luke's literary achievement. However, Parsons seems to overlook the theological motivation of the two ascension narratives. Specifically, he neglects the heaven references in the ascension narratives and thus misses the theological significance of the ascension of Jesus.

The above review shows that these scholars more or less overlook the heaven references in the ascension narrative, even though they are important for understanding Luke's message. By neglecting the heaven references in the ascension accounts, these scholars inevitably downplay the theological significance of the ascension of Jesus.

It is Matthew Sleeman who pays more attention to the heaven references in the ascension narratives. He is reckoned as the first scholar who applies Soja's modern geographical theory to the study of Acts. His geographical analysis of Acts 1:1–11:18 suggests that Jesus's ascension into heaven establishes the spatiality of Acts. The heavenly location of Christ is decisive for our understanding of places and spaces in the book of Acts.[20]

Adopting Soja's tripartite model of spatiality,[21] Sleeman provides a spatial reading of the first half of Acts (1:1–11:18). His study is innovative in that he revolutionarily shows the significance of the heaven reference in

---

16. M. C. Parsons, *The Departure of Jesus in Luke-Acts: The Ascension Narratives in Context* (Sheffield: JSOT Press, 1987), 125.
17. Ibid., 66–73, 93–94, 96–102.
18. Ibid., 155–186.
19. Ibid., 189–199.
20. Sleeman, *Geography and the Ascension Narrative*, 5, 12.
21. According to Soja, there are three spaces. The first-space is the empirical realm, the second-space is the theoretical realm, and the third-space belongs to the creative realm. Ibid., 43.

the ascension narrative of Acts. Sleeman seeks to establish "heaven" as a significant geographical marker. He asserts that, "the fourfold mention of οὐρανός in Acts 1:10–11 is a more than sufficient narrative marker in this regard."[22] The heavenly Christ narrated in Acts 1:6–11 provides the third spatial basis upon which the rest of the action in Acts 1:1–11:18 is theologically oriented. The heavenly Christ dominants the spaces of "Temple," "Sanhedrin," "Εκκλησια," (Acts 2:1–6:7) "Samaria," "Desert," and "Saul" (Acts 8:4–9:31). Sleeman argues that the risen Lord centers the spaces. Sleeman also examines Acts 9:32–11:18, where the Gentiles are included. He asserts that, "up to the point of Acts 11:18 the spatial ordering laid out in 1:6–11 appears complete, at least in embryo."[23] Based on Soja's modern geographical theory, Sleeman enables readers to make more sense of the role of the risen Christ in the narrative than any previous theory. He introduces a new methodology that opens a window for us to read and think about the texts in a new light. However, some weaknesses of Sleeman's work need to be noted.

First, Sleeman asserts that "the fourfold mention of "heaven (οὐρανός) in Acts 1:10–11 is a more than sufficient narrative marker" and thus introduces an overarching heaven motif for the entire Book of Acts.[24] The heaven motif is no doubt important for the Book of Acts. This motif is also significant for Luke's gospel since there are forty heaven references in Luke as we demonstrated in our earlier study. How does the heaven motif function as a whole in Luke's two-volume work? What will the big picture of the heaven motif look like when one considers the entire Lukan corpus? Sleeman neglects Luke's gospel.

Moreover, Sleeman focuses on heaven references exclusively within Acts 1:1–11:18. He asserts that "the references to heaven subside within the narrative" after 11:18 and that "[t]he remaining narrative of Acts will not add anything substantially new."[25] It is true that most of the heaven references in Acts appear in 1:1–11:18, but, one should not overlook the significance

---

22. Ibid., 58.
23. Ibid., 254.
24. Ibid., 58.
25. Ibid., 254, 257.

of the heaven references in the second half of Acts (e.g. 14:15; 17:24; 19:35; 22:6),[26] which contribute to the heaven motif in Luke-Acts as a whole.

Finally, Sleeman's entire spatial study focuses solely on Acts 1:1–11:18. He claims at the end of his study that "at 11:18 the spatial ordering laid out in 1:6–11 appears complete, at least in embryo, from all three Sojan perspectives. The remaining narrative of Acts will not add anything substantially new to this embryonic vista."[27] This claim seems to downplay the significance of the second half of Acts where there are more spaces that should be discussed. Examination of spaces covered by Paul in his three mission journeys will undoubtedly add *something new* to the spatial reading of Acts. Does the heavenly Christ who dominates the spaces of "Temple," "Sanhedrin," "Samaria," "Desert," "Saul," and so forth also dominate Lystra, Athens, and Ephesus in which the apostle Paul employs the word heaven in combating the idols of the nations? Using Sleeman's geographical language, one wonders how the "heavenly Christ" dominates "the third-space" of the idols where the anti-idol polemic in the second half of Acts plays an important role in the growth of the early Christian movement. Using Sojan spatial geographical theory, in which third-space is a realm of imagination – the creative, Sleeman needs to spatialize the demonic realm which Luke lays out in his gospel and in Acts. Robert O'Toole rightly comments, "The methodology used by most researchers seems too limited. They spend a good deal of time discussing Luke's treatment of the ascension and exaltation, but they do not study these two events in Luke-Acts as a whole."[28] This critique applies to Sleeman's study. Sleeman focuses on the ascension of Jesus solely in the Book of Acts. He should not overlook the one in the gospel of Luke.

The above review demonstrates that scholars have acknowledged the importance of the ascension of Jesus. They have studied the ascension narrative from different perspectives and have indeed contributed to scholarship in various ways (Lohfink, Zwiep, Parsons). However, by and large they have overlooked the references to heaven in the ascension narratives (Lohfink,

---

26. Though the reference to heaven does not appear in Acts 19:35 but the term διοπετοῦς does relate to heaven reference. We will study this term in its due course.

27. Sleeman, *Geography and the Ascension Narrative*, 254.

28. Robert F. O'Toole, "Luke's Understanding of Jesus' Resurrection-Ascension-Exaltion," *BTB* 9 (1979): 111.

Parsons). Zwiep has noted the significance of the heaven reference, but he has relied so heavily on the Jewish ascension background, which leads him to a narrow understanding of the heaven references – heaven is simply "a temporary waiting place" of Jesus for his second coming. Sleeman has captured the importance of the heaven references in the ascension narrative. His spatial reading of the first half of Acts has been revolutionary and has brought forth the theological significance of the heavenly-ascended Jesus. However, his geographical methodology is questionable. The downplaying of the heaven references in the second half of Acts prevents him from understanding the significance of the heaven references in the book of Acts as a whole. And his overlooking of the heaven references in Luke's gospel deprives him from obtaining a holistic understanding of the significance of the heaven references.

Having studied the scholarship on the ascension of Jesus, next we will demonstrate that the two ascension narratives are actually describing the same event.

Double Accounts, One Event (*Luke 24:50–53* and *Acts 1:9–11*)

Luke is the only evangelist who provides a visible ascension of Jesus, and he does it twice. One is at the end of his gospel (Luke 24:50–51); the other is at the beginning of Acts (1:9–11). The double ascension accounts are actually depicting the same event – the ascension of Jesus. First, we will study textual variants in Luke 24:51 to show that this verse does describe the ascension of Jesus. Then, we will examine the "discrepancies" between the two ascension accounts (Luke 24:50–53 and Acts 1:9–11) and will show that they are actually describing the same event.

Textual Study of Luke 24:51

The earliest acknowledgment of a discrepancy between the two ascension narratives of Jesus, perhaps, could be traced back to the second century. The Western reading (D) of Luke 24:51 deletes the words "he parted from them and was carried up into heaven" (διέστη ἀπ' αὐτῶν καὶ ἀνεφέρετο εἰς τὸν οὐρανόν) in order to eliminate the ascending event due to the different timing of the ascension according to Acts 1:9–11. Internal and external evidences support the longer reading, though a scholarly consensus has not yet been reached.²⁹ The longer reading is preferred for the following reasons. First, according to a basic criterion of textual criticism, "the more difficult reading is to be preferred."³⁰ The omission of the phrase καὶ ἀνεφέρετο εἰς τὸν οὐρανόν in ℵ and D seems to be an attempt to harmonize the text with Acts 1:3, where the ascension comes at the end of a forty-day period.³¹ Second, and significantly, the Papyrus Bodmer XIV (P⁷⁵), a text that dates back to 200 CE, contains this clause.³² Third, the longer Markan ending of the gospel also supports the longer reading of Luke 24:51. Mark 16:19 says, "After the Lord Jesus had spoken to them, he was taken up into heaven and he sat at the right hand of God" (Ὁ μὲν οὖν κύριος Ἰησοῦς μετὰ τὸ λαλῆσαι αὐτοῖς ἀνελήμφθη εἰς τὸν οὐρανὸν καὶ ἐκάθισεν ἐκ δεξιῶν τοῦ θεοῦ).³³ Given that the longer ending is likely an early work that is dependent upon Luke's gospel, this is further external evidence in support of the longer reading of Luke 24:51. Finally, the evidence of Acts 1:2 supports the longer reading of Luke 24:51. Scholars argue that Acts 1:2 is a reference to Luke 24:51.³⁴ Therefore, the longer reading is preferred. Luke does provide the ascension of Jesus at the end of his gospel (Luke 24:50–53).

The So-Called Discrepancies

The so-called discrepancies between the two ascension narratives have long been noted and well-discussed. The most obvious discrepancies are as follows. First is the period of time (forty days) between the resurrection and the ascension. In Luke 24:50–53, it seems that the ascension occurs on Easter Sunday. In Acts 1:1–11, the ascension happens forty days after the resurrection. Second is the place of the ascension. In the gospel, the ascension occurs in Bethany. In Acts, the place is Mount Olivet. In what follows we will argue that there is no contradiction between the two accounts. They are actually depicting one event.

---

29. Metzger, *Textual Commentary*, 189; Marshall, *Luke*, 990.
30. Metzger and Ehrman, *Text of the New Testament*, 302.
31. Marshall, *Luke*, 909.
32. J. A. Fitzmyer, "The Ascension of Christ and Pentecost," *TS* 45 (1984): 416.
33. With regard to the longer ending of Mark's gospel, scholars hold different opinions. But most take the longer ending as inauthentic.
34. Fitzmyer, "Ascension and Pentecost," 418; Dunn, "Ascension of Jesus," 303.

The time of the ascension

Did it happen on Easter Sunday? In this section we will argue that the ascension does not occur on Easter Sunday; rather, it occurs forty days after the resurrection. We will show that "the difficult reading" of Luke 24:51 does not mean the ascension of Jesus occurs on Easter Sunday. The texts of Luke 24:36–49 and 24: 50–51 do not exclude a period of time between Jesus's appearance to the disciples and the ascension event. A surface reading of Luke 24 may give the impression that the ascension of Jesus occurs on the first Easter Sunday.[35] But this is unlikely. First, a study of the particle δέ will demonstrate that there is an interval between Jesus's appearance to his disciples and the ascension. The particle δέ in verse 50 simply indicates a transition. It means "then" in this context, and thus introduces a new occasion.[36] In terms of time consideration, the transition could be consecutive or separative. Here the term δέ is separative. The three occurrences of δέ in Luke 23:56 and 24:1–2 illustrate this point. The term δέ in Luke 23:56 connects two consecutive events, namely the event of seeing the tomb of Jesus and the event of these women going home (Luke 23:55–56). The appearance of δέ in Luke 24:1, however, introduces two events separated by almost three days (from Good Friday to Easter Sunday) (Luke 23:56–24:1). Interestingly, the δέ in Luke 24:2 again introduces two consecutive events – the women's approach to the tomb and their finding the stone rolled away. Thus, one can see that when the word δέ connects two episodes the episodes are separated in time, but when it occurs within an episode it refers to an immediately subsequent event. In Luke 24:50, Luke employs the term δέ at the beginning of an episode, which may indicate that some time has passed. Another example is in Luke 12:13 where there are also two events.[37] Therefore one cannot conclude based on the term δέ that the appearance of Jesus on the road to Emmaus in Luke 24:36–49 and the ascension of Jesus in Luke 24:50–53 are two consecutive events. C. F. D. Moule rightly asserts: "The

---

35. Fitzmyer, "Ascension and Pentecost," 417.

36. Plummer, *Luke*, 564.

37. See also Luke 13:6 (two events); 13:10; Acts 6:8 (there is a time interval between "the growth of the church" in Acts 6:7 and "the arrest of Stephen" in Acts 6:8); 9:10 (following the narrative of Saul's encounter with Jesus in Acts 9:1–9); and Acts 24:17, where the term δέ now occurs with a temporal phrase, "after some years" (δι' ἐτῶν δὲ πλειόνων).

ascension is described as a decisive and deliberate withdrawal from sight, to be distinguished from the mere 'disappearance' in the Emmaus story."[38]

Furthermore, Luke provides an explicit time span for the appearances of Jesus after the resurrection in Acts 1:3: "He [Jesus] appeared to them over a period of forty days" (δι' ἡμερῶν τεσσεράκοντα ὀπτανόμενος αὐτοῖς). Jesus's Emmaus appearance is only one of many occasions of Jesus appearing to his disciples. In the following section we will unpack this more.

Thus the above study shows that the event of the ascension of Jesus does not occur on Easter Sunday. The following study will demonstrate that the ascension of Jesus happens after a period of forty days.

Did it happen forty days after the resurrection? We will demonstrate that the ascension of Jesus occurs forty days after his resurrection. First of all, Acts explicitly tells the readers when the ascension happens. Acts 1:3 says, "After his suffering, he showed himself to these men and gave many convincing proofs that he was alive. He appeared to them over a period of forty days (δι' ἡμερῶν τεσσεράκοντα ὀπτανόμενος αὐτοῖς) and spoke about the kingdom of God (καὶ λέγων τὰ περὶ τῆς βασιλείας τοῦ θεοῦ)." Moreover, it would be unreasonable for Jesus to reveal himself to so many people in different occasions on the same day. Jesus appears to two disciples on the road to Emmaus (Luke 24:13–35). Thus, we see that it is more reasonable for Jesus to appear to his disciples and instruct them during a period of time than to do all of these activities within one single day. Donne rightly asserts, "The deletion of a period will create more problems than it would solve, since it would be impossible to fit all the post-resurrection appearances into a single day."[39]

Second, it is unlikely that the forty days of appearances come after the ascension event. Zwiep takes the view that "the post-resurrection appearances recorded in Luke-Acts are all manifestations of the already exalted Lord from heaven; the ascension rounds off the last one."[40] Likewise, Henk Jan de Jonge in a recent article argues that "the forty days are not the term fixed for the ascension; they are not linked with the ascension at all. They are linked

---

38. C. F. D. Moule, "Ascension: Acts 1:9," *ExpTim* 68 (1957): 205–209.

39. Brian K. Donne, "Significance of the Ascension of Jesus Christ in the New Testament," *SJT* 30 (1977): 558.

40. Zwiep, *The Ascension of the Messiah*, 197.

with the post-Easter, post-ascension appearances."[41] For de Jonge, Jesus was already exalted and glorified at the moment of his resurrection. When Jesus disappears he goes to heaven; when he appears he comes down from heaven. He repeatedly asserts that the ascension is merely Jesus's third/last appearance.[42] De Jonge's opinion is problematic. First, there is no scriptural evidence that Jesus ascends to heaven right after his resurrection. Second, besides the second coming of Jesus, it is hard to find a scripture passage that depicts a bodily descension of Jesus from heaven after his ascension. The only bodily descending of the ascended Jesus would be his second coming (Luke 21:25–28; Acts 3:21). Thus, de Jonge's understanding of the forty days of appearances is unconvincing.

Finally, Acts 1:2 explicitly says that after "giving instruction to the disciples" (ἐντειλάμενος τοῖς ἀποστόλοις) "he was taken up" (ἀνελήφθη). The reason why Luke prefers not to mention the forty-day period at the end of his gospel is due to his theological concerns that we will discuss later. Therefore, our study shows that Jesus ascends to heaven forty days after his resurrection. Next we will study the so-called different locations of the ascension.

The location of the ascension

Another issue is the seemingly different locations of the ascension. The place of the ascension in Luke 24 is Bethany while in Acts 1 it is Mount Olivet. The seemingly different ascension locations may lead readers to think that there were two ascension events. But this seems unlikely. Geography can provide the answer. The fact is that both places are closely connected. Bethany is on the eastern side of Mount Olivet, which extends its long slope to the east of Jerusalem.[43] Luke probably chooses Bethany at the end of his gospel and Mount Olivet at the beginning of Acts for his theological concerns.[44]

The above study demonstrates that the two ascension accounts are actually depicting the same event, the ascension of Jesus. Luke 24:50–53 does

---

41. H. J. de Jonge, "The Chronology of the Ascension Stories in Luke and Acts," *NTS* 59 (2013): 166.

42. Ibid., 166, 167, 170.

43. Grant R. Osborne, *The Resurrection Narratives: A Redactional Study* (Grand Rapids: Baker, 1984), 137; F. J. Foakes-Jackson and Kirsopp Lake, *The Beginnings of Christianity. vol. 1, The Acts of the Apostles* (London: Macmillan, 1933), 21–22.

44. P. A. van Stempvoort, "Interpretation of the Ascension in Luke and Acts," *NTS* 5 (1958): 30–42; Pervo, *Acts*, 46.

contain the ascension of Jesus, though it is a brief narration. Luke 24:50–53 does not indicate that the ascension occurs on Easter Sunday; rather, the ascension is a separate event from the event in Luke 24:36–49. The ascension narrative in Acts 1:9–11 is a detailed one. Jesus has been taken up to heaven after a period of forty days. Our studies demonstrate that the two ascension narratives are actually describing the same event.[45] Next we will consider why Luke provides two different versions of the same ascension – one at the end of his gospel and another at the beginning of Acts.[46]

Literary Function

Having showed that the two ascension accounts are actually describing the save event, in the following, we will demonstrate that Luke closes his gospel and starts the book of Acts with ascension narratives because of his literary and theological concerns. Scholars are often too hasty to judge the two versions of the ascension account. For instance, Haenchen observes variations between the two narratives and asserts that "it must be admitted that the two-fold account of the Ascension constitutes a greater stumbling block."[47] Then he concludes that Luke is a free writer who does not care about the consistency of the ascension story.[48] This is largely due to Haenchen's ignorance of the principles of ancient history writing. As a historian, Luke follows the convention of history writing in his own days. Lucian advises the historian, "the first and second topics must not merely be neighbors but have common matter and overlap."[49] The double narratives of the ascension connect the two volumes together as one literary work. T. S. Eliot asserts: "What we call

---

45. Osborne, *Resurrection Narratives*, 136–137; Parsons, *The Departure of Jesus*, 193–198; J. F. Maile, "The Ascension in Luke-Acts," *TynBul* 37 (1986): 55.

46. The Lukan ascension account and other New Testament ascension accounts (e.g. 1 Thess 1:9–10; 1 Cor 15:3–10; Rom 1:3–4; Eph 1:19–21; Phil 6–11) differ in that Luke provides an earthly, visible version of the ascension while the epistles give a heavenly, invisible version of the ascension. The difference is because "The epistles are doctrinal rather than historical, and theological identification in them does not necessarily imply chronological historical events. The Gospels, on the other hand, are more historical." See Osborne, *Resurrection Narratives*, 138. Brian K. Donne comments on this issue. It could be concluded that these New Testament writers have different theological motivations. See also Donne, "Ascension of Jesus Christ," 555–568.

47. Haenchen, *Acts*, 146.

48. Ibid.

49. Samosata's treatise, *How to Write History* 55. This has been acknowledged by some scholars. See Witherington, *The Acts of the Apostles*, 107; Johnson, *The Acts of the Apostles*, 28.

the beginning is often the end. And to make an end is to make a beginning. The end is where we start from."[50] This is why Luke closes his first volume with the ascension narrative and starts the second volume with the same event. With regard to the variations between the two narratives, Marguerat rightly asserts, "Narrative repetition [is] never the return of the same."[51]

The two ascension narratives function as a literary device of redundancy to bring forth the emphasis.[52] Parsons, after examining the two narratives of the ascension in their narrative contexts, concludes, "The ascension narratives represent Luke at his literary best. Through the literary device of redundancy in the ascension narrative, he both ties his two volumes together with repetition, yet moves ahead to tell the tale of the early church."[53]

Therefore, one finds that Luke, the author of Luke-Acts,[54] follows a literary convention of antiquity in composing his two-volume work. He applies the ascension narrative to end his gospel and to start Acts. More importantly, Luke, as a theologian, employs the two ascension narratives for his theological concerns. Before investigating Luke's theological concerns, it is helpful to study the relationship between the resurrection and the ascension of Jesus.

Ascension and Resurrection

What is the relationship between the ascension and the resurrection of Jesus? Some hold that they are one event. Some state that they are separate events. In what follows, we will demonstrate that the ascension and the resurrection are separate events. For Luke, the ascension is a visible event as described in Acts 1:6–11 (cf. Luke 24:50–53) apart from the resurrection.

De Jonge is probably too hasty to say that the resurrection-ascension/exaltation is a single event of Jesus.[55] In the following section we will argue that Luke distinguishes between the ascension and the resurrection. First,

---

50. Quoted in Parsons, *The Departure of Jesus*, 199.

51. Marguerat, *The First Christian Historian*, 132.

52. Robert C. Tannehill, "The Composition of Acts 3–5: Narrative Development and Echo Effect," *SBLSP* (1984): 238–240.

53. Parsons, *The Departure of Jesus*, 198.

54. We acknowledge that God is the divine author of Luke-Acts. He inspires Luke to write the two-volume work.

55. Jonge, "Chronology of the Ascension," 167.

Luke takes the ascension and resurrection as two separate events. Moreover, he explicitly narrates a visible ascension.

Resurrection and Ascension: Two Events

Luke separates the ascension from the resurrection. This can be discerned in Luke's gospel and in the book of Acts.

Luke 24:13–35

Luke alone provides a detailed account of the post-resurrection appearance of Jesus in Luke 24:13–35.[56] Jesus had been resurrected in Luke 24:1–12. The resurrected Jesus appeared to two disciples. "Jesus himself came up and walked along with them" (Ἰησοῦς ἐγγίσας συνεπορεύετο αὐτοῖς) (24:15). Jesus talked to them and explained Scripture to them (24:17–29). Jesus also conducted Holy Communion with them (24:30). This vivid description of the appearance of Jesus occurs between the resurrection and the ascension.

The temporal marker "the same day" (αὐτῇ τῇ ἡμέρᾳ) indicates that the ascension occurred after the resurrection. "The same day" refers to "the first day of the week" (Τῇ δὲ μιᾷ τῶν σαββάτων) (24:1), on which the resurrection occurred (24:2–12). After the resurrection, Jesus appeared to the two disciples on the road to Emmaus. The event of this appearance of Jesus happened between the resurrection and the ascension. Thus this indicates that the resurrection and the ascension are separate events. The following study will make this point clearer.

Luke 24:36–49

In Luke 24:36–49 the resurrected Jesus appeared to more disciples. He showed his hands and feet to them (24:39). Jesus even ate in the presence of his disciples. Luke 24:43 says, "He took it and ate in their presence" (λαβὼν ἐνώπιον αὐτῶν ἔφαγεν). Thus another appearance of Jesus occurred between the resurrection and the ascension.

Acts 1:3

A post-resurrection appearance of Jesus to his disciples is also narrated in Acts 1:3. It says, "After his suffering, he showed himself to these [men]

---

56. Only two verses depict the appearance of Jesus in Mark 16:12–13. Matthew totally omits this episode.

and gave many convincing proofs that he was alive" (οἷς καὶ παρέστησεν ἑαυτὸν ζῶντα μετὰ τὸ παθεῖν αὐτὸν ἐν πολλοῖς τεκμηρίοις). Here, the word "suffering" (τὸ παθεῖν) refers to the entire passion of Jesus.[57] It includes the death and resurrection of Jesus. The temporal clause μετὰ τὸ παθεῖν αὐτόν indicates that Jesus showed himself to these men after his death and resurrection (τὸ παθεῖν αὐτὸν).

Furthermore, Luke explicitly indicates the time period between the resurrection and the ascension. Acts 1:3b says, "For forty days he appeared to them speaking about the kingdom of God" (δι' ἡμερῶν τεσσεράκοντα ὀπτανόμενος αὐτοῖς καὶ λέγων τὰ περὶ τῆς βασιλείας τοῦ θεοῦ). The term διά indicates an interval in which multiple appearances of Jesus occurred.[58] The "forty days" explicitly indicates the interval between the resurrection and the ascension of Jesus.

Our study demonstrates that Luke depicts the events of the resurrection and the ascension as two separate events. Next our study will demonstrate that Luke presents a vivid event of the ascension.

The Ascension

The ascension of Jesus is explicitly described in Luke 24:50–53 and Acts 1:9–11. Five heaven references in the ascension narratives – one in Luke 24:51 and four in Acts 1:9–11 – should be considered as explicit indicators of the ascension of Jesus.

Luke 24:50–53

The heaven reference in Luke 24:51 points to the ascension of Jesus. Luke 24:51 says, "While he was blessing them, he left them and was taken up into heaven" (καὶ ἐγένετο ἐν τῷ εὐλογεῖν αὐτὸν αὐτοὺς διέστη ἀπ' αὐτῶν καὶ ἀνεφέρετο εἰς τὸν οὐρανόν). The term heaven refers to the destination of the ascending Jesus. The aorist tense of the verb διέστη describes the setting apart of Jesus from his disciples. It depicts the overall picture of the ascension of Jesus. The passive verb ἀνεφέρετο is a divine passive, with God the Father

---

57. C. K. Barrett, *A Critical and Exegetical Commentary on the Acts of the Apostles, vol. 1: Preliminary Introduction and Commentary on Acts 1–14,* ICC (Edinburgh: T&T Clark, 1994), 69.

58. Ibid., 70.

doing the "lifting up." The imperfect tense of the verb ἀνεφέρετο describes the gradual process of Jesus's going up into heaven.

Acts 1:9–11

The narrative in Acts 1:9–11 depicts the same event of Jesus's going up but provides more details of the ascension. First some terms suggest the upward memvement of Jesus. First, the aorist verb ἐπήρθη gives a general sense of "going up." The passive voice again indicates a divine action. Second, the verb ὑπολαμβάνω indicates the upward motion. Phrases like "they were gazing up into heaven" (ἀτενίζοντες ἦσαν εἰς τὸν οὐρανὸν) and "looking into heaven" (ἐμβλέποντες εἰς τὸν οὐρανόν) also indicate the upward direction. Third, the two present participles, πορευομένου and πορευόμενον, describe the process of the ascending of Jesus (Acts 1:10–11). Fourth, the text indicates clearly that Jesus "was taken up from you into heaven" (ἀναλημφθεὶς ἀφ' ὑμῶν εἰς τὸν οὐρανὸν). The same verb, ἀναλαμβάνω, occurs in Acts (1:2; 1:22; cf. Mark 16:19). Finally, the term "cloud" (νεφέλη) suggests this reading. It is the cloud that "takes up" (ὑπέλαβεν) Jesus. The cloud, according to Jewish tradition, serves as a vehicle of the ascension.[59] More importantly, it indicates the epiphany of God. This term elsewhere in the gospel of Luke (Luke 9:34–35; 21:27) accompanies divine epiphanies.[60]

The study of these terms shows the ascension of Jesus. The investigation of these verbs and participles shows that Jesus is "going up" into heaven. The cloud is the vehicle that takes Jesus up to heaven.

Second, the fourfold appearance of the phrase "into heaven" (εἰς τὸν οὐρανὸν) indicates the event of the ascension of Jesus. The first two appearances of this phrase refer to the direction in which the disciples are gazing (1:10–11).[61] In Acts 10:16, the same verb describes upward motion: "the sheet was taken up to heaven" (ἀνελήμφθη τὸ σκεῦος εἰς τὸν οὐρανόν).[62] As J. G. Davies comments, "Luke is deliberately making a distinction between the resurrection and the ascension of Jesus. Such spatial categories clearly

---

59. Zwiep, *The Ascension of the Messiah*, 104.

60. This tradition could also be evidenced in some OT passages: Exod 16:10; 24:16; Num 16:42; Isa 4:5; Ezek 10:4.

61. Bovon, *Luke 3*, trans. James Crouch (Minneapolis: Fortress), 412.

62. For more discussion of ascension vocabulary see Zwiep, *The Ascension of the Messiah*, 80–117; Lohfink, *Die Himmelfahrt Jesu*, 170–171.

conveyed to the onlookers the entry of the Risen Lord from this world of time and space into the heavenly sphere."[63]

The last two occurrences describe the place where Jesus is going (1:11). Acts 1:11 says, "This same Jesus, who has been taken from you into heaven, will come back in the same way you have seen him go into heaven" (οὗτος ὁ Ἰησοῦς ὁ ἀναλημφθεὶς ἀφ᾽ ὑμῶν εἰς τὸν οὐρανὸν οὕτως ἐλεύσεται ὃν τρόπον ἐθεάσασθε αὐτὸν πορευόμενον εἰς τὸν οὐρανόν). Luke later provides the place where Jesus is. Jesus ascends to the right hand of God. Acts 2:33 says, "He [Jesus] has been exalted to the right hand of God" (τῇ δεξιᾷ οὖν τοῦ θεοῦ ὑψωθείς) (cf. 2:34). Acts 5:31 reads, "God exalted him [Jesus] to his right hand" (ὁ θεὸς ὕψωσεν τῇ δεξιᾷ αὐτοῦ). Stephen is an eyewitness to the location of Jesus: Acts 7:55–56 relates that Stephen saw "the Son of Man [Jesus] standing at the right hand of God" (τὸν υἱὸν τοῦ ἀνθρώπου ἐκ δεξιῶν ἑστῶτα τοῦ θεοῦ). Thus the phrase "into heaven" (εἰς τὸν οὐρανὸν) indicates the event of the ascension of Jesus.

Third, Luke employs extensive visual vocabulary to stress that the ascension is a real event (Acts 1:9–11). The following phrases link to Jesus's going "up into heaven" (εἰς τὸν οὐρανόν): "while they were watching" (βλεπόντων αὐτῶν); "from their sight" (ἀπὸ τῶν ὀφθαλμῶν αὐτῶν), "looking intently" (ἀτενίζοντες), "looking" ([ἐμ]βλέποντες), and "you have seen" (ἐθεάσασθε). By using these phrases Luke purposely emphasizes the reality of the ascension of Jesus.[64] The ascension is a different event from the resurrection. The fourfold emphasis on seeing highlights the reality of the ascension of Jesus.[65]

Finally, the absence of eyewitnesses in other ascension stories, such as in the OT, Second Temple literature and Greco-Roman literature, supports that the ascension of Jesus is a real and unique event. First, Elisha's witnessing of Elijah's ascension is described only once. 2 Kings 2:10 says, "If you see me when I am taken up from you" (ἐὰν ἴδῃς με ἀναλαμβανόμενον ἀπὸ σου). Elisha saw the ascension of Elijah (Ελισαιε ἑώρα) and then he saw him no more (οὐκ εἶδεν αὐτόν) (2 Kgs 2:12). Another point is that Elisha is the only person who witnesses this event, whereas in Acts there are many eyewitnesses:

---

63. Donne, "Ascension of Jesus Christ," 559.
64. Walton, "The Heavens Opened," 65.
65. One may say that these expressions can represent a "visual" resurrection. But our previous study demonstrated that the resurrection and the ascension are separate events.

his disciples and other followers. Second, there are no eyewitnesses of the taking up of Enoch, either in Genesis 5:24 or in the pseudepigraphic accounts of the ascension of Enoch. *1 En.* describes a dream or visionary ascension (14:8–9 and 39:3–8). *2 En.* 67: 1–3 describes the taking up of Enoch into the highest heaven. There is darkness when God takes Enoch away. People look for Enoch, but they cannot figure out how Enoch has been taken away. They find a scroll that says "the invisible God," and they glorify God and go home. There is no "seeing" action mentioned. Enoch's ascension has no eyewitnesses. Last, there are no eyewitnesses of the ascension/deification of the Roman emperors. There is a belief that "the soul of [Julius] Caesar . . . had been taken to heaven."[66] Plutarch describes Romulus' being caught up into heaven. There "he was to be a benevolent god for them instead of a good king," but there is no eyewitness of his ascension.[67] Only later does someone see Romulus, and he must swear an oath that it is true that "as he was travelling on the road, he had seen Romulus coming to meet him, fair and stately to the eye as never before, and arrayed in bright and shining armor."[68] Because of the lack of eyewitnesses, some believe Romulus was murdered (cf. Ovid, *Fast.* 2:491–492; Livy, 1.16).[69] With regard to the deification of Augustus, Suetonius writes, "There was even an ex-praetor who took oath that he had seen the form of the Emperor, after he had been reduced to ashes, on his way to heaven."[70] Again due to the lack of other eyewitnesses the person has to take an oath to affirm that he has seen the ascension of Emperor Augustus.

Thus, our study of the appearances of Jesus to his disciples and the "forty days" interval demonstrates that the ascension and the resurrection are separate events. The heaven reference and some terms in Luke 24:50–53 support that the ascension is a separate event. Some of the terms in Acts 1:9–11 and especially the phrase "into heaven" also suggest this reading. Our investigation of the ascension stories in the Jewish and Greco-Roman world shows that eyewitnesses of ascensions are rare. This also supports that the

---

66. Suetonius, *Jul.* 88.
67. Plutarch, *Rom.* 27:6–7.
68. Plutarch, *Rom.* 28:1.
69. Ibid., 27:8.
70. Suetonius, *Aug.* 100:4.

ascension of Jesus is a visible, real event. The ascension of Jesus is separate from the resurrection. Luke does provide a visible ascension event at the end of his gospel and at the beginning of Acts.

The Resurrection

While Luke gives a real and unique description of the ascension of Jesus, he also provides a detailed account of the resurrection of Jesus (Luke 24:1–12). In addition to stating that the resurrection occurred (Luke 24:5; cf. Matt 28:6), Luke provides a lengthy narrative of the post-resurrection events. He devotes twelve verses to the resurrection, whereas Matthew and Mark each provide only eight. Furthermore, Luke emphasizes the scene of the empty tomb by relating it twice (Luke 24:3, 12), whereas Matthew and Mark describe it only once (Matt 28:6; Mark 16:6). In addition, Luke stresses the resurrection after the crucifixion in words not contained in Mark and Matthew (Luke 24:6). Space does not allow us to provide a full comparison of the Lukan resurrection account with the Matthean and Markan accounts. The above study shows that Luke does give a detailed version of the resurrection of Jesus. For Luke, the detailed description of the post-resurrection scene confirms the resurrection of Jesus. This also indicates that the ascension is an event different from the resurrection.

Summary

Therefore, the ascension is a separate event from the resurrection for Luke. Luke provides a unique ascension account of Jesus, and he does so twice. Luke put so much weight on the ascension of Jesus for his theological concerns. To this we now turn.

Luke's Theological Concerns

Having studied the literary importance of the two ascension accounts and the ascension as a separate event, in this section we will show the Luke's theological motivations in reporting the ascension of Jesus. Luke, as a historian as well as a theologian, writes his history book with theological concerns.[71] Parsons rightly observes that outside Luke-Acts, "[n]one of the Synoptic

---

71. Osborne, *Resurrection Narratives*, 138.

Gospels ends with the ascension and none of the apocryphal books of Acts starts with the ascension narrative."[72]

The theological significance of the ascension of Jesus has been well acknowledged. Maddox asserts, "the ascension is the major bridge from volume one to volume two: it is the necessary climax of the one and starting-point of the other."[73] Zwiep states, "Whatever one may say about traditions and sources of the ascension narratives, the way Luke has positioned the ascension texts at the key points of his two-volume work suggests that the ascension of Jesus is of central significance to Luke."[74] B. K. Donne asserts, "Theologically and empirically the Ascension of Jesus Christ is at the very heart of the New Testament."[75] Similarly, Maile states, "Luke has undoubtedly shaped the ascension narratives in his own way to present his own theological emphases."[76] Some scholars have recognized specific theological motivations in the ascension narrative.

Ascension and Parousia

Some assert that Luke's interest in the ascension is eschatological. Zwiep locates the Lukan ascension story in the context of the Jewish apocalyptic tradition (*4 Ezra*, *2 Bar* and *2 En.*).[77] He concludes that "[t]he ascension of Jesus is reserved for a future reentry, namely the eschaton."[78] He holds that Luke faces the problem of the delay of the Parousia.[79] For, Zwiep, "The rapture-preservation paradigm enabled Luke to maintain the certainty of the promised Parousia.[80]

De Jonge holds that "the main intention of Acts 1:9–11 is not to depict the ascension, but to encourage his readers and hearers to hold on to their hopes for the coming of Jesus in the future."[81] Luke is aware of the delay of

---

72. Parsons, *The Departure of Jesus*, 193.
73. Robert Maddox, *The Purpose of Luke-Acts* (Vandenhoeck & Ruprecht, 1982), 10.
74. Zwiep, *The Ascension of the Messiah*, 115.
75. Brian K. Donne, *Christ Ascended* (Paternoster, 1983), 67.
76. Maile, "Ascension," 37.
77. Zwiep, *The Ascension of the Messiah*, 196.
78. Ibid., 63, 79.
79. Ibid., 177–180, 197.
80. Ibid., 197.
81. Jonge, "Chronology of the Ascension," 171.

the Parousia and wants to reaffirm the expectation of Jesus's intervention at the end of time for his own day. His argument is that "Luke could have the two men say anything, however, the fact [is] that Luke chooses to make them say 'He will come in the way you saw him go.'"[82]

Wilson admits that there is a problem of the delay of the Parousia. This problem could lead to two extreme trends of eschatology. One is "the fervent renewal of Apocalypticism, false Messiahs who claimed that the End was near or already here."[83] It is to this trend that Luke addresses Acts 1:6–8. Another trend is denial of the coming of the Parousia. This is what Acts 1:11 addresses.[84] For Wilson, Luke uses the ascension to correct the false views of eschatology held by his audience.

While Luke clearly links the ascension of Jesus to eschatology in Acts 1:11, to say that the ascension concerns primarily the eschaton misses Luke's main theological motivation.

Ascension and the ecclesia

Other scholars propose that the ascension account is driven by an ecclesial concern. Dunn comments that "there is evidently a theological motivation at work here . . . Luke was content for the narrative of the ascension to be a pawn in an ecclesiastical game."[85] P. A. van Stempvoort discerns a specific theological significance for the ascension narratives in Luke-Acts. He asserts that the ascension narrative in Acts emphasizes the ecclesiastical perspective.[86] While the ascension of Jesus certainly relates to the church, this relationship cannot fully explain Luke's emphasis on the ascension narratives.

More significant is the relationship between the ascension narratives and salvation history. Some have noticed this connection.[87] Fitzmyer says, "The ascension of Christ acts as a caesura marking off another phase of salvation

---

82. Ibid.

83. S. G. Wilson, "Ascension: A Critique and An Interpretation," *ZNW* 59 (1968): 279–280.

84. Ibid., 280.

85. Dunn, "Ascension of Jesus," 304.

86. Stempvoort, "Interpretation of the Ascension in Luke and Acts," 39.

87. R. Schwindt, "Bibelhermeneutische Überlegungen zur Himmelfahrtserzählung Apg 1, 4–11," *SNTSU* 35 (2010): 161–176.

history that is now beginning."[88] It is insightful to recognize the link between the ascension and salvation history. But in what sense does the ascension connect to salvation? This question has yet to be answered.

Others have taken a further step in showing that the ascension of Jesus connects heaven and earth. Osborne rightly comments, "Luke's ascension scene then is a kind of link between heaven and earth, the climax of God's redemptive plan, yet an event which initiates *a new phase of salvation-history in the age of universal mission.*"[89] Flender comments that Luke 24 describes the ascension from an earthly point of view, while Acts 1 describes it from a heavenly point of new (the appearance of two angles).[90] Conzelmann points out that the ascension marks the limit of his stay on earth and the beginning of the heavenly reign of Jesus.[91] These scholars have discerned the significance of the ascension in linking heaven and earth. They rightly point to an area that deserves more scholarly attention.

It is Matthew Sleeman who acknowledges the significance of the heaven references in the ascension narrative in Acts 1:9–11. He applies Soja's modern geography theory to the ascension text and has provided a "spatialized reading" of the ascension narrative.[92] Sleeman's tripartite geographical study of the ascension narrative is laudable.

Sleeman provides a "high" Christology. His geographical analysis of Acts 1:1–11:18 suggests that Jesus's ascension into heaven establishes the spatiality of Acts. The heavenly location of Christ is decisive for the understanding of place and space.[93] The role of the heavenly Christ in Acts 1:6–11 is third-spatial, theologically orienting the rest of the action in Acts 1:1–11:18. He challenges the assumption that absence means inactivity and presence equals activity. Sleeman notably brings out the importance of the heavenly

---

88. Fitzmyer, *Acts*, 201.

89. Osborne, *Resurrection Narratives*, 144. Italics mine.

90. Flender, *Theologian of Redemptive History*, 12–13. Flender takes the position of the shorter reading of Luke 24:51). Thus he thinks that the term "heaven" does not occur in Luke 24:50–53.

91. Conzelmann, *Theology*, 204.

92. According to Soja's tripartite model of spatiality, first space is the empirical, second space the theoretical, and third space the creative realm. See Sleeman, *Geography and the Ascension Narrative*, 43.

93. Ibid., 5, 12.

Christ upon the growth of the earthly ecclesia. However, he fails to explain how the heavenly-exalted Jesus enables the growth of the church on earth. Besides, Sleeman fails to explain how the ascension of Jesus connects to Luke's gospel. Sleeman's reading of Acts "under a Christological heaven"[94] is actually only a reading of the first half of Acts, since he leaves the second half of Acts (from Acts 11:19 onward) unexamined.

The above survey demonstrates the following. The ascension event connects heaven and earth (Osborne, Flender, Conzelmann). It is also closely associated with salvation history (Fitzmyer). This event also brings forth the centrality of the heavenly Christ (Sleeman). But two questions require further examination: (1) in what sense does the ascension connect heaven and earth? And (2) how does this event relate to salvation history? The heaven references in the ascension narrative connect back to the heaven references in the gospel and anticipate other heaven references in the rest of Acts. These heaven references contribute to the heaven motif that goes through the entire Lukan corpus. This is the area that has yet to be explored.

In what sense does the ascension of Jesus climax the gospel and start the book of Acts? What does the ascension mean for Jesus? What theological concerns does the ascension of Jesus convey for Luke? In chapter 2 we demonstrated that the heaven/highest (Luke 2:14) brings forth the eschatological peace on earth. In chapter 3 we demonstrated that the heaven reference in Luke 10:18 points to the victory of God in heaven and its impact on earth. At the crucial juncture of Luke's two volume work, one finds the references to heaven in the ascension narratives. Luke intentionally employs the heaven references in the ascension narratives to introduce yet another stage in the Lukan narrative in that heaven points to the exaltation of the cosmic Lord. The impacts of the exalted heavenly Christ are well documented in the book of Acts. First is the inclusion of the Gentiles (Acts 10–11) especially when Paul's calling to the Gentiles is depicted as a vision from heaven (Acts 9, 22, 26). Second is the criticism of idols. The criticism of idols of the various nations becomes the affirmation of the cosmic lordship (Acts 14:15; 17:24). Finally, it is interesting that the fall of Artemis is described as a fall from

---

94. Ibid., 79–80.

heaven (Acts 19:35). With these theological concerns we will first turn to the study of the exaltation of Jesus.

Ascension and Exaltation of Jesus

As we have demonstrated, the resurrection and the ascension are two separate events. Luke portrays the ascension as a visible event of Jesus. The ascension brought the resurrection of Jesus to its climax as many scholars have acknowledged. Luke considers that the resurrection is not the culmination of God's power in Jesus Christ.[95] As Osborne rightly states, "For Luke the ascension is the climax of God's redemptive plan, yet an event which initiates a new phase of salvation-history in the age of universal mission. The ascension is the 'capstone' of the resurrection."[96] Franklin makes a similar assertion concerning the ascension: "for Luke's scheme the resurrection, though of vital importance, has nevertheless a clearly-defined significance."[97] Flender also comments: "The resurrection of Jesus forfeits to the exaltation its cosmic character of introducing the world to come. The resurrection of Jesus is offered to the individual as the eschatological message of the new life in Christ, while the exaltation is Jesus's entrance into the divine world."[98] The ascension of Jesus has significant theological concerns for Luke. Next, our study will first demonstrate that the heaven references in the ascension narratives point to the exaltation of Jesus. Then we will study the phrase "at the right hand of God" and will demonstrate that this shows the enthronement of Jesus. The ascension points to the exaltation of Jesus. We will first examine the phrase "into heaven."

Εἰς Τὸν Οὐρανὸν

The following examination of the phrase "into heaven" (εἰς τὸν οὐρανὸν) in the ascension narratives, in other passages in Luke-Acts, in the LXX, and in the Pseudepigrapha will demonstrate that this phrase points to the place where God is.

---

95. Osborne, *Resurrection Narratives*, 145.
96. Ibid., 144–145.
97. Eric Franklin, *Christ the Lord: A Study in the Purpose and Theology of Luke-Acts* (Philadelphia: Westminster, 1975), 31.
98. Flender, *Theologian of Redemptive History*, 19.

The Ascension Narratives

All four references to heaven in the ascension narrative (Acts 1:9–11) appear in the phrase "into heaven" (εἰς τὸν οὐρανόν) and point to the exaltation of Jesus. This phrase points not only to the direction in which Jesus went but also to the destination of the ascending Jesus. In Luke 24:50 and Acts 1:11, the term εἰς describes Jesus who "goes through humiliation to the upper world."[99] The preposition εἰς has a significant theological role in the New Testament.[100] In Acts 1:10, Luke uses the verb "stare" (ἀτενίζω) to depict the disciples when "they [the apostles] are staring into heaven" (ἀτενίζοντες ἦσαν εἰς τὸν οὐρανὸν). Strelan asserts that the verb "stare" (ἀτενίζω) connotes an epiphany or manifestation of divine power. The disciples are actually looking into the heavenly world.[101] The appearances of heaven emphasize the destination of the ascending Jesus. They indicate "the heavens where God's throne is."[102] The phrase "into heaven" (εἰς τὸν οὐρανὸν) in other passages in Luke-Acts also indicates the exaltation of Jesus.

Other Passages in Luke-Acts

The phrase "into heaven" (εἰς τὸν οὐρανὸν) elsewhere in Luke-Acts also refers to the place where God is. In Luke 2:15, it says, "When the angels had left them and gone into heaven" (Καὶ ἐγένετο ὡς ἀπῆλθον ἀπ' αὐτῶν εἰς τὸν οὐρανὸν οἱ ἄγγελοι). Jesus, "taking the five loaves and the two fish and looking up to heaven, gave thanks" (λαβὼν δὲ τοὺς πέντε ἄρτους καὶ τοὺς δύο ἰχθύας ἀναβλέψας εἰς τὸν οὐρανὸν εὐλόγησεν) (Luke 9:16). The tax collector, as a sinner, "would not even look up to heaven" (οὐκ ἤθελεν οὐδὲ τοὺς ὀφθαλμοὺς ἐπᾶραι εἰς τὸν οὐρανόν) (Luke 18:13). Acts 7:55 says that Stephen "looked up to heaven and saw the glory of God, and Jesus standing at the right hand of God" (ἀτενίσας εἰς τὸν οὐρανὸν εἶδεν δόξαν θεοῦ καὶ Ἰησοῦν ἑστῶτα ἐκ δεξιῶν τοῦ θεοῦ). One New Testament passage says explicitly that heaven is God's throne (μήτε ἐν τῷ οὐρανῷ, ὅτι θρόνος ἐστὶν τοῦ θεοῦ) (Matt 5:33).

---

99. Oepke, "εἰς," *TDNT*, 2:421–422.
100. Oepke, "εἰς," *TDNT*, 2:420.
101. Rick Strelan, "Strange Stares: Atenizein in Acts," *NovT* 41 (1999): 255.
102. Rick Strelan, *Strange Acts: Studies in the Cultural World of the Acts of the Apostles*, BZNW (Berlin: Walter de Gruyter, 2004), 39.

Our study of the phrase, εἰς τὸν οὐρανὸν, points to the place where God dwells. The following study of this phrase in the LXX and Pseudepigrapha also illustrates this point.

The Septuagint
The phrase "into the heaven" (εἰς τὸν οὐρανόν) in the LXX is often used in reference to the place where God dwells. A couple of examples will suffice. In a dream, Jacob saw a ladder that reaches to heaven (εἰς τὸν οὐρανόν) where God is (Gen 28:12). Elijah is taken up "into heaven" (εἰς τὸν οὐρανὸν) (2 Kgs 2:1; 2:11). More explicitly is 2 Chronicles 30:27, where it says, "The priests and the Levites stood to bless the people, and God heard them, for their prayer reached heaven, his holy dwelling place" (καὶ ἀνέστησαν οἱ ἱερεῖς οἱ Λευῖται καὶ ηὐλόγησαν τὸν λαόν καὶ ἐπηκούσθη ἡ φωνὴ αὐτῶν καὶ ἦλθεν ἡ προσευχὴ αὐτῶν εἰς τὸ κατοικητήριον τὸ ἅγιον αὐτοῦ εἰς τὸν οὐρανόν). The Psalmist says, "If I go up to the heavens, you are there" (ἐὰν ἀναβῶ εἰς τὸν οὐρανόν σὺ εἶ ἐκεῖ) (Ps 139:8). Isaiah 14:13 also supports this reading: "You said in your heart, 'I will ascend to heaven; I will raise my throne above the stars of God; I will sit enthroned on the mount of assembly, on the utmost heights of the sacred mountain'" (σὺ δὲ εἶπας ἐν τῇ διανοίᾳ σου εἰς τὸν οὐρανὸν ἀναβήσομαι ἐπάνω τῶν ἄστρων τοῦ οὐρανοῦ θήσω τὸν θρόνον μου καθιῶ ἐν ὄρει ὑψηλῷ ἐπὶ τὰ ὄρη τὰ ὑψηλὰ τὰ πρὸς βορρᾶν). In 3 Macc 5:9 says that "[p]rayer went up into heaven" (ἡ λιτανεία ἀνέβαινεν εἰς τὸν οὐρανόν). This is also found in 3 Macc 5:25: "Stretching out hands to heaven he implored the Almighty God once more to help them speedily" (τείνοντες τὰς χεῖρας εἰς τὸν οὐρανὸν ἐδέοντο τοῦ μεγίστου θεοῦ πάλιν αὐτοῖς βοηθῆσαι συντόμως) (3 Macc 5:25; see also 4 Macc 4:11). Therefore one finds that the phrase εἰς τὸν οὐρανὸν points to the place where God dwells.

The Pseudepigrapha
The use of the phrase "into heaven" (εἰς τὸν οὐρανόν) in the Pseudepigrapha also supports our argument. In *4 Bar.*, it says, "When people look up into heaven they pray to God" (καὶ ἄρας τοὺς ὀφθαλμοὺς αὐτοῦ εἰς τὸν οὐρανόν, προσηύξατο). "You are God who bestows a reward to those who love you" (Σὺ ὁ θεὸς ὁ παρέχων μισθαποδοσίαν τοῖς ἀγαπῶσί σε) (*4 Bar.* 6:5–6).

In the Pseudepigrapha the use of the phrase "into heaven" in ascension contexts strongly supports a reference here to the exaltation of Jesus. In ascension contexts, this phrase often refers to the person who ascends to meet God or to be with God. Enoch says that when "winds lifted [him] up into heaven" (ἄνεμοι ἐπῆράν με εἰς τὸν οὐρανόν) (*1 En.* 14:8–25), he saw "the Great Glory sitting upon the lofty throne" (ἡ δόξα ἡ μεγάλη ἐκάθητο ἐπὶ θρόνον ὑψηλόν) (*1 En.* 25:3; cf. 84:2). When Ezra has been taken into heaven (ἀνελήφθην οὖν εἰς τὸν οὐρανόν), he meets God and interacts with God.[103] In Apocalypse of Sadrach, Sadrach ascends into heaven and meets God. Sadrach 2:3 says, "The angel, having stretched out his wings, took him and went up into the heavens, and the flame of the divinity stood here and the Lord said to him, "Welcome, my dear Sadrach" (ὁ ἄγγελος ἔλαβεν αὐτὸν καὶ ἀνῆλθεν εἰς τοὺς οὐρανούς, καὶ ἔστη ἐν αὐτῷ ἡ φλὸξ τῆς θεότητος. Καὶ λέγει αὐτὸν ὁ κύριος· Καλῶς ἦλθες, ἀγαπητέ μου, Σεδράχ) (2:3–5; 3:1). Baruch is led into heaven and sees God. He relates, "The angel led me up into heaven" (ὁ ἄγγελος ἤγαγέν με εἰς οὐρανόν) where he watched Michael standing "before the heavenly God" (ἔμπροσθεν τοῦ ἐπουρανίου θεοῦ) (*3 Bar.* 11:1–9). The heavenly being, the archangel Michael, the commander-in-chief, ascended into heaven and stood before God (Ὁ ἀρχιστράτηγος ἀνῆλθεν εἰς τὸν οὐρανὸν καὶ ἔστη ἐνώπιον τοῦ θεοῦ) (*T. Ab.* 4:5; 8:1; 20:12). In *4 Bar.*, when God returns, he goes up into heaven (ταῦτα εἰπὼν ὁ κύριος ἀνέβη εἰς τὸν οὐρανόν) (3:17). Levi sees the scene "and the angel opened for me the gates of heaven and I saw the Most High sitting on the throne (Καὶ ἤνοιξέ μοι ὁ ἄγγελος τὰς πύλας τοῦ οὐρανοῦ· καὶ εἶδον τὸν ναὸν τὸν ἅγιον, καὶ ἐπὶ θρόνου δόξης τὸν ὕψιστον) (*T. Levi* 5:1). Therefore, the context of other ascension stories shows that when people ascend to heaven they are with God.

Summary

Our study of the phrase εἰς τὸν οὐρανὸν in the ascension narratives, in other passages in Luke-Acts, in the Old Testament, in the LXX, and in the Pseudepigrapha demonstrates that it points to the place where God is. Our study of the phrase "at the right hand of God" will demonstrate the exaltation of Jesus.

---

103. *Gk. Apoc. Ezra* 1:7–20.

"At the Right Hand of God"

One can observe that the phrase εἰς τὸν οὐρανόν also depicts angels or persons (Elijah, Enoch) who depart from the earth to heaven. But neither angels, Elijah or Enoch is depicted as occupying the place of "the right hand of God." Luke 2:15 says that "the angels went away from them into heaven" (ἐγένετο ὡς ἀπῆλθον ἀπ' αὐτῶν εἰς τὸν οὐρανὸν οἱ ἄγγελοι). In 2 Kings 2:11, "Elijah was taken up into heaven by whirlwind" (ἀνελήμφθη Ηλιου ἐν συσσεισμῷ ὡς εἰς τὸν οὐρανόν) (cf. 2:1). Enoch says, "winds lifted me up into heaven" (ἄνεμοί ἐπῆράν με εἰς τὸν οὐρανόν) (*1 En.* 14:8–25). Only Jesus was depicted as going "into heaven" (εἰς τὸν οὐρανὸν) and occupying the place of "the right hand of God" (τῇ δεξιᾷ τοῦ θεοῦ).

The phrase "at the right hand of God" (τῇ δεξιᾷ τοῦ θεοῦ) occurs two times in Luke (20:42; 22:69) and five times in Acts (2:33, 34; 5:31; 7:55, 56). Our following study will demonstrate that this phrase expresses the exalted status of the risen Jesus.

Luke 20:42

The position of "the right hand of God" that Jesus will obtain is prophesied by King David. David says, "The Lord said to my Lord: 'Sit at my right hand'" (εἶπεν κύριος τῷ κυρίῳ μου· κάθου ἐκ δεξιῶν μου) (Luke 20:42). The first "Lord" is God the Father and the second one is Jesus.

Luke 22:69

Jesus's position "at the right hand of God" is also foretold by Jesus. Luke 22:69 says, "The Son of Man will sit at the right hand of the power of God" (ἔσται ὁ υἱὸς τοῦ ἀνθρώπου καθήμενος ἐκ δεξιῶν τῆς δυνάμεως τοῦ θεοῦ). Jesus says "the power of God" to indicate that he co-reigns with God the Father as the cosmic Lord, as we will demonstrate shortly.

The two occurrences of the phrase "at the right hand of God" in Luke's gospel predict the future exalted position that Jesus will obtain. The occurrences of this phrase in Acts evidence the exalted Jesus.

Acts 2:33

First, the phrase "at the right hand" is an allusion to Psalm 110:1. Peter's point is that the resurrected Jesus has been exalted to the right hand of God (i.e. the throne) as the Davidic Messiah. The purpose of the quotation of

Psalm 110:1 is to argue for the exaltation of Jesus. Psalm 110:1 may be the most alluded to or quoted Christological passage in the New Testament.[104] Jesus indicates in his address to Jewish leaders (Luke 20:42–44; cf. Matt 22:43–44; Mark 12:36) that David is the speaker of Psalm 110. Psalm 110:1 has been considered as a royal psalm written in the pre-exilic period.[105] This psalm was likely used in a context of enthronement of kings.[106] This prophetic psalm is one of the "direct forecasts of a coming personal Messiah."[107] "Sitting at the right hand of God" has the background of an enthronement ceremony for a Davidic king.[108] The right hand should be taken as a dative of place.[109] Jesus has been exalted at the right hand of God the Father. This means the heavenly Jesus co-reigns with God in heaven. Jesus is called both "Lord and Messiah" (κύριον καὶ χριστὸν) (Acts 2:36). The conviction that Jesus sits at the right hand of God is found in other places.[110]

Second, the context of Acts 2:33 (2:32–36) indicates the enthronement of Jesus. Jesus is the one to whom God promises the throne of David. Acts 2:30 says, "God had promised him on oath that he would place one of his descendants on his throne" (ὅρκῳ ὤμοσεν αὐτῷ ὁ θεὸς ἐκ καρποῦ τῆς ὀσφύος αὐτοῦ καθίσαι ἐπὶ τὸν θρόνον αὐτοῦ). This is an allusion to Psalm 132:11 (LXX 131:11), which is a messianic prediction. "The LORD swore an oath to David, a sure oath that he will not revoke: 'One of your own descendants I will place on your throne'" (ὤμοσεν κύριος τῷ Δαυιδ ἀλήθειαν καὶ οὐ μὴ ἀθετήσει αὐτήν ἐκ καρποῦ τῆς κοιλίας σου θήσομαι ἐπὶ τὸν θρόνον σου). The term throne (θρόνος) echoes back to Luke 1:32 where it says, "The Lord God will give him the throne of his father David" (δώσει αὐτῷ κύριος ὁ θεὸς τὸν

---

104. William R. G. Loader, "Christ at the Right Hand: Ps 110:1 in the New Testament," *NTS* 24 (1978): 199.

105. Herbert W. I. V. Bateman, "Psalm 110:1 and the New Testament," *BSac* 149 (1992): 441.

106. Leslie C. Allen, *Psalms 101–150*, WBC 21 (Waco, TX: Word, 1983), 111; Mitchell Joseph Dahood, *Psalms, III: 101–150*, AB (Garden City, NY: Doubleday, 1970), 114.

107. Walter C. Kaiser, Jr., *The Uses of the Old Testament in the New* (Chicago: Moody, 1985), 131–132. Kaiser's comments on 1 Pet 1:10–12 show that the suffering and the glorification of Jesus are separated events. See ibid., 19–21.

108. F. F. Bruce, *The Acts of the Apostles: The Greek Text with Introduction and Commentary* (Grand Rapids: Eerdmans, 1990), 127.

109. Conzelmann, *Acts*, 30.

110. Acts 2:24–33; 5:31; 7:55–56; Eph 1:20–21; Col 3:1; Heb 1:3; 8:1; 10:12; 12:2; 2 Pet 3:22.

θρόνον Δαυὶδ τοῦ πατρὸς αὐτοῦ). Luke 1:32 makes clear that it will be Jesus, as the descendant of David, who will sit on the throne. Another "throne" reference shows that this throne is not an earthly one; rather it is in heaven. Acts 7:49 says, "Heaven is my throne" (ὁ οὐρανός μοι θρόνος). Jesus has done what David never achieved, namely rule on the heavenly throne as the lord/king.[111] Thus, Acts 2:22–36, especially the quotation of Psalm 109:1 (LXX), explicitly provides the enthronement picture of the victorious king. Thus, our study illustrates the exaltation of Jesus. Jesus has been enthroned at the right hand of God.

Acts 5:30–32

Acts 5:30–32 should be considered as the second explicit passage regarding the exaltation of Jesus in Acts. This passage evidences the exaltation of Jesus. Compared to Acts 2:22–26, Peter simplifies the accounts of the death and resurrection of Jesus in this passage. This is due probably to the different audience. Here the audience is the whole council and the whole body of elders of Israel that may be acquainted with these facts (cf. Matt 28:11–13).

In Acts 5:30, the exaltation is mentioned with an active verb, and the agent is clarified as God (cf. Acts 2:33). It is God who has exalted Jesus. The same verb, ὑψόω, recurs. The place of the risen Jesus is "the right hand of God" (cf. 2:33). Here, Peter further specifies the title of Jesus as "Prince and Savior" (ἀρχηγὸν καὶ σωτῆρα), which deserves more discussion.

Ἀρχηγός

The term ἀρχηγός occurs only twice in Luke-Acts (Acts 3:15; 5:31). Elsewhere in the New Testament this term appears in Hebrews (2:10; 12:2). It contains the meaning of "author" or "originator." Deities are often addressed as ἀρχηγός, like Zeus and Apollo.[112] Johnston argues for the meaning of ἀρχηγός as "prince" after examining it in the OT.[113] Paul-Gerhard Müller prefers rendering ἀρχηγός as "leader."[114] Flender argues that the resurrection

---

111. Schnabel, *Acts*, 148. For Fitzmyer, the word ἀναλαμβάνω (to take up) implies that he is "enthroned." See Fitzmyer, "Ascension and Pentecost," 412.
112. Delling, "ἀρχηγός," *TDNT*, 1:487.
113. George Johnston, "Christ as Archegos," *NTS* 27 (1981): 381–385.
114. Paul-Gerhard Müller, *Christos Archēgos: der religionsgeschichtliche und theologische Hintergrund* (Bern: Lang, 1973), 272–273.

and exaltation are different events. Exaltation occurs after the resurrection (Acts 5:30). The significance of the exaltation for Jesus is that he becomes the ruler (ἀρχηγός) (Acts 5:31).[115] It seems that all these meanings apply to ἀρχηγός. The context is in favor of the meaning "ruler," as Flender shows. First, Peter's speech here is against the Jewish rulers (ἄρχοντες) who try to order them not to preach the name of Jesus (Acts 4:8, 18). The fact that the terms "the kings" (οἱ βασιλεῖς) and "the rulers" (οἱ ἄρχοντες) appear in Acts 4:26 also supports this reading. The earthly rulers or leaders are opposing the real leader (i.e. Jesus Christ). Second, 5:29 further challenges the rulers that it is God who has the authority, rather than the earthly rulers. Finally, verse 31 supports this reading. The place of "the right hand of God" indicates that the risen Jesus co-reigns with God the Father. Jesus is the ruler. Therefore, the best understanding of the term ἀρχηγός is "ruler."

Σωτήρ

The risen Jesus is designated as "Savior" (σωτήρ). This title echoes back to Luke 2:11, which says, "Today in the town of David a Savior has been born to you; he is Christ the Lord" (ἐτέχθη ὑμῖν σήμερον σωτὴρ ὅς ἐστιν χριστὸς κύριος ἐν πόλει Δαυίδ). The purpose of the birth of Jesus is to bring salvation on earth. This does not mean that Jesus brought salvation when he was exalted at the right hand of God. Jesus is Savior at his birth (Luke 2:11) and granted repentance when he was on earth (Luke 5:32). Here Peter may indicate that the salvation is now available to all humanity, especially to the Gentiles.[116] The exaltation of Jesus makes salvation available to all.[117]

Therefore, the two titles of Jesus as the "Ruler" and "Savior" demonstrate the exalted status of Jesus.

Acts 7:55–56

The exalted status of Jesus is evidenced in Acts 7:55 where Stephen says, "Behold, I see heaven opened and the Son of Man standing at the right hand of God" (ἰδοὺ θεωρῶ τοὺς οὐρανοὺς διηνοιγμένους καὶ τὸν υἱὸν τοῦ ἀνθρώπου ἐκ δεξιῶν ἑστῶτα τοῦ θεοῦ) (cf. 7:56). The risen Lord Jesus has been exalted,

---

115. Flender, *Theologian of Redemptive History*, 105.
116. Pervo, *Acts*, 145.
117. Fitzmyer, *Acts*, 338.

obtaining the glorious position of the right hand of God. This is the only use of the title "Son of Man" for Jesus outside of the Gospels. It recalls the anticipations of Jesus's enthronement in the Gospel of Luke.[118] Stephen "saw the glory of God" (εἶδεν δόξαν θεοῦ) (Acts 7:55). This is the realization of Jesus's glory anticipated in his Transfiguration where Peter and two others saw "his glory" (εἶδον τὴν δόξαν αὐτου) (Luke 9:32).[119] Jesus has entered his glory with God and has become the glorified Son of Man.[120]

Summary

The above study demonstrates the exalted status of the risen Jesus. The ascension leads Jesus to the exaltation. Of course the exaltation of Jesus cannot be apart from the cross and the resurrection. The reference to heaven in the ascension narrative points to the exaltation of Jesus. The exalted status of the risen Jesus is evidenced in Luke-Acts. The risen Jesus has not only been exalted but also become the cosmic Lord. To this we now turn.

The Cosmic Lord

Having argued that the heaven references in the ascension narratives point to the exaltation of Jesus, in this section we will study passages that contain a heaven reference or the terms God/Lord and will demonstrate that the heavenly-exalted Jesus is the cosmic Lord.

The Cosmic God/Lord

The cosmic God is already indicated in the Gospel of Luke. This notion is well documented in the book of Acts.

Luke

The notion of the cosmic God has already been indicated in Luke's gospel. Our study of the terms, ὁ ὕψιστος and passages (10:15, 18, 21) that contain reference to heaven or God demonstrates this point.

---

118. Beverly Roberts Gaventa, *The Acts of the Apostles*, ANTC (Nashville: Abingdon, 2003), 131; William S. Kurz, *The Acts of the Apostles*, CBC (Collegeville, MN: Liturgical Press, 1983), 133.

119. Bruce, *The Acts of the Apostles*, 210. There has been much debate on why the Son of Man is standing. It is more likely that Jesus is standing to receive Stephen's spirit. For more discussion, see Bock, *Acts*, 311–312; Barrett, *Acts of the Apostles, vol. 1*, 384–385.

120. Peterson, *Acts*, 246.

"The Most High God" (ὁ ὕψιστος)

The Lukan use of the term "the Most High" (ὁ ὕψιστος) suggests the notion of the cosmic Lord. First, the term has a strong sense of cosmology. The basic meaning of ὕψιστος is "highest" or "loftiest."[121] Second, that Luke uses the term "Most High" more frequently than Matthew and Mark suggests this point. Luke uses the term ὕψιστος seven times in his gospel. Matthew uses it only once in Matthew 21:9, where it refers to the high heaven (cf. Mark 11:10 and Luke 19:38). Matthew never uses it as a synonym for God. Mark uses this term twice (5:7; 11:10), once to refer to the high heaven (11:10) and once as a synonym for God (5:7). Only Luke uses "the Most High" repeatedly as a synonym for God. God is "the Most High" (ὁ ὕψιστος) (Luke 1:32, 35, 76; 6:35; 8:28). Jesus "will be called the Son of the Most High" (υἱὸς ὑψίστου κληθήσεται) (1:32; 8:28). Luke could have used the term "God" like Matthew and Mark do, but he prefers the term "Most High" as a synonym for God. Thus, the fact that Luke chooses the term "the Most High" in his gospel suggests the notion of the cosmic God.

Other passages

Luke 10:15 suggests that God is the cosmic Lord. God has sovereignty over heaven and hades. Luke 10:15 says, "And you, Capernaum, will you be lifted up to heaven? No, you will go down to ades." It is not possible for the prideful Capernaum to reach heaven. Rather, God sends her to hades. God is in control of heaven and hades. God is cosmic in a sense of universal sovereignty.

Luke 10:18 indicates the cosmic Lord. As studied earlier, Satan, the enemy of God, has fallen from heaven. Heaven is no longer a place for Satan. God is in charge of heaven. God's sovereignty is over Satan and his evil forces. This is explicitly expressed in Luke 11:14–23, where the sovereignty of God over demons is highlighted.[122] God is cosmic in terms of his sovereignty in heaven over evil forces.

Luke 10:21 also indicates that God is cosmic. Jesus addresses the Father as "the Lord of heaven and earth" (κύριε τοῦ οὐρανοῦ καὶ τῆς γῆς). This passage

---

121. Bertram, "ὕψιστος," *TDNT*, 8:615.
122. Pao, *Isaianic New Exodus*, 209.

indicates that God has sovereignty over heaven and earth. The notion that God is cosmic has been explicitly indicated.

The above study shows that God is the Most High God who is above all and everything. God has sovereignty over heaven and earth. God has sovereignty over evil forces. The cosmic Lord is addressed in the gospel. The Lord is cosmic. The lordship of the exalted Jesus over the cosmos is well documented in Acts.

Acts

Compared to Luke, the cosmic Lord is more explicitly documented in the book of Acts. We will study Stephen's speech and other passages to demonstrate this point.

Stephen's speech

The cosmic Lord is explicitly demonstrated in Stephen's speech. First, Acts 7:49 depicts a clear image of the cosmic Lord: "Heaven is my throne, and the earth is my footstool." The heaven references here are closely connected to the heaven references in the ascension narrative in Acts 1:9–11.

Second, the quotation also suggests the cosmic Lord. Acts 7:49–50 is a quotation from Isaiah 66:1–2a. Stephen's point in this quotation is not, as some hold, to criticize the temple,[123] but to assert that God could not be confined to a specific locale (c.f. 1 Kgs 8:27b; 2 Chr 6:18b).[124] God should not be put in a box.[125] His presence exists throughout all heaven and earth. The quotation of Isaiah 66:1–2a virtually depicts an image of the cosmic Lord.

Third, the context of Acts 7:49–50 supports that God is cosmic. The description of the appearance of God in the speech of Stephen (Acts 7:2–53) demonstrates a cosmic Lord. The God of glory appears to Abraham in Mesopotamia (7:2). God is with Joseph in Egypt (7:9). God speaks to Moses at Mount Sinai (7:31–32). God is with Israel in the wilderness (7:44). Up to this point, Stephen makes the point that God does not restrain himself to a certain place (i.e. "house" [οἶκον]). Acts 7:48 says, "Yet the Most High

---

123. Pervo, *Acts*, 191; Timothy C. G. Thornton, "Stephen's Use of Isaiah 66:1," *JTS* 25 (1974): 432–434; Conzelmann, *Acts*, 56; Mallen, *The Reading and Transformation*, 114.

124. Bock, *Acts*, 303–304.

125. Witherington, *The Acts of the Apostles*, 273.

does not dwell (κατοικεῖ) in that which is made with hands." This indicates that God is cosmic.

Fourth, the phrase "the Most High" (ὁ ὕψιστος) also supports the reading of the cosmic God/Lord. Stephen's accusers refer to God as τὸν θεόν. Stephen refers to God as "ὁ θεὸς/τοῦ θεοῦ" eighteen times (Acts 7:2, 6, 7, 9, 17, 20, 25, 32[x2], 37, 42, 45, 46[x2], 55[x2], 57). The only exception is when Stephen uses the term "the Most High" (ὁ ὕψιστος) to refer God (Acts 7:48). "The Most High" has a strong Greek cosmological flavor as we have demonstrated earlier. The Lukan change of reference to God shows the transcendence of God.[126] Luke's use of "the Most High" underlines God's transcendence and sovereignty.[127]

Finally, Acts 7:55–56 shows the cosmic Lord. As demonstrated earlier, the risen Jesus has been exalted to the right hand of God. He co-reigns with God the Father. The cluster of heaven references appearing in the speech of Stephen (Acts 7:55–56) supports that the Lord is cosmic. Jesus's sitting at the right hand of God indicates that the exalted Jesus co-reigns with God. The risen Jesus has been exalted to the same status as God the Father. Characteristics that refer to God such as the sovereignty, authority, and transcendence, are also applied to the risen Jesus.

Therefore, in Stephen's speech, the notion of the cosmic God/Lord has been demonstrated in many ways. The notion of the cosmic Lord is also indicated in other passages in Acts.

Other passages

Acts 4:12 shows the notion of the cosmic Lord. It says salvation comes from no one else under heaven, but Jesus only. The phrase "under heaven" (ὑπὸ τὸν οὐρανὸν) is an "exclusive and universal claim."[128] The exclusive claim underlines that it is only Jesus in the universe that can bring salvation to the world.[129] The cosmic lordship is stressed from a salvific point of view.

Acts 4:24–30 suggests the cosmic lordship of the exalted Jesus. The Lord is claimed as the "sovereign Lord who made heaven and earth" (δέσποτα, σὺ

---

126. Dennis D. Sylva, "The Meaning and Function of Acts 7:46–50," *JBL* 106 (1987): 267.

127. Schnabel, *Acts*, 385.

128. Pao, *Isaianic New Exodus*, 210.

129. C. H. Pinnock, "Acts 4:12: No Other Name Under Heaven," *ThS* 10 (2003): 19–28.

ὁ ποιήσας τὸν οὐρανὸν καὶ τὴν γῆν καὶ τὴν θάλασσαν καὶ πάντα τὰ ἐν αὐτοῖς) (Acts 4:24). The term δέσποτα indicates that some one has legal authority and power over persons or subjects.[130] The term ὁ ποιήσας shows that God is the Creator of the universe. Obviously, the Creator rules over the creation. The δέσποτα rules over the creation. Peter applies the title "sovereign Lord" (δέσποτα) and "the maker" (ὁ ποιήσας) of heaven and earth to show that God is the ruler of the cosmos. God is in control of earthly Jewish rulers. This passage stresses the cosmic lordship from a creation perspective.

Acts 9:5 indicates that the heavenly exalted Jesus is cosmic. Acts 9:5 says, "'Who are you, Lord?' he [Saul] asked. 'I am Jesus, whom you are persecuting,' he replied" (εἶπεν δέ· τίς εἶ, κύριε; ὁ δέ· ἐγώ εἰμι Ἰησοῦς ὃν σὺ διώκεις). The heavenly Jesus presents himself in his followers who are living on earth. This is another case that shows the cosmic Lord. The cosmic Jesus is active on earth. He heals Aeneas (Acts 9:34). His name overpowers the evil spirits (Acts 16:19; 19:13, 17).[131] The cosmic Lord is presented in a sense of a universal presence. Parsons asserts that "the risen Lord is a character who is 'absent but curiously present'"[132] The presence and absence are ambivalent: Jesus by the ascension becomes universally absent but also universally present.[133] Sleeman rightly states that "the heavenly Christ, hidden from sight and yet sovereign and transformative within earthly spaces."[134] The cosmic Lord is also indicated in other passages.

Acts 10:36 affirms the notion of the cosmic lordship of Jesus. The exalted Jesus is declared as "Lord of all" (οὗτός ἐστιν πάντων κύριος). This title of Jesus connects with the Roman imperial cult propaganda.[135] J. R. Howell moves beyond Rowe's study by examining its context. His study demonstrates that Luke says "he [Jesus] is the Lord of all" to criticize the Roman centurion in particular and the Roman benefaction system in general, since centurions were exercising authority and benefaction on the emperor's behalf.

---

130. Rengstor, "δεσπότης," *TDNT*, 2:44–49.

131. Sleeman, *Geography and the Ascension Narrative*, 199–202.

132. Parsons, *The Departure of Jesus*, 161.

133. Lukas Ohly, "Kontrast-Harmonie: Ein Beitrag zur Theologie der Himmelfahrt Christi," *NZTR* 49 (2007): 484–498.

134. Sleeman, *Geography and the Ascension Narrative*, 257.

135. C. K. Rowe, "Luke-Acts and the Imperial Cult: A Way through the Conundrum?," *JSNT* 27 (2005): 279–300; Bock, *Acts*, 397.

Howell further points out that the centurion, Cornelius, has to admit Jesus as his Lord.[136] While the expression, "Jesus is the Lord of all" indeed criticizes imperial authority, Luke's agenda is broader than that. It is not an accident that this title, "Lord of all," appears in the account of the conversion of the first Gentile. In this context "all" (πάντων) would include both Jews and Gentiles. The inclusion of Gentiles is stressed. Thus, Jesus becomes the Lord of all in a sense that both Jews and Gentiles are under his sovereignty when it comes to salvation.[137] This claims the cosmic lordship from the view of salvation.

The anti-idol polemic in Acts 14:8–15 and 17:22–34 expresses the notion of the cosmic Lord. Acts 14:15 says, "The living God, who made heaven and earth and the sea and everything in them" (θεὸν ζῶντα, ὃς ἐποίησεν τὸν οὐρανὸν καὶ τὴν γῆν καὶ τὴν θάλασσαν καὶ πάντα τὰ ἐν αὐτοῖς). This anti-idol polemic stresses the Creator God and at the same time asserts the cosmic lordship of Jesus.

One can also find the notion of the cosmic Lord in Acts 17. Acts 17:24 says, "The God who made the world and everything in it is the Lord of heaven and earth and does not live in temples built by hands" (ὁ θεὸς ὁ ποιήσας τὸν κόσμον καὶ πάντα τὰ ἐν αὐτῷ, οὗτος οὐρανοῦ καὶ γῆς ὑπάρχων κύριος οὐκ ἐν χειροποιήτοις ναοῖς κατοικεῖ). This anti-idol polemic claims that God is the creator of the cosmos and at the same time asserts the cosmic lordship of Jesus.

Summary

Therefore, the above study shows the cosmic Lord. Stephen's speech, especially in Acts 7:49–50, explicitly portrays the cosmic Lord. The risen Lord is present in the cosmos (9:5). The cosmic lordship of God is expressed in a salvific (4:12) and in a general way (10:36). The cosmic lordship is also demonstrated from the perspective of creation (14:15; 17:24). We see that the cosmic Lord has been explicitly depicted in the book of Acts.

We have seen that the heaven references in the ascension narrative refer to the exaltation of the risen Jesus. We have also demonstrated that by the

---

136. J. R. Howell, "The Imperial Authority and Benefaction of Centurions and Acts 10.34–43: A Response to C. Kavin Rowe," *JSNT* 31 (2008): 25–51.

137. Pao, *Isaianic New Exodus*, 210.

ascension Jesus is now at his exalted status and co-reigns with God the Father. The exalted Jesus is the cosmic Lord. It is time to investigate the heaven references in the second half of Acts. A heaven references occur repeatedly in the visions of Paul and Peter (Acts 9:1–9, cf. 22:6–16; 26:12–18; Acts 10:9–16). A heavenly vision challenges Paul who opposes the Way and changes him to bring salvation to both Jews and Gentiles. A heavenly vision also challenges Peter and other Jewish Christian leaders of their notion of the exclusion of Gentiles from salvation. Heaven references also appear in the anti-idol polemical passages in the three missionary journeys of the apostle Paul (Acts 14:8–18; 17:22–34; 19:21–41). The anti-idol polemic challenges the idols of nations and affirms the cosmic lordship of God. First we will study the heavenly visions of Paul and Peter.

Visions from Heaven: The Inclusion of the Gentiles

The heaven references in the ascension narrative point to the exaltation of the risen Jesus. The heaven references in the visions of Paul and Peter reveal the active role of the cosmic/heavenly Lord. The heavenly-exalted Jesus challenges Paul and calls him to bring salvation to Jews and Gentiles. Heaven is still fighting for the sake of the eschatological kingdom. First we will examine the heavenly vision of Paul.

The Heavenly Vision of Paul (Acts 9:1–9; 22:6–16; 26:12–18)

The significance of the reference to heaven in Acts 9:3 has often been downplayed by scholars. By and large, the connection between the heaven reference in this vision and Jesus's ascension has been neglected.[138] Barrett provides a comparison of the three accounts of the vision, and unfortunately his examination excludes the reference to heaven.[139] Only a few scholars have paid attention to the connections between the heaven reference in this vision and the ascension of Jesus. Schnabel asserts, "The light from heaven is the appearance of the exalted Jesus (v. 5)."[140] However, he fails to discuss how these heaven references connect to each other. Sleemann acknowledges the connection between the heaven reference in Acts 9:3 and the ascension of

---

138. Conzelmann, *Acts*, 71; Barrett, *Acts of the Apostles, vol. 1*, 449; Bruce, *The Acts of the Apostles*, 234; Fitzmyer, *Acts*, 425; Bock, *Luke 1:1–9:50*, 356–357.

139. Barrett, *Acts of the Apostles, vol. 1*, 439–440.

140. Schnabel, *Acts*, 443.

Jesus.¹⁴¹ He provides a geographical understanding of their relationship. He claims, "Indeed, the unseen but sovereign aspect of heaven is a key touchstone to establishing ascension geography as both material and ideational, *and more.*"¹⁴² The heaven reference in Acts 9:3 is the "Christological intervention in space."¹⁴³ He insightfully discerns the theological significance of the heaven reference in Acts 9:3. In the following we will argue first that the vision is the intervention of the heavenly-exalted Jesus. Second, we will show that the exalted Jesus challenges and changes Saul. Finally, we will demonstrate that the purpose of the intervention of the heavenly-exalted Jesus is for a kingdom/salvation concern in that Paul should bring salvation first to the Jews and then to the Gentiles.

The intervention of the heavenly-exalted Jesus

First we will show the connection between the heaven reference in the vision and the ascension of Jesus. Reference to heaven first appears in the vision of Saul in Acts 9:3, and it recurs in Paul's two recollections of this vision (Acts 22:6–16 and 26:12–23).¹⁴⁴ Heaven references in Acts 9:3 and 22:6 recall those in the ascension of Jesus (Acts 1:9–11). As we have shown, the heaven references in the ascension narrative point to the exaltation of the risen Jesus. And the risen Jesus has been exalted to the right hand of God and he has been enthroned and is co-reigning with God the Father. The exalted Jesus is a cosmic Lord. Thus, the recurrence of the heaven reference links to the exalted cosmic Jesus. Next, we will demonstrate that the exalted Jesus appears to Saul from heaven in this vision.

Second, the "light from heaven" in Acts 9:3 is the Christophany.¹⁴⁵ This is the appearance of the exalted Jesus. Several points support this reading. First of all, in the OT, "light" is a common feature of God. Psalm 27:1 (26:1

---

141. Sleeman, *Geography and the Ascension Narrative*, 199.

142. Ibid., 259. Italics original.

143. Ibid., 199.

144. For a comparison of the three visionary narratives see, Charles W. Hedrick, "Paul's Conversion/Call: A Comparative Analysis of the Three Reports in Acts," *JBL* 100 (1981): 415–432; John B. F. Miller, *Convinced That God Had Called Us: Dreams, Visions, and the Perception of God's Will in Luke-Acts*, Biblical Interpretation Series 85 (Leiden: Brill, 2007), 195–199; N. T. Wright, *The Resurrection of the Son of God*, COQG 3 (Minneapolis; London: Fortress, 2003), 388–393.

145. Conzelmann, *Acts*, 71; Bock, *Luke 1:1–9:50*, 357.

LXX) says, "The Lord is my light and salvation" (Ὁ Κύριος εἶναι φῶς μου καὶ σωτηρία μου) (cf. 78:14, LXX 77:14). Isaiah 9:2 says, "The people walking in darkness have seen a great light" (Ὁ λαὸς ὁ περιπατῶν ἐν τῷ σκότει εἶδε φῶς μέγα) (cf., 42:16; 60:1, 20). Micah 7:8 says, "The LORD will be my light" (ὁ Κύριος θέλει εἶσθαι φῶς εἰς ἐμέ). Second, "the light from heaven" (φῶς ἐκ τοῦ οὐρανοῦ) (Acts 9:3; 22:6) further suggests that it is a divine figure who appears from heaven. Heaven is the place where the exalted Jesus reigns. In Acts 26:13 Saul says, "I saw a light brighter than the sun from heaven shining around me" (οὐρανόθεν ὑπὲρ τὴν λαμπρότητα τοῦ ἡλίου περιλάμψαν με φῶς) indicates that this is not an ordinary light. Third, that the voice comes from the light further supports that a figure appears. "He [Saul] heard a voice [of the Lord] say to him" (ἤκουσεν φωνὴν λέγουσαν αὐτῷ) (Acts 9:4; 22:7; 26:14). Fourth, the following narrative explicitly indicates that this figure is the exalted Jesus who appears from heaven. Acts 9:5 says, "Who are you, Lord?' Saul asked. 'I am Jesus, whom you are persecuting,' he replied" (εἶπεν δέ· τίς εἶ, κύριε; ὁ δέ· ἐγώ εἰμι Ἰησοῦς ὃν σὺ διώκεις). (cf. 22:8; 26:15). Finally, Paul's recollection of this vision in 1 Corinthians 9:1 says, "Have I not seen Jesus our Lord?" (Οὐχὶ Ἰησοῦν χριστὸν τὸν κύριον ἡμῶν ἑώρακα;).[146] Acts 9:7 says, "The men traveling with Saul stood there speechless; they heard the sound but did not see anyone" This implies that Saul has seen a real subject, namely, the exalted Jesus.

Finally, the vision in Acts 22:17–21 points the intervention of the exalted Jesus. The vision occurs at the occasion when Paul was praying in the temple (22:17). In the vision, it is the exalted Jesus who comes down directly from heaven and appears to Paul from heaven even though the term "heaven" does not occur. Paul addresses him as κύριε (22:19). Paul's testimony is about Jesus, and verse 18 says, "They will not accept your testimony about me" (οὐ παραδέξονταί σου μαρτυρίαν περὶ ἐμοῦ). In this vision the inclusion of the Gentiles is stressed. The exalted Jesus commands Paul, "Go; I will send you far away to the Gentiles" (πορεύου, ὅτι ἐγὼ εἰς ἔθνη μακρὰν ἐξαποστελῶ σε) (22:21). Thus, it is the exalted Jesus who appears to Paul from heaven and commissions him to bring salvation to the Gentiles.

---

146. Schnabel, *Acts*, 443.

Heaven references here connect to the ascension of Jesus. It is the heavenly-exalted Jesus who appears to Saul, or as Sleemann rightly asserts, "the heavenly Christ, hidden from sight and yet sovereign and transformative within earthly spaces."[147]

The challenge of this heavenly vision

The heavenly-exalted Jesus as the cosmic Lord challenges the opponents on earth. The cosmic Lord challenges Saul, the opponent of the Way and also challenges to Jewish leaders. The following points demonstrate the challenges to Saul.

First, Acts 26:14 supports this notion. "It is hard for you to kick against the goads" (σκληρόν σοι πρὸς κέντρα λακτίζειν) (Acts 26:14). Fitzmyer takes this sentence to mean "it is useless for you to try to resist this heavenly call."[148] This seems unlikely. It is more likely that Paul's persecuting the followers of Jesus is hard and harmful for him since this is against the will of God. A Greek proverb tells that all life has been determined by gods. This text indicates the futility and harmfulness of acting against the will of a deity.[149] This phrase has the notion of opposition of a human being to deity.[150] Garrett even asserts that this phrase has diabolic connotations.[151]

Second, the context shows that Saul's persecuting the believers of Jesus (the Way) is useless and is also harmful to him. The immediate context says, "Saul, Saul, why are you persecuting me?" supporting this point. Saul intends to crash down the Way (Acts 8:1, 3; 9:1–2). But he is actually against the risen Jesus, the cosmic Lord.

Third, the blindness of Saul is also in favor of this point. Due to the heavenly light (Acts 22:11), Saul "opened his eyes but could see nothing" (ἀνεῳγμένων δὲ τῶν ὀφθαλμῶν αὐτοῦ οὐδὲν ἔβλεπεν) (Acts 9:8a). He needs others to lead him by the hand into Damascus (χειραγωγοῦντες δὲ αὐτὸν εἰσήγαγον εἰς Δαμασκόν) (Acts 9:8b). His blindness is harmful for him. This also supports our reading.

---

147. Sleeman, *Geography and the Ascension Narrative*, 257.

148. Fitzmyer, *Acts*, 758.

149. Lothar Schumid, "κέντρον," *TDNT*, 3:664.

150. Simon Kistemaker, *Exposition of the Acts of the Apostles*, NTC (Grand Rapids: Baker, 1990), 552–553.

151. Garrett, *Demise of the Devil*, 84.

Fourth, Gamaliel's statement (Acts 5:38–39) is in favor of this point. He says, "For if their purpose or activity is of human origin, it will fail" (ὅτι ἐὰν ᾖ ἐξ ἀνθρώπων ἡ βουλὴ αὕτη ἢ τὸ ἔργον τοῦτο, καταλυθήσεται). "But if it is from God, you will not be able to stop these men; you will only find yourselves fighting against God" (εἰ δὲ ἐκ θεοῦ ἐστιν, οὐ δυνήσεσθε καταλῦσαι αὐτούς, μήποτε καὶ θεομάχοι εὑρεθῆτε). The fact is this is God's purpose. Saul is against God. Thus, Saul will not be able to stop these men. Rather, Saul finds himself fighting against God.

Finally, there is no indication of the resistance of Paul in the text. Rather, Saul asks, "what shall I do, Lord?" (τί ποιήσω, κύριε;) (Acts 22:10a). The Lord says to him to get up and to go to Damascus (Acts 22:10b). The following verses tell that Paul does exactly what Jesus tells him (Acts 22:11–16). Elsewhere, Paul himself declares that "I was not disobedient to the vision from heaven" (οὐκ ἐγενόμην ἀπειθὴς τῇ οὐρανίῳ ὀπτασίᾳ) (Acts 26:19). On the other hand, Luke does relate the resistance of Ananias (Acts 9:13–14). Ananias rejects what the Lord commands him to do, "get up and go" (ἀναστὰς πορεύθητι), which could be translated as "go at once" (Acts 9:11).[152] His rejection makes Jesus say the "go" command" (πορεύου) twice. And this time Jesus also explains why Ananias has to go. It is because "This man is my chosen instrument to carry my name before the Gentiles and their kings and before the people of Israel. I will show him how much he must suffer for my name" (Acts 9:15–16). Then Ananias departs and fulfills what Jesus commands him (Acts 9:17–19a).

The appearance of the exalted Jesus to Saul is to challenge Saul's persecution of the followers of Jesus. The encounter of the heavenly Jesus makes a dramatic change in Saul's life. The heavenly Jesus not only challenges Saul but also challenges earthly Jewish authorities.

The cosmic Lord not only challenges Saul but also challenges the authority of the Jewish leaders, as Acts 9:1–2 indicates. The high priest (ὁ ἀρχιερεύς) of Acts 9:1 would be the same high priest who participates in the crucifixion of Jesus.[153] The dramatic change of Saul would affect a challenge to the

---

152. Schnabel, *Acts*, 447.

153. The high priest might have been Jonathan, son of Ananus, who was in this office from 36–37 CE but it was probably the same high priest, Caiaphas, who was in this office from 18–36 CE. Josephus, *Ant.* 18.4.3.

authority of the Jewish leadership. Saul, instead of following the authority of the high priest, now follows the heavenly Jesus.

The heavenly vision challenges Saul as well as the earthly authority of the high priest. The heavenly vision also dramatically changes Saul into an instrument to bring salvation to Jews and Gentiles. Next we will study the significance of this heavenly vision.

The significance of the heavenly vision

The significance of this heavenly vision could be demonstrated as follows. First, Saul is saved. Acts 9:17–19 narrates the salvation of Paul. After Ananias lays hands on Saul, Saul immediately regains sight (εὐθέως ἀνέβλεψέν) and is baptized (καὶ ἀναστὰς ἐβαπτίσθη). And probably at the time of baptism Paul is filled with the Holy Spirit (πλησθῆς πνεύματος ἁγίου). The following narrative depicts the change in Paul. The word "immediately" (εὐθέως) recurs in Acts 9:20 to describe what Paul is doing that is exactly opposite to what he did before the vision. Acts 9:20 says, "At once he began to preach in the synagogues that Jesus is the Son of God" (καὶ εὐθέως ἐν ταῖς συναγωγαῖς ἐκήρυσσεν τὸν Ἰησοῦν ὅτι οὗτός ἐστιν ὁ υἱὸς τοῦ θεοῦ). Paul's preaching that "Jesus is the Messiah" (οὗτός ἐστιν ὁ χριστός) is so powerful that Jews plot to kill him (συνεβουλεύσαντο οἱ Ἰουδαῖοι ἀνελεῖν αὐτόν) (Acts 9:23). This indicates that Saul as the persecutor of the Way has become persecuted because of the Way. Paul is so eager to proclaim Jesus as the Messiah that he even risks his life by going up to Jerusalem (Acts 9:26–30).

Second, Paul is commissioned. The encounter of the heavenly-exalted Jesus not only changes Saul but also reveals to him a greater plan. Acts 9:15 says, "This is my chosen instrument to carry my name before the Gentiles and kings and before the children of Israel" (σκεῦος ἐκλογῆς ἐστίν μοι οὗτος τοῦ βαστάσαι τὸ ὄνομά μου ἐνώπιον ἐθνῶν τε καὶ βασιλέων υἱῶν τε Ἰσραήλ). Paul's retellings of his calling affirm the commission of Paul. The first retelling of the heavenly vision is Acts 22:6–16. Paul is commissioned to bring salvation to Jews and Gentiles (22:17–21).

Compared to the first recounting, the second one (Acts 26:12–18) speaks more explicitly of Paul's commission.[154] According to Acts 26:17–18, Paul has been commissioned to preach salvation to "his people" (Jews) and to

---

154. Hedrick, "Paul's Conversion," 424–425.

Gentiles (non-Jews). This time the audience consists of both Jews and Gentiles (Acts 25:23). It should be noted that toward the end of Paul's speech, he defends himself before King Agrippa, "So then, King Agrippa, I was not disobedient to the vision from heaven" (Ὅθεν, βασιλεῦ Ἀγρίππα, οὐκ ἐγενόμην ἀπειθὴς τῇ οὐρανίῳ ὀπτασίᾳ) (Acts 26:19). One perceives that the authority of the heavenly vision surpasses the authority of the earthly king. The sovereignty of the cosmic Lord has been indicated. The three missionary journeys narrated evidence exactly what Paul has been commissioned for (Acts 13:3–14:28; 15:36–18:22; 18:23–21:16). Paul's three missionary journeys show that he preaches salvation to the Gentiles. Paul has done exactly what he has been commissioned to do in Acts 26:15–18.

Third, Paul's Gentile mission is stressed in 22:21. It says, "Then he said to me, 'Go; I will send you far away to the Gentiles'" (καὶ εἶπεν πρός με· πορεύου, ὅτι ἐγὼ εἰς ἔθνη μακρὰν ἐξαποστελῶ σε). There, Paul "has been assigned to do" (τέτακταί ποιῆσαι) this (Acts 22:10). Ananias tells Paul, "you will be his witness to all men of what you have seen and heard" (ὅτι ἔσῃ μάρτυς αὐτῷ πρὸς πάντας ἀνθρώπους ὧν ἑώρακας καὶ ἤκουσας).

Thus, the heavenly vision not only challenges Saul by changing him from a persecutor of the Way to a follower of the Way. The heavenly vision also commissions Saul to bring salvation to both Jews and Gentiles.

Uniqueness of the heavenly vision

As we have seen, none of the ascension stories in Jewish and Greco-Roman literature is quite like the story of the ascension of Jesus. Here we will show that the reappearance of Jesus in the heavenly vision is also unique compared to that of Romulus. Plutarch narrates that Julius has seen Romulus in his ascension: "As he was travelling on the road, he had seen Romulus coming to meet him, fair and stately to the eye as never before, and arrayed in bright and shining armor."[155] Livy records the appearance of the deified Romulus to Julius.

> Romulus, the father of our City, descended from heaven at dawn this morning and appeared to me, in awe and reverence I stood before him, praying for permission to look upon his

---

155. Plutarch, *Rom.* 28:1.

face without sin. "Go," he said, "go and tell the Romans that by heaven's will my Rome shall be capital of the world. Let them learn to be soldiers. Let them know, and teach their children, that no power on earth can stand against Roman arms." After speaking these words, he was taken up again into heaven.[156]

There are some similarities between Paul's encounter of the exalted Jesus and Julius' encounter of Romulus. But the dissimilarities are telling. First, the reappearance of Romulus lacks the description of the light brighter than the sun. Second, there is no narration of the influence of the great light on the man who sees it. Third, the Romulus appearance does not effect dramatic changes for the person who encounters the supposedly deified person. Finally, the most telling one is that the reappearance of Romulus fails to provide any other eyewitnesses.

Kingdom concern: heaven and earth

The kingdom concern is addressed explicitly in the commission to Paul. Acts 9:15 says: "This is my chosen instrument to carry my name before the Gentiles and kings and before the children of Israel" (σκεῦος ἐκλογῆς ἐστίν μοι οὗτος τοῦ βαστάσαι τὸ ὄνομά μου ἐνώπιον ἐθνῶν τε καὶ βασιλέων υἱῶν τε Ἰσραήλ). The retellings of the commission affirm the commission of Paul. In the first retelling of the heavenly vision, Paul is commissioned to bring salvation to Jews and Gentiles (22:17–21). In the second retelling in 26:16–18 the commission to Paul is further stated. Paul has been commanded to bring salvation to the Jews and also to the Gentiles.

The three missionary journeys evidence the realization of the commission. Even at the end of the Lukan writings, one finds that Paul "boldly preached the kingdom of God and taught about the Lord Jesus Christ" (κηρύσσων τὴν βασιλείαν τοῦ θεοῦ καὶ διδάσκων τὰ περὶ τοῦ κυρίου Ἰησοῦ Χριστοῦ μετὰ πάσης παρρησίας). Thus we see the kingdom concern of this heavenly vision.

Summary

This study of the heavenly vision of Paul shows the following. First, the heavenly Jesus challenges Saul and Jewish authorities. Second, it changes Saul to be a follower of Christ and commissions him to bring salvation to

---

156. Livy, *Rom.* 1.16.7

both Jews and Gentiles. Third, our study shows the uniqueness of the reappearance of the exalted Jesus. Finally, the purpose of this heavenly vision concerns the kingdom of God. Paul has been assigned to preach the gospel to Jews and Gentiles. The Gentile inclusion opens a new era of salvation history. Now we turn to study the heavenly vision of Peter.

The Heavenly Vision of Peter (Acts 10:9–16, 11:1–18)

Similar to the heaven references in the vision of Saul, the reference to heaven in the vision of Peter connects it to the ascension of Jesus in Acts 1:9–11. Many scholars acknowledge the importance of this heavenly vision. By and large, however, they overlook the relationship between the heaven references here and the ascension narrative. This downplays the theological significance of this heavenly vision in Luke-Acts. It is Sleeman who has studied the connection between the heaven reference and the ascension of Jesus from a modern geographical point of view and provides a spatial reading of this heavenly vision.[157] He states that "Peter is experiencing a Christophany . . . The vision reveals *Jesus's* global influence (cf. 19:15)."[158] The references to heaven in Acts 10:11, 16 (cf. 11:5, 9, 10) again are the intervention of the exalted Jesus.

The intervention of the heavenly Jesus

In Acts 10 we have another appearance of the exalted Jesus, this time to Peter. Of course this is not a physical appearance and thus not the second coming of Jesus (Acts 1:11). First, this vision is from heaven (ἐκ τοῦ οὐρανοῦ) (10:11; cf. 11:5). The phrase "from heaven" is a theological marker in Acts (9:3; 11:9; 22:6). The opening of heaven (ἀνεῳγμένον) is another theological marker (Luke 3:21; Acts 10:11) and Stephen also sees "the heavens opened" (τοὺς οὐρανοὺς διηνοιγμένους) (Acts 7:56). Walton asserts that this is "heaven invading earth."[159] Second, the voice that speaks comes from heaven (φωνὴ ἐκ τοῦ οὐρανοῦ) (11:9). Peter's address, "Lord" (κύριε) (10:13–14; 11:8), shows explicitly that the voice is from the exalted Jesus. Third, the term God (θεός) in the following narrative indicates that this is Jesus who speaks here.

---

157. Sleeman, *Geography and the Ascension Narrative*, 226–229.
158. Ibid., 226.
159. Walton, "The Heavens Opened," 68.

In Acts 10:15, it says, "Do not call anything impure that God has made clean" (ἃ ὁ θεὸς ἐκαθάρισεν, σὺ μὴ κοίνου) (10:15). Thus we see that the vision is the intervention of the heavenly-exalted Jesus.

The significance of this heavenly vision

The significance of this heavenly vision is twofold. First, it challenges Peter. Second, it challenges other Jewish Christian leaders.

The challenge to Peter is clear from a number of points. First is Peter's strong resistance to the vision. To the command of the Lord, "Get up, Peter. Kill and eat," Peter replies, "Surely not, Lord! I have never eaten anything impure or unclean" (μηδαμῶς, κύριε, ὅτι οὐδέποτε ἔφαγον πᾶν κοινὸν καὶ ἀκάθαρτον). These strong negative terms, μηδαμῶς and οὐδέποτε indicate the strong resistance of Peter to eating unclean creatures.[160] The text that follows suggests that Peter denies the command three times (Acts 10:15–16; 11:9–10). "This happened three times, and immediately the sheet was taken back to heaven" (τοῦτο δὲ ἐγένετο ἐπὶ τρίς καὶ εὐθὺς ἀνελήμφθη τὸ σκεῦος εἰς τὸν οὐρανόν).

Second is Peter's threefold resistance to the Lord. At first, Peter is perplexed (διηπόρει) about the vision (Acts 10:17). Later Peter perceives the meaning of the vision by saying, "God has shown me that I should not call any man impure or unclean" (ὁ θεὸς ἔδειξεν μηδένα κοινὸν ἢ ἀκάθαρτον λέγειν ἄνθρωπον) (Acts 10:28). Peter gradually comprehends that he should not consider people (Gentiles) as unclean. Peter understands "that God is not partial" (ὅτι οὐκ ἔστιν προσωπολήμπτης ὁ θεός) (Acts 10:34). The fact that "the Holy Spirit came on all who heard the message" (ἐπέπεσεν τὸ πνεῦμα τὸ ἅγιον ἐπὶ πάντας τοὺς ἀκούοντας τὸν λόγον) (Acts 10:44) confirms Peter's understanding of the vision.

The retelling of the vision indicates that Peter holds strongly the notion of the exclusion of Gentiles from salvation. Jews consider the Gentiles as unclean or profane. The concept of holiness is well documented in the OT.[161] Humans are divided into three categories. The holy (the priests); the

---

160. The pure and profane animals connect to the holiness of the Jews. See Exod 22:29–31; Lev 11:44–45; 20:22–26; Deut 14:4–21. See Schnabel, *Acts*, 488–490.

161. Lev 11:1–47; Deut 14:3–20.

pure (Israel) and the profane (the Gentiles).¹⁶² The divisions correspond to three kinds of animals. Holy animals are those sacrificed to God. The pure animals are described in Leviticus 11. Israelites can eat only pure/clean animals. The rest of the animals are considered unclean. Those are animals that Gentiles eat.¹⁶³

This vision indicates that God has declared that all animals including birds are clean (Acts 10:15). The Jewish dietary laws are abandoned. The implication is that the obstacle between Jews and Gentiles is removed. Peter said, "God showed me that I should not call anyone profane or unclean" (κἀμοὶ ὁ θεὸς ἔδειξεν μηδένα κοινὸν ἢ ἀκάθαρτον λέγειν ἄνθρωπον) (Acts 10:28).

Peter gradually apprehends the meaning of the heavenly vision and takes his action accordingly (Acts 10:34–48). Peter preaches Jesus Christ to bring the peace/salvation to the Gentiles. He is the Lord of all (οὗτός ἐστιν πάντων κύριος). This phrase in the context indicates the inclusion of Gentiles in particular and of all human beings in general. Using Sleeman's geographical language, the vision challenges Peter's "mental map."¹⁶⁴

Thus we see that the heavenly Jesus challenges Peter on the exclusion of the Gentiles from salvation. Next, we will show that the exalted Jesus also challenges the notion of other Jewish Christian leaders.

The heavenly vision not only challenges Peter but also challenges the other Jewish Christians leaders. Following the instruction of the heavenly visions, Peter and Paul preach the gospel to the Gentiles. The inclusion of the Gentiles creates a sharp dispute and debate within the early church. When Peter goes up to Jerusalem, "the circumcised believers criticized him" (διεκρίνοντο πρὸς αὐτὸν οἱ ἐκ περιτομῆς) (Acts 11:2). The inclusion of the Gentiles is of no small issue at that time, as Acts 15 indicates. Acts 15:2 says, "This brought Paul and Barnabas into sharp dispute and debate with them" (γενομένης δὲ στάσεως καὶ ζητήσεως οὐκ ὀλίγης τῷ Παύλῳ καὶ τῷ Βαρναβᾷ πρὸς αὐτούς). The consequence of preaching to the Gentiles is that "[t]he apostles and elders met to consider this question" (Acts 15:6).

Peter's recounting of this heavenly vision to the Jerusalem church (Acts 11:1–18) indicates this point. First, the source of the vision is stressed. It is

---

162. Schnabel, *Acts*, 489.
163. For more discussions see ibid., 488–490.
164. Sleeman, *Geography and the Ascension Narrative*, 228.

from heaven. Peter makes slight changes in his recounting of the vision. The first change is that Peter says that the object was "coming down from heaven (καθιεμένην ἐκ τοῦ οὐρανοῦ) (Acts 11:5). Another change is in 11:9 where Peter says the voice was from heaven (φωνὴ ἐκ τοῦ οὐρανοῦ). By making these changes Peter emphasizes the invitation of God.[165]

Second, the audience in the text supports this point. According to Acts 11:2 Peter explains things to circumcised believers. It is this party of Christians who criticizes Peter for bringing salvation to Gentiles. Peter's retelling of the vision brings the result that "[w]hen they heard this, they had no further objections and praised God, saying, 'So then, God has granted even the Gentiles repentance unto life'" (Ἀκούσαντες δὲ ταῦτα ἡσύχασαν καὶ ἐδόξασαν τὸν θεὸν λέγοντες· ἄρα καὶ τοῖς ἔθνεσιν ὁ θεὸς τὴν μετάνοιαν εἰς ζωὴν ἔδωκεν) (Acts 11:18). Peter's retelling of the heavenly vision is vital. Sleeman rightly asserts, "Peter is at a highly significant crossroads, and auditors do not know what will happen if Peter rejects the as yet unknown implication of the vision."[166] The repetition of the vision of Peter "is a clear indication that such a vision cannot and must not be opposed."[167]

The narrative of the first missionary journey of Paul and Barnabas (Acts 13:3–14:28) supports the heavenly vision of Peter. Their missionary work is summarized in Acts 15:12b where Barnabas and Paul relate "as many as the miraculous signs and wonders God had done among the Gentiles through them" (ὅσα ἐποίησεν ὁ θεὸς σημεῖα καὶ τέρατα ἐν τοῖς ἔθνεσιν δι' αὐτῶν). Their telling of salvation coming upon the Gentiles makes "[t]he whole assembly become silent as they listen" (Ἐσίγησεν δὲ πᾶν τὸ πλῆθος καὶ ἤκουον) (Acts 15:2a).

The heavenly Jesus not only challenges Peter's Jewish notion of the exclusion of the Gentiles, but he also challenges that of other Christian leaders. This heavenly vision breaks down human obstacles.

Kingdom concern: heaven and earth

Along with the vision of Paul, the vision of Peter also concerns the salvation of humanity. In this vision, the inclusion of the Gentiles is stressed. For Peter,

---

165. Miller, *Convinced That God Had Called Us*, 215.
166. Sleeman, *Geography and the Ascension Narrative*, 229.
167. Strelan, "Strange Stares," 164.

to bring salvation to the Jews is not a problem at all. But preaching to the Gentiles is totally out of his mind (cf. Acts 10:45). God has made all the animals clean (Acts 10:15). Peter should not call any man impure or unclean (Acts 10:28). God shows no partiality (οὐκ ἔστιν προσωπολήμπτης ὁ θεός) (Acts 10:34). The out pouring of the Holy Spirit upon the Gentiles further affirms the inclusion of Gentiles revealed in the heavenly vision (Acts 10:44).

Summary

Therefore, the heavenly-exalted Jesus challenges Saul. He changes Saul from persecutor of the gospel to bold preacher of this gospel. The heavenly Jesus commissions Paul to bring salvation to the Jews and Gentiles. Paul has done exactly what he has been told. The heavenly vision of Peter changes both Peter's notion of the exclusion of the Gentiles and that of other Jewish Christian leaders. These heavenly visions to Paul and Peter concern the expansion of the kingdom of God. The heavenly Jesus encounters the human opponent (Saul) that intends to hamper the kingdom of God. The exalted Jesus challenges a human notion (of Peter) that hinders the spread of the kingdom of God. Next, we will study anti-idol polemic to demonstrate that the heavenly-exalted Jesus as cosmic Lord challenges the idols of the nations. The anti-idol polemic affirms the cosmic lordship of God.

Cosmic Lordship of Christ: Anti-Idol Polemic

The preceding study demonstrated that the exalted Jesus is the cosmic Lord. The cosmic Lord challenges Paul and Peter. In what follows we will argue that the cosmic Lord also challenges the idols of the nations. The anti-idol polemic critiques idols and thus affirms the cosmic lordship of God.

The anti-idol polemic has gained scholarly attention but still suffers from insufficient scholarly examination. Pao notices the significance of this topic in the Lukan writings. He has convincingly argued that the anti-idol polemic in Luke-Acts is deeply rooted in the book of Isaiah. It relates to the sovereignty of the risen Jesus over the nations. The critique of the idols shows their powerlessness and affirms the cosmic lordship of Yahweh. The anti-idol polemic connects to the new exodus motif in Luke-Acts.[168] Pao's

---

168. Pao, *Isaianic New Exodus*, 181–216.

study brings forth the theological significance of the anti-idol polemic and contributes to Lukan scholarship in this regard.

Litwak provides a case study of the anti-idol polemic in Acts 17:22–31. He argues that Luke uses the Scripture of Israel (Isaiah) to present Paul's speech as prophetic. In this prophetic speech, Luke shows the continuity of the anti-idol polemic of Israel's prophets in the past in order to validate the faith of his audience as the true people of God.[169] Litwak's study brings forth the theological significance of the anti-idol polemic at the ecclesiological level. Plötz also studies Paul's speech at Areopagus and argues that Paul criticizes all idol worship.[170]

Sleeman notices the significance of the heaven references in Luke-Acts. However, he examines only those in the first half of Acts (1–11). He overlooks the heaven references in the rest of Acts (12–28), especially the heaven references in the anti-idol passages in Acts 14, 17 and 19. At the end of his study, he asserts that "the remaining narrative of Acts will not add anything substantially new to this embryonic vista."[171] Without examining the heaven references in the anti-idol passages it is hard for Sleeman to make this assertion. Our study will demonstrate that the heaven references in the anti-idol polemic indeed bring something new.

In this section it will be argued that the heaven references in the second half of Acts (14:15; 17:24; 19:35) contribute to the larger heaven motif in the Lukan writings. The heaven references in the anti-idol polemic critique the idols of the nations and therefore affirm the cosmic lordship of God. The cosmic lordship of God cannot be challenged. The context of these heaven references shows that the realization of the eschatological kingdom cannot be deterred. Our attention will first turn to the heaven references in these anti-idol passages. And then we will give attention to each anti-idol polemical speech.

---

169. Kenneth D. Litwak, "Israel's Prophets Meet Athens' Philosophers: Scritural Echoes in Acts 17:22–31," *Bib* 85 (2004): 199–216.

170. K. Plötz, "Die Areopagrede des Apostels Paulus: Ein Beispiel urkirchlicher Verkündigung," *IKaZ* 17 (1988): 111–117.

171. Sleeman, *Geography and the Ascension Narrative*, 254.

Heaven References

The studies in previous chapters show that heaven is not simply a static dwelling place of God. Heaven is dynamic. Heaven has brought down salvation on earth, as we have shown in chapter 2. Heaven is not static but is still fighting. Satan has fallen from heaven, as we demonstrated in chapter 3. Heaven is not static but is pointing to the exaltation of the risen Lord, as we showed so far in this chapter. References to heaven and earth appearing in the anti-idol polemic contribute to the heaven motif in that they point to the Creator God who is cosmic and is the only God that deserves human worship. The cosmic lordship of God cannot be challenged.

It is interesting that the heaven references in anti-idol polemic appear alongside references to earth. The first heaven and earth pair appears in Acts 14:15 where Paul declares God as the one "who made heaven and earth and the sea and everything in them" (ὃς ἐποίησεν τὸν οὐρανὸν καὶ τὴν γῆν καὶ τὴν θάλασσαν καὶ πάντα τὰ ἐν αὐτοῖς) in his combat against idol worship in Lystra. Similarly, Paul designates God as "the Lord of heaven and earth" (οὗτος οὐρανοῦ καὶ γῆς ὑπάρχων κύριος) when he argues with philosophers in Mars Hill in Athens (17:24). A reference to heaven appears in the last anti-idol polemical passage in Ephesus where the goddess Artemis is described as falling from heaven (19:35). Next, we will study each anti-idol passage respectively.

Criticism of the Worship of Zeus and Hermes in Acts 14:8–18

The anti-idol polemic first appears in Paul's first missionary journey in Lystra in southern Asia Minor (Acts 14:15). Paul's healing of the crippled man in Lystra (14:8–10) provokes the reaction of the inhabitants of Lystra (14:11–13) and the subsequent response of Paul (14:14–18).[172] In what follows, it will be demonstrated that idols of Zeus and Hermes have been denounced in every aspect possible. The anti-idol polemic demonstrates the sovereignty of the cosmic Lord. The lordship of God cannot be challenged.

---

172. For the plot of this narrative, see C. Dionne, "L'épisode de Lystre (Ac 14, 7–20a): Une Analyse Narrative," *Science et Esprit* 57 (2005): 5–33. Dionne explores the five parts of Acts 14:7–20: the preaching of the good news (Acts 14:7); the healing miracle (14:8—10); the reaction of the Lycaonians (14:11–13); the response of the apostles (14:14–18); and the arrival of the Jews (14:19–20). Dionne demonstrates that these episodes are interrelated and unified as a whole.

Criticism of idols

The following study demonstrates that the idol Zeus is lambasted from every aspect possible.

First we will examine the term τὰ μάταια. This term refers to Zeus and Hermes (Acts 14:15). Paul points out that the Lycaonians ought "to turn away from worthless things" (ἀπὸ τούτων τῶν ματαίων ἐπιστρέφειν). The term μάταια can refer to either persons or things as "idle, empty, fruitless, useless, and powerless."[173] The word μάταια is often used in the LXX to refer to idols. This is evidenced in the Pentateuch. Leviticus 17:7 says, "They must no longer offer any of their sacrifices to the goat idols to whom they prostitute themselves" (καὶ οὐ θύσουσιν ἔτι τὰς θυσίας αὐτῶν τοῖς ματαίοις οἷς αὐτοὶ ἐκπορνεύουσιν). Here the Hebrew word is שְׂעִירִים that refers to idols. In the Historical Books, one also finds this use. In 1 Kings 16:13, the sins of Baasha and the nation bring "the Lord God of Israel to anger with their idols" (τοῦ παροργίσαι κύριον τὸν θεὸν Ισραηλ ἐν τοῖς ματαίοις αὐτῶν). In the Wisdom Books, Psalm 23:4 (LXX 24:4) says, "he who has clean hands and a pure heart, who does not lift up his soul to an idol" (ὃς οὐκ ἔλαβεν ἐπὶ ματαίῳ τὴν ψυχὴν αὐτοῦ). This use is also found in the prophets, especially in the book of Isaiah, to which Luke heavily alludes. In Isaiah, the term τὰ μάταια refers to idols. "Men shall cast out the detestable silver and gold which they made to worship as idols" (ἐκβαλεῖ ἄνθρωπος τὰ βδελύγματα αὐτοῦ τὰ ἀργυρᾶ καὶ τὰ χρυσᾶ ἃ ἐποίησαν προσκυνεῖν τοῖς ματαίοις) (Isa 2:20). Isaiah 44:9 says, "Those who fashion graven idols are nothing" (οἱ πλάσσοντες καὶ γλύφοντες πάντες μάταιοι).[174] Jonah 2:8 (9) says, those who regard vain idols forsake their faithfulness (φυλασσόμενοι μάταια καὶ ψευδῆ ἔλεος αὐτῶν ἐγκατέλιπον).[175]

Second, τὰ μάταια refers to Zeus and Hermes in this context.[176] The structure of this sentence supports this point. Paul and Barnabas are preaching good news to the Lycaonians so that "they should turn from these worthless

---

173. BDAG, 621.

174. Cf. 2 Chr 11:15; Ps 23(24):4; Hos 5:11; Amos 2:4; Isa 30:14; 44:9; Jer 2:5; 8:19.

175. Philo also uses this word to refer idols. *Som.* 1:244.

176. For Schnabel, the term ματαία refers to "Zeus and Hermes, together with the sacrificial bulls, the garland, the procession, the altar of sacrifice, and the temple." This seems unlikely. Schnabel, *Acts*, 609; Peterson, *Acts*, 409. See also Bauernfeind, "μάταιος," *TDNT* 4:522.

things to the living God" (ἀπὸ τούτων τῶν ματαίων ἐπιστρέφειν ἐπὶ θεὸν ζῶντα) (Acts 14:15). The two prepositional phrases, ἀπὸ τῶν ματαίων and ἐπὶ θεὸν ζῶντα, which surround the infinitive "to turn" (ἐπιστρέφειν) are contrasted with each other. Here "the living God" is contrasted to "idols." This indicates that "the worthless things" are idols (i.e. the false deities of Zeus and Hermes). Second, the context is also in favor of this reading. The further description of "the living God" supports this point. The living God is the Creator God (Acts 14:15) and also the provisioning God (14:16–17). These features of the living God are over against the characteristics of Zeus that we will discuss more in the next section.

Therefore, the term τὰ μάταια refers to idols in general and here it refers to Zeus and Hermes in particular. Next our study will consider the criticism of Zeus.

Having studied the term τὰ μάταια, next we will focus on the criticism of Zeus. First, the designation, "the living God" contains an implicit criticism of Zeus. The God who is living critiques the fake deities of Zeus and Hermes. The God Paul describes to the crowd is "the living God" (θεὸς ζῶν). The designation of God as "the living God" declares that God is the one true God. The phrase, "the living God" (θεὸς ζῶν), is an allusion to Deuteronomy 6:4 where it says, "the Lord our God, the Lord is one" (κύριος ὁ θεὸς ἡμῶν κύριος εἷς ἐστιν). This particular designation (θεὸς ζῶν) occurs often "in the contexts affirming the sovereignty of Yahweh over against idols."[177] Two of the occurrences in the LXX appear explicitly in anti-idol contexts (Jer 10:10–11; Hos 1:10). Other occurrences are found in places where the saving power of "the living God" is clearly indicated (1 Sam 17:26; Josh 3:10; Dan 6:20, 26). This one true God (monotheon) that Paul and Barnabas are proclaiming critiques to the two gods of Zeus and Hermes (the pantheon notion).[178] On the other hand, this designation of "the living God" has the implication that Zeus and Hermes are not living.[179] Zeus has been considered a god who gives life, as his name indicates.[180] The term Zeus derives from the

---

177. Pao, *Isaianic New Exodus*, 203.

178. Zeus is the chief god in the Greek religion. Hermes is considered the messenger of the gods. See Bruce, *The Acts of the Apostles*, 322.

179. Fitzmyer, *Acts*, 532.

180. Peterson, *Acts*, 409; Witherington, *The Acts of the Apostles*, 426.

Greek word ζωή. The notion that the living God stands against the lifeless idols exists in Old Testament. Isaiah 37:17 says the living God can hear and see (εἰσάκουσον κύριε εἴσβλεψον κύριε) (Isa 37:17). But "idols are the works of human hands, wood and stones" (τὰ εἴδωλα ἦσαν ἔργα χειρῶν ἀνθρώπων ξύλα καὶ λίθοι) (Isa 37:19). Another instance is in Daniel 5:23, where Daniel says to Belshazzar, "[Y]ou do not praise the living God" (τῷ θεῷ τῷ ζῶντι οὐκ εὐλογήσατε) but "all idols made by human hands" (πάντα τὰ εἴδωλα τὰ χειροποίητα τῶν ἀνθρώπων) "which cannot see or hear or understand" (οἵτινες δὲν βλέπουσιν οὐδὲ ἀκούουσιν οὐδὲ νοοῦσι). There the living God contrasts sharply with the dead idols.[181] Therefore, the phrase "the living God" (θεὸς ζῶν) exposes Zeus and Hermes as false and dead deities.

Second, the Creator God contrasts the created Zeus/gods. Another aspect of the anti-idol polemic is the designation of the Creator God, the God "who created heaven and earth and the sea and everything in them" (ὃς ἐποίησεν τὸν οὐρανὸν καὶ τὴν γῆν καὶ τὴν θάλασσαν καὶ πάντα τὰ ἐν αὐτοῖς) (Acts 14:15). The reference to the Creator God echoes Genesis 1–2 in general, where God created heaven and earth and everything in them.[182] This is also an allusion to Exodus 20:11, where it says, "For in six days the LORD made the heavens and the earth, the sea, and all that is in them" (ἐν γὰρ ἓξ ἡμέραις ἐποίησεν κύριος τὸν οὐρανὸν καὶ τὴν γῆν καὶ τὴν θάλασσαν καὶ πάντα τὰ ἐν αὐτοῖς). The first four commandments focus on God himself. The first commandment declares the one true God (Exod 20:1–2). The second commandment contains anti-idol polemic, taking up a pretty lengthy paragraph (vv. 4–6) compared to other commandments. Idols can be in the form of anything "that is in heaven above, or that is on the earth beneath, or that is in the water under the earth" (παντὸς ὁμοίωμα ὅσα ἐν τῷ οὐρανῷ ἄνω καὶ ὅσα ἐν τῇ γῇ κάτω καὶ ὅσα ἐν τοῖς ὕδασιν ὑποκάτω τῆς γῆς). In other words, apart from the Creator God, anything that people worship is an idol. The recurrence of the same phrase in the fourth commandment (v. 11), "God made the heaven and the earth, the sea, and everything in them" (ἐποίησεν κύριος τὸν οὐρανὸν καὶ τὴν γῆν καὶ τὴν θάλασσαν καὶ πάντα τὰ ἐν αὐτοῖς), depicts the mighty work done in six days by God. The phrase reaffirms the

---

181. Bock, *Acts*, 478.
182. Litwak, "Israel's Prophets Meet Athens' Philosophers," 204.

second commandment in that anything besides God that is worshiped is an idol. One finds that the allusion to Exodus 20:11 asserts the lordship of the Creator God.

The God "who made heaven and earth, the sea, and everything in them" (τὸν ποιήσαντα τὸν οὐρανὸν καὶ τὴν γῆν τὴν θάλασσαν καὶ πάντα τὰ ἐν αὐτοῖς) in Psalm 146[145]:6 points to the sovereignty of the Creator God. At the end of this psalm, it says, "The LORD reigns forever, for all generations" (βασιλεύσει κύριος εἰς τὸν αἰῶνα εἰς γενεὰν καὶ γενεάν) (Ps 146:10). That God is the Creator declares that anything apart from God is created, a creature of God. The Creator God denounces the created Zeus and Hermes and criticizes the worship of human beings.[183] The designation of the Creator God undoubtedly affirms the sovereignty of God.[184] The Creator God also critiques Zeus' cosmology. Schnabel comments, "Zeus is aether, Zeus is earth, Zeus is sky, Zeus is everything."[185]

Third, it has been acknowledged that Acts 14:16–17 addresses general revelation and God's care for all human beings (natural theology).[186] But, one should not overlook that this passage further vilifies Zeus. Zeus has been worshiped as a deity who gives rain and snow and thus provides harvest and fruit.[187] Zeus controls rains and snow.[188] J. P. Brown compares Yahweh, Zeus, and Jupiter and finds that they all have the common features of control over the elements, throwing down "thunders and lightning, snow and hail, rain and dew" from heaven.[189] Zeus is also revered as the sky father.[190] Scholars often overlook the heaven reference here.[191] The adverbial form of the heaven reference (οὐρανόθεν) is used by Homer and Aristotle as the

---

183. David B. Sloan, "The Understanding of the Psalms in Luke-Acts" (Ph.D. diss., Trinity International University, 2012): 306.

184. Pao, *Isaianic New Exodus*, 204; Schnabel, *Acts*, 610.

185. Schnabel, *Acts*, 610.

186. Witherington, *The Acts of the Apostles*, 425.

187. E. J. Schnabel, *Early Christian Mission. Vol. 2: Paul and the Early Church*, 2 (Downers Grove, IL: InterVarsity, 2004), 1118.

188. Homer, Iliad 10:57; 16:297–330.

189. J. P. Brown, "Yahweh, Zeus, Jupiter: The High God and the Elements," *ZAW* 106 (1994): 175–197.

190. Walter Burkert, *Greek Religion: Arahaic and Classical*, trans. John Raffan (Cambridge: Harvard University Press, 1985), 126.

191. Sleeman, *Geography and the Ascension Narrative*, 254.

dwelling place of gods.¹⁹² This notion is found in the LXX. In 4 Macc 4:10, when the temple was desecrated "angels on horseback appeared from heaven" (οὐρανόθεν ἔφιπποι προυφάνησαν ἄγγελοι) to defend the Holy Place. The only occurrence in Philo's work is in *Som.* 1.112 where is says, "By [God's] mercy for mankind, he sends [his light] from heaven" (δι' ἔλεον τοῦ γένους ἡμῶν εἰς νοῦν τὸν ἀνθρώπινον οὐρανόθεν ἀποστέλλει). The only two occurrences in the New Testament are here and Acts 26:13. There Paul says that he has seen a light "from heaven" (οὐρανόθεν). The term οὐρανόθεν in Acts 14:17 asserts that it is the God who has been granting "rain and fruitful seasons from heaven to you, satisfying your heart with food and gladness" (οὐρανόθεν ὑμῖν ὑετοὺς διδοὺς καὶ καιροὺς καρποφόρους, ἐμπιπλῶν τροφῆς καὶ εὐφροσύνης τὰς καρδίας ὑμῶν). The notion of the God who controls rain from heaven is not foreign to Luke. One finds this notion at the beginning of the gospel. "Heaven was shut for three years and six months" (ἐκλείσθη ὁ οὐρανὸς ἐπὶ ἔτη τρία καὶ μῆνας ἕξ) (Luke 4:25). The context shows that it is God who prevented heaven from giving rain on the land of Israel. God controls heaven. This denounces the notion that it is Zeus who grants these things. As Breytenbach rightly asserts, Acts 14:17 "criticizes the belief of the inhabitants in southern Asia Minor that Zeus, the heavenly deity, is in control of weather and vegetation."¹⁹³

Particularly, Acts 14:14–18 lambastes Zeus who has been the most widely worshiped male deity in Asia Minor.¹⁹⁴ Zeus has been portrayed on reliefs as an elderly, bearded man.¹⁹⁵ The healing miracle of the lame man in Lystra (Acts 14:8–10) vilifies Zeus' inability as a relief deity. The healing miracle demonstrates that Paul and Barnabas are preaching the good news of salvation: "To turn away from these idols to the living God" (ἀπὸ τούτων τῶν ματαίων ἐπιστρέφειν ἐπὶ θεὸν ζῶντα). They are messengers, not from Zeus, but from the living, Creator God. Salvation is from God who sent Jesus as Savior.

---

192. Traub, "οὐρανόθεν," *TDNT*, 5:542

193. C. Breytenbach, "Zeus und der lebendige Gott: Anmerkungen zu Apostelgeschichte 14.11–17," *NTS* 39 (1993): 409. In the original German: "Daß hier gegen Glauben de landbevölkerung im südlichen Kleinasien polemisiert wird, die in Zeus die himmliche Gotteit über Wetter und Wegetation sieht."

194. Witherington, *The Acts of the Apostles*, 422. Keener, *Acts, vol. 2*, 2153.

195. *ABD*, 4:427.

Finally, Paul and Barnabas assert to the Lycaonians, "we are men with the same nature as you" (ἡμεῖς ὁμοιοπαθεῖς ἐσμεν ὑμῖν ἄνθρωποι). Paul and Barnabas refused to be worshiped as deities (Acts 14:14–15). "Tearing their clothes" (διαρρήξαντες τὰ ἱμάτια αὐτῶν), they "rushed out into the crowd" (ἐξεπήδησαν εἰς τὸν ὄχλον), "crying out" (κράζοντες). The narrative of actions shows their strong refusal of being worshiped lest they commit idolatry.[196]

One might wonder why Paul and Barnabas do not introduce Jesus Christ to the Lycaonians. It would be no use for them to preach Jesus Christ at that occasion since Paul is addressing to a purely pagan audience.[197] This speech is not Christological, but rather theological.[198] In Christian preaching monotheism is the first theme to introduce.[199] This could be evidenced in the work of Josephus.[200] Having studied the criticism of Zeus, we turn to the kingdom concern.

Kingdom concern

Kingdom concern in this passage is evidenced in the following. First, Paul urges the Lycaonians to "turn from these worthless things to the living God" (ὑμᾶς ἀπὸ τούτων τῶν ματαίων ἐπιστρέφειν ἐπὶ θεὸν ζῶντα) (Acts 14:15). Paul was preaching (εὐαγγελιζόμενοι) to them salvation. Second, the context of this passage is in favor of this reading. Acts 14:7 says, "They continued to preach the good news there" (κἀκεῖ εὐαγγελιζόμενοι ἦσαν) in Lystra. The healing of the crippled man (Acts 14:8–10) is one of the "signs and wonders" (σημεῖα καὶ τέρατα) that "testifies to the word of grace" (i.e. the gospel) (μαρτυροῦντι [ἐπὶ] τῷ λόγῳ τῆς χάριτο) (Acts 14:3). Finally, the larger context also supports this point. Paul and Barnabas establish a church in the city of Lystra. Paul later visits believers in Lystra when he returns to

---

196. Bruce, *The Acts of the Apostles*, 323.
197. Ibid.; Witherington, *The Acts of the Apostles*, 425; Dean Philip Bechard, "Paul Among the Rustics: The Lystran Episode (Acts 14:8–20) and Lucan Apologetic," *CBQ* 63 (2001): 90. Bechard insightfully comments that "Paul and Barnabas crossed a cultural frontier and entered a region well-renowned for the rustic simplicity and primitive lifestyle of its largely uncivilized inhabitants."
198. Fitzmyer, *Acts*, 532.
199. Barrett, *Acts of the Apostles*, vol. *1*, 681.
200. F. Gerald Downing, "Common Ground with Paganism in Luke and in Josephus," *NTS* 28 (1982): 546–559. Downing examines the speeches in Acts 14:11–13 and 17:22–31 and concludes that these speeches resemble Josephus, *Ant.* 8.100–130, not only in details, but also in the structure of the argument.

Antioch from Derbe (Acts 14:21–23). Paul visits Lystra again on his journey from Syria to Asia Minor (Acts 16:1–3). Paul's intimate coworker, Timothy has been recruited there.[201]

Therefore, this narrative brings a sharp contrast between the Greek view of deities and the Jewish/Christian view of the living God.[202] This challenges Zeus in every aspect possible. The powerlessness of the idols is in sharp contrast to the power of the living God. The anti-idol polemic virtually affirms the universal sovereignty of God. His cosmic lordship cannot be challenged by Zeus. The concern of this anti-idol polemic is to bring salvation to the local people. Having studied the anti-idol polemic in Acts 14, now it is time to move on to another anti-idol passage.

Criticism of the Idols of the Nations (Acts 17:22–31)

In the following we will argue that the recurrence of the anti-idol polemic challenges the idols of the nations. This again affirms the lordship of the cosmic God.

Criticism of the idols of the nations

It is well acknowledged that Acts 17:22–31 has been foreshadowed by Acts 14:15–17.[203] In the following, we will demonstrate that the anti-idol polemic in Acts 17:22–31 denounces the idols of the nations in a more profound way compared to that in Acts 14.

First, the audiences are different. In Lystra, Paul addresses rural Lycaonians. They are "unsophisticated."[204] People in Lystra do not use Greek as their daily language but, speak the native Lycaonian language (Acts 14:11).[205] The fact that there is no mention of the synagogue in Lystra but that there is in Athens (17:17) also indicates that residents in Lystra are less civilized than

---

201. Schnabel, *Early Christian Mission*, 1119.

202. L. H. Martin, "Gods or Ambassadors of God? Barnabas and Paul in Lystra," *NTS* 41 (1995): 156.

203. Conzelmann, *Acts*, 111; Witherington, *The Acts of the Apostles*, 425; Fitzmyer, *Acts*, 532.

204. Bechard, "Paul Among the Rustics," 84–101.

205. Fox states, "[t]o all but a few of the highly educated, the gods were indeed a potential presence whom a miracle might reveal." Robin Lane Fox, *Pagans and Christians* (New York: Alfred A. Knopf, 1987), 140.

the Athenians.²⁰⁶ In Athens, he speaks to urban philosophers who are seeking to know new things. As the context indicates, they desire to get knowledge of gods. They say to Paul, "May we know" (δυνάμεθα γνῶναι) (17:19), and, "We want to know" (βουλόμεθα γνῶναι) (Acts 17:20). They are very religious people. Luke applies the term "very religious" (δεισιδαιμονεστέρους) to describe their religiousness (Acts 17:22), a term that occurs only here in the NT and LXX.

Furthermore, the idols in these two episodes are different. In Lystra, idols are specified as Zeus and Hermes (Acts 14:13). In Athens, the idols are many as indicated by the description of Athens as "a city full of idols" (κατείδωλον οὖσαν τὴν πόλιν) (Acts 17:16). Athens is "a luxuriant forest of idols."²⁰⁷ No specific idols are mentioned. Numerous idols represent the idols of all nations.

To the philosophical audience, Paul addresses them in a philosophical way. Dibelius describes this speech as "a Hellenistic speech about the true knowledge of God."²⁰⁸ Paul argues for the existence of God in a way familiar to the Greek philosophers.²⁰⁹

Cosmic Lord vs. Idols. Paul chooses different words to describe the Creator God. Paul explicitly asserts that God is Creator in Acts 17:24. Paul also emphasizes that the Creator God is the cosmic Lord, even more clearly here than in Acts 14:15. The term "cosmos" (κόσμος) demonstrates this point (Acts 17:24). Luke carefully employs this term, which occurs only here in Acts, to show that God is cosmic. "The God who created the cosmos and everything in it" (ὁ θεὸς ὁ ποιήσας τὸν κόσμον καὶ πάντα τὰ ἐν αὐτῷ) (Acts 17:24a). Compared to the designation of God in Acts 14:15, where it says God "created heaven and earth and the sea and everything in them" (ἐποίησεν τὸν οὐρανὸν καὶ τὴν γῆν καὶ τὴν θάλασσαν καὶ πάντα τὰ ἐν αὐτοῖς), Paul replaces "heaven and earth and the sea" with the term "cosmos" (κόσμος). The term κόσμος is one of the most important terms in

---

206. This also could be because there are fewer Jews there.

207. Joshua W. Jipp, "Paul's Areopagus Speech of Acts 17:16–34 as Both Critique and Propaganda," *JBL* 131 (2012): 570.

208. Martin Dibelius, et al., *Studies in the Acts of the Apostles* (New York: Charles Scribner's Sons, 1956), 57.

209. Fitzmyer, *Acts*, 532.

Greek philosophy. Its religious significance should not be overlooked.[210] It has the spatial sense of "universe" in the Hellenistic world.[211] Here the term denotes the universe that consists of heaven and earth and all the individual creatures (πάντα τὰ ἐν αὐτῷ).[212]

The Creator God vs. Created Idols (Acts 17:24). Paul asserts that God is the Creator (17:24a) and the Lord of heaven and earth (17:24b). "God does not dwell in temples made by hands" (ὁ θεὸς οὐκ ἐν χειροποιήτοις ναοῖς κατοικεῖ) (17:24c). The whole verse of 17:24 echoes Isaiah 66:1–2 and 1 Kings 8:27 (cf. 1 Chr 6:18). In Isaiah 66:1–2, the Lord declares, "since my hand made all these things and so they came into being" (πάντα γὰρ ταῦτα ἐποίησεν ἡ χείρ μου καὶ ἔστιν ἐμὰ πάντα ταῦτα λέγει κύριος) (Isa 66:2a), then "[h]eaven is my throne, and the earth is my footstool, where is the house you will build for me? And where is a place that I may rest?" (ὁ οὐρανός μοι θρόνος ἡ δὲ γῆ ὑποπόδιον τῶν ποδῶν μου ποῖον οἶκον οἰκοδομήσετέ μοι ἢ ποῖος τόπος τῆς καταπαύσεώς μου) (66:1). The anti-idol polemic alludes to 1 Kings 8:27 where Solomon asserts, "But will God really dwell on earth? The heavens, even the highest heaven, cannot contain you. How much less this temple I have built" (ὅτι εἰ ἀληθῶς κατοικήσει ὁ θεὸς μετὰ ἀνθρώπων ἐπὶ τῆς γῆς εἰ ὁ οὐρανὸς καὶ ὁ οὐρανὸς τοῦ οὐρανοῦ οὐκ ἀρκέσουσίν σοι πλὴν καὶ ὁ οἶκος οὗτος ὃν ᾠκοδόμησα τῷ ὀνόματί σου). The term "handmade" (χειροποίητος) is often connected to idolatry. This usage is evidenced in the Pentateuch (Lev 26:1; cf. 26:30) and more often in Isaiah. "The idols will totally disappear" (τὰ χειροποίητα πάντα κατακρύψουσιν) (2:18). "Idols of Egypt will tremble before him [God]" (σεισθήσεται τὰ χειροποίητα Αἰγύπτου ἀπὸ προσώπου αὐτοῦ) (Isa 19:1). "All the images of its gods lie shattered on the ground" (τὰ χειροποίητα αὐτῆς συνετρίβησαν εἰς τὴν γῆν) (21:9). "Men will deny the idols" (ἀπαρνήσονται οἱ ἄνθρωποι τὰ χειροποίητα) (31:7). "They bow down and worship idols" (χειροποίητα καὶ κύψαντες προσκυνοῦσιν) (46:6). This use is also seen in Daniel (5:4, 23; 6:28). When Paul says, "He does not dwell in temples made by hands" (οὐκ ἐν χειροποιήτοις ναοῖς κατοικεῖ) (Acts 17:24c), he declares that the cosmic Lord cannot be boxed in temples (cf. 7:48 – the Most High does not dwell in houses made by hands).

---

210. Sasse, "κόσμος," *TDNT*, 3:869.
211. Ibid., 871.
212. Ibid., 884.

God the Giver, not A Recipient (Acts 17:25). Every act of idolatry involves sacrifice to idols. Idols are recipients. Here the assertion is that "he [God] is not served by human hands, as if he needed anything" (οὐδὲ ὑπὸ χειρῶν ἀνθρωπίνων θεραπεύεται προσδεόμενός τινος). This is "because he himself gives all men life and breath and everything else" (αὐτὸς διδοὺς πᾶσι ζωὴν καὶ πνοὴν καὶ τὰ πάντα). God does not need any human care (οὐδὲ ὑπὸ χειρῶν ἀνθρωπίνων θεραπεύεται). God gives to humans not only lives but also everything they need. This attacks the sacrificial system that exists in every practice of idol worship.

The Creator God Reigns over Humankind (Acts 17:26). In line with Acts 17:25 in which God is the life giver, Acts 17:26 further asserts that God is sovereign over all human beings. "God has made every nation from one man" (ἐποίησέν τε ἐξ ἑνὸς πᾶν ἔθνος ἀνθρώπων) "to inhabit the whole surface of the earth" (κατοικεῖν ἐπὶ παντὸς προσώπου τῆς γῆς). "He determined the times set for them and the exact places where they should live" (ὁρίσας προστεταγμένους καιροὺς καὶ τὰς ὁροθεσίας τῆς κατοικίας αὐτῶν). This is again based on Genesis 1–10 in general and, in particular, Genesis 2:7–8; Genesis 5 and 10; and Deuteronomy 32:8, "for the Most High divided the nations as he separated the sons of Adam."

God Reveals Himself to Humankind (Acts 17:27–28). Not only is God the Creator, who is over all human beings, but he also reveals himself to humankind. Acts 17:27 says, "God is not far from each one of us" (οὐ μακρὰν ἀπὸ ἑνὸς ἑκάστου ἡμῶν ὑπάρχοντα). We are related to him. "For in him we live and move and have our being" (ἐν αὐτῷ γὰρ ζῶμεν καὶ κινούμεθα καὶ ἐσμέν). Paul further quotes Aratus' poem "we are his offspring" (τοῦ γὰρ καὶ γένος ἐσμέν) to substantiate his argument.[213]

Idols Are Nothing (Acts 17:29). Another criticism of idols is found in Acts 17:29. Paul says, since we are offspring of God, "We should not think that the divine being is like gold or silver or stone – an image made by man's design and skill" (οὐκ ὀφείλομεν νομίζειν χρυσῷ ἢ ἀργύρῳ ἢ λίθῳ, χαράγματι τέχνης καὶ ἐνθυμήσεως ἀνθρώπου, τὸ θεῖον εἶναι ὅμοιον). This alludes to the anti-idol polemic of Isaiah 40:18–19 where it says, "To whom, then, will you compare God? What image will you compare him to? As for an idol, a

---

213. This quotation is taken from line five of the astronomical poem by Aratus of Soli in Cilicia (300 BCE). See Schnabel, *Acts*, 737.

craftsman casts it, and a goldsmith overlays it with gold and fashions silver chains for it." Similar anti-idol polemical vocabulary could be found in Isaiah 46:5–6 and Isaiah 44:19. Paul's message alludes to the anti-idol polemic in Isaiah to argue that manmade idols are nothing.[214]

God Has the Final Say – the Judgment (Acts 17:31). "For he has set a day when he will judge the world with justice by the man he has appointed" (καθότι ἔστησεν ἡμέραν ἐν ᾗ μέλλει κρίνειν τὴν οἰκουμένην ἐν δικαιοσύνῃ, ἐν ἀνδρὶ ᾧ ὥρισεν). The one who will judge the world is Jesus, whom "God raised him from dead" (ὁ θεὸς ἀνέστησεν αὐτὸν ἐκ νεκρῶν) (Acts 17:31). The risen Jesus will judge those who do not repent of worshiping idols. Acts 17:30 says, "In the past God overlooked such ignorance, but now he commands all people everywhere to repent" (τοὺς μὲν οὖν χρόνους τῆς ἀγνοίας ὑπεριδὼν ὁ θεός, τὰ νῦν παραγγέλλει τοῖς ἀνθρώποις πάντας πανταχοῦ μετανοεῖν). The judgment of idol worshipers denounces idols. Worship should be given only to the one true God. The cosmic lordship cannot be challenged. Paul's Areopagus speech criticizes all the pagan religion.[215]

Kingdom concern

The purpose of the anti-idol polemic is stated in Acts 17:30: "he commands all people everywhere to repent" (τὰ νῦν παραγγέλλει τοῖς ἀνθρώποις πάντας πανταχοῦ μετανοεῖν). Note the term "everywhere" (πανταχοῦ), which Luke employs four times (Luke 9:6, Acts 24:3; 28:22 and here). But only here does Luke combine the adjective "all" (πᾶς) with the adverb "everywhere" to say "all and every" (πάντας πανταχοῦ).[216] This phrase occurs only here in the NT and can be found nowhere in the LXX. It is Philo who employs this phrase frequently to bring the notion of wholeness.[217] Josephus also uses this

---

214. Litwak, "Israel's Prophets Meet Athens' Philosophers," 209.

215. C. Kavin Rowe, *World Upside Down: Reading Acts in the Graeco-Roman Age* (Oxford; New York: Oxford University Press, 2009), 41.

216. In 1 Corinthians, Paul "teaches everywhere in every church" (πανταχοῦ ἐν πάσῃ ἐκκλησίᾳ διδάσκω). The only occurrence of the term πανταχοῦ in the LXX is in Isa 42:22.

217. *Opif.* 1:63 says, "But it does not form completely" (πλὴν οὐ πανταχοῦ πάντα διεπλάττετο). Cf. οὐ γὰρ πανταχοῦ πάντα (*Unchangeable* 152); πανταχοῦ πάντες (*Joseph* 44; *Moses* 2:12); πανταχοῦ πάντων (*Moses* 2:12; *Virtues* 226); πανταχοῦ πάντων (*Embassy* 16, 48); πανταχοῦ πᾶσιν (*Moses* 2:65; cf. *Decalogue* 178; *Virtues* 140); πανταχοῦ πᾶσι (*Embassy* 89); πανταχοῦ πάντα (*Spec. Laws* 4:85); πανταχοῦ πάντας (*Virtues* 175; *Flaccus* 1; *Embassy* 152, 159, 204, 370; *Providence* 2:11); etc.

term to show the same notion.²¹⁸ Paul declares that "God commands "all the people from everywhere to repent" (ὁ θεός παραγγέλλει τοῖς ἀνθρώποις πᾶσιν πανταχοῦ μετανοεῖν). This is an inclusive declaration.

Paul introduces the truth of the gospel to pagan philosophers. Paul "preaches Jesus and the resurrection" (τὸν Ἰησοῦν καὶ τὴν ἀνάστασιν εὐηγγελίζετο) (Acts 17:18). Paul does bring something new to them so that they can embrace a new way of life by repenting of worshiping idols.²¹⁹ Paul's Areopagus speech is successful, as Acts 17:34 indicates: "A few men became followers of Paul and believed. Among them was Dionysius, a member of the Areopagus, also a woman named Damaris, and a number of others."

Criticism of Artemis (Acts 19:23–41)

The last anti-idol narrative is set in Ephesus during Paul's third missionary journey. It is interesting that the famous goddess Artemis is described as "falling from heaven" (τοῦ διοπετοῦς). This fall from heaven recalls the fall of Satan from heaven in Luke 10:18, as we demonstrated in the previous chapter that God won the victory over Satan in heaven. The account of the Ephesian riot is not simply one more attempt of early Christianity to legitimize itself.²²⁰ More importantly, it is a critique of the most famous idol in Asia Minor, Artemis. This anti-idol polemic further affirms the cosmic lordship of God.

In the third missionary journey, Paul makes a lengthy stay in Ephesus. The riot occurs at the end of his stay (54–57 CE). Having spent three months arguing about the kingdom of God in a synagogue, Paul spent about three years doing the same thing outside the synagogue. Paul's preaching of the word of God brings the result that "all the Jews and Greeks who lived in the province of Asia heard the word of the Lord" (πάντας τοὺς κατοικοῦντας τὴν Ἀσίαν ἀκοῦσαι τὸν λόγον τοῦ κυρίου, Ἰουδαίους τε καὶ Ἕλληνας) (Acts 19:10). It is Paul's powerful preaching that causes the Ephesian riot and ensures this anti-idol polemic.

---

218. *Ant.* 17:143; cf. τὰ πάντα πανταχοῦ (*Ant.* 17:143); πᾶσιν πανταχοῦ (*J.W.* 5:310); πάντα δὲ καὶ πανταχοῦ (*Ag. Ap.* 2:294).

219. Rowe, *World Upside Down*, 41.

220. Fitzmyer, *Acts*, 655–656.

In what follows, we will demonstrate the criticism of Artemis. First, we study the influence of Artemis and the importance of Ephesus.

Artemis

Compared to the other two anti-idol narratives (Acts 14:8–18; 17:22–31), the narrative in Acts 19:23–40 has the following features by which Luke attacks the idol, Artemis, in a different way.

Luke uses mouths of a silversmith and a town clerk to bring forth the status of Artemis as a deity. First, Artemis has been described as μεγαλειότης. This term is often used to describe the greatness of God (Luke 9:43). Elsewhere in the New Testament Peter relates his witness of the greatness of the Lord Jesus Christ using this word (2 Pet 1:16). This usage could also be found in the LXX.[221]

Second is the term, "to worship" (σέβω) (Acts 19:27). This term is often used in connection with the worship of God. A few instances will suffice. Acts 18:13 speaks of how Paul is persuading "men to worship God." In Acts 16:14 Lydia is called "a worshiper of God" (σεβομένη τὸν θεόν). Acts 17:4 likewise speaks of "a great number of God-fearing Greeks" (τῶν τε σεβομένων Ἑλλήνων πλῆθος πολύ).[222]

Third, the influence of Artemis is tremendous. Artemis is described as a goddess "that the whole of Asia and the whole world worships" (ἣν ὅλη ἡ Ἀσία καὶ ἡ οἰκουμένη σέβεται) (Acts 19:27). This shows how wide is the worship of Artemis. Artemis probably began to be worshiped as early as the eighth century BCE.[223] The temple that is located just outside the city of Ephesus is well-known as one of the seven wonders of the ancient world. This temple is a political, religious, and cultural symbol.[224] The fact is that Artemis of the Ephesians enjoyed great renown in the whole Mediterranean world.[225] The Ephesians considered Artemis *Soteria* of their city.[226] Oster

---

221. 1 Esd 4:40.

222. See also Acts 13:50; 17:17; 18:7, 13.

223. Lynn R. LiDonnici, "The Images of Artemis Ephesia and Greco-Roman Worship: A Reconsideration," *HTR* 85 (1992): 389–415.

224. C. L. Brinks, "'Great Is Artemis of the Ephesians': Acts 19:23–41 in Light of Goddess Worship in Ephesus," *CBQ* 71 (2009): 781.

225. Richard Oster, "The Ephesian Artemis as an Opponent of Early Christianity," *JAC* 19 (1976): 24–44.

226. Jean-Pierre Vernant, "The Encyclopedia of Religion," *Artemis* 1: 420–421.

comments that Artemis of Ephesus is "an indispensable pillar in the cultural structure and life of Asia, and was therefore a crucial factor in the lives of all . . . whom Christianity hoped to convert."[227]

Thus, we see that Artemis has been considered as a female deity and has gained such a wide worship in the ancient Mediterranean world. Next, we will study the importance of the city Ephesus.

Ephesus

Having studied Artemis, to note the importance of Ephesus will contribute to the criticism of Artemis. Ephesus is the first city to be granted the title of "temple warden." Ephesus is the largest city in Asia Minor and is an important commercial center.[228] The nearly-three-year-long stay of Paul in Ephesus indicates its strategic importance for the preaching of the word of God.

The Uniqueness of This Anti-Idol Polemic. Compared to the other two anti-idol passages, Luke makes Paul stay out of the scene. Though Paul wants to go into the crowd (Παύλου δὲ βουλομένου εἰσελθεῖν εἰς τὸν δῆμο) (19:30), "his disciples would not permit him" (οὐκ εἴων αὐτὸν οἱ μαθηταί). "Even some officials of the province begged him not to venture into the theater" (τινὲς δὲ καὶ τῶν Ἀσιαρχῶν παρεκάλουν μὴ δοῦναι ἑαυτὸν εἰς τὸ θέατρον) (19:31). Paul has no chance to address the mob. Furthermore, criticism is presented by the silversmith and the Roman town clerk, who represent the message of Paul as "man-made gods are no gods at all" (οὐκ εἰσὶν θεοὶ οἱ διὰ χειρῶν γινόμενοι) (Acts 19:26), which is a belief of both Jews and Christians. This was likely Paul's daily argument (καθ' ἡμέραν διαλεγόμενος) in the lecture hall of Tyrannus where he preached "for two years, so that all the Jews and Greeks who lived in the province of Asia heard the word of the Lord" (ἐπὶ ἔτη δύο, ὥστε πάντας τοὺς κατοικοῦντας τὴν Ἀσίαν ἀκοῦσαι τὸν λόγον τοῦ κυρίου, Ἰουδαίους τε καὶ Ἕλληνας) (19:9–10). The claim that "man-made gods are no gods at all" directly attacks the idol Artemis, which was made by the silversmith Demetrius, "a silversmith who made silver shrines of Artemis" (ἀργυροκόπος, ποιῶν ναοὺς ἀργυροῦς Ἀρτέμιδος) (Acts 19:24), as well as the other related workmen (19:25a). The text indicates that the business of making idols was quite successful (19:25b). Although this

---

227. Oster, "Ephesian Artemis," 34.
228. Brinks, "Artemis of the Ephesians," 783.

statement appears in the narrative of Paul's ministry in Ephesus, a similar statement is expressed in Paul's preaching to Gentiles in Lystra and Athens (Acts 14 and 17). Other attacks are hinted at in the context (Acts 19:1–23). The fact that Luke let the unbelievers utter the criticism of idols here differs from the other two narratives. These criticisms have actually challenged the idol – the goddess Artemis. We will show this point in the following.

Criticism of Artemis. Luke has argued for the superiority of Christianity over Judaism, over pagan religion, and over magic. Luke, in this narrative, denounces Artemis and her followers. Jesus the Lord has successfully challenged evil spirits (19:12) and his lordship has been attested (19:13–16). The result of the preaching of Paul is described in this way: "This became known to all the Jews and Greeks living in Ephesus" (τοῦτο δὲ ἐγένετο γνωστὸν πᾶσιν Ἰουδαίοις τε καὶ Ἕλλησιν τοῖς κατοικοῦσιν τὴν Ἔφεσον) (19:17). The summary statement in 19:20 – "In this way the word of the Lord spread widely and grew in power" (οὕτως κατὰ κράτος τοῦ κυρίου ὁ λόγος ηὔξανεν καὶ ἴσχυεν) – sets the stage for the riot.

First, the fact that the silversmith needs to defend the idol making business indicates that idolatry has already been threatened. Demetrius takes an action by calling together the idol-making men (τοῖς τεχνίταις) in order to make "a not small disturbance to the Way" (τάραχον οὐκ ὀλίγον περὶ τῆς ὁδοῦ) (19:23). The idol of Artemis has already been challenged.

Second, the Word has conquered the world. Using the word of Demetrius, "this fellow Paul has convinced and led astray a large number of people not only in the city of Ephesus but in the whole province of Asia" (οὐ μόνον Ἐφέσου ἀλλὰ σχεδὸν πάσης τῆς Ἀσίας ὁ Παῦλος οὗτος πείσας μετέστησεν ἱκανὸν ὄχλον) (19:26b). And this has become a reality that "you can see and hear" (θεωρεῖτε καὶ ἀκούετε) (19:26a).

Third, the following verse makes this point explicit. Acts 19:27 shows the danger to their trade and especially to the temple of Artemis. Luke employs various words to depict the danger to the trade and to the temple. The trade is in "disrepute" (ἀπελεγμός) (Acts 19:27). More importantly, the temple of the great Artemis will be reckoned as nothing (ἀλλὰ καὶ τὸ τῆς μεγάλης θεᾶς Ἀρτέμιδος ἱερὸν εἰς οὐθὲν λογισθῆναι). The meaning of the word "nothing" (οὐθὲν) needs to be noted. This word is used in an anti-idol context in Isaiah 40:17–23: "God brings princes and rulers to nothing" (ὁ διδοὺς ἄρχοντας εἰς οὐδὲν ἄρχειν τὴν δὲ γῆν ὡς οὐδὲν ἐποίησεν) (Isa 40:23). Further, the challenge would be that "[h]er majesty is to be dethroned" (μέλλειν τε καὶ καθαιρεῖσθαι τῆς μεγαλειότητος αὐτῆς) (Acts 19:27). The conjunction, "but also" (ἀλλὰ καί), puts more weight on the latter point than on the former, this can be seen in Luke's other uses of this phrase. Acts 21:13 says, "I am ready not only to be bound, but also to die in Jerusalem for the name of the Lord Jesus" (ἐγὼ γὰρ οὐ μόνον δεθῆναι ἀλλὰ καὶ ἀποθανεῖν εἰς Ἰερουσαλὴμ ἑτοίμως ἔχω ὑπὲρ τοῦ ὀνόματος τοῦ κυρίου Ἰησοῦ). Acts 26:29 says, "I pray God that not only you but all who are listening to me today may become what I am" (οὐ μόνον σὲ ἀλλὰ καὶ πάντας τοὺς ἀκούοντάς μου σήμερον γενέσθαι). Acts 27:10 says, "not only of the cargo and the ship, but also of our lives" (οὐ μόνον τοῦ φορτίου καὶ τοῦ πλοίου ἀλλὰ καὶ τῶν ψυχῶν ἡμῶν). These passages show that the phrase following "but also" is emphasized. Finally, the text that follows also supports this reading. When they heard this, they were furious and began shouting, "Great is Artemis of the Ephesians" (Μεγάλη ἡ Ἄρτεμις Ἐφεσίων), and "crying out for two hours" (ἐπὶ ὥρας δύο κραζόντων) (19:34). Therefore, the threat to Artemis is stressed.

Further Criticism of Artemis. Further criticism of Artemis can be seen in the following ways. First, the term διοπετοῦς is a criticism of the idol Artemis. This term is used to describe objects such as meteorites that have fallen from heaven and are honored as gods. These fallen images may take human likeness.[229] The term διοπετοῦς can be found in the NT only in Acts. But the notion of an image from heaven has some parallels.[230] This may indicate that this object (idol) is not made by human hands, thus invalidating the critique that "images made by human hands are not gods at all."[231] But the "falling from heaven," or as some would say, "falling from Zeus," is another criticism of Artemis. Falling from Zeus would indicate that she is inferior to Zeus, and Zeus has already been criticized by Paul in Acts 14. Subsequently Artemis is criticized. It is more likely, however, that Artemis is falling from heaven. It should be noted that her fall from heaven is reminiscent of Satan's falling from heaven in Luke 10:18. We have demonstrated that the fall of

---

229. Peterson, *Acts*, 549; Barrett, *Acts of the Apostles, vol. 2*, 936.
230. Fitzmyer, *Acts*, 661. See also BDAG, 250–251.
231. Barrett, *Acts of the Apostles, vol. 2*, 936.

Satan from heaven symbolizes the victory of God in heaven. This notion applies here that Artemis' fall from heaven is the victory of the cosmic Lord.

Brinks points out that the purpose of the narrative of Acts 19:23–41 is this: "the God of the Christians is challenging the power and supremacy of the goddess of the Ephesians . . . showing how the power of the Christian God is threatening to eclipse the power of even the great Artemis of the Ephesians."[232]

The fact is that the Christian God has introduced such a threat to Artemis of the Ephesians that a riot results. When this ends, "the riot is quelled, the pagan mob is sent home empty-handed and red-faced, and the Christians come out clean."[233] The Artemis that holds honor above all gods is indeed in danger of losing out to the cosmic God of the Christians. The history of the burning down of Ephesus proves it. The temple of Artemis gets destroyed in 262 CE. Modern excavations of the temple show some evidence of this. On one statue the name of Artemis was erased for fear of offending Christianity.[234]

Luke boldly challenges the most widely worshiped goddess (Artemis) in the known world. As Brinks concludes,

> The Artemis cults had spread so that she was worshiped in one form or another throughout much of the known world. Her presence was in the religious, social, political, and economic life of Ephesus, and her magnificence lent prestige to the entire city. She was a force to be reckoned with for the early Christians, and Luke boldly met that force head-on, his story of the rioting silversmiths in Ephesus challenging the notion of Artemis's supremacy in Ephesus, in Asia, and in the whole world . . . [T]he message of the story is that Paul's God, not Artemis, is the one worthy of worship in Ephesus, in Asia, and in the whole world.[235]

---

232. Brinks, "Artemis of the Ephesians," 791–792.

233. Scott Shauf, *Theology as History, History as Theology: Paul in Ephesus in Acts 19*, BZNW (Berlin; New York: de Gruyter, 2005), 263.

234. Clive Foss, *Ephesus after Antiquity: A Late Antique, Byzantine and Turkish City* (Cambridge: Cambridge University Press, 1979), 60. The temple of Artemis was destroyed in 262 CE when the Ostrogoths, seizing the opportunity afforded by civil war within the Roman Empire, attacked the city of Ephesus. The site of the temple was buried for a millennium and a half, the excavations of which turned up several statues of Artemis that had been defaced or engraved with crosses. See ibid., 60, 70, 82.

235. Brinks, "Artemis of the Ephesians," 794.

The speech of the town clerk further challenges Artemis and her worshipers. The Way is not condemned. The Demetrius speech implies a tangible success of Paul's missionary work in the city of Ephesus.[236]

Kingdom concern

The context of the anti-idol polemic concerns the preaching of the word of God. Acts 19:9–10 says Paul's two year preaching in the lecture hall of Tyrannus makes all the residents of Asia hear the word of God. The miracles God does through Paul also gain some believers in Ephesus (Acts 19:18). The narrative of the aftermath of the riot indicates that Paul's evangelizing in Ephesus has gained some believers. Acts 20:1 indicates that Paul sent disciples to encourage the believers in Ephesus.

Brinks's study shows that "the main thrust of the narrative is a contrast between the Ephesian goddess, worshiped by 'all Asia and the world' (19:27), and the God for whom Paul has gained converts among 'all the residents of Asia' (19:10).'"[237] God is beginning to gain ground.[238] The Demetrius speech implies a tangible success of Paul's missionary work in the city of Ephesus.[239]

Summary

The anti-idol polemic in Acts 14:8–20 criticizes Zeus as the most influential male idol in every aspect possible. It also stresses that the cosmic God is the living God and the Creator God. Human worship should be given only to the one true God. This anti-idol polemic challenges idol worship and affirms the cosmic lordship of God. Paul appeals to people in Lystra to turn away from idol worship to worshiping God alone.

The anti-idol polemic in Acts 17:22–34 denounces the idols of all the nations in a general sense. The cosmic Lord is again designated as the Creator God who makes heaven and earth and everything in them. Human worship should be ascribed only to the risen Lord (17:31). His cosmic lordship cannot be challenged by the various idols of the nations. The kingdom concern of this anti-idol polemic is that people (the Athenians) should worship their "unknown" – the resurrected Jesus whom Paul preaches.

---

236. Schnabel, *Early Christian Mission*, 1224.
237. Brinks, "Artemis of the Ephesians," 786.
238. Ibid., 792.
239. Schnabel, *Early Christian Mission*, 1224.

The anti-idol polemic in Acts 19:23–41 criticizes the most influential female idol, Artemis of Ephesus, who had been worshiped in Asia and in the whole world (19:27). The goddess Artemis has fallen from heaven (19:35). She has already been defeated by the cosmic Lord in heaven (cf. Luke 10:18). The cosmic Lord has gained the ground of Ephesus that Artemis once occupied. This anti-idol polemic also concerns the kingdom of God.

The anti-idol polemic affirms the universal lordship of God. This also concerns the kingdom of God. By critiquing idols, a call for turning away from idols to the cosmic Lord has been made. The exalted cosmic Lord challenges and dominates the space of idols using Sleeman's geographical language. The aim of the anti-idol polemic in Acts is "to underscore the power and sovereignty of the risen Jesus over all the opposing forces."[240]

Conclusion

In this chapter, we first reviewed the scholarship on the ascension narratives. The review shows that many scholars have studied the ascension narratives from various perspectives and have contributed to Lukan scholarship accordingly. However, the study of the heaven references has been mostly overlooked. A few scholars have sensed the relationship between the heaven references in the ascension narratives and Luke's theological concerns, but the manner in which the heaven references in the ascension narratives contribute to the heaven motif remains unexamined. This makes our study of the ascension narratives from the perspective of heaven necessary.

Second, we studied the ascension narratives in Luke-Acts and demonstrated that the two accounts are actually describing one event, the ascension of Jesus. The ascension narratives have not only a literary function but more importantly a theological function in Luke-Acts. Luke explicitly views the ascension apart from the resurrection. The ascension for Luke is the climax of the resurrection.

Third, our study demonstrated that the ascension of Jesus leads to his exaltation. The heaven reference in the ascension narratives (Luke 24:50–53; Acts 1:9–11) points to the exaltation of Jesus. Our study of other passages that reference heaven or use the term God or Lord demonstrated the exalted

---

240. Pao, *Isaianic New Exodus*, 208.

status of the risen Jesus. The heavenly ascended Jesus has been exalted to the right hand of God.

Fourth, our studies have demonstrated that the exalted Jesus is the cosmic Lord. The cosmic Lord is evidenced by many passages in Luke and Acts that contain heaven references. The heavenly Jesus commissions Paul to bring salvation to the Jews and Gentiles. Paul has done exactly what he has been told. The heavenly vision of Peter changes Peter's notion of the exclusion of the Gentiles and that of other Jewish Christian leaders. These heavenly visions to Paul and Peter concern the expansion of the kingdom of God. The heavenly Jesus encounters the human opponent (Saul) that intends to hamper the kingdom of God. The exalted Jesus challenges the human notion (of Peter) who hinders the spread of the kingdom of God. Our studies of the heavenly visions of Paul and Peter demonstrate that the cosmic Lord challenges the earthly obstacles from human beings (Paul and Peter) and changes them for the expansion of salvation (i.e. the kingdom concern).

Finally, our study of the anti-idol polemic in Acts 14:8–20 showed that it provides a critique of Zeus, the most influential male idol, in every aspect possible. It stresses that the cosmic Lord is the one true living God. People should worship the true God and him alone. It also affirms the cosmic lordship of God (the exalted Jesus). The purpose of this anti-idol polemic is the kingdom concern.

The anti-idol polemic in Acts 17:22–34 critiques the idols of all nations in a general sense. The cosmic Lord is again designated as the Creator God who makes heaven and earth and everything in them. Worship should only be ascribed to the risen Lord (17:31). The cosmic lordship cannot be challenged by various idols of the nations. People (the Athenians) should worship their "unknown" – the resurrected Jesus whom Paul preaches. The kingdom concern is obvious in this anti-idol polemic.

The anti-idol polemic in Acts 19:23–41 critiques the most important female idol, Artemis of Ephesus, who had been worshiped in Asia and in the whole world (19:27). The goddess Artemis has fallen from heaven (19:35). She has already been defeated by the cosmic Lord in heaven (cf. Luke 10:18). The cosmic Lord has gained the ground of Ephesus that Artemis had once occupied. This anti-idol polemic also concerns the kingdom of God.

Our studies of the anti-idol polemics in Acts 14, 17 and 19 demonstrate that the cosmic Lord critiques the idols of the nations. The cosmic lordship of God cannot be challenged by the various idols of the nations. The anti-idol polemic thus affirms the cosmic lordship of Yahweh. The concern of the anti-idol polemic is for the preaching of the kingdom of God.

CHAPTER 5

Heaven Must Receive Jesus Until the Restoration of All

Acts 3:21

Introduction

The reference to heaven in Acts 3:21 connects closely to the heaven reference in the ascension narrative (Luke 24:50–53; Acts 1:9–11). As we have shown, Jesus has ascended to heaven. The ascension brings the exaltation of Jesus. He has been enthroned as the Davidic king. He reigns over not only the whole of Israel but also the Gentiles. He is the Lord of all (Acts 10:36). He is the cosmic Lord. His cosmic lordship cannot be challenged. Jesus remains in heaven where he has been exalted and is sitting at the right hand of God as leader and savior (Acts 2:33; 5:31). Jesus, who has been exalted will remain in heaven until his second coming. The remain-in-heaven Jesus as the cosmic Lord is still working on earth as we have shown in chapter 4. The reference to heaven in Acts 3:21 points to another stage of the realization of God's eschatological kingdom on earth: the unfulfilled or not-yet-fulfilled, element of the kingdom of God.

While acknowledging the spatial aspect of the heaven reference, the temporal aspect should also be noted. The following studies will demonstrate the not-yet-realized part of the kingdom of God. First, we will examine the eschatological references in the programmatic passage, Acts 3:21. Then we will study eschatological references in Luke 17:20–37; 21:25–28; and Acts

2:17–21 respectively since these passages contain temporal markers – "times/time" or "days/day" – that relate to the second coming of Jesus.

Acts 3:21

Acts 3:21 is one of the programmatic passages in Luke-Acts that contain a reference to heaven. It contains the divine plan, as the term δεῖ indicates, and a reference to heaven (οὐρανός). Acts 3:21, together with 3:20, has been acknowledged to contain "the most difficult and most controversial aspect of Lucan theology today."[1] To understand Acts 3:21 one needs to study the text (Acts 3:21) and its context (Acts 3:17–26). Some key terms or phrases in this passage need to be studied first in order to understand Acts 3:21. Temporal markers like καιροί, χρόνος, ἡμέραι; their related phrases, καιροὶ ἀναψύξεως and χρόνοι ἀποκαταστάσεως; the term "all" (πάντων); the preposition "until" (ἄχρι); the relative pronoun ὧν; and the phrase ἐλάλησεν ὁ θεὸς διὰ στόματος τῶν ἁγίων ἀπ' αἰῶνος αὐτοῦ προφητῶν are keys to understanding this passage and Lukan eschatology.[2]

Temporal Markers in *Acts 3:17–26*

The temporal references in Acts 3:17–26 are critical for one's understanding of Acts 3:21. These references indicate the not-yet-fulfilled part of the kingdom of God. Three explicit temporal references occur in this passage: καιροί (Acts 3:19); χρόνοι (Acts 3:21); and αἱ ἡμέραι (Acts 3:24). First, we will the study the singular and plural forms of καιρός. Second, we will examine the singular and plural forms of χρόνος. Third, we will examine the two phrases καιροὶ ἀναψύξεως and χρόνοι ἀποκαταστάσεως. Finally, we will study the expression, τὰς ἡμέρας ταύτας.

The two temporal markers καιρός and χρόνος have attracted scholarly attention. John Marsh argues for a distinction between the two words. The term χρόνος is for chronological time, and the term καιρός is for realistic time.[3] This notion has been challenged by James Barr.[4] Barr agrees with the

---

1. Fitzmyer, *Luke 1–9*, 231.
2. William S. Kurz, "Acts 3:19–26 as a Test of the Role of Eschatology in Lukan Christology," *SBLSP* (1977): 309.
3. John Marsh, *The Fulness of Time* (New York: Harper & Brothers, 1952), 19–21.
4. James Barr, *Biblical Words for Time* (London: SCM, 1969), 33.

classical meaning of καιρός in the sense of "opportunity, critical time,"[5] and argues that the more commonly used temporal marker χρόνος has the sense of "date."[6] Barr understands the phrase χρόνους ἢ καιροὺς in Acts 1:7 as "dates and times."[7] Neither Marsh nor Barr focuses on the singular terms, καιρός and χρόνος. They both neglect to distinguish between the singular and plural forms of these two terms. Further, both of them overlook the Lukan use of these temporal references. Therefore, a study of how Luke uses these terms will surely be helpful for understanding Acts 3:21.

Καιροί

The following study will show that the plural form καιροί refers to an extended period of time. The plural form occurs only once in Luke's gospel in Luke 21:24, where it indicates a period of time. The city of Jerusalem will be trampled down "until the times of the Gentiles are fulfilled" (ἄχρι οὗ πληρωθῶσιν καιροὶ ἐθνῶν). The plural form also appears in Acts 1:7; 3:20; 14:17; 17:26. The most explicit references are in Acts 14:17 and 17:26. Acts 14:17 says that God gives "fruitful times" (καιροὺς καρποφόρους) to human beings as a witness of his kindness. Most translators render καιρούς as "fruitful seasons."[8] Acts 17:26 says God determines "times and boundaries" (καιροὺς καὶ τὰς ὁροθεσίας) for men to dwell. The context shows that καιρούς refers to a pretty lengthy time span, covering the time from the beginning of the first man Adam to the various nations on earth (Acts 17:26). The plural forms in Acts 1:7 and 3:20 also indicate "a period of time," as will be shown later.

Thus, we see that the plural form, καιροί, refers to *"a period of time."*[9] Sometimes it refers to a short period. Sometimes it refers to a lengthy period. Next, we will examine the singular form, καιρός, to show that it refers to *"a particular moment."*

---

5. Ibid.
6. Ibid., 35–36.
7. Ibid., 49.
8. See NIV; NASB; ESV; KJV; NKJV; etc.
9. Cf. Gen 1:14.

Καιρός

The singular form, καιρός, occurs eleven times in Luke and five times in Acts. First, the singular form refers to a particular moment at which an event occurs. Zechariah will be silent until the time that John the Baptist is born (Luke 1:20). Good servants are those who give their food allowance "at the proper time" (ἐν καιρῷ) (Luke 12:42). The event of the visitation of Jesus to Jerusalem will take place at a certain point of time (Luke 19:44). Similar uses can be found in Luke 12:42, 56; 13:1; 18:30; 20:10; 21:8. The deliverance of Israel by Moses takes place at a particular time (Acts 7:20; cf. 12:1; 19:23; 24:25). Second, occasionally the term is used with prepositions for "a period of time." Luke 8:13 says, "They believe for a while, but in the time of testing they fall away" (οἳ πρὸς καιρὸν πιστεύουσιν καὶ ἐν καιρῷ πειρασμοῦ ἀφίστανται). Elymas will not see the sun "for a while" (ἄχρι καιροῦ) (Acts 13:11).

Therefore, one finds that in most cases the singular form, καιρός, refers to a certain moment in time. When it is used in a prepositional phrase it can refer to a period of time.

This study of the two forms of καιρός shows that the plural form, καιροί, refers to a *period* of time, while the singular form, καιρός, often refers to *a certain moment* of time, though the singular form can refer to a period of time in a preposition phrase. Next, we will study the plural and singular forms of χρόνος.[10]

Χρόνοι

Like καιρός, the temporal marker χρόνος appears frequently in Luke-Acts.[11] The plural form occurs six times and the singular eighteen times. The plural form, χρόνοι occurs three times in Luke (8:29; 20:9; 23:8). In Luke 8:29, the term χρόνοις is modified by the adjective πολλοῖς, which expresses the frequency of the occurrence of events. The capture of the man by the evil spirit happened "many times" (πολλοῖς γὰρ χρόνοις). The plural form with the adjective ἱκανός refers to a period of time. The landlord goes away for

---

10. Delling, "καιρός," *TDNT*, 3:459–460.

11. The term (χρόνος) occurs seven times in Luke (1:57; 4:5; 8:27, 29; 18:4; 20:9; 23:8) and seventeen times in Acts (1:6, 7; 1:21; 3:21; 7:17, 23; 8:11; 13:18; 14:2, 28; 15:33; 17:30; 18:20, 23; 19:22; 20:18; 27:9).

"a long time" (χρόνους ἱκανούς) (Luke 20:9). Herod has wanted to see Jesus for "a long time" (ἱκανῶν χρόνων) (Luke 23:8). The plural form occurs three times in Acts (1:7; 3:21; 17:30). The occurrence in Acts 17:30 refers to a long period of time, the past generations (τοὺς χρόνους).[12] We will study the plural form in Acts 1:7 and 3:21 later.

Χρόνος

The singular form χρόνος occurs more frequently than the plural form. The singular form in Luke and Acts has the following meanings. First it refers to a certain point in time. A certain time comes for Elizabeth to give birth (ὁ χρόνος τοῦ τεκεῖν) (Luke 1:57). "In a moment of time" (ἐν στιγμῇ χρόνου), Satan shows Jesus all the kingdom of the world (Luke 4:5). "The time draws near" (ἤγγιζεν ὁ χρόνος) for God to fulfill his plan (Acts 7:17). Second, the singular form with prepositions or adjectives refers to a period of time. "For a while" (ἐπὶ χρόνον) the city judge refuses a request (Luke 18:4). Jesus was accompanied by certain people "all the time" (ἐν παντὶ χρόνῳ) that he went in and out (Acts 1:21). Simon, the magician, has amazed the people "for a long time" (διὰ τὸ ἱκανῷ χρόνῳ) (Acts 8:11, cf., Luke 8:27; Acts 14:3; 14:28; 20:18; 27:9). Third, sometimes the singular form, χρόνος, alone can refer to "a period of time." Judas and Silas "spent some time" (ποιήσαντες δὲ χρόνον) in Antioch (Acts 15:33). Paul has been requested "to stay a longer time" (πλείονα χρόνον μεῖναι) in Ephesus (Acts 18:20). Paul has been "spending some time" (ποιήσας χρόνον) in Antioch (Acts 18:23). Paul "stayed for some time" (ἐπέσχεν χρόνον) in Asia (Acts 19:22). Finally, the term χρόνος together with a number of years refers to an age of a person or a time span of years. Moses was "forty years old" (τεσσερακονταετὴς χρόνος) (Acts 7:23). God put up with Israel for "about forty years" (ὡς τεσσερακονταετῆ χρόνον) (Acts13:18).[13]

Therefore, the plural form, χρόνοι, is often used to indicate a *period* of time (Luke 21:24, Acts 14:17; 17:26). In most cases, the singular form, χρόνος, can refer to a *particular moment*. Sometimes χρόνος alone can refer

---

12. We will study the occurrences in Acts 1:7 and 3:21 later. The plural form refers to "seasons," a long period of time. Ps 103:19 (LXX) says, "He made the moon for all seasons" (ἐποίησεν σελήνην εἰς καιρούς).

13. The singular form χρόνος can refer to "a period of time" in Second Temple Judaism and in Qumran literature. See Delling, "χρόνος," *TDNT*, 9:587.

to a period of time, and when it is used with prepositions or adjectives it can refer to a period of time. The singular form together with a number of years refers to a *time span* of years.

Having studied the two terms, καιρός and χρόνος, in Luke-Acts, next we will study passages that contain both temporal terms in order to discern the distinction between these terms.

Passages containing both terms in Luke

Καιρός and χρόνος occur together in Luke 4; 8; 18; and 20. In Luke 4, Satan shows Jesus all the kingdoms of the world "in a moment of time" (ἐν στιγμῇ χρόνου) (Luke 4:5), and later Satan leaves Jesus "until an opportune time" (μέχρι καιροῦ) (4:13). In chapter 8, Jesus says, "They believe for a while, but in the time of testing they fall away" (οἳ πρὸς καιρὸν πιστεύουσιν καὶ ἐν καιρῷ πειρασμοῦ ἀφίστανται) (Luke 8:13), and then a certain man is said to have had demons "for a long time" (χρόνῳ ἱκανῷ) (Luke 8:27). In chapter 18, a certain city judge refused a request "for some time" (ἐπὶ χρόνον) (Luke 18:4), and then the disciples are told that they will receive many times more "in this present time" (ἐν τῷ καιρῷ τούτῳ) (Luke 18:30). In chapter 20, "a man went away for a long time" (ἀπεδήμησεν χρόνους ἱκανούς) (Luke 20:9) and then sent a servant "at the time [of harvest]" (καὶ καιρῷ) (Luke 20:10).

Our study of these verses shows that Luke prefers to use καιρός when he describes a *certain point* of time (Luke 4:5, 13; 18:30; 20:10) but will use either term with a preposition or adjective for a *period* of time (8:13; 8:27; 18:4; 20:9).

Passages containing both terms in Acts

Both temporal markers occur in Acts 1; 3; 7; 13; 17; and 19. Acts 1:6–7 says, "So when they met together, they asked him, 'Lord, are you at this time going to restore the kingdom to Israel?' He said to them: 'It is not for you to know the times or dates the Father has set by his own authority'" (Οἱ μὲν οὖν συνελθόντες ἠρώτων αὐτὸν λέγοντες· κύριε, εἰ ἐν τῷ χρόνῳ τούτῳ ἀποκαθιστάνεις τὴν βασιλείαν τῷ Ἰσραήλ; εἶπεν δὲ πρὸς αὐτούς· οὐχ ὑμῶν ἐστιν γνῶναι χρόνους ἢ καιροὺς οὓς ὁ πατὴρ ἔθετο ἐν τῇ ἰδίᾳ ἐξουσίᾳ). While not denying their concern for the restoration of the kingdom to Israel, Jesus first corrects their understanding of the timing and then tells them how to restore the kingdom to Israel (1:8). Instead of following the disciples in using the singular χρόνος, Jesus applies the plural forms χρόνους and καιρούς. The following verse indicates that the restoration takes a period of time: "You shall be my witnesses both in Jerusalem, and in all Judea and Samaria" (ἔσεσθέ μου μάρτυρες ἔν τε Ἰερουσαλὴμ καὶ [ἐν] πάσῃ τῇ Ἰουδαίᾳ καὶ Σαμαρείᾳ) (Acts 1:8). The events of "witnessing" in Jerusalem, Judea, and Samaria take some time. We see that the plural forms χρόνους and καιρούς refer to a period of time.

Acts 7:17 says, "As the time drew near for God to fulfill his promise to Abraham, the number of our people in Egypt greatly increased" (Καθὼς δὲ ἤγγιζεν ὁ χρόνος τῆς ἐπαγγελίας ἧς ὡμολόγησεν ὁ θεὸς τῷ Ἀβραάμ, ηὔξησεν ὁ λαὸς καὶ ἐπληθύνθη ἐν Αἰγύπτῳ). The phrase "the time draws near" (ἤγγιζεν ὁ χρόνος) refers to the period of time in which God has almost fulfilled his promise to Abraham.[14] It is the time period from Joseph to Moses.[15] Acts 7:20 says, "At the time Moses was born" (Ἐν ᾧ καιρῷ ἐγεννήθη Μωϋσῆς). The term χρόνος with numbers refers to a period of years (Acts 7:20). Moses was "forty years old" (τεσσερακονταετὴς χρόνος) (7:23; cf. 13:18). In chapter 13, Elymas is told that he will be blind "until a certain point of time" (ἄχρι καιροῦ) (Acts 13:11). Then Paul says God has taken care of his people for "forty years" (τεσσερακονταετῆ χρόνον) in the desert (Acts 13:18). Here we see that καιρός refers to a certain point in time and χρόνος with a number of years refers to "a period of time."

In Acts 17:26, Paul says God "determined the allotted times" (ὁρίσας προστεταγμένους καιροὺς) for every nation. In Acts 17:30, he says, "In the past times God overlooked the ignorance" (τοὺς μὲν οὖν χρόνους τῆς ἀγνοίας ὑπεριδὼν ὁ θεός) (Acts 17:30). The plural forms καιρούς and χρόνους refer to a long period of time – from the time of Adam to the time of Paul's speaking.

Finally, in chapter 19 it says, "He [Paul] stayed in Asia for a while" (αὐτὸς ἐπέσχεν χρόνον εἰς τὴν Ἀσίαν) (Acts 19:22). Here the singular form of χρόνος refers to the period of time in which the Ephesian riot happened (Acts 19:21–41).[16] The following verse says, "At that time there arose a great disturbance about the Way" (Ἐγένετο δὲ κατὰ τὸν καιρὸν ἐκεῖνον τάραχος

---

14. Schnabel, *Acts*, 372–373.

15. Alexander, *Acts*, 269.

16. Barrett, *Acts of the Apostles, vol. 2*, 921.

οὐκ ὀλίγος περὶ τῆς ὁδοῦ) (Acts 19:23). The singular form of καιρός refers to the point of time at which the Ephesian riot started.

This study of passages in Acts shows the following. First, Luke prefers to use the term καιρός when he describes a *certain point* of time (7:20; 13:11; 19:23). Second, Luke sometimes uses the singular form χρόνος for a *period* of time (7:17; 19:22). Third, Luke employs χρόνος with numbers for a *time span* of years. Finally, the plural forms of these two terms refer to a *period* of time and can be used interchangeably (1:6–7; 7:26, 30).

Summary

The above study can be summarized as follows. First, Luke uses the singular forms of καιρός and χρόνος for a *certain point* of time. Second, Luke employs the plural forms καιροί and χρόνοι to refer a *period* of time. Third, Luke prefers to use καιρός for a certain point of time. He prefers to use χρόνοι or sometimes χρόνος for a period of time. Finally, Luke employs plural forms, χρόνοι and καιροί, to express a period of time, and he uses them interchangeably.

Having studied the two terms, next we will first investigate two phrases related to the two temporal references: "times of refreshing" (καιροὶ ἀναψύξεως) and "times of restoration" (χρόνων ἀποκαταστάσεως). Then we will study another temporal phrase "these days" (τὰς ἡμέρας ταύτας).

Temporal Phrases

Having studied the singular and plural forms of καιρός and χρόνος, next we will study two phrases that relate to these two temporal markers: "times of refreshing" (καιροὶ ἀναψύξεως) and "times of restoration" (χρόνων ἀποκαταστάσεως). First, we will examine "times of refreshing" (καιροὶ ἀναψύξεως).

Καιροὶ ἀναψύξεως

Having studied the temporal marker καιροί, we now take ἀναψύξεως into consideration so as to get a better understanding of the phrase.

Ἀνάψυξις

Since the noun ἀνάψυξις occurs only here in the NT, a study of the verb could shed light on the meaning of the noun. The basic meaning of the verb ἀναψύχω is "to cool by blowing" or "to dry."[17] A study of the use of the verb in the LXX sheds more light on the present text. This verb is found in Exodus 23:12 to describe being refreshed on the Sabbath: "On the seventh day rest, so that your ox and your donkey may rest and the slave born in your household, and the alien as well, may be refreshed." God himself rested and was refreshed on the seventh day after creating the heavens and the earth (Exod 31:17). After drinking the water God provided, "Samson's strength returned and he was refreshed" (ἐπέστρεψεν τὸ πνεῦμα αὐτοῦ ἐν αὐτῷ καὶ ἀνέψυξεν) (Judg 15:19). When David played music for Saul, the evil spirit left and Saul "was refreshed" (ἀνέψυχεν Σαουλ) (1 Kgs 16:23). In 2 Kings 16:14, David refreshes himself at Jordan River after being weary from his travels. The verb also means "to breathe" (2 Macc 4:46; 13:11) or "to gain strength" (Ps 38:14). The only occurrence of the verb in the NT is in 2 Timothy 1:16 where Paul says that "he [Onesiphorus] often refreshed me" (πολλάκις με ἀνέψυξεν). Thus, the basic meaning of the term ἀναψύχω is "to refresh" the body either by rest, music, water or fresh air.

While the basic meaning of the verb is helpful for understanding the noun ἀνάψυξις, a study of the noun in the LXX will shed still more light on the understanding of Acts 3:19–21. The term ἀνάψυξις occurs elsewhere only in Exodus 8:11 (LXX), where it says, "There was relief" (γέγονεν ἀνάψυξις). The noun refers to relief from the plague of frogs. Fitzmyer describes it as "the breathing space" that has been granted to Pharaoh after the second plague of frogs.[18] This term has the notion of freedom/relief from something bad.

Our study of the verb ἀναψύχω in the LXX shows that it means "to refresh" someone by something good for the body. Our study of the noun ἀνάψυξις in Exodus 8:11 shows that it means "freedom/relief" from bad things. Bearing this in mind, next we will study the context of Acts 3:20 to discern the meaning of ἀνάψυξις in this instance.

The term ἀνάψυξις occurs only in Acts 3:20 in the NT. The context of this verse helps us to discern the meaning of this term here. Peter urges his Jewish audience to "repent and turn so that [their] sins can be wiped out" (μετανοήσατε καὶ ἐπιστρέψατε εἰς τὸ ἐξαλειφθῆναι ὑμῶν τὰς ἁμαρτίας)

---

17. Homer, *Odyssey*, 4:568 and Herodotus, *History*, 8:59.3.
18. Fitzmyer, *Acts*, 288.

(Acts 3:19). In this context, the "refreshment" is the result brought about by the wiping out of sins. It is freedom from sins, which is the salvation brought about by Jesus.[19] The only way to have sins wiped out is "to repent and turn" (i.e. to believe in Jesus).[20] "To repent and turn" indicates both a change of mind and accompanying actions.[21] In Acts 3:20, the refreshing is related to forgiveness of sins (v. 19c).[22] Repentance leads to life, as Acts 11:18 says: "God granted to the Gentiles repentance to life" (τοῖς ἔθνεσιν ὁ θεὸς τὴν μετάνοιαν εἰς ζωὴν ἔδωκεν). The conjunction ὅπως indicates the result of verse 19. The phrase "from the face of the Lord" (ἀπὸ προσώπου τοῦ κυρίου) (Acts 3:20) tells the source of the refreshment. The term "Lord" (κύριος) refers to Yahweh. Thus, ἀνάψυξις refers to the salvation from God that comes through Jesus Christ.[23] The refreshment is the result of being freed from sins, "the bad thing" human beings experience. Human beings will get "refreshed" by good things (i.e. salvation).

We have shown that the plural form καιροί refers to "a period of time." The term ἀνάψυξις refers to the salvation brought by Jesus. Thus, "times of refreshing" (καιροὶ ἀναψύξεως) means "a period of time of salvation." In other words, it is the messianic era.

Who will experience the refreshment?

The context shows that it is the people of Israel that will be refreshed. First, the audience is Israelites (3:12). Peter speaks to the "men, Israelites" (ἄνδρες Ἰσραηλῖται) about how the lame man got perfect health (3:13–16). Peter later addresses them as "brothers" (ἀδελφοί) (3:17). This further clarifies that the audience is Jewish like Peter. Second, the context shows that Peter urges the Israelites "to repent and turn" so that the times of refreshment may come upon them. Thus, we see that the recipients of "the refreshment" are people of Israel.

---

19. Schweizer, "ἀνάψυξις," *TDNT*, 9:664.

20. Haenchen, *Acts*, 208.

21. Conzelmann, *Acts*, 29.

22. John R. W. Stott, *The Spirit, the Church, and the World: The Message of Acts* (Downers Grove: IVP, 1990), 94.

23. Peace is one of the Lukan ways to depict salvation as we have demonstrated in chapter 2. Cf. the link to the eschatological peace in Luke 2:14.

When will "the times of refreshment" occur?

As we have shown, "the times of refreshing" refers to the era of salvation. The recipients of the salvation are the people of Israel. Next, we will show that the time for the people of Israel to receive salvation has already started. This era began at the first coming of Jesus in Luke 2:14. Jewish people have obtained the eschatological peace. Simeon has experienced the refreshment by experiencing the eschatological peace/salvation (Luke 2:29). The sinful woman has gotten refreshment by obtaining salvation (Luke 7:50). The hemorrhaging woman has enjoyed the refreshment by getting the eschatological peace/salvation (Luke 8:48). Later, three thousand Jews have gotten the refreshment (Acts 2:41). And so many others have gotten refreshed, as documented in the book of Acts.

Therefore, the word "times" refers to a period of time in which the individual events of repentance occur. The term "refreshment" refers to relief/deliverance from bad or evil things. The phrase "times of refreshing" expresses a period of time of being refreshed by being freed from something bad. In this context this phrase refers to a period of time of freedom from sins. In other words, "times of refreshment" refers to a period of time in which people can be refreshed by repenting of their sins by believing in Jesus Christ. This period of time refers to the salvation period, or the messianic era. The context of this phrase indicates that "times of refreshment" points to the time span in which the people of Israel can receive salvation. "Times of refreshment" speaks of present and future events that are occurring. This is "a period of time and a cluster of events."[24] The events include the individual repentance of the Jews.[25] The era of salvation has begun and is ongoing.

---

24. Hans F. Bayer, "Christ-centered Eschatology in Acts 3:17–26," in *Jesus of Nazareth* (Grand Rapids: Eerdmans, 1994), 247.

25. Acts 1:6 suggests that even the apostles are holding the messianic expectation that the coming Messiah is to restore the kingdom to Israel. The restoration consists of the regathering of the people of Israel and the restoration of the land. The expectation of the coming of the Messiah has been held by the Palestinian Jews since around the time of Jesus. They have been waiting for the Messiah as the agent of Yahweh to restore Israel and bring about the triumph of God's power and dominion. Fitzmyer, *Luke 1–9*, 471. This expectation exists in Qumran literature (1QS 9:11; 1QSa 2:14; CD 20:1) and in *Pss. Sol.* (17:23, 36; 18:6, 8). There clearly exists the expectation of a messiah or messiahs in Palestine around the time of Jesus. The OT theme of a Davidic king as the anointed one had been developed by that time. See Fitzmyer, *Luke 1–9*, 471–472.

Having studied the phrase "times of refreshing" and its meaning in this context, next we will examine another phrase, "times of restoration" (χρόνοι ἀποκαταστάσεως), and its context to discern its meaning.

Χρόνοι ἀποκαταστάσεως

Our earlier study of the two temporal references demonstrated that both plural forms suggest *a period of time*. Luke employs these plural forms interchangeably. The singular forms, however, often refer to *a particular/decisive moment*. The plural form χρόνοι, like καιροί, refers to a period of time. Issues surrounding this phrase are as follows. First, what does the term ἀποκαταστάσεως mean? Second, to what does the term πάντων refer? Third, what does the relative pronoun ὧν modify? Fourth, how does the word ἄχρι inform our understanding of this phrase?

Ἀποκατάστασις

First, we will examine the term ἀποκατάστασις. Since the noun form occurs only here in the NT and does not appears in LXX, its use in extra-biblical literature may provide a clue to understanding its meaning. LSJ adduces examples to provide the basic meaning of "restoration of property," "re-establishment," "recovery from illness," "return to original position" or "restoration of sun and moon after eclipse."[26]

Josephus employs this word to refer to "the restoration of the Jews" (τῆς τῶν Ἰουδαίων ἀποκαταστάσεως) after the Babylonian exile."[27] The context shows that this is the restoration of captive Jews to their homeland and the return, under the decree of King Darius, to their normal state of making sacrifices at the temple.[28] The main ideas are being set free and returning to the normal state. Josephus also uses this term to refer to "the restoration of Jerusalem" (τὴν τῶν Ἱεροσολύμων ἀποκατάστασιν)."[29] The context indicates that the word refers to the restoration of the destroyed Jerusalem to its normal state.[30]

---

26. LSJ, 201.
27. *Ant.* 11:63.
28. *Ant.* 11:60–62.
29. *Ant.* 11:98.
30. *Ant.* 11:97.

The verbal forms appear elsewhere in the Bible. The two forms of the verb ἀποκαθιστάνω and ἀποκαθίστημι occur in the OT and the NT. The verb ἀποκαθίστημι in the OT can mean "to restore" the nation of Israel to the land (Jer 16:15; 23:8; 24:6; 27:19; 29:6; Ezek 17:23), "to heal" (Exod 4:7; Lev 13:16; Jer 15:19), or "to restore" all (Mal 3:23 LXX). The verb ἀποκαθιστάνω in the NT can mean "to heal" from illness (Matt 12:13; cf. Mark 3:5; Luke 6:10; Mark 8:25), "to restore" all by Elijah (Matt 17:11; Mark 9:12), "to restore" a person to a community (Heb 13:19) or "to restore" the kingdom to Israel (Acts 1:6). Thus, we see that the verb has the force of delivering/liberating in order to restore something to its original state.

This understanding is evidenced by Luke's programmatic quotation of Isaiah 61:1–2 in Luke 4:18. This quotation contains the motif of restoration. The coming of Jesus is "to proclaim freedom for the prisoners and recovery of sight for the blind, to release the oppressed" (κηρύξαι αἰχμαλώτοις ἄφεσιν καὶ τυφλοῖς ἀνάβλεψιν, ἀποστεῖλαι τεθραυσμένους ἐν ἀφέσει). We may render this passage as "Jesus comes to restore freedom to the captives, to restore sight for the blind and to restore freedom to the oppressed." This is the literal understanding of the term "restore." The following quotation of Isaiah 58:6 in Luke 4:19 leads us to understand the restoration beyond its literal meaning. The coming of Jesus is "to proclaim the year of the Lord's favor" (κηρύξαι ἐνιαυτὸν κυρίου δεκτόν) (Luke 4:19). "The year of the Lord's favor" in the Isaianic context refers to the year of release. And here it suggests the time of the acceptance of people by God. Therefore, "the restoration" refers to the salvation from God that comes by Jesus Christ. This salvation can liberate or deliver people from the state of oppression of sins, which Luke expresses by "captivity," "blindness," and "oppression" (Luke 4:18).

Further, the preceding healing of the man born lame (Acts 3:1–10) symbolizes the "restoration of the man" being not merely physically restored but more importantly spiritually restored to God by the name of Jesus (Acts 3:16).[31] Luke's description of the lame man, "leaping and walking and prais-

---

31. Dennis Hamm, "Acts 3:12–26: Peter's Speech and the Healing of the Man Born Lame," *PRSt* 11 (1984): 200–201.

ing God," echoes the particular wording of Isaiah 35:6, which anticipates the coming day of salvation.[32]

Therefore, the word "restoration" refers to deliverance or liberation – both physical and spiritual. Luke emphasizes more the spiritual side, which is the deliverance/liberation from sins. In this context, it refers to the salvation of God brought by Jesus Christ"[33] Because the plural form χρόνοι refers to a period of time, the phrase "the times of restoration" (χρόνων ἀποκαταστάσεως) means *a period of time of salvation*. In other words, this phrase points to the messianic era.

Having studied the phrase "the times of restoration" (χρόνων ἀποκαταστάσεως), we will examine the term πάντων to discern what things are being restored.

The restoration of what? – the term πάντων

Much debate hangs on the term πάντων. Grammatically, the plural form πάντων could be either masculine or feminine or neuter. Scholars hold various views on it. It could refer to things or humans or even places.[34] Generally, there are four views. We will take each view into consideration and will argue that the term πάντων refers to all peoples – both Jews and Gentiles.[35] The inclusion of Gentiles is emphasized.

Πάντων Refers to "All That Scripture Spoke of." The first view is that πάντων refers to "all that Scripture spoke of."[36] This view seems unlikely for the following reasons. First, the reference to Scripture in Acts 3:21 is a reference to what Scripture says about the coming of the Messiah, his ministry and his suffering, and these are not the things that will be restored in Acts 3:21. That this is what the reference to Scripture in Acts 3:21 refers to is clear from the context as well as from similar expressions in Luke-Acts.

---

32. Alan J. Thompson, *The Acts of the Risen Lord Jesus: Luke's Account of God's Unfolding Plan* (Nottingham: Apollos, 2011), 156.

33. This era has already begun. The Gentiles have obtained "restoration/salvation." The inclusion of the Gentiles is well documented in the book of Acts.

34. Sleeman, who proposes a geographical reading of Acts, holds that the "all" refers to "all places." Sleeman, *Geography and the Ascension Narrative*, 109.

35. This does not mean that "all human beings" will be saved, but only those who believe in Jesus regardless of Jews and Gentiles.

36. Conzelmann, *Acts*, 29; I. Howard Marshall, *The Acts of the Apostles: An Introduction and Commentary* (Leicester: InterVarsity, 1980), 94; Barrett, *Acts of the Apostles, vol. 1*, 206.

Acts 3:22 relates "the raising up of the Messiah." Acts 3:23 speaks of the ministry of the Messiah. Those who do not listen to the Messiah will be cut off. Acts 3:24 says that all the prophets have prophesied these days in which these things happen. Besides, the typology of Moses supports the reading that "what the prophets spoke of" refers to Jesus and his ministry. For Acts 3:12, 26, the most instructive parallel is Acts 7:35 – this Moses whom they refused God sent as both ruler and deliverer. Luke uses Moses typologically to speak of Jesus.

The larger Lukan corpus supports this reading. What the holy prophets have spoken of in Luke 1:69–70 is the raising up of salvation, which, in context, happens at the birth of Jesus. In Luke 18:31 Jesus refers to everything the prophets predicted about the Son of Man, which there includes the maltreatment, death and resurrection of Jesus (Luke 18:32–34). Luke 24:25, 27 refers to "all that the prophets have spoken" (πᾶσιν οἷς ἐλάλησαν οἱ προφῆται), in speaking of Jesus's birth, ministry, suffering, resurrection and ascension. Here the suffering and the exaltation of Jesus are emphasized (ἔδει παθεῖν τὸν χριστὸν καὶ εἰσελθεῖν εἰς τὴν δόξαν αὐτοῦ) (Luke 24:26). In Acts 13:29, the phrase "all the things that are written about him" (πάντα τὰ περὶ αὐτοῦ γεγραμμένα) refers to his maltreatment, suffering and death (Acts 13:29).

Similar expressions in Luke-Acts also favor this reading. What all the prophets testify in Acts 10:43 is the salvation of all who believe in Jesus. In Acts 26:22–23 they testify to Jesus's salvific work: "But I have had God's help to this very day, and so I stand here and testify to small and great alike. I am saying nothing beyond what the prophets and Moses said would happen – that the Christ would suffer and, as the first to rise from the dead, would proclaim light to his own people and to the Gentiles." What Paul preaches is the same thing that Acts 28:23 speaks of: "about Jesus from the Law of Moses and from the Prophets" (περὶ τοῦ Ἰησοῦ ἀπό τε τοῦ νόμου Μωϋσέως καὶ τῶν προφητῶν). Luke 24:26–27 also confirms this point, "Did not the Christ have to suffer these things and then enter his glory? And beginning with Moses and all the Prophets, he explained to them what was said in all the Scriptures concerning himself" (οὐχὶ ταῦτα ἔδει παθεῖν τὸν χριστὸν καὶ εἰσελθεῖν εἰς τὴν δόξαν αὐτοῦ; καὶ ἀρξάμενος ἀπὸ Μωϋσέως καὶ ἀπὸ πάντων τῶν προφητῶν διερμήνευσεν αὐτοῖς ἐν πάσαις ταῖς γραφαῖς τὰ περὶ ἑαυτοῦ). Thus, we see that what "the Scripture spoke of" is the coming of the Messiah and his work.

Second, the context does not favor this view. Scholars who hold this view argue that the relative pronoun ὧν modifies πάντων instead of χρόνων. But Barrett contends, "It does not make sense to speak of the restoration of all the things that God spoke through the prophets."[37] Furthermore, Luke would normally use the verb πληρόω or τελέω for the fulfillment of OT Scripture. For example, Luke 4:21 says, "Today this Scripture is fulfilled in your hearing" (σήμερον πεπλήρωται ἡ γραφὴ αὕτη ἐν τοῖς ὠσὶν ὑμῶν). Acts 1:16 says, "The Scripture has to be fulfilled" (ἔδει πληρωθῆναι τὴν γραφήν). Acts 13:27 says, "They fulfilled the voice of the prophets" (τὰς φωνὰς τῶν προφητῶν ἐπλήρωσαν). Luke 18:31 says, "Everything that is written by the prophets about the Son of Man will be fulfilled" (τελεσθήσεται πάντα τὰ γεγραμμένα διὰ τῶν προφητῶν τῷ υἱῷ τοῦ ἀνθρώπου). Acts 13:29 says, "They fulfilled all the things written about him" (ἐτέλεσαν πάντα τὰ περὶ αὐτοῦ γεγραμμένα). Nowhere does Luke employ the term ἀποκατάστασις for the fulfillment of what "the prophets spoke of."

Finally, if this view were correct one would need to understand the term ἀποκαταστάσεως as "fulfillment," but our previous study of this term does not support that definition. Therefore, the view that "all things" refers to "all that Scripture spoke of" is unlikely.

Πάντων Refers to "All Israel." Some scholars hold the view that the term πάντων refers to "all Israel."[38] Reasons for this view are as follows. First, the context suggests that the term πάντων refers to people instead of "things," since the purpose of the speech is to urge people to repent. Second, the audience is indeed the people of Israel (Acts 3:12). Peter urges his fellow Jews to repent and turn to restore their relationship to their God.[39] This view seems possible but not probable for the following reasons.

First, while the audience is the people of Israel upon whom the blessings of God will first come, the following text speaks of the blessings that will come upon "all the families of the earth" ([ἐν]ευλογηθήσονται πᾶσαι αἱ πατριαὶ τῆς γῆς) (Acts 3:25). Here the singular σπέρμα refers to Jesus Christ

---

37. Barrett, *Acts of the Apostles, vol. 1*, 206.
38. Witherington, *The Acts of the Apostles*, 187.
39. Keener, *Acts, vol. 2*, 1112.

(cf. Acts 13:23). Acts 3:26 suggests the order of the blessings: "To you first, God, after raising his servant, sent him to bless you" (ὑμῖν πρῶτον ἀναστήσας ὁ θεὸς τὸν παῖδα αὐτοῦ ἀπέστειλεν αὐτὸν εὐλογοῦντα ὑμᾶς). Taking these two verses together; one may discern the order of the blessings of God by sending Jesus. The covenant people (Israelites) get the blessings (salvation) first and then the Gentiles (all the families of the earth).

Second, that the salvation comes upon all human beings has been well documented in Luke and Acts. The salvation is for "all the peoples" (πάντων τῶν λαῶν) (Luke 2:29–31). Jesus will bring salvation to the Gentiles (ἐθνῶν) and the Israelites (τοῦ λαοῦ σου Ἰσραήλ) (Luke 2:32). "All flesh" (πᾶσα σάρξ) will see the salvation (Luke 3:6). Jesus will be witnessed (preaching salvation) to the ends of the earth (ἕως ἐσχάτου τῆς γῆς) (Acts 1:8). Salvation to the Jews first and then to the Gentiles has been well evidenced by Paul in his missionary trips.

Therefore, this view is laudable in that it sees πάντων referring to people, but it seems that πάντων refers not to "all Israel," but to "all human beings." To this we now turn.

Πάντων Refers to All Human Beings. The third view is that πάντων refers to all human beings, both Jews and Gentiles.[40] Our study will demonstrate that this reading is more likely, though not many scholars agree to it. Johnson holds this view,[41] but he does not provide sufficient arguments to substantiate it.

First, grammatically this reading is possible. The term πάντων can be neuter, or masculine. Barrett asserts, "There is indeed no reason why πάντων should not be taken as masculine rather than . . . neuter," thus referring to "*[a]ll men*, the whole human race."[42] One should not exclude the understanding of πάντων as masculine.

Second, two observations suggest that πάντων refers to "people." The first observation is that the focus of Peter's speech is on the repentance of the people of Israel. Peter addresses the "men, Israelites" (ἄνδρες Ἰσραηλῖται) who have been astonished by seeing the miracle of the healing of a crippled beggar (3:12). Then he introduces Jesus and his rejection, crucifixion, and

---

40. Johnson, *The Acts of the Apostles*, 69.
41. Ibid.
42. Barrett, *Acts of the Apostles, vol. 1*, 207.

resurrection. At last he urges the Jews to repent of their sins and turn to God by believing in Jesus (3:19–21).[43] By doing so the "times of refreshment" (i.e. salvation) could come upon them. The repentance theme concerns only people. In the context they are Jews. The second observation is that the immediate context supports this reading. We have shown that "the times of refreshing" relates to ὑμῖν, which are the Jews (Acts 3:20). "The times of refreshing" (salvation) will come upon those who repent. "The times of refreshing" and "the times of restoration" parallel each other. The latter mirrors the former but goes deeper to include the Gentiles in the kingdom of God.[44] Pairing is typical of Luke.[45] Because "times of refreshing" relates to people, "times of restoration" should also relate to people.

Third, the following context suggests that πάντων refers to all human beings. A few points need to be noted. First, Acts 3:25 continues to relate the salvific work of God through Jesus Christ. The phrase "in your [Abraham's] descendant" (ἐν τῷ σπέρματί σου) refers to Jesus Christ. Acts 13:23 makes this point clear when it says, "From this man's [David's] descendant God has brought to Israel the Savior Jesus, as he promised" (τούτου ὁ θεὸς ἀπὸ τοῦ σπέρματος κατ' ἐπαγγελίαν ἤγαγεν τῷ Ἰσραὴλ σωτῆρα Ἰησοῦν). Acts 3:25 says, "All the families of the earth will be blessed" ([ἐν]ευλογηθήσονται πᾶσαι αἱ πατριαὶ τῆς γῆς). Here, the inclusion of Gentiles is indicated.

Second, Acts 3:26 indicates a chronological order of salvation history that further substantiates this reading. God has raised "his servant" (τὸν παῖδα), Jesus, and sent him to the Jews first (πρῶτον) (Acts 3:26). This is the first coming of Jesus (Luke 2). Through his ministry, Jesus has brought blessings to Jews first by turning them from their wicked ways. This indicates that Jesus will then bless others (all the families of the earth). The blessings will be first to the people of Israel and then to the Gentiles.

Third, Acts 3:25 suggests the order of the blessings by God. God's people will be blessed first since they have the covenant that God made with their ancestors. And then the blessings will fall upon all the families of the earth. This refers to the inclusion of the Gentiles. Acts 15:17 explicitly relates the

---

43. Witherington, *The Acts of the Apostles*, 187.

44. Max Turner, *Power from on High: the Spirit in Israel's Restoration and Witness in Luke-Acts*, JPThSup (Sheffield: Scheffield Academic, 1996), 309; Fitzmyer, *Acts*, 288.

45. Flender, *Theologian of Redemptive History*, 8.

inclusion of the Gentiles. It says, "All the Gentiles" (πάντα τὰ ἔθνη) "who call on my name" (ἐφ' οὓς ἐπικέκληται τὸ ὄνομά μου) (Acts 15:17) will be saved. That the wider mission to the Gentiles is well documented in the book of Acts evidences this point.[46] Thus πάντων refers to all human races.

Fourth, the term πάντων that appears in the context of this passage supports this reading. The term πᾶς occurs repeatedly in Acts 3, most often to refer to people (Acts 3:9, 11, 16, 18, 23, 24, and 25).[47] The only exception is verse 22, where it refers to "all the words that he [Jesus] spoke" (πάντα ὅσα ἂν λαλήσῃ). The term refers to all the people who witnessed the healing miracle (3:9, 11, 16, and 18). In one instance it refers to "all the prophets" (πάντες δὲ οἱ προφῆται) (3:24). In the other two cases this term refers to "all human beings" (Acts 3:23, 25). Acts 3:23 says "everyone" (πᾶσα ψυχὴ) who failed to listen to the Prophet Jesus will be utterly cut off. Acts 3:25 says, "all the families of the earth will be blessed" ([ἐν]ευλογηθήσονται πᾶσαι αἱ πατριαὶ τῆς γῆς) by Jesus Christ. Thus one finds that none of the occurrences refers to "everything/all things." The only exception is that this term refers to "all the words" (Acts 3:22). The two occurrences in Acts 3:23, 25 refer to all people, including both Jews and Gentiles. Thus the term πάντων more likely refers to all human beings.

Fifth, the use of the term "all" in Acts 2 also supports this point. The programmatic Joel quotation says, "And everyone who calls on the name of the Lord will be saved" (καὶ ἔσται πᾶς ὃς ἂν ἐπικαλέσηται τὸ ὄνομα κυρίου σωθήσεται). The term refers to all human beings. The expression, "all the house of Israel" (πᾶς οἶκος Ἰσραὴλ) in Acts 2:36 refers to people. Acts 2:39 says, "The promise is for you and your children and for all who are far off – for all whom the Lord our God will call" (ὑμῖν γάρ ἐστιν ἡ ἐπαγγελία καὶ τοῖς τέκνοις ὑμῶν καὶ πᾶσιν τοῖς εἰς μακράν, ὅσους ἂν προσκαλέσηται κύριος ὁ θεὸς ἡμῶν). This is another passage that indicates explicitly that the term refers to all the people. Acts 2:43 says, "Everyone was filled with awe" (ἐγίνετο δὲ πάσῃ ψυχῇ φόβος). Acts 2:44 says, "All the believers" (οἱ πιστεύοντες).

---

46. Witherington, *The Acts of the Apostles*, 187.

47. Not counting the one in verse 21, seven out of nine occurrences of this term refer to people.

Sixth, the OT background also favors this reading. The restoration of πάντων has its OT background. Bruce takes Malachi 4:5 (LXX 3:23) to support his view of "the restoration of all things."⁴⁸ The following study will show that πάντων refers to "all human beings." The expectation was that Elijah would come to "restore all people" (Mark 9:12; Matt 17:11 and Mal 4:5; cf. Sir 48:10). Elijah has been taken away into heaven, and one day he will return from heaven (2 Kgs 2:11). Two points need to be noted. First, Mark 9:12 and Matthew 17:11 do relate the coming of Elijah to restore πάντων. The text speaks explicitly that "Elijah will come first, and he has come." Matthew 11:14 relates that John the Baptist is the Elijah (cf. Luke 1:16–17). Second, what will Elijah restore when he comes? This seems a tough question.⁴⁹ The answer lies in both the OT and the NT. Malachi 3:23 (LXX) says, "He will turn the hearts of the fathers to their children, and the hearts of the children to their fathers" (ὃς ἀποκαταστήσει καρδίαν πατρὸς πρὸς υἱὸν καὶ καρδίαν ἀνθρώπου πρὸς τὸν πλησίον αὐτοῦ). The coming of Elijah is to bring good personal relationships between people.⁵⁰ Mark 9:12 says, "To be sure, Elijah does come first, and restores all" (Ἠλίας μὲν ἐλθὼν πρῶτον ἀποκαθιστάνει πάντα). Matthew 17:11 says, "To be sure, Elijah comes and will restore all" (Ἠλίας μὲν ἔρχεται καὶ ἀποκαταστήσει πάντα). Matthew 17:13 clarifies that the already coming Elijah refers to John the Baptist. Luke 1:16–17 tells what John the Baptist will do. John, like Elijah ("with the spirit and power of Elijah"), will go before Jesus "to turn the hearts of parents to their children, and the disobedient to the wisdom of the righteous" (ἐπιστρέψαι καρδίας πατέρων ἐπὶ τέκνα καὶ ἀπειθεῖς ἐν φρονήσει δικαίων) (Luke 1:17). The phrase "the disobedient to the wisdom of the righteous" corresponds to the clause "to give his people the knowledge of salvation through the forgiveness of their sins" (τοῦ δοῦναι γνῶσιν σωτηρίας τῷ λαῷ αὐτοῦ ἐν ἀφέσει ἁμαρτιῶν αὐτῶν) (Luke 1:17). Luke 1:16 clearly says, "He will turn many sons of Israel to the Lord their God" (πολλοὺς τῶν υἱῶν Ἰσραὴλ ἐπιστρέψει ἐπὶ κύριον τὸν θεὸν αὐτῶν).⁵¹ We see that what Elijah

---

48. Bruce, *The Acts of the Apostles*, 144.
49. Marshall, *Luke*, 59.
50. Ibid., 60.
51. Luke seems to try to avoid the notion of "the renewal of all things" in Matthew. In Matt 19:28, it says, "Jesus said to them, 'I tell you the truth, at the renewal of all things,

restores is relationships between people. The relevant NT passages make it clear that it is the good relationship of men with God. The above Lukan passages further make clear that this restoration refers to salvation. Only by salvation can people (Jews and Gentiles) restore the relationship with God.[52]

Finally, other evidence supports this reading. The idea of the renewal of all things appears in Matthew 19:28. It says, "Jesus said to them, 'I tell you the truth, at the renewal of all things, when the Son of Man sits on his glorious throne, you who have followed me will also sit on twelve thrones, judging the twelve tribes of Israel,'" (ὁ δὲ Ἰησοῦς εἶπεν αὐτοῖς· ἀμὴν λέγω ὑμῖν ὅτι ὑμεῖς οἱ ἀκολουθήσαντές μοι ἐν τῇ παλιγγενεσίᾳ, ὅταν καθίσῃ ὁ υἱὸς τοῦ ἀνθρώπου ἐπὶ θρόνου δόξης αὐτοῦ, καθήσεσθε καὶ ὑμεῖς ἐπὶ δώδεκα θρόνους κρίνοντες τὰς δώδεκα φυλὰς τοῦ Ἰσραήλ). Here three points need to be said. First is that the term παλιγγενεσία is different from ἀποκαταστάσεως. The former has the meaning of regeneration (cf. Tit 3:5). The latter refers to restoration. Besides, Matthew 19:28 relates the time when Jesus sits on his throne. At that time "all things are renewed." As for Acts 3:21, the time is about the second coming of Jesus.

Therefore, the study of the preceding text (Acts 3:17–19) shows that πάντων refers to people. The examination of the text that follows (Acts 3:22–26) demonstrates that πάντων refers to "all human beings" (i.e. both Jew and Gentiles). The study of the OT background and relevant NT passages also supports the reading that πάντων refers to "all human races." The inclusion of Gentiles is stressed.

Πάντων Refers to "All Things." The fourth view held by most scholars is that the term πάντων refers to "all things."[53] Origen seems to be the first to propose the concept of "the restoration of all things."[54] Haenchen asserts that Acts 3:21 concerns the restoration of the original order of creation.[55] The

---

when the Son of Man sits on his glorious throne, you who have followed me will also sit on twelve thrones, judging the twelve tribes of Israel.'" The idea of the renewal of all things is also found in Rom 8:18–23 and Heb 2:5–8.

52. The belief that a particular prophet will come and bring a new age is deeply embedded in Samaritan thought. Charles H. H. Scobie, "Origins and Development of Samaritan Christianity," *NTS* 19 (1973): 390–414.

53. Bruce, *The Acts of the Apostles*, 144; Haenchen, *Acts*, 208; Fitzmyer, *Acts*, 288. See also most of the translations.

54. *De principiis* 1.6.1–4; 2.3.1–5.

55. Haenchen, *Acts*, 208.

phrase "the restoration of all" means "universal cosmic restoration," namely "the new heaven and new earth."[56] Pelikan even asserts boldly that the Bible as a whole supports the idea of the restoration of all things.[57]

There might be an OT background here. Fitzmyer argues that the notion of the coming Elijah could be found vaguely in Jewish prophetic and apocalyptic writings (Mal 3:24 (LXX); Isa 62:1–5; 65:17; 66:22; *1 En.* 45:4–5; 96:3; 2 Esd 7:75; 91–95).[58] Black points out that cosmic renewal is a Jewish hope.[59]

Reasons for holding this view can be summarized as follows. First, some NT passages speak of the restoration of "everything/all things/creation," such as Romans 8:18–23; Revelation 21–22. Second, some OT texts foretell the "restoration of all things" (Mal 3:23; Isa 62:1–5; 65:17; 66:22). Finally, passages from the Second Temple literature vaguely refer to the restoration of all things. But the arguments that support the idea that πάντων refers to "all human beings" also denounce the view that πάντων refers to "all things" in those passages. The view that πάντων refers to "everything" lacks support from the context. The scrutiny of the OT background and the relative NT passages is not in favor of this reading. It seems that these scholars have read the meaning of "all things" into πάντων in this passage. Luke probably has not yet developed the universal restoration theology as Paul and John have done in Romans 8:18–23 and Revelation 21–22.

Therefore, the term πάντων should be understood to refer to "all human beings." "The restoration of all human beings" means "the restoration of Jews and Gentiles." This does not mean that "all human beings" will be saved. Only those who repent by accepting Jesus Christ will have their sins wiped out. Then they can have their relationship with God restored. Having studied the term πάντων, next we will examine the term ὧν.

---

56. Fitzmyer, *Acts*, 289.
57. Jaroslav Pelikan, *Acts* (Grand Rapids: Brazos, 2005), 66–68.
58. Fitzmyer, *Acts*, 289.
59. Matthew Black, *Scrolls and Christian Origins: Studies in the Jewish Background of the New Testament* (New York: Scribner, 1961), 135–136.

The term ὧν

There is no consensus as to what the relative pronoun ὧν modifies. Some hold that ὧν modifies "all" (πάντων).[60] Some argue that it modifies "times" (χρόνων)."[61]

The following study of the pronoun ὧν will demonstrate that it links not to "all" (πάντων) but to "times" (χρόνων).[62] First, the context supports that the relative pronoun ὧν refers to χρόνων rather than πάντων. The temporal marker "these days" (τὰς ἡμέρας ταύτας) further confirms this point. All the prophets from Samuel onward predicted "these days," a time span, in which all human beings will be blessed (Acts 3:24–25).

Second, the relative pronoun ὧν does not necessarily refer to the word or phrase that immediately precedes it. Acts 8:24 says that Simon asks Peter to pray to the Lord "that none of the things spoken fall upon me" (ὅπως μηδὲν ἐπέλθῃ ἐπ' ἐμὲ ὧν εἰρήκατε). Here the term ὧν does not refer to ἐμέ but to μηδέν. In Acts 26:22 Paul says, "I am saying nothing beyond what the prophets and Moses said would happen" (οὐδὲν ἐκτὸς λέγων ὧν τε οἱ προφῆται ἐλάλησαν μελλόντων γίνεσθαι καὶ Μωϋσῆς). In some cases ὧν can refer to the noun immediately preceding it (Luke 5:9; 13:1; 15:16; 19:37; Acts 1:1; 10:39; 21:19; 22:10; 26:2), but this is not always the case. The pronoun ὧν can refer to a noun a few words away.

Finally, this makes better sense in the context. Since the term πάντων is a part of the phrase χρόνων ἀποκαταστάσεως πάντων and its emphasis falls on the word χρόνων.

The context shows that ὧν refers to χρόνων instead of to πάντων. Grammatically, ὧν can modify a word or words that do not immediately precede it. This understanding makes better sense of the text. What the prophets foretold is Jesus and his ministry (i.e. salvation to human beings). Having studied the term ὧν next we will examine ἄχρι, which is crucial for understanding Acts 3:21.[63]

---

60. Conzelmann, *Acts*, 29; Haenchen, *Acts*, 208.
61. Barrett, *Acts of the Apostles, vol. 1*, 206; Zwiep, *The Ascension of the Messiah*, 110.
62. Bock, *Acts*, 177; Otto Bauernfeind, *Kommentar und Studien zur Apostelgeschichte* (Tubingen: J C B Mohr [Paul Siebeck], 1980), 69.
63. Pao, *Isaianic New Exodus*, 134.

Ἄχρι

The preposition ἄχρι occurs fifteen times in Acts.[64] It could be used with place, person or time.[65] In Acts it is mostly used with time.[66] The term ἄχρι with a time reference marks the end of a continuous extent of time.[67] The usage in Acts 3:21 belongs to this category. Our previous study of the time reference shows that χρόνων refers to "a period of time." The phrase ἄχρι χρόνων ἀποκαταστάσεως πάντων has often been translated as "until the times of the restoration of all things," as in most of the English versions.[68] This translation is actually misleading. It gives the impression that "times" (χρόνων) is "a certain point of time." A better understanding of the phrase ἄχρι χρόνων ἀποκαταστάσεως πάντων is "until the end of the times of the restoration of all people."[69]

The preposition ἄχρι occurring with a singular temporal marker means "until a certain point of time." Luke 17:27 says, "Until the day Noah entered the ark" (ἄχρι ἧς ἡμέρας εἰσῆλθεν Νῶε εἰς τὴν κιβωτόν). Acts 1:2 says, "Until the day Jesus was taken up into heaven" (ἄχρι ἧς ἡμέρας ἀνελήμφθη).

The preposition ἄχρι occurring with plural temporal markers means "until the end of a period of time." For instance, the phrase ἄχρι ἡμερῶν πέντε in Acts 20:6 parallels the phrase in Acts 3:21. They both have ἄχρι with a plural temporal marker. In Acts 20:6 the temporal marker is ἡμερῶν while in Acts 3:21 it is χρόνων. The phrase ἄχρι ἡμερῶν πέντε should be translated "until the end of five days." The rendering "within five days" (NAB) seems to miss the target. The rendering "in five days" (KJV, NJV) is little better than the rendering of NAB. The translation "five days later" (NIV, NJB) is the closest to its meaning. The best translation should be "at the end of the five days."

---

64. Acts has more occurrences of this term (fifteen) than any other NT book. Second place goes to the book of Revelation, with eleven occurrences.

65. A. T. Robertson, *A Grammar of the Greek New Testament in the Light of Historical Research* (New York: George H Doran, 1919), 639.

66. The term ἄχρι is associated with a place in Acts 13:6 and 28:15; with a person in Acts 7:18; 11:5; 22:4; and 22:22; and with time in Acts 1:2; 2:29; 3:21; 13:11; 20:6; 23:1; 26:22; 27:33.

67. *BDAG*, 160.

68. See almost all the Bible versions.

69. Of course, not every person will be saved, but only those who believe in Jesus.

This rendering makes better sense of the context. Paul and Luke sailed from Philippi after the days of Unleavened Bread to Troas, where the other five people had gone ahead to wait for them (20:4–5). They sailed for five days. At the end of the five days they reached Troas, and then the five men joined them (20:6), and they stayed in Troas for seven days. Carroll rightly observed that ἄχρι with the plural ἡμερῶν certainly means "after."[70] We see that "at the end of five days" also means "after five days." This strongly suggests that the phrase ἄχρι χρόνων in Acts 3:21 means "at the end of the period of time" or "after the period of time," since these are the only two instances of ἄχρι with plural temporal markers.[71]

Another point is that during "the five days" the sailing event continues day after day. Until the end of the five days, they reached Troas. And then the event of sailing ends.

Therefore, the term ἄχρι with the plural temporal marker χρόνων means "until the end of a period of time." The phrase ἄχρι χρόνων ἀποκαταστάσεως πάντων means "until the end of the restoration of all human beings."[72] During this period of time, the event of the repentance of Jews and Gentiles occurs repeatedly until the end of this period of time at which the Parousia happens.[73]

When will the times of restoration start?

The Restoration of Israel. In Luke's gospel, one finds the refreshment/restoration of the people Israel. At the birth of Jesus, the angel Gabriel announces that Jesus will reign over the house of Jacob forever (βασιλεύσει ἐπὶ τὸν οἶκον Ἰακὼβ εἰς τοὺς αἰῶνας), that is, the house of Israel (Luke 1:33). Throughout the whole gospel individual Israelites have been restored/refreshed. It is in the book of Acts that the restoration of Israel becomes more explicit.

---

70. John T. Carroll, *Response to the End of History: Eschatology and Situation in Luke-Acts,* 92 (Atlanta: Scholars Press, 1988), 145.

71. Ibid.

72. Again, this does not mean every single human being will be saved. It means that both Jews and Gentiles could be saved by accepting Jesus Christ.

73. Scholars who overlooked the plural χρόνων and ἄχρι thought that "until times of refreshing" points only to the future event of Jesus. See Arthur W. Wainwright, "Luke and the Restoration of the Kingdom to Israel," *ExpTim* 89 (1977): 77; Larry R. Helyer, "Luke and the Restoration of Israel," *JETS* 36 (1993): 328.

At the beginning of Acts, the apostles ask about the restoration of the kingdom to Israel by asking "Lord, are you at this time going to restore the kingdom to Israel (κύριε, εἰ ἐν τῷ χρόνῳ τούτῳ ἀποκαθιστάνεις τὴν βασιλείαν τῷ Ἰσραήλ;) (Act 1:6).[74] Without denying the restoration of the kingdom to Israel, Jesus corrects their wrong perception of the timing. He answers, "It is not for you to know the seasons or times the Father has set by his own authority (οὐχ ὑμῶν ἐστιν γνῶναι χρόνους ἢ καιροὺς οὓς ὁ πατὴρ ἔθετο ἐν τῇ ἰδίᾳ ἐξουσίᾳ) (Act 1:7). The change of χρόνῳ to χρόνους ἢ καιρούς indicates that the restoration to the kingdom to Israel will not happen at a point of time; rather, it takes "a period of time" which has begun already. The text that follows (Acts 1:8) shows three things. First, it tells the disciples that the restoration of the kingdom is realized by the witness of Jesus (i.e. preaching the gospel). Second, this further confirms this notion of the restoration of Israel. Finally, it provides the chronological order of the restoration of the kingdom. Acts 1:8 contains "one city, two regions."[75] The restoration is realized in Jerusalem in Acts 2, when the Spirit is poured out and three thousand are refreshed. The restoration of Samaria is realized in Acts 8, as Pao rightly asserts, "This blanket statement [Acts 8:14] concerning the conversion of an entire city or region appears only here in the narrative of Acts; and this peculiar fact can only be understood when the symbolic value of the name 'Samaria' is recognized."[76] The restoration of the kingdom to Israel is evidenced in the rest of the narrative of Acts.[77] Jesus corrects the wrong notion of the kingdom's essence. Stott points out that "the kingdom of God is spiritual in its character, . . . international in its membership, gradual

---

74. N. T. Wright's understanding of the restoration of Israel is this: "Israel's god has restored his kingdom for his people." N. T. Wright, *The New Testament and the People of God*, COQD 1 (Minneapolis: Fortress, 1989), 375. Wright asserts that "this is how the kingdom is being restored to Israel: by its representative Messiah being enthroned as the world's true lord." Wright, *The Resurrection*, 655. Our study shows that his view is problematic.

75. Pao, *Isaianic New Exodus*, 127.

76. Ibid., 128.

77. "After this I will return and rebuild David's fallen tent. Its ruins I will rebuild, and I will restore it" (μετὰ ταῦτα ἀναστρέψω καὶ ἀνοικοδομήσω τὴν σκηνὴν Δαυὶδ τὴν πεπτωκυῖαν καὶ τὰ κατεσκαμμένα αὐτῆς ἀνοικοδομήσω καὶ ἀνορθώσω αὐτήν) (Acts 15:16). See also Acts 28:30–31, where Paul "welcomed all who came to see him proclaiming the kingdom of God and teaching the truth about the Lord Jesus Christ" (ἀπεδέχετο πάντας τοὺς εἰσπορευομένους πρὸς αὐτόν, κηρύσσων τὴν βασιλείαν τοῦ θεοῦ καὶ διδάσκων τὰ περὶ τοῦ κυρίου Ἰησοῦ Χριστοῦ)."

in its expansion."⁷⁸ The refreshment/restoration of the people of Israel has already begun. God has not only started the restoration of the Israelites but also initiated the restoration of the Gentiles. To this we now turn.

The Restoration of Gentiles. The restoration of the Gentiles has been indicated early in Luke's Gospel. Luke 2:32 says that Jesus will be "a light for revelation to the Gentiles" (φῶς εἰς ἀποκάλυψιν ἐθνῶν). Luke 3:6 restates that "all flesh shall see the salvation of God" (ὄψεται πᾶσα σὰρξ τὸ σωτήριον τοῦ θεοῦ). It is in the book of Acts that the restoration of the Gentiles becomes clearer. The inclusion of Gentiles is stated in Acts 1:8, where it says, "you will be my witnesses in Jerusalem, and in all Judea and Samaria, and to the ends of the earth" (ἔσεσθέ μου μάρτυρες ἔν τε Ἰερουσαλὴμ καὶ [ἐν] πάσῃ τῇ Ἰουδαίᾳ καὶ Σαμαρείᾳ καὶ ἕως ἐσχάτου τῆς γῆς). As Pao asserts, this verse contains "one city, two regions, and a reference to the Gentiles. This is not geographical but theopolitical terms."⁷⁹

The believing eunuch illustrates the inclusion of Gentile outsiders in Acts 8:26–40, which was anticipated in Isaiah 56. That Gentiles receive salvation has been fully narrated in Acts 10–11. And it has also been well narrated in the book of Acts in the three mission journeys of Paul (Acts 13–21). Even at the end of Acts, Luke provides a hint that the restoration of Gentiles (as well as Jews) is an ongoing process. Paul preaches to all who come to him "the kingdom of God with boldness and without hindrance" (κηρύσσων τὴν βασιλείαν τοῦ θεοῦ μετὰ πάσης παρρησίας ἀκωλύτως) (Acts 28:30–31).

Therefore, the above study shows that the restoration of "all human beings," both Jews and Gentiles, has begun. Having studied the two temporal markers, the two related phrases and other terms, next we will examine the third temporal marker.

Τὰς ἡμέρας ταύτας

The expression "these days" refers to the days that God sent Jesus to the people of Israel (3:22). It also refers to the times in which "if the Jews do not listen to the Messiah, the Moses-like prophet, they will be cut off from the kingdom blessing (3:23). Peter speaks out that the salvation is present and also future. He continues to urge his Jewish audience to repent in order to

---

78. Stott, *Message of Acts*, 40–45.
79. Pao, *Isaianic New Exodus*, 127.

get the kingdom blessing (Acts 3:24–26). "These days" generally refers to "the messianic days."[80] This is an era in which people can repent and turn from their sins so that "the times of refreshing" may come to the Jewish people. "The times of restoration" may come upon all human races.

The third-time reference (ἡμέραι) is correlated with that in verses 20 (καιροί) and 21 (χρόνοι) so that "it becomes apparent that in verse 21 Peter does not speak exclusively of the future but includes the present."[81]

The above study could be summarized as follows. Linguistically, the references behind the two phrases χρόνων ἀποκαταστάσεως and καιροὶ ἀναψύξεως are not foundationally different, and many scholars rightly argue that these two phrases express the same idea.[82] It is true that these two phrases contain the same period of time as the temporal markers indicate. During that period of time people are able to repent and convert before the end.[83]

Theologically, the two terms, "times of refreshing" and "times of restoration," do convey the same emphasis. "Times of refreshing" refers to "a period of time" by which people could obtain salvation. The context suggests that in this period of time all the human beings can obtain salvation. "Times of restoration" likewise refers to "a period of time by which people could obtain salvation." The context suggests that in this period of time all human beings can obtain salvation. The inclusion of Gentiles is emphasized.

Summary

The two temporal phrases, "times of refreshment" and "times of restoration," correspond to each other. They refer to the same period of time that is the salvation era. This era has started by the first coming of Jesus and will last till the second coming of Jesus (Acts 3:19–21). Throughout this period, events of individual repentance of both Jews and Gentiles will happen. The third temporal marker, "these days," also corresponds to the other two temporal markers. The phrase "these days" suggests the already-realized salvation era on earth. Having studied the temporal markers, next we will examine Acts

---

80. Bock, *Acts*, 180. See also Keener, *Acts, vol. 2*, 1118.
81. Turner, *Power from on High*, 309–10; Bayer, "Eschatology," 247–248.
82. Bruce, *The Acts of the Apostles*, 144; Schnabel, *Acts*, 76; Conzelmann, *Acts*, 29.
83. Fitzmyer, *Acts*, 288.

3:17–26 and will show that the two comings of Jesus have been indicated in this passage.

The First and Second Comings of Jesus in *Acts 3:17–26*

Scholars have rightly discerned that Acts 3:17–26 introduces an eschatological theme, the first and second coming of Jesus.[84]

The First Coming of Jesus

The first coming of Jesus has been indicated in this passage. First, Peter explains to the Israelites the rejection of Jesus (Acts 3:13–15) and his suffering (Acts 3:18). The Messiah has come and suffered according to the predestination of God. "But this is how God fulfilled what he had foretold through the mouth of all the prophets, saying that his Christ would suffer" (ὁ δὲ θεός, ἃ προκατήγγειλεν διὰ στόματος πάντων τῶν προφητῶν παθεῖν τὸν χριστὸν αὐτοῦ, ἐπλήρωσεν οὕτως) (Acts 3:18). This passage speaks of the first coming of Jesus and his death.

Second, the first coming of the Messiah has been foretold by the prophets and has now been fulfilled. Acts 3:22 says, "For Moses said, 'The Lord your God will raise up for you a prophet like me from among your own people'" (Μωϋσῆς μὲν εἶπεν ὅτι προφήτην ὑμῖν ἀναστήσει κύριος ὁ θεὸς ὑμῶν ἐκ τῶν ἀδελφῶν ὑμῶν ὡς ἐμέ). Acts 3:22 connects to verse 18 instead of 21.[85] The verb ἀναστήσας echoes ἀναστήσει κύριος ὁ θεὸς ὑμῶν in verse 2, referring not to the resurrection of Jesus but to his coming and his ministry (cf. 13:33).[86] The quotation of Deuteronomy 18:15–20 refers to Jesus, who is the prophet like Moses and who has been rejected and has accomplished the work of deliverance for the Israelites. God has indeed raised Jesus Christ as the one likes Moses. In Acts 3:24, Samuel, though he does not directly prophesy regarding the Christ, prophesies regarding King David in whose line Jesus will become the eternal king.[87]

All the prophets from Samuel onward predicted these days (Acts 3:24). The blessings will occur through the seed (σπέρμα) of Abraham (Jesus, the singular), and all the people of the earth will be benefited (3:25). The

---

84. Bock, *Acts*, 166.
85. Haenchen, *Acts*, 209.
86. Bruce, *The Acts of the Apostles*, 146.
87. Bock, *Acts*, 180; Schnabel, *Acts*, 218.

converted Jews are the first recipients of the blessings mediated by God's raising up of his servant and sending him to them (3:26). "These days" in Acts 3:24 is a reference to the times of Jesus's first coming and his ministry (his death, resurrection, ascension). During the time span of these days (like the days of Noah and Lot) people may believe in Jesus and thus get the blessings of God's promise to Abraham, or they will be rooted out (3:22–23). The raising of the Moses-like prophet and the raising of the servant of God are the same event.[88]

Finally, Acts 3:26 further speaks of the first coming of the Messiah. It says "When God rose up his servant, he sent him first to you to bless you by turning each of you from your wicked ways" (ὑμῖν πρῶτον ἀναστήσας ὁ θεὸς τὸν παῖδα αὐτοῦ ἀπέστειλεν αὐτὸν εὐλογοῦντα ὑμᾶς ἐν τῷ ἀποστρέφειν ἕκαστον ἀπὸ τῶν πονηριῶν ὑμῶν). Here the verb "raise up" (ἀνίστημι) echoes ἀναστήσει κύριος ὁ θεὸς ὑμῶν in verse 22, where God will raise up a prophet like Moses. This term does not necessarily refer to the resurrection of Jesus but his first coming and his ministry.[89] Some scholars argue that the word "raise up" refers to the resurrection.[90] This seems unlikely.

Thus, the study shows that Acts 3:17–26 speaks of the first coming of Jesus. It has been foretold by the prophets and has been now fulfilled.

The Second Coming of Jesus

Many scholars rightly understand Acts 3:21 to refer to the second coming of Jesus, namely the Parousia. Verse 21 says that the Jesus whom God once sent to Israel is now in heaven and will return after the restoration of all. The term heaven in verse 21 recalls the heaven reference in the ascension narrative (Luke 24:50–53; Acts 1:9–11). As we showed there, Jesus ascended to heaven, bringing about the exaltation of Jesus, who remains in heaven sitting at the right hand of God (Acts 2:33; 5:31). Acts 3:20 indicates the ultimate returning of Jesus.[91]

Further, the preposition "until" (ἄχρι) suggests a future event, and it begins at the present time. The translation "until" (ἄχρι) also supports this

---

88. Kurz, "Eschatology in Lukan Christology," 311.
89. Bruce, *The Acts of the Apostles*, 146.
90. Bock, *Acts*, 178; Witherington, *The Acts of the Apostles*, 187.
91. Bock, *Acts*, 175.

interpretation. A close parallel is Acts 20:6, where it says, "until the end of five days" (ἄχρι ἡμερῶν πέντε) Paul reached Troas. As we demonstrated earlier, the idea that Jesus will come "until the end of the period of restoration of all" means Jesus will come after the restoration of all human beings."[92]

Having studied the three temporal markers, the two phrases, "times of refreshing" and "times of restoration"; and the terms πάντων, ὧν, and ἄχρι, the first and second coming of Jesus in Acts 3:17–26, now we will provide our understanding of this entire verse (Acts 3:21) in reference to the significance of the heaven language in Acts.

Acts 3:21

Acts 3:21 says, "Whom [Jesus] heaven must receive until the restoration of all" (ὃν δεῖ οὐρανὸν μὲν δέξασθαι ἄχρι χρόνων ἀποκαταστάσεως πάντων). A couple of points need to be noted. First, the reference to heaven recalls the ascension narrative (Acts 1:9–11). As we showed in chapter 4, Jesus ascended to heaven, is exalted and is sitting at the right hand of God as the cosmic Lord.

Second, it is surprising that the heaven reference is personified. In this sentence οὐρανόν serves as the subject. Walter Robert Shade comments on Acts 3:21 that "a non-personal thing [in this case, heaven] makes a poor subject for a verb like receive that is normally the prerogative of persons, not things."[93] Shade takes that "heaven" is a periphrasis for God.[94] It is true that the verb "receive" usually takes persons as subjects, but to say that "heaven" is a periphrasis for God is to miss Luke's theological concerns, which we will demonstrate in the following.[95] The verb δεῖ with the infinitive suggests this point. The verb δέχομαι has often been used with a personal subject in Luke-Acts. Luke uses this verb exclusively of a person who receives or welcomes somebody (Luke 2:28; 9:5; 9:48 [x4]; 9:53; 10:8, 10; 16:4; Acts 7:59) or something, mostly the Word of God (Luke 8:13; 18:17; Acts 7:38;

---

92. Again, this does not mean "all human beings" will be saved. Only those who repent and believe in Jesus can be restored (saved).

93. Walter Robert Shade, III, "The Restoration of Israel in Acts 3:12–26 and Lukan Eschatology" (Ph.D. diss., Trinity Evangelical Divinity School, 1994): 73.

94. Ibid.

95. Luke does not like Matthew who uses heaven as a paraphrase for God. One obvious example is when Luke employs "the kingdom of God" instead of "the kingdom of heaven."

8:14; 11:1; 17:11). Other cases are people who receive something (Luke 16:4, 6, 7, 9 and Acts 22:5; 28:21). Heaven, like a person, receives and keeps the exalted Jesus.

That Luke elsewhere uses anthropomorphic rhetoric supports this reading. Luke refers to the Word as a person (Acts 6:7; 12:24; 19:20). Acts 6:7 says, "The Word of God was growing" (ὁ λόγος τοῦ θεοῦ ηὔξανεν). Another case is Acts 12:24, where he says, "But the word of God grew and multiplied" (Ὁ δὲ λόγος τοῦ θεοῦ ηὔξανεν καὶ ἐπληθύνετο). Luke uses exactly the same phrase, ηὔξησεν καὶ ἐπληθύνθη, to describe the growth and multiplication of the people of Israel in Acts 7:17: "the people grew and multiplied" (ηὔξησεν ὁ λαὸς καὶ ἐπληθύνθη). Again one finds the personifying of the Word in Acts 19:20.[96]

Another anthropomorphous case is the Way. The Way terminology in Acts has been considered as a reference to Jesus.[97] Lyonnet studies Acts 22:4, 8 and argues that to persecute the Way is tantamount to persecuting Jesus.[98] Pao has convincingly argued that "the Way" identifies the "true people of God."[99] Thus, we see that the Way is personified. Luke again uses anthropomorphic rhetoric in Acts 3:21.

Third, the verb δεῖ suggests divine determination. Δεῖ is a "must" for Luke, not merely a "shall."[100] That Luke uses δεῖ more than any other NT writer suggests that δεῖ plays an important part in his narrative.[101] The motif of "the divine must" is critically important for Luke to present the history of salvation. It is used time and again for the divine intervention of God's

---

96. Pao, *Isaianic New Exodus*, 147–180.

97. Eero Repo, *Der "Weg" als Selbstbezeichnung des Urchristentums: Eine traditionsgeschichtliche und semasiologische Untersuchung* (Helsinki: Suomalainen Tiedeakatemia, 1964), 182–184.

98. Stanislas Lyonnet, "'La voie' dans les Actes des Apôtres," *RSR* 69 (1981): 149–164.

99. Pao, *Isaianic New Exodus*, 60–68.

100. Henry Joel Cadbury and Paul N. Anderson, *The Making of Luke-Acts* (Peabody: Hendrickson, 1999), 305.

101. Kenneth Bass, "The Narrative and Rhetorical Use of Divine Necessity in Luke-Acts," *Journal of Biblical and Pneumatological Research* 1 (2009): 51. This term occurs forty times in Luke-Acts, versus eight times in Matthew, six times in Mark, ten times in John, twenty-four times in the Pauline corpus, five times in the general epistles, and seven times in Revelation.

saving acts.[102] Luke uses δεῖ in relation to Jesus in Luke 9:22, where Jesus says that "the Son of Man must suffer . . . die . . . and be raised" (δεῖ τὸν υἱὸν τοῦ ἀνθρώπου πολλὰ παθεῖν καὶ ἀποδοκιμασθῆναι ἀπὸ τῶν πρεσβυτέρων καὶ ἀρχιερέων καὶ γραμματέων καὶ ἀποκτανθῆναι καὶ τῇ τρίτῃ ἡμέρᾳ ἐγερθῆναι). He also uses this word in Luke 13:33; 17:25; 22:37; 24:7, 26, 44; Acts 17:3. Luke employs δεῖ to express other divine things (Acts 1:16; 14:22; 23:11; 27:24). That heaven receives Jesus for a period of time is a divine providence. It is a must for Jesus to remain in heaven for a while.

Thus, Acts 3:21 could be understood as, "By God's will, heaven must retain Jesus until the end of the time in which both Jews and Gentiles obtain their salvation that God proclaimed by the mouth of the holy prophets long ago." The times of refreshing/restoration have begun with the first conversions and continue until the return of Jesus.[103]

Summary

This section can be summarized as follows. First, both plural forms, καιροί and χρόνοι, refer to a period of time. The two phrases "Times of refreshing" (καιροὶ ἀναψύξεως) and "times of restoration" (χρόνων ἀποκαταστάσεως) relate to each other. They both indicate the messianic era in which people can restore their relationship with God by "repenting and turning" from their sins (believing in Jesus). "Times of refreshing" speaks of the time span in which individual acts of repentance of the Jews occur. "Times of restoration" refers to the same messianic era in which all human races (both Jews and Gentiles) can restore their relationship with God by believing Jesus. Whereas "times of refreshing" emphasizes the repentance of the Jews, "times of restoration" stresses the inclusion of Gentiles.

Second, our study also shows that "the times of refreshing" (i.e. the messianic era) have been initiated by the birth and the ministry of Jesus, who has brought the eschatological peace upon the Jews in the Gospel of Luke. "The times of restoration" have also begun and are signified by the inclusion of Gentiles, as is well documented in the book of Acts. "The restoration" refers to the "re-establishment" of the relationship of people with God.

---

102. Charles H. Cosgrove, "The Divine Dei in Luke-Acts: Investigations into the Lukan Understanding of God's Providence," *NovT* 26 (1984): 189–190.

103. Kurz, "Eschatology in Lukan Christology," 310.

Here, it refers to salvation coming upon Gentiles. The "all" refers to all human beings, including "both Jews and Gentiles." The plural form "times" refers to a period of time, and "the restoration of all" will take place for a period of time during which a cluster of events (repentance and turning to God/conversion to Jesus Christ) will occur. "Times of restoration" speaks of present and future events. This is "a period of time and a cluster of events."[104]

Third, the first and second comings of Jesus are both noted in Acts 3:17–26. The temporal marker "these days" (Acts 3:24) indicates the first coming of Jesus and the messianic era he brought in. The second coming of Jesus is also indicated in this passage (Acts 3:20–21). Between the two comings are "the times of refreshing" and "the times of restoration," in which both Jews and Gentiles repent and receive the remission of their sins by believing in Jesus. The events of repentance occur repeatedly until the end of the times, when Jesus comes again. During "the times of refreshing" and "the times of restoration" Jesus remains in heaven and works as the cosmic Lord until the end of this period of time that is the Eschaton.

Peter's speech shows that the salvation of the Jews and of all the people (Gentiles) becomes a present reality that has begun at the first coming of Jesus (the Messiah). The process of the realization of the kingdom of God is ongoing in terms of the repeated events of individual repentance (times of refreshing and times of restoration). This cluster of events will keep happening until the second coming of the Messiah. Next we will examine other eschatological passages in Luke-Acts. First we will take Luke 17:22–37 into consideration.

Luke 17:22–37

Luke 17:22–37 is one of the eschatological passages in Luke-Acts. The text explicitly speaks of the final revelation of the Son of Man (17:30). It is interesting that this passage contains both plural and singular temporal markers, "the days" and "the day." In this section, first we will examine the temporal markers to show that "the days" refers to a period of time and "the day" refers to a decisive point of time. This is in line with our understanding of "the times" and "the time" (Acts 3:20–21) in our earlier study. Then, we

---

104. Bayer, "Eschatology," 247.

will study the phrases "the days of the Son of Man" and "the day of the Son of Man" and will demonstrate that the former refers not only to the earthly time of Jesus, but also to the entire messianic era, whereas the latter refers to the final revelation, the second coming of Jesus.

Temporal Markers

The pattern of the juxtaposition of "the days" (αἱ ἡμέραι) and "the day" (ἡ ἡμέρα) reappears in this passage. We will show that Luke uses "the days" (αἱ ἡμέραι) to refer to *a period of time* and "the day" (ἡ ἡμέρα)" to refer to *a decisive moment*.

"The days" (αἱ ἡμέραι) and "the day" (ἡ ἡμέρα) repeatedly occur in this passage (17:22[x2], 24, 26[x2], 27, 28, 29, 30, 31). Jesus compares "the days of the Son of Man" to "the days of Noah" (Luke 17:26–27) and to "the days of Lot" (Luke 17:28–29). Three points need to be made. First, it is clear that "the days of Noah" and "the days of Lot" express *periods of time*. Second, during the days of Noah, people were "eating and drinking, and marrying and being given in marriage" (Luke 17:27). People were doing their daily activities without paying attention to Noah's preaching. These activities happened repeatedly until a point of time (Luke 17:27). Likewise, in the days of Lot, people follow their daily routine without paying heed to the warning of Lot (Gen 19:12–22). Third, the days of Noah are characterized by the possibility of obtaining deliverance from the flood through Noah's preaching.[105] Unfortunately people did not pay attention to Noah's preaching. Similarly, the days of Lot are characterized by the possibility of being delivered from the fire from heaven by listening to Lot's warning (Gen 19:12–22).

"The Day of the Son of Man" is like "the day of Noah" and "the day of Lot."[106] "The day of Noah" has the following features. First, it is a decisive moment. The day of Noah indicates a decisive point of time. On that day Noah entered his ark (Gen 7:7). Likewise, the day of Lot is also a decisive moment. It refers to the time when Lot left Sodom (Gen 19:22–23). Second, the day of Noah and the day of Lot are signified by unexpected judgments.

---

105. Nolland, *Luke 9:21–18:34*, 698.

106. One may notice that here the verb is ἔσται. The future tense should be understood as a "gnomic future" that expresses "the days of the Son of Man" like "the days of Noah and Lot." Wallace, *Greek Grammar* 571. See also James Hope Moulton, *A Grammar of New Testament Greek, vol. 3: Syntax* (Edinburgh: T&T Clark, 1963), 86.

On the day when Noah entered the ark, the disaster of flood came (Gen 7:11–12). On the day when Lot left Sodom sulfur and fire rained down from heaven upon Sodom (Gen 19:24).

"The days of the Son of Man," like "the days of Noah/Lot," refers to "a period of time." This is the period of time that Jesus lives on earth (Luke 17:26): the birth, ministry, suffering, and resurrection. It also includes the period of the church.[107] "The days of the Son of Man" are also characterized by the possibility of deliverance. During this time span, some people responded to the preaching of Jesus and his followers and thus attained the kingdom of God. But most people failed to pay attention to the preaching of Jesus. In other words, this period of time (the days of the Son of Man) denotes the messianic era.

"The Day of the Son of Man" is "a decisive moment." It is the final revelation of Jesus (17:30). This is the second coming, which is unexpected, sudden, eye-catching, glorious and celestial (17:23–24). "The Day of the Son of Man" refers to the same thing as the second coming of Jesus of Acts 1:11.[108] The Day of the Lord often connotes the Day of Judgment (Isa 39:6; Jer 7:23; Hos 9:7; Amos 4:2).

In the days of the Son of Man, as in the days of Noah and of Lot, events happened and happened up to the decisive point, the day of the Son of Man, or the day of Noah or of Lot. "The days of the Son of Man" refers to the manifestation of the kingdom of God. The second coming of the Son of Man at the end of time is the completion of the kingdom of God.

The temporal marker "the days" refers to a period of time. "The day" means a decisive moment. "The days of the Son of Man" refers to the first coming of Jesus and the subsequent messianic era he brought. "The Day of the Son of Man" refers to the second coming of Jesus.

Linguistically, this study of the plural and singular temporal markers further substantiates our understanding of the plural and singular forms of "time" in Acts 3:20–21. The plural form refers to a period of time in which events occur. The singular form refers to a particular moment at which decisive event happens. Theologically, "the days of the Son of Man," like the

---

107. Green, *The Gospel of Luke*, 632.
108. Fitzmyer, *Luke 10–24*, 1168.

days of Noah and of Lot, corresponds with "the times of refreshment and the times of restoration." "The days of the Son of Man" refers to the messianic era in which the kingdom of God has been realized. "The Day of the Son of Man" refers to the second coming of Jesus (Acts 3:20–21).

The Context of *Luke 17:22–37*

The context concerns the kingdom of God (Luke 17:20–21). Pharisees ask Jesus when the kingdom of God will come. They think that the kingdom of God comes at the end of the times (the day). Jesus corrects them by saying that "the kingdom of God is among you/in you" (17:21). Perceiving that the Pharisees' understanding of the kingdom of God may also be the disciples' understanding, Jesus explains to his disciples about the coming of the kingdom of God (Luke 17:22–37). Jesus uses "the days of the Son of Man" and "the Day of the Son of Man" to show that the kingdom of God comes as "the days of the Son of Man" (the first coming and the ministry of Jesus until the second coming). The climax of the coming of the kingdom of God happens at "the Day of the Son of Man" (the second coming of Jesus)." Luke again employs the pattern of temporal markers to make this point.

Summary

This examination of Luke 17:20–37 shows the following. First, the temporal marker "these days" refers to a period of time like "the days of Noah" and "the days of Lot." The singular form "the day" refers to a decisive moment of time. This supports our understanding of "the times of refreshing" and "the times of restoration." Second, the phrase "the days of the Son of Man" refers to the messianic era. The phrase "the Day of the Son of Man" refers to the second coming of Jesus at the end of time, similar to "the day of Noah" and "the day of Lot." Finally, our study of the context shows that the kingdom of God has been realized at the time of Jesus. In other words, the messianic era has started in the days of the Son of Man. Luke uses the juxtaposition of the plural (the days) and the singular (the day) to refer to the era of salvation and the end of time (the Parousia) respectively.

Luke 21:25–28

Another eschatological discourse in Luke 21:25–28 also resembles the pattern of the plural and singular forms of temporal marker. A couple of points need to be noted.

Temporal Markers

First, the plural form "the days" refers to "a period of time" in which events occur. Luke 21:6 says, "The days will come" (ἐλεύσονται ἡμέραι) "in which not one stone will be left on another; every one of them will be thrown down" (ἐν αἷς οὐκ ἀφεθήσεται λίθος ἐπὶ λίθῳ ὃς οὐ καταλυθήσεται). Luke 21:24 says the destruction of Jerusalem will come "until the times of the Gentiles are fulfilled" (ἄχρι οὗ πληρωθῶσιν καιροὶ ἐθνῶν). In this period of time, serious events will happen to the Gentiles. The singular temporal marker "the time/day" (ὁ καιρός)" refers to the ultimate end. The singulars in 21:8 and 34 refer to the final day (i.e. the Parousia). In Luke 21:8, the singular "the time" (ὁ καιρὸς) refers to the second coming of Jesus though it is a false prediction. In Luke 21:34 "the day" (ἡ ἡμέρα) refers to the ultimate end (the second coming).[109]

Second, it is interesting that Luke uses "the days" (ἡμέραι) and "the times" (καιροί) interchangeably in this eschatological discourse. This is further evidence that "the times" (καιροί) refers to a period of time (Luke 21:6). The interchangeable use of the singular temporal markers "the time" (ὁ καιρὸς) and "the day" (ἡ ἡμέρα) can also be found in this passage. They both refer to the ultimate end of the times (i.e. the second coming of Jesus). Luke 21:8 says, "The time is near" (ὁ καιρὸς ἤγγικεν). "The time" refers to the second coming of the Son of Man.[110] This is the ultimate end.[111] The synoptic parallel in Matthew 24:3–8 speaks of the second coming of the Lord.[112] According to Luke 21:34–35, "that day will close on you unexpectedly like a trap" (ἐπιστῇ ἐφ' ὑμᾶς αἰφνίδιος ἡ ἡμέρα ἐκείνη ὡς παγίς).[113]

---

109. Kurz, "Eschatology in Lukan Christology," 319.
110. Carroll, *Luke*, 416; Bock, *Luke 9:51–24:53*, 1664.
111. Carroll, *Luke*, 416.
112. Osborne, *Matthew*, 866, 871.
113. Nolland, *Luke 18:35–24:53*, 1012; Carroll, *Luke*, 420.

Summary

In sum, a study of Luke 21:25–28 demonstrates the following. First, Luke employs a plural temporal marker (days, times) to refer to a period of time and a singular form to express a moment of time. This supports our understanding of "the times of refreshing" and "the times of restoration." Second, the fact that Luke interchangeably uses "the days" and "the times" to refer "a period of time" further substantiates our understanding of "the times" in Acts 3:20–21. Finally, singular temporal markers refer to the second coming of the Son of Man." Next we will examine another eschatological passage, Acts 2:17–21.

Acts 2:17–21

The Joel quotation (Joel 2:28–32; LXX 3:1–5) in Acts 2:17–21 is programmatic for Lukan eschatology. It is interesting that this eschatological passage again has the plural and singular temporal markers, "the days" and "the day." First, we will study the temporal markers.

Temporal Markers

The Joel quotation in Acts 2:17–21 contains plural and singular temporal markers: "the days" (2:17) and "the day" (2:20). We will show that the plural, "the days," refers to a period of time, while "the day" refers to a decisive point of time.

"The days" appears in the phrase "in the last days" (ἐν ταῖς ἐσχάταις ἡμέραις) (2:17), appended to the beginning of the Joel quotation.[114] The text that follows shows that "the days" refers to a period of time in which God pours his Spirit upon all human beings (2:17). During this period of time "everyone who calls on the name of the Lord will be saved" (ἔσται πᾶς ὃς ἂν ἐπικαλέσηται τὸ ὄνομα κυρίου σωθήσεται) (2:21). In other words, in this period of time every person could obtain salvation. Thus, we see that "the days" refers to the messianic era.

"The day" appears in the phrase "the great and glorious day of the Lord" (ἡμέραν κυρίου τὴν μεγάλην καὶ ἐπιφανῆ) (2:20). Peter is in line with the

---

114. Luke modifies Joel 3:1 (LXX) by replacing μετὰ ταῦτα with ἐν ταῖς ἐσχάταις ἡμέραις for his own theological purposes, as our study will demonstrate.

LXX, which is slightly different from the MT, which refers to the day as "great and terrible." "The great and glorious day of the Lord" refers to the second coming of Jesus (c.f. Luke 17:24 and Acts 1:11).[115] "The day" (ἡ ἡμέρα) refers to a specific day on which Jesus will return.[116] Thus we see that "the day" refers to "a decisive point of time" in which the Parousia occurs. Kurz argues that "the great and glorious day of the Lord" in the Joel quotation (Acts 2:20) equals the sending of Christ at the end of time (Acts 3:20).[117]

This study shows that Luke again uses the juxtaposition of the plural and the singular, "the days" and "the day." "The days" (ἡμέραι) refers to the messianic era during which people could obtain salvation. "The day" (ἡμέρα) is "the decisive moment" in which the second coming of Jesus occurs. This understanding of these temporal markers is again in line with our understanding of the temporal markers in Acts 3:20–21; Luke 17:20–37; 21:25–28. Next, we will demonstrate that "the period of the days" has already started.

The Last Days – Inaugurated

The following points will demonstrate the inauguration of the last days. First, this quotation shows that the present times about which Peter speaks are the last days. The context of the quotation is that Joel urges the people of Israel who will suffer the impending locust disaster to repent; otherwise worse things will happen to them on the day of the Lord. The Joel quotation functions as an OT prophecy fulfilled in the NT.[118] Rese argues that Peter uses this quotation to explain what was happening at Pentecost.[119] In the last days, God will pour out his Spirit on "all flesh" (πᾶσαν σάρκα) regardless of gender, age, and social status (Acts 2:17–18). This is being fulfilled at Pentecost and afterward. This is evidenced in Acts 2:38; 10:44; 11:15–18. The inclusion of Gentiles evidences this point. The "signs" (τέρατα) and

---

115. Barrett, *Acts of the Apostles, vol. 1*, 138.
116. Our following study will provide evidence for this point.
117. Kurz, "Eschatology in Lukan Christology," 309.
118. Bock, *Acts*, 108; Craig A. Evans, "The Prophetic Setting of the Pentecost Sermon," *ZNW* 74 (1983): 213–225; Schnabel, *Acts*, 133.
119. Martin Rese, *Alttestamentliche Motive in der Christologie des Lukas* (Gutersloh: Gerd Mohn, 1969), 45–55; Robert B. Sloan, ""Signs and Wonders" : A Rhetorical Clue to the Pentecost Discourse," *EvQ* 63 (1991): 225–240.

"wonders" (σημεῖα) have been fulfilled in the ministry of Jesus and in his death (Acts 2:19). The cosmic signs, "the darkness of the sun and the blood of the moon," have happened during the death of Jesus (Luke 23:44–45).[120] "The cloud of smoke" and "the fire" denote the manifestation of God on Mount Sinai (Exod 19:18). The phenomenon that occurs at Pentecost suggests a theophany on the day of Pentecost (Acts 2:20).[121] All these things happen "before the great and glorious day of the Lord comes" (πρὶν ἐλθεῖν ἡμέραν κυρίου τὴν μεγάλην καὶ ἐπιφανῆ) (Acts 2:20). This is the day of the second coming of Jesus. Peter finally proclaims his major concern that "everyone who calls on the name of the Lord will be saved" (καὶ ἔσται πᾶς ὃς ἂν ἐπικαλέσηται τὸ ὄνομα κυρίου σωθήσεται) (Acts 2:21). "The Lord" is Jesus Christ. The term "everyone" (πᾶς) emphasizes the availability of salvation to the entire human race. The context makes this point clear (Acts 2:17–18, 21, 39). That salvation is for all is one of Luke's theological concerns in Luke-Acts as we have already shown (cf. Luke 2:31; 3:6; Acts 3:21; 10:44).

Second, a feature of the last days is the opportunity to obtain salvation through repentance. The theme of repentance prevails in Acts 2. In Peter's Pentecost speech, this term repeatedly appears and refers to all the people. "God says, I will pour out my Spirit on all people" (λέγει ὁ θεός, ἐκχεῶ ἀπὸ τοῦ πνεύματός μου ἐπὶ πᾶσαν σάρκα). Acts 2:21 further confirms the reading. It says, "And everyone who calls on the name of the Lord will be saved" (καὶ ἔσται πᾶς ὃς ἂν ἐπικαλέσηται τὸ ὄνομα κυρίου σωθήσεται). The term πᾶς refers to all human beings. "All the house of Israel" (πᾶς οἶκος Ἰσραὴλ) (Acts 2:36) refers to all the people of Israel. Acts 2:39 says, "The promise is for you and your children and for all who are far off – for all whom the Lord our God will call" (ὑμῖν γάρ ἐστιν ἡ ἐπαγγελία καὶ τοῖς τέκνοις ὑμῶν καὶ πᾶσιν τοῖς εἰς μακράν, ὅσους ἂν προσκαλέσηται κύριος ὁ θεὸς ἡμῶν).

One more point needs to be made. "The last days" have not been started at the outpouring of the Holy Spirit, which is a prominent sign of the last days. Schnabel rightly asserts, "Peter links the last days not with the coming of the Holy Spirit but with the entire ministry of Jesus. This was a common early Christian conviction that was often expressed: the ministry, death,

---

120. Bock, *Acts*, 116.
121. Schnabel, *Acts*, 139.

resurrection, and ascension of Jesus, the Messiah and Savor, with the climax of the coming of the Spirit on Pentecost, constitute the beginning of the final epoch in history when God has acted in a decisive manner to bring salvation through his Son."[122]

Therefore, we see that for Luke "in the last days" (ἐν ταῖς ἐσχάταις ἡμέραις) God fulfills his promise of salvation to human beings through Jesus. The last days have begun with Jesus. As both Annette Steudel and J. J. Collins have demonstrated from their study of this motif in early Jewish literature, the end of days is most often described as a time of testing as well as a time of incipient salvation or restoration for Israel.[123] "The last days" (αἱ ἐσχάται ἡμέραι) (2:17) have already been inaugurated in the coming of Jesus and his ministry and suffering, resurrection and ascension.[124] "The days" (αἱ ἡμέραι) refers to the messianic era. "The coming of the great and glorious day of the Lord" (ἐλθεῖν ἡμέραν κυρίου τὴν μεγάλην καὶ ἐπιφανῆ) (Acts 2:20) refers to the second coming of Jesus (c.f. Luke 17:24 and Acts 1:11).[125]

Kurz argues that the time of the sending of the Christ (Acts 3:20) is the final event, described as the day of the Lord in Joel's quotation (Acts 2:20). Luke employs the singular and plural forms of ἡμέρα in the Joel quotation in the following way. Luke juxtaposes the plural and singular forms to show that multiple events lead up to the end. For Luke, the programmatic Joel quotation distinguishes the plural – for the series of events and prolonged time span leading up to the end and cosmic occurrences (Acts 2:17–20a) – from the singular – for the ultimate Day of the Lord (Acts 2:20b), which will occur in a definitive way at their end.[126]

---

122. Ibid., 135.

123. Michael E. Fuller, *The Restoration of Israel: Israel's Re-gathering and the Fate of the Nations in Early Jewish Literature and Luke-Acts,* BZNW 138 (Berlin: de Gruyter, 2006), 261.

124. Schnabel, *Acts*, 139.

125. Barrett, *Acts of the Apostles, vol. 1*, 138.

126. Kurz, "Eschatology in Lukan Christology," 309–310. D. L. Tiede argues that "today," the temporal marker of Jesus's teaching in Luke 4:21 (cf. 19:9; 23:43) introduces the beginning of the fulfillment of the messianic era. Tiede observes that "today" is a catchword for Lukan eschatology that has been realized in Jesus and extended to human history. See David L. Tiede, *Prophecy and History in Luke-Acts* (Philadelphia: Fortress, 1980), 39–55.

Summary

In sum, our study of the programmatic Joel 3:1–5 (LXX) quotation in Acts 2:17–21 demonstrates the following. First, Luke employs the temporal markers "the days" to depict the messianic era, during which many events of repentance occur. Luke uses "the day" to refer to the end of the times, at which Jesus will come again (i.e. the Parousia). This is in line with our understanding of the temporal markers in Acts 3:17–26; Luke 17:22–37 and 21:25–28. Second, for Luke "the days" are the last days that have been inaugurated in the coming of salvation to human beings. The pouring out of the Holy Spirit is one of the signs of the last days. Luke juxtaposes the plural and singular forms to depict that multiple events lead up to the end and to depict the end itself. Third, the Joel quotation also shows that the eschatological salvation is for "all flesh" (2:17). Salvation comes to the Jews first and then to the Gentiles. This corresponds with "the times of refreshment" and "the times of restoration" (3:20–21). The period of salvation will be accompanied by events of repentance until the end of time, at which the second coming of Jesus occurs.

Conclusion

In this chapter, we have studied the programmatic passage, Acts 3:21, and other related passages (Luke 17:20–37; Luke 21:25–28 and Acts 2:17–21). Our study shows the following.

First, the singular forms καιρός and χρόνος refer to a certain point of time. The plural forms καιροί and χρόνοι refer to a period of time. The term ἀνάψυξις refers to the rebuilding of relationships with God. The related phrase, "times of refreshing" (καιροὶ ἀναψύξεως), means "a period of time of salvation." The term ἀποκαταστάσεως refers to deliverance or liberation from sins. In this context, it refers to the salvation of God brought about by Jesus Christ. The phrase "times of restoration" (χρόνων ἀποκαταστάσεως) is a period of time of salvation. Linguistically, "times of refreshing" (καιροὶ ἀναψύξεως) and "times of restoration" (χρόνων ἀποκαταστάσεως) have no fundamental distinction. They both refer to the messianic era. These two phrases do have their own theological emphases. The former expresses the salvation of the people of Israel, while the latter the salvation of all human beings, stressing the inclusion of Gentiles.

Second, our study demonstrates that the salvation era (times of refreshment/restoration) has already started with acts of repentance and conversion to Jesus Christ. The refreshment/restoration is a process instead of a certain event. Salvation (eschatological peace) has come first upon the covenant people, as evidenced in Luke's gospel and also in the book of Acts, and then upon the Gentiles. The order of the salvation of Jews first and then Gentiles has been indicated in the Gospel of Luke and has been well documented in the book of Acts. The Israelites have the first privilege; they also have the first responsibility for their response to the offer of salvation.[127] During the period of time (times of refreshment and times of restoration) the event of repentance of individual Jews and Gentiles occurs again and again. The events of repentance have happened in the past, are happening now and will be happen in the future.

Third, the first and second comings of Jesus are both expressed in Acts 3:17–26. The overall message of Peter's speech at Solomon's portico evidences the first coming of Jesus. This is prophesied in time past and has been now realized (Acts 3:22–26). The second coming of Jesus has been indicated in Acts 3:20–21. Heaven will keep Jesus until the end of the restoration of both Jews and Gentiles who shall obtain salvation.

Fourth, the reference to heaven in Acts 3:21 recalls the heaven references in the Ascension narratives (Luke 24:51 and Acts 1:9–11). The exalted Jesus co-reigns with God the Father in heaven. Heaven has been anthropomorphized. Heaven is not a static place; rather, it is dynamic. The Lukan use of the verb δεῖ suggests that heaven's keeping of Jesus is by divine determination.

Our study of Luke 17:22–37 shows the following. First, the temporal marker "these days" refers to a period of time but the singular form, "the day," refers to a decisive moment of time. Luke juxtaposes the plural and singular forms to show (1) that multiple events lead up to the end and (2) the end itself. This is in line with our understanding of the temporal markers in Acts 3:17–26. Second, the phrase "the days of the Son of Man" refers to the messianic era. This corresponds to the phrases, "the times of refreshing"

---

127. Bruce, *The Acts of the Apostles*, 146.

and "the times of restoration." The phrase "the Day of the Son of Man" refers to the second coming of Jesus at the end of time. Finally, our study of the context shows that the kingdom of God has been realized at the time of Jesus. In other words, the messianic era has started in the days of the Son of Man. This reading is also harmonious with our understanding of the already-inaugurated "times of refreshing/restoration."

Our study of Luke 21:25–28 demonstrates the following. First, Luke employs the plural temporal markers, "the days," and "the times," to refer to a period of time. He uses the singular form, "the time" or "the day," to express a decisive moment of time. This supports our understanding of "the times of refreshing" and "the times of restoration." Second, the fact that Luke interchangeably uses "the days" and "the times" to refer a period of time further substantiates our understanding of "the times" in Acts 3:20–21. Finally, the singular temporal marker, "the time" or "the day" refers to the second coming of Jesus.

Our study of the Joel quotation in Acts 2:17–21 demonstrates the following. First, Luke again uses a plural temporal reference (ἡμέραι) to express a period of time and the singular form (ἡμέρα) to designate the ultimate end. This further supports our reading of the temporal markers in Acts 3:17–26. The plural "times" refers to a period of time during which the events of repentance occur until the ultimate end. Second, for Luke "the days" are the last days that have been inaugurated in the coming of salvation upon human beings. The outpouring of the Holy Spirit is one of the signs of the last days. Luke juxtaposes the plural form – to show that multiple events lead up to the end – and the singular form for this end.

The χρόνοι and the καιροί have begun at the conversions of Jews first and then Gentiles. This is the messianic era that is inaugurated by the first coming of Jesus. The event of repentance happens again and again. The occurrences of conversion gradually reach their definitive completion and lead up to the final return of Jesus at the end point.[128] Heaven will keep Jesus for a certain period of time during which Jewish and Gentile individuals obtain their salvation. "The sending of the Christ will occur at the end of

---

128. Kurz, "Eschatology in Lukan Christology," 310–311.

the times of fulfillment/restoration, as their definitive climax."[129] But the text of Acts 3:20–21 does not give any hint of the length of time of Jesus's stay in heaven before the Parousia.[130]

The kingdom of God has been manifested on earth but has not yet been fully accomplished. The ultimate end is yet to come.

Excursus: Lukan Eschatology

The term "eschatology" is ambiguous in that it may refer to events during the last days of the present age or to events occurring at the Parousia. No consensus has yet been reached on the use of the term eschatology. This lack of clarity lies primarily in the relationship between the etymology of the word and the theology of the New Testament texts. The phrase τὰ ἔσχατα refers to "the last things," while eschatology is the study of the last things.

A narrow definition of eschatology confines it only to the Parousia. For Carroll, the eschaton is "the final consummation of God's plan and the end of history."[131] A broad definition leads to a more nuanced discussion of eschatological themes in New Testament theology. Anders Eyvind Nielsen takes an exegetical approach.[132] For Nielsen, the term "eschatology" must be reserved to a greater degree for a quality definition rather than a time definition, thus avoiding a chronological fixing of the concept. He applies a wide-ranging definition that covers "the meeting between God's eternity and man's temporality, between God's future and man's present."[133] This definition allows a functional feature of apocalyptic eschatology, namely the meeting between God's eternity and man's temporality, between God's future

---

129. Ibid.

130. Gerhard Schneider, *Die Apostelgeschichte 1: Einleitung, Kommentar zu Kap 1,1–8,40* (Fribourg, Switzerland: Herder, 1980), 336–337.

131. John T. Carrol, *Response to the End of History: Eschatology and Situation in Luke-Acts,* SBLDS 92 (Decatur: Scholars, 1988), 87–94. There are four issues associated with the eschatology: the timing of the eschatological program; the content of it – what did Luke expect to happen, and to whom – an individual or cosmic scope of salvation; the destiny of Israel, of unbelieving Jews or Gentile believers (the nature of judgment and restoration); and the significance of the eschaton – what is the weight of the eschatological program and its completion in Luke-Acts. The fourth is the situation of eschatology in Luke's total perspective.

132. Anders Eyvind Nielsen, *Until It Is Fulfilled: Lukan Eschatology according to Luke 22 And Acts 20,* WUNT 2.126 (Tübingen: Mohr Siebeck, 2000).

133. Ibid., 25.

and man's present. In this context the horizontal transcendent moment as collective eschatology, and the vertical moment as individual eschatology, do not necessarily exclude one another.

Review of Scholarship

Temporal Approaches

In general, scholarship on Lukan eschatology could be classified into two main groups: temporal (horizontal) and spatial (vertical) approaches. Most Lukan scholars focus on the temporal aspect. There are subgroups within this group. First is the Bultmann camp that argued for an un-eschatological Luke. Leading scholars were Hans Conzelmann, E. Käsemann, and E. Haenchen.[134] Bultmann argued that the author of Luke-Acts had no interest in eschatology since he wrote the book of Acts as the sequence of his Gospel. Along this line, students of Bultmann launched and promoted the un-eschatological Luke. P. Vielhauer argued that, judging by the fact of Acts, it is apparent that Luke's concern was un-eschatological. Käsemann spoke more clearly that Luke did not possess any vital interest in the eschatological hope (the Parousia).[135] It was Hans Conzelmann who detected "the Parousia problem" and provided a more coherent and consistent thesis that the imminent eschatological hope gave way to salvation history. Luke moved the eschaton to a distant future. Luke replaced the Parousia with the Holy Spirit. Conzelmann's position remains the best known and the one against which others are offered. Was the delay of the Parousia a significant problem for Luke's church? In response to Conzelmann, others suggested that "eschatology in Luke cannot so easily be relegated to an appendix. The End, though postponed, is not dismissed; history is not unaffected by eschatology; and the kingdom, though transcendent, already exerts its influence over history. In truth, Luke's eschatology is more complicated than Conzelmann allows."[136]

---

134. Haenchen, in his magisterial commentary of Acts of the Apostles, based on Acts 1:9–12, argued that the apostles were forbidden to stare at heaven "because it expresses the imminent expectation." Luke opposed the imminent Parousia hope and advocated a "new form of the Christian hope, which renounced all dating of the Parousia." See Haenchen, *Acts*, 150, 152.

135. Ernst Käsemann, *Essays on New Testament Themes*, SBT (Naperville: Alec R Allenson, 1964), 15–57.

136. Franklin, *Christ the Lord*, 11–12.

The second subgroup, represented by F. O. Francis, A. J. Mattill, John Carroll and others, advocated a consistent imminent eschatology.[137] Francis studied Acts 2:16–21 (Joel 3:1–5 [LXX]) and Luke 21, and argued that the eschaton will come speedily though not immediately.[138] Francis understood the coming of the kingdom of God as the second coming of Jesus.[139] There is a paradox between history and eschatology.[140] France emphasized the temporal aspect of eschatology. A. J. Mattill argued that there is evidence of an imminent expectation in Acts 17:31: "He has fixed a day on which he will judge the world in righteousness by a man whom he has appointed." Mattill insisted that the phrase "he will judge" indicates that the judgment is imminent.[141] Mattill's conclusion was that Luke-Acts was written "for the purpose of effecting the immediate end." Luke fervently desired the fulfillment of the kingdom, but he was convinced that the eschaton could not come about until the completion of the world mission. Thus, he wrote in order to urge the early completion of the mission. "It may even be that Luke had hopes of bringing about the day of the Lord ahead of schedule."[142]

Within this subgroup, John T. Carroll also argued for an imminent eschatology. What is different from Conzelmann with regard to the delay issue for Carroll is that "delay does not oppose but undergirds expectation of an imminent End in Luke's own situation."[143] Luke correlates eschatological claims with believers' present manner of life.[144] Carroll modifies Conzelmann's thesis as follows: first he accepts that Luke tones down his eschatology that was inaugurated for Jesus's audience, that is, in Luke's past.

---

137. A. J. Mattill, "Naherwartung, Fernerwartung, and the Purpose of Luke-Acts: Weymouth Reconsidered," *CBQ* 34 (1972): 276–293. Mattill argued that the imminent hope dominated Luke's eschatological perspective. R. H. Smith also argued that Luke emphasized the imminent hope. Robert H. Smith, "Eschatology of Acts and Contemporary Exegesis," *CTM* 29 (1958): 641–663. Robert H. Smith, "History and Eschatology in Luke-Acts," *CTM* 29 (1958): 881–901.

138. Fred O. Francis, "Eschatology and History in Luke-Acts," *JAAR* 37 (1969): 55, 58–59.

139. Ibid., 61.

140. Ibid., 62.

141. A. J. Mattill, *Luke and the Last Things: A Perspective for the Understanding of Lukan Thought* (Dillsboro, NC: Western North Carolina Press, 1979), 44–51.

142. Ibid., 233.

143. Carrol, *The End of History*, 166.

144. Ibid., 167.

For Carroll, Luke makes Jesus tone down the *Naherwartung* for his audience in order to actualize it for the audience in the evangelist's own time. "The crucial moment for eschatology is the present time of response to Jesus, of the summons to repentance and to a faithful, vigilant manner of life."[145] "Chronology remains a matter of the freedom and prerogative of God."[146] Carroll's view has been criticized for insisting on a fixated chronological view of eschatology.[147]

In the middle ground between the first and second subgroups is the third subgroup. Scholars like S. G. Wilson proposed a two-strand, two-document, and two-stage eschatology. In Luke's gospel there are passages governed by the delay of the Parousia (Luke 9:27; 19:11, 41–42; 21:20–24; and 22:69). However, there are other passages supporting the imminent expectation (Luke 10:9–11; 12:38–40, 41–48; 12:54–13:9; 18:8; and 21:32). Thus Wilson finds a dual situation that requires Luke to offer a dual response. In this camp, the temporal aspect of eschatology was also the focus.

Fourth, H. Farrell examined several passages (Luke 1–2; 4:16–30; 9:27; 17:20–21; and Acts 2:16) and argued that "the present realization of the kingdom of God in Jesus and the church is the dominant motif in Luke's thought."[148] Farrell followed the thesis proposed by Conzelmann that the delay of the Parousia motivated Luke to write Luke-Acts. Farrell seems to have followed Wilson in suggesting that Luke fought "a battle on two fronts." There was the false teaching that the End was imminent or immediate. In response to this Luke clarified that the Parousia has yet to come, even though it is imminent. Farrell's view of Lukan eschatology was similar to Dodd's, which we will discuss later. Farrell followed the temporal line while ignoring passages with spatial concerns.

Maddox also advocated a realized eschatology of Luke. From the presence of the Holy Spirit, the terminology of fulfillment and the concepts of judgment and salvation, he argued that eschatology is already a present reality.[149]

---

145. Ibid., 163–164.
146. Ibid., 165.
147. Nielsen, *Until It Is Fulfilled*, 15.
148. H. Farrell, "The Eschatological Perspective of Luke-Acts" (Ph.D. dissertation, Boston: Boston University, 1972). 86–87.
149. Maddox, *The Purpose*, 137–145.

Maddox defined eschatology as the kingdom of God. The future consummation was a prominent and lively hope for Paul, Mark and Matthew, but for Luke and John, the kingdom of God was "already a present reality."[150] Maddox touched on one spatial account in Acts 2:1–13 for his argument that the descending of the Holy Spirit was a "last day" event, but he neglected the role of Jesus and the defeat of Satan in Lukan eschatology. As such, Maddox' treatment of eschatology was far from sufficient.[151] Maddox left other spatial passages unexamined.[152]

Another advocate of realized eschatology is C. H. Dodd. Dodd used his eschatology as the basis for interpreting the parables.[153] Conversely, he tested the validity of his realized eschatology by his interpretation of parables. Dodd argued that "the Kingdom of God was proclaimed as a present fact, which human beings must recognize, whether by their actions they accept or reject it."[154] His argument was based on Mark 1:14–15. For Dodd, the perfect verb ἤγγικεν means "to reach" or "to arrive". This verb is no different than the aorist verb ἔφθασεν in Matthew 12:28 and its parallel, Luke 21:20. Both indicate the "arrival" of something expected. We should translate these verses, "The Kingdom of God has come."[155] This reality did not depend on any condition. This contrasts the opinion of the Jews who held that the observance of the Torah is required for one's entrance into the kingdom.[156] Dodd used Luke 10:9–11, 23–24 (the certainty that the kingdom has come) to support his argument.[157] The kingdom was eschatological and had come in Jesus himself.[158] This reality was present regardless of its rejection or acceptance by human beings. Jesus's disciples have seen and heard that the kingdom is here (Luke 11:31–32 and Matt 12:41–42) – the something

---

150. Ibid., 137.

151. Maddox discuss the descending of the Holy Spirit in less than three pages. See ibid., 137–139.

152. Passages like "the birth of Jesus (Luke 2:1–20); "the descending of the Holy Spirit" (Luke 3:21–22; Acts 2:1–13)."

153. The title of his book indicates this point. C. H. Dodd, *The Parables of the Kingdom* (London: Nisbet, 1935).

154. Ibid., 44.

155. Ibid.

156. Ibid., 41–42.

157. Ibid., 45.

158. Ibid.

greater is indeed the kingdom of God that the prophets and kings longed to see. "The eschaton has moved from the future to the present, from the sphere of expectation into that of realized experience."[159] "The kingdom of God" language represents the ministry of Jesus as realized eschatology.[160]

Like many scholars, Dodd took Matthew 12:28 as a key passage.[161] One passage was privileged arbitrarily; other texts were interpreted in accordance with it. Arguments based on one passage are insufficient. Dodd confined his study to the Gospel of Luke. He neglected the second volume of the Lukan writings. One wonders whether passages in Acts would be informative for Lukan eschatology. Dodd's understanding (and definition) of the kingdom of God seems to confine the expression to too narrow a sense. He failed to deal with others aspects, such as the eschatological spirit, the restoration of Israel, the inclusion of Gentiles and the judgment. After all, the aim of the study of eschatology (the kingdom of God) was for the purpose of his understanding of the parables. Dodd did not provide a coherent and comprehensive understanding of Lukan eschatology.

The fifth subgroup is a corrective to over-realized eschatology. C. H. Talbert was one of a few scholars who did not follow the delay of the Parousia thesis proposed by Conzelmann. He detected another problem in Luke's church that eschatology was over-emphasized – a kind of Gnostic understanding of eschatology. Some in Luke's church were misinterpreting Jesus's words (Luke 17:20–21) to underscore the claim to have experienced the eschaton now. For Luke the question was not the delay of the Parousia, rather the heretic pressure of over-realized eschatology.[162] There was an erroneous perception that the ascension was the Parousia and/or that the decent of the

---

159. Ibid., 50. The realization of the kingdom of God is at present in Jesus's saying, "The blind see, the lame walk, the lepers are cleansed, the deaf hear, the dead are raised, the poor have the Gospel preached to them" (Luke 7:22–23). Also see Mark 9:1, "There are some of those standing here who will not taste death until they have seen that the Kingdom has come with power." Matt 8:11 and Luke 13:28–29 are also relevant "Many will come from east and west and sit at meat with Abraham, Isaac and Jacob in the kingdom of God."

160. Ibid., 51.

161. Schweitzer took Mark 1:14 as his key passage and W. G. Kümmel took Mark 9:1 as his key passage.

162. Charles H. Talbert, "Redaction Critical Quest for Luke the Theologian," *Perspective* 11 (1970): 173–174.

Holy Spirit was the Parousia.[163] Talbert defined eschatology as the second coming of Jesus (i.e. the Parousia). He identified the kingdom of God with the Parousia.[164] He seems to have been in dialogue only with Conzelmann, but his detection of a heretical problem lacks convincing evidence. He has likely gone too far to say that some in Luke's church took Luke 17:20–21 to underscore their now-realized eschatology.[165] Passages that contain the final consummation should also be taken into consideration. Like many others, Talbert followed the temporal approach and overlooked the heaven passages.

Spatial Approaches

The other group of scholars examined the spatial aspect of Lukan eschatology. Scholars like H. Flender and E. Franklin focused on the ascension as the center of Luke's eschatology.

Helmut Flender asserted that "[t]he real problem exercising the community was not the continuation of time, but the certainty of Christ's final victory."[166] Conzelmann took the delay of the Parousia as the historical key to Luke's writings, and a theological reflection on the meaning of history (issuing in a three-period scheme) as its result. Flender picked up the exaltation of Christ to be the key to Luke's Christology and eschatology. For Flender, there was a shift of weight from the Parousia to ascension. "Functions previously assigned to Christ at the Parousia are transferred to the exaltation . . . For Luke exaltation and Parousia are identical, Jesus's goal is achieved with his exaltation. The Parousia is the manifestation on earth of the Lordship into which Jesus has entered in heaven."[167] Luke emphasized the importance of the exaltation of Christ for his theology. Flender argued that "in it the Parousia becomes as it were a reality in heaven, the already completed event of salvation."[168] The eschatology was realized with the exaltation of Jesus and "the days of the Son of Man" refer to the exaltation of Jesus." Thus Luke 17:22ff is the description of the ascension.[169] For Flender, "Christ, now en-

---

163. Ibid., 173–176.
164. Ibid., 173, 176, 180.
165. Ibid., 179–181.
166. Flender, *Theologian of Redemptive History*
167. Ibid., 95–96, 99, 94, note 3.
168. Ibid., 106.
169. Ibid., 95.

throned in haven, keeps alive the expectation of his coming on earth."[170] The spatial juxtaposition of earth and heaven encompasses the temporal aspect of eschatology.[171] Flender focused on the ascension of Christ and his attention to the spatial aspect is refreshing. However, his study of eschatology that was based on only two passages (Luke 19:38; Acts 1:9–11) is insufficient. One may question whether there are any other passages that contain spatial aspects that would contribute to his eschatology. The second problem is his definition of eschatology; for Flender, it seems that the word "eschatology" is a synonym of "exaltation" or "ascension" or "Parousia." What is the role of the Holy Spirit in Lukan eschatology? Where is there room for the birth of Jesus in eschatology? Third, "eschatology" for Flender is stripped of any temporal considerations. It is true that Luke emphasizes the spatial aspect of eschatology; however, Luke does not exclude the temporal aspect.[172]

Conclusion

The foregoing review of Lukan scholarship on eschatology shows the following. First, there is no consensus on the definition of eschatology. Eschatology is identified with the Parousia (Conzelmann, Carroll, Francis, Wilson), the kingdom of God (Farrell, Maddox, Dodd, Talbert), the encounter between the eternal God and human beings (Anders) or the Ascension (Flender, Franklin). Second, two camps could be drawn based on the focus on temporal or spatial aspects. For the temporal camp, the Parousia was moved to the distant future (un-eschatological: Conzelmann, Käsemann, Haenchen and other followers of Conzelmann); the Parousia was imminent, though not necessarily immediate (imminent eschatology: Francis); or the Parousia was already realized (the present fulfillment eschatology: Farrell, Maddox, Dodd [the kingdom of God]; Flender and Franklin [the ascension]). For the spatial camp, Flender and Franklin focused on the vertical aspect, emphasizing the ascension of Jesus.

For the many who have investigated Lukan eschatology from a temporal perspective, the main issue for Luke is the delay of the Parousia. Only a few

---

170. Ibid., 99.

171. Ibid., 61–62, note 6.

172. The individual eschatology: J. Dupont and G. Schneider. Maddox provided a helpful discussion on this issue. He argued that the idea of "individual eschatology" in not unique to Luke. See Maddox, *The Purpose*, 103–105.

scholars focused on the spatial dimension (Flender, Franklin, Maddox). Among them, Flender and Franklin examined the ascension narrative of Jesus and emphasized the pivotal role of the ascended Jesus in Lukan eschatology. Maddox took another spatial passage (the descent of the Holy Spirit) and studied the eschatology of Luke-Acts. The shift from temporal to spatial is promising, and their studies are insightful.

The significance of the present project lies in the fact that eschatology has not yet been fully discussed through an examination of the heaven motif. This project therefore also contributes to the study of Lukan eschatology. While not overlooking the spatial aspect of the reference to heaven, Luke focuses on temporal aspect. Heaven points to the arrival of God's eschatological kingdom on earth (i.e. the inauguarated eschatology). A few comments are in order, then, regarding the definition of eschatology, the timing of eschatology and its completion, the significance of eschatology and the *Sitz im Leben* of Luke.

First, the *definition* of eschatology in this project is the intrusion of heaven onto earth, inaugurating the kingdom of God upon earth (i.e. the presence of the eschatological kingdom of God on earth). Lukan eschatology focuses more on content: the interrelationship between heaven and earth that deals with the progression of the realization of the kingdom of God on earth, the salvation of the people of Israel and of the Gentiles, and the Parousia.

Second, the *timing* of eschatology and its completion is as follows. Jesus, the heavenly glory, by his birth (i.e. his first coming) has brought the eschatological peace to earth and thus initiated the eschatological kingdom of God on earth. The manifestation of the eschatological kingdom of God on earth signifies the beginning of "the last days." Luke does not provide any hint of how long heaven will hold Jesus (Acts 3:21) until his final return (i.e. his second coming). Rather, Luke focuses more on the progression of the realization of the kingdom of God on earth than the end of the times (i.e. the eschaton).

Third, the *significance* of eschatology is as follows. Luke has presented a realized eschatology. The last days have already been inaugurated. The kingdom of God has been manifested on earth, but it has not yet been fully accomplished. The ultimate end is yet to come. Luke put more weight on the individual repentance of both Jews and Gentiles (the restoration of all human beings) than on the Parousia.

Finally, we will comment on the *Sitz im Leben* of Luke. Was there a problem of the delay of the Parousia? Has the Parousia been delayed? The answer is probably "no," since there is no explicit evidence in Luke-Acts that Jesus was expected to return soon and so had to postpone his return. From the perspective of heaven, when Jesus was on earth he did his ministry and after his suffering he was resurrected and, more importantly, he ascended into heaven and was exalted. The heavenly-exalted Jesus is the cosmic Lord. He seems to be absent from earth but actually presents himself everywhere in the cosmos. He combines heaven and earth together. His followers in some way represent his presence on earth. While not denying the second coming of Jesus, Luke puts more weight on the materialization of the kingdom of God on earth. For Luke, the physical appearance of Jesus (i.e. the second coming gives way to his cosmic existence).

CHAPTER 6

Summary and Conclusion

Summary

In chapter 1 we demonstrated that Luke uses heaven language frequently in his two-volume work. More importantly, Luke places the references to heaven in crucial narratives in Luke-Acts, including the narratives of the birth of Jesus (Luke 2:8–21), the fall of Satan (Luke 10:17–20), the ascension (Luke 24:50–53 and Acts 1:9–11), Peter's speech in Solomon's Portico (Acts 3:11–26), the vision of Stephen (Acts 7:55–57), the vision of Paul (Acts 9:1–9, and 22:6–16; 26:12–18), and the vision of Peter (Acts 10:9–16 and 11:4–10). Our study also demonstrated that the heaven motif runs throughout the entire Lukan narrative and that Luke employed this heaven motif for his theological purposes. The review of scholarly literature demonstrated that the heaven motif in the Lukan corpus has not yet been examined, partially impoverishing Lukan scholarship, especially in regard to Luke's presentation of salvation history.

In chapter 2 we examined the first programmatic passage, Luke 2:14. Our study has demonstrated that the heaven motif and the peace motif exist in Luke 2:14. The peace motif in Luke-Acts is actually the outworking of this programmatic passage. The heaven motif is therefore expressed by the peace motif. The glory of God in heaven is manifested on earth through various means. First, the birth of Jesus signifies the invasion of the heavenly glory on earth (Luke 2:14; 1:78–79; 2:29–32). The purpose of this invasion is to bring the eschatological peace to earth. Those who reject the heavenly glory are therefore rejecting this eschatological peace (Luke 19:38) and as such will be judged. Second, the heavenly glory is made manifest by this eschatological peace on earth among the Jews in the healing ministries of Jesus (Luke 7:50 and 8:48), thus signifying the presence of this heavenly glory on earth. Third, the heavenly glory is also expressed by this peace in the ministries of the disciples of Jesus (Luke 10:5–6), which stress the spread of the heavenly glory on earth among more people. Fourth, the heavenly glory is materialized by peace on earth, where Jews and Samaritans have been reunited, thus signifying the restoration of the nation Israel (Acts 9:31). Finally, the heavenly glory is manifested on earth by peace among Gentiles, highlighting the inclusion of the Gentiles and thus stressing the ecclesiological implications (Acts 10:36).

The heavenly hymn concerns "heaven" and "earth." It introduces the heaven motif and the peace motif. The glory of the highest heaven has been manifested on earth by the eschatological peace/salvation. Heavenly glory brings the eschatological peace down to earth.

In chapter 3 we investigated the second programmatic passage, Luke 10:18. Our study demonstrated the following. First, Satan's fall from heaven is an actual event. Second, Jesus saw the fall of Satan from heaven when his disciples were performing exorcisms. Third, the fall of Satan from heaven symbolizes the victory of God in heaven. The power of God has overcome Satan in heaven and its impact is well felt on earth. Fourth, each act of exorcising is a lethal attack on Satan and his dominion and is a sign from heaven (i.e. an event of Satan's fall from heaven), thus signifying the victory of God in heaven, the impact of which on earth is the realization of the eschatological kingdom of God. The heaven reference here points to the victory of God in heaven.

In chapter 4 we examined the ascension narratives (Luke 24:50–51; Acts 1:9–11). Out study has demonstrated the following. First, the ascension of Jesus projects to yet another stage of Luke's narrative: the exaltation of Jesus. Heaven here points to the exaltation of the cosmic Lord. The heavenly-exalted Jesus has challenged Saul (Acts 9:1–9; 22:6–16; and 26:12–18), the opponent of the Christian movement, and changed him to be a gospel bearer to preach the kingdom of God to both Jews and Gentiles. The heavenly-exalted Lord has also challenged Peter (Acts 10:9–16; 11:4–10), who has the notion of excluding the Gentiles, to preach the kingdom of God to the Gentiles. The challenge of the cosmic lord to Saul and Peter concerns the realization of the kingdom of God on earth and also stresses the inclusion of Gentiles. The cosmic lord also challenges the idols of the nations (Acts 14:8–18; 17:22–31; and 19:23–41). The anti-idol polemic criticizes idols and calls for people to turn away from idol worship to worship the one true God. The purpose of the anti-idol polemic is for the realization of the kingdom of God on earth.

In chapter 5 our study of the final programmatic passage, Acts 3:21, demonstrated the following. First, "the times of refreshment" and "the times of restoration" refer to a period of salvation (i.e. the messianic era that has been initiated by the first coming of Jesus). The times of refreshment/restoration is characterized by the individual repentance/conversion of Jews and Gentiles. Salvation comes upon Jews first and then Gentiles. During the times of refreshment/restoration, acts of repentance by individual Jews and Gentiles repeatedly occur. Acts of repentance have happened in the past (from the first coming of Jesus Christ), continued (during the ministry of Jesus) and are happening now and will happen in the future (church period) until the second coming of Jesus (the Parousia). The reference to heaven points to the unfulfilled elements of the kingdom of God since heaven is an eschatological/temporal concept, as we demonstrated in previous chapters.

The occurrences of conversion gradually reach their definitive completion and lead up to the final sending of Jesus at the end point. Heaven must keep Jesus for a certain period of time, during which individual Jews and Gentiles obtain their salvation. Heaven will release him at the end of the times of refreshing/restoration, as their definitive climax (Acts 3:20–21). But when will this happen? The text of Acts 3:20–21 does not give any hint of the length of time of Jesus's stay in heaven before the Parousia. The kingdom of God has been manifested on earth, but it has not yet been fully accomplished. The ultimate end is yet to come.

Conclusion

Through an examination of each programmatic passage, its context in Luke-Acts, and a wider background of Second Temple and Graeco-Roman literature, our study demonstrated that heaven is not simply a static place where God is or the symbol of God's power. Heaven is more dynamic for Luke. Heaven has invaded earth by the birth of Jesus (the heavenly glory) and brought the eschatological peace down to earth, thus inaugurating the messianic era on earth. Heaven points to the cosmic warfare over Satan and his forces. Its impact is to bring the eschatological kingdom of God on earth. Heaven is active in that the heavenly-exalted cosmic Lord continues challenging the human opponents and conquering the evil forces in order to materialize the kingdom of God on earth. Heaven is active in that it keeps Jesus until salvation history comes to its fullness (i.e. the number of saved Jews and Gentiles comes to its fullness). Then Heaven will send Jesus for the second coming (the Parousia). Heaven has brought the eschatological kingdom of God down to earth. Heaven continues to materialize the eschatological kingdom of God on earth until the times of its manifestation on earth are fully accomplished.

Implications for the Study of the Lukan Ecclesiology

By examining the heaven motif, this study demonstrated that Luke's ecclesiological concern for all human beings appears at the very beginning of the Lukan narrative. The glory of heaven invades the earth at the birth of Jesus, bringing the eschatological peace on earth to all upon whom God's favor rests. Luke's concern for the salvation to all human beings is indicated in the symbolic mission of the seventy(-two), whose exorcisms cast Satan down from heaven. It is made even more explicit by the heavenly visions of Paul and Peter. Paul has been challenged and turned to be a missionary to bring the gospel to Jews and especially to Gentiles. Peter has been challenged and turned to bring salvation to the first Gentile, Cornelius. The anti-idol polemic further confirms the concern for all human beings. "God commands all people from everywhere to repent" (ὁ θεός παραγγέλλει τοῖς ἀνθρώποις πάντας πανταχοῦ μετανοεῖν), regardless of where they live, in rural Lystra, in highly-civilized Athens, or in the world-renowned Ephesus. Salvation from heaven is about and for all human beings on earth. Luke is concerned with much more than the Roman Empire. Luke has a larger agenda – not only will Jews be saved, but Gentiles will also be saved. The criticism of the idols of the nations (especially idols within the Roman Empire) implies the criticism of the Roman Empire and its emperors.

Implications for the Study of Luke-Acts

In recognizing the heaven motif, this study provides a fresh way to study Luke-Acts. By studying the Lukan redaction of the references to heaven in his gospel, one can discern Luke's own theological concerns. By examining the heaven references in the book of Acts, one can see that Luke carefully places the references to heaven in crucial narratives to bring forth his theological purpose. The references to heaven that appear in the end of the gospel and at the beginning of the book of Acts seamlessly connect the two as a whole literary work. More importantly, the references to heaven which constitute the heaven motif overarch the two-volume work in which Luke presents his main theological concern – salvation history. Applying the perspective of heaven makes Luke different from other ancient historians while Luke follows some of the ancient history conventions.

Implications for Evangelization

Heaven is not a static place but a dynamic one. Heaven provides salvation to human beings. God has gained the victory over Satan in heaven. The resurrected Jesus seems to be absent from the earth, but the heavenly-exalted Jesus is the cosmic Lord. He has cosmic lordship. He is active and continues working in the cosmos. He challenges all the human and demonic opponents for his kingdom's sake. His salvific work continues until the restoration of all human beings who should obtain salvation. Luke provides a "high Christology." The heavenly-exalted Jesus still challenges human obstacles and conquers evil forces to materialize the kingdom of God on earth. Jesus's followers, as the representatives, are partaking in the battle against Satan and his followers. We have been given authority over Satan and his followers. God has won the battle against Satan and his forces, though the ultimate victory has not yet come.

Implications for the Persecuted Church

The heavenly-exalted Jesus is the cosmic Lord. He is in heaven, and he challenges and conquers any opponents, even the unseen evil forces. He can also challenge our present opponents, just as he transforms Paul from a gospel persecutor to a gospel preacher. Earth (Christians) connects to heaven (the heavenly-exalted Jesus). Furthermore, our cosmic Lord is with his followers. Those who persecute the followers of Jesus are actually persecuting the cosmic Lord. As the Lord asked Saul, "why are you persecuting me? (Acts 9:4)." Christians will never ever be alone! We are connected to heaven, though we are still on earth. That heaven is anthropomorphized is meaningful for the persecuted church. Heaven will execute justice for the righteous. Heaven will bring judgment upon the unrighteous.

Implication for Contextualization

In a Chinese context, heaven is always anthropomorphized to provide salvific/rescue actions, mercy and justice. When people are confronted with hard situations, especially the threatening of life, they usually cry, "Heaven, rescue/save me." When people experience miserable circumstances, they kneel down, spread their hands, gaze to heaven and cry, "Heaven, have mercy on me!" When people undergo mistreatment, they cry, "Heaven, execute justice/righteousness!" When an evil person dies, people will say, "The high heaven has eyes, and he punished the evil one who deserved the punishment." When people face disasters such as severe drought, flood, earthquake or hail, people will say, "Heaven punishes since we have sinned." When people swear, they say, "Heaven knows." People try to avoid "cursing words" since we have the notion: "Heaven can hear." The personified heaven is also witnessed by the Temple of Heaven (literally "Altar of Heaven") in Beijing where ancient Emperors in China worshiped once a year to Heaven for good harvest. Heaven is anthropomorphized. This is in line with the Chinese understanding of heaven.

Areas for Further Research

First, our initial study showed that the Lukan use of the heaven language is different from that of Matthew and Mark. For instance, Luke does not use "the kingdom of heaven;" rather, he uses "the kingdom of God." While Matthew uses nearly all of the heaven references of Mark (seventeen out of nineteen), Luke uses only eleven of them (eleven out of nineteen). A comparative study of the references to heaven in the Synoptic Gospels may discern the different theological concerns of the evangelists and thus contribute to scholarship on the Synoptic Gospels. Similarly, a study focusing on the references to heaven in the Gospel of Mark may discern Mark's theological concerns and thus contribute to Markan scholarship. Further, a study of the references to heaven or of the heaven motif in other NT books, especially in the Gospel of John, Ephesians, the book of Hebrews and of course the book of Revelation, may open new windows for scholarship of these books. For Chinese scholars, a comparative study of the references to heaven and the traditional Chinese understanding of heaven would be interesting, especially a comparison with Taoist understandings of heaven. This would be a very useful bridge-building exercise for the evangelizing of the Chinese.

Bibliography

Aitken, William Ewart Maurice. "Beelzebul." *Journal of Biblical Literature* 31 (1912): 34–53.
Aland, Kurt. *Synopsis of the Four Gospels: Greek-English Edition of the Synopsis Quattuor Evangeliorum with the Text of the Revised Standard Version.* New York: United Bible Societies, 1973.
Aland, Kurt, and Eberhard Nestle. *Novum Testamentum Graece.* 27th ed. Stuttgart: Deutsche Bibelgesellschaft, 2001.
Allen, Leslie C. *Psalms 101–150.* Word Biblical Commentary 21. Waco, TX: Word, 1983.
Alter, Robert. *The Art of Biblical Narrative.* New York: Basic, 1981.
Aune, David E. *The New Testament in Its Literary Environment.* Library of Early Christianity. Philadelphia: Westminster, 1987.
———. *Revelation 6–16.* Word Biblical Commentary 52B. Dallas: Word, 1998.
Baarlink, Heinrich. "Friede im Himmel: die lukanische Redaktion von Lk 19:38 und ihre Deutung." *Zeitschrift für die neutestamentliche Wissenschaft und die Kunde der älteren Kirche* 76 (1985): 170–186.
Barr, James. *Biblical Words for Time.* Studies in Biblical Theology. London: SCM, 1969.
Barrett, C. K. *The Acts of the Apostles: A Shorter Commentary.* London: T&T Clark, 2002.
———. *A Critical and Exegetical Commentary on the Acts of the Apostles, vol. 1: Preliminary Introduction and Commentary on Acts 1–14.* International Critical Commentary. Edinburgh: T&T Clark, 1994.
———. *A Critical and Exegetical Commentary on the Acts of the Apostles, vol. 2: Introduction and Commentary on Acts 15–28.* International Critical Commentary. Edinburgh: T&T Clark, 1994.
Bass, Kenneth. "The Narrative and Rhetorical Use of Divine Necessity in Luke-Acts." *Journal of Biblical and Pneumatological Research* 1 (2009): 48–68.
Bateman, Herbert W. I. V. "Psalm 110:1 and the New Testament." *Bibliotheca Sacra* 149 (1992): 438–453.

Bauckham, Richard. *The Climax of Prophecy: Studies on the Book of Revelation.* Edinburgh: T&T Clark, 1993.

Bauernfeind, Otto. *Kommentar und Studien zur Apostelgeschichte.* Tubingen: J. C. B. Mohr [Paul Siebeck], 1980.

Bayer, Hans F. "Christ-centered Eschatology in Acts 3:17–26." In *Jesus of Nazareth*, 236–250. Grand Rapids: Eerdmans, 1994.

Beale, Gregory K. *The Book of Revelation: A Commentary on the Greek Text.* New International Greek Testament Commentary. Grand Rapids: Eerdmans, 1999.

Beale, Gregory K., and Donald A. Carson, eds. *Commentary on the New Testament Use of the Old Testament.* Grand Rapids, MI; Nottingham: Baker; Apollos, 2007.

Bechard, Dean Philip. "Paul among the Rustics: The Lystran Episode (Acts 14:8–20) and Lucan Apologetic." *Catholic Biblical Quarterly* 63 (2001): 84–101.

Biguzzi, Giancarlo. "Witnessing Two by Two in the Acts of the Apostles." *Biblica* 92 (2011): 1–20.

Bird, Michael F. "Mission as an Apocalyptic Event: Reflections on Luke 10:18 and Mark 13:10." *Evangelical Quarterly* 76 (2004): 117–134.

Black, C. Clifton. *The Rhetoric of the Gospel: Theological Artistry in the Gospels and Acts.* St Louis: Chalice, 2001.

Black, David Alan, and David R. Beck, eds. *Rethinking the Synoptic Problem.* Grand Rapids: Baker, 2001.

Black, David Alan, and David S. Dockery, eds. *New Testament Criticism & Interpretation.* Grand Rapids: Zondervan, 1991.

Black, Matthew. *Scrolls and Christian Origins: Studies in the Jewish Background of the New Testament.* New York: Scribner, 1961.

Bock, Darrell L. *Acts.* Baker Exegetical Commentary on the New Testament. Grand Rapids: Baker, 2007.

———. *Luke 1:1–9:50.* Baker Exegetical Commentary on the New Testament. Grand Rapids: Baker, 1994.

———. *Luke 9:51–24:53.* Baker Exegetical Commentary on the New Testament. Grand Rapids: Baker, 1996.

Bovon, François. *Luke 1, A Commentary on the Gospel of Luke 1:1–9:50.* Translated by Christine M. Thomas. Hermeneia. Minneapolis: Fortress, 2002.

———. *Luke 3.* Translated by James Crouch. Hermeneia: A Critical and Historical Commentary on the Bible. Minneapolis: Fortress.

———. *Luke the Theologian: Fifty-five Years of Research (1950–2005).* 2d ed. Waco, TX: Baylor University Press, 2006.

Breck, John. "Chiasmus as a Key to Biblical Interpretation." *St Vladimir's Theological Quarterly* 43 (1999): 249–267.

Breytenbach, C. "Zeus und der lebendige Gott: Anmerkungen zu Apostelgeschichte 14.11–17." *New Testament Studies* 39 (1993): 396–413.

Brinks, C. L. "'Great Is Artemis of the Ephesians': Acts 19:23–41 in Light of Goddess Worship in Ephesus." *Catholic Biblical Quarterly* 71 (2009): 776–794.

Brown, J. P. "Yahweh, Zeus, Jupiter: The High God and the Elements." *Zeitschrift für die Alttestamentliche Wissenschaft* 106 (1994): 175–197.

Brown, Raymond Edward. *The Birth of the Messiah: A Commentary on the Infancy Narratives in the Gospels of Matthew and Luke*. Anchor Bible Reference Library. New York: Doubleday, 1993.

Bruce, F. F. *The Acts of the Apostles: The Greek Text with Introduction and Commentary*. Grand Rapids: Eerdmans, 1990.

———. *The Book of the Acts*. New International Commentary on the New Testament. Grand Rapids: Eerdmans, 1988.

Bruckner, James K. *Exodus*. New International Biblical Commentary. Peabody: Hendrickson, 2008.

Bultmann, Rudolf Karl. *The History of the Synoptic Tradition*. New York: Harper & Row, 1963.

———. *The History of the Synoptic Tradition*. Oxford: Basil Blackwell, 1968.

Burkert, Walter. *Greek Religion: Arahaic and Classical*. Translated by John Raffan. Cambridge: Harvard University Press, 1985.

Cadbury, Henry Joel. *Making of Luke-Acts*. New York: Macmillan, 1958.

———. *The Style and Literary Method of Luke. I, The Diction of Luke and Acts*. Harvard Theological Studies 6. Cambridge: Harvard University Press, 1919.

———. *The Style and Literary Method of Luke. II*. Harvard Theological Studies 6. Cambridge: Harvard University Press, 1920.

Cadbury, Henry Joel, and Paul N. Anderson. *The Making of Luke-Acts*. Peabody: Hendrickson, 1999.

Calvin, John. *Acts of the Apostles, 1–13*. Calvin's Commentaries. Edinburgh: Oliver & Boyd, 1965.

Carrol, John T. *Response to the End of History: Eschatology and Situation in Luke-Acts*. Society of Biblical Literature Dissertation Series 92. Decatur: Scholars, 1988.

Carroll, John T. *Luke: A Commentary*. 1st ed. The New Testament Library. Louisville, KY: Westminster, 2012.

———. *Response to the End of History: Eschatology and Situation in Luke-Acts*. Dissertation Series 92. Atlanta: Scholars Press, 1988.

Carson, Donald A., and Douglas J. Moo. *An Introduction to the New Testament*. Leicester: Apollos, 2006.

Chafer, Lewis Sperry. "Angelology." *Bibliotheca Sacra* 98 (1941): 389–420.
Charlesworth, James H. *The Old Testament Pseudepigrapha*. Vol. 2. Expansions of the "Old Testament" and Legends. London: Darton, 1985.
———, ed. *The Old Testament Pseudepigrapha*. Vol. 1. Apocalyptic Literature and Testaments. Garden City: Doubleday, 1983.
Clark, Kenneth Willis. "Realized Eschatology." *Journal of Biblical Literature* 59 (1940): 367–383.
Conzelmann, Hans. *Acts of the Apostles*. Hermeneia. Philadelphia: Fortress, 1987.
———. *Die Mitte der Zeit: Studien zur Theologie des Lukas*. Beiträge zur historischen Theologie. Tübingen: Mohr Siebeck, 1954.
———. *The Theology of St Luke*. Translated by George Buswell. New York: Harper & Row, 1960.
Cosgrove, Charles H. "The Divine Dei in Luke-Acts: Investigations into the Lukan Understanding of God's Providence." *Novum Testamentum* 26 (1984): 168–190.
Craddock, Fred B. *Luke*. Interpretation Bible Commentary. Louisville: Westminster, 1990.
Dahood, Mitchell Joseph. *Psalms, III: 101–150*. Anchor Bible. Garden City, NY: Doubleday, 1970.
Danker, Frederick W. *Jesus and the New Age: A Commentary on St Luke's Gospel*. Philadelphia: Fortress, 1988.
Dart, John. "Scriptural Schemes: The ABCBAs of Biblical Writing." *Christian Century* 121 (2004): 22–25.
De Villiers, Pieter G. R. "Peace in Luke and Acts: A Perspective on Biblical Spirituality." *Acta Patristica et Byzantina* 19 (2008): 110–134.
De Wette, Wilhelm Martin Leberecht, and Frederick Frotheringham. *An Historico-Critical Introduction to the Canonical Books of the New Testament*. 5th ed. Boston: Crosby, 1858.
Delorme, Jean. "Intertextualities about Mark." In *Intertextuality in Biblical Writings*, 35–42. Kampen, Netherlands: J. H. Kok, 1989.
Derrenbacker, Robert A., Jr. *Ancient Compositional Practices and the Synoptic Problem*. Bibliotheca Ephemeridum Theologicarum Lovaniensium. Leuven: Peeters, 2005.
Dibelius, Martin. *Die Formgeschichte des Evangeliums*. 4th ed. Tübingen: J. C. B Mohr, 1961.
Dibelius, Martin, Heinrich Greeven, and Mary Ling. *Studies in the Acts of the Apostles*. New York: Charles Scribner's Sons, 1956.
Dibelius, Martin, and K. C. Hanson. *The Book of Acts: Form, Style, and Theology*. Fortress Classics in Biblical Studies. Minneapolis: Fortress, 2004.
Dionne, C. "L'épisode de Lystre (Ac 14, 7–20a): Une Analyse Narrative." *Science et Esprit* 57 (2005): 5–33.

Dodd, C. H. *The Parables of the Kingdom*. London: Nisbet, 1935.
Donne, Brian K. *Christ Ascended*. Paternoster, 1983.
———. "Significance of the Ascension of Jesus Christ in the New Testament." *Scottish Journal of Theology* 30 (1977): 555–68.
Downing, F. Gerald. "Common Ground with Paganism in Luke and in Josephus." *New Testament Studies* 28 (1982): 546–559.
———. "Redaction Criticism: Josephus' Antiquities and the Synoptic Gospels, pt 1." *Journal for the Study of the New Testament* (1980): 46–65.
———. "Redaction Criticism: Josephus' Antiquities and the Synoptic Gospels, pt 2." *Journal for the Study of the New Testament* (1980): 29–48.
Dozeman, Thomas B. *Exodus*. Eerdmans Critical Commentary. Grand Rapids: Eerdmans, 2009.
Dunn, James D. G. "The Ascension of Jesus: A Test Case for Hermeneutics." In *Auferstehung*, edited by Hermann Lichtenberger Friedrich Avenaris, 301–322. Tübingen: Mohr Siebeck, 2001.
Ellis, E. Earle. *The Gospel of Luke*. Marshall, Morgan & Scott, 1981.
Emmrich, Martin. "The Lucan Account of the Beelzebul Controversy." *Westminster Theological Journal* 62 (2000): 267–279.
Evans, C. F. *Saint Luke*. London: SCM, 1990.
Evans, Craig A. *Luke*. Edited by W. Ward Gasque. New International Biblical Commentary. Peabody: Hendrickson, 1990.
———."The Prophetic Setting of the Pentecost Sermon." *Zeitschrift für die neutestamentliche Wissenschaft und die Kunde der älteren Kirche* 74 (1983): 148–150.
Fanning, Buist M. *Verbal Aspect in New Testament Greek*. Oxford: Clarendon, 1990.
Fitzmyer, J. A. "The Ascension of Christ and Pentecost." *Theological Studies* 45 (1984): 409–440.
Fitzmyer, Joseph A. *The Acts of the Apostles*. 1st ed. The Anchor Bible 31. New York: Doubleday, 1998.
———. *The Gospel according to Luke 1–9*. Anchor Bible. Garden City: Doubleday, 1981.
———. *The Gospel according to Luke 10–24*. Anchor Bible 28A. New York: Doubleday, 1985.
———. *Luke the Theologian: Aspects of His Teaching*. London: Geoffrey Chapman, 1989.
Flender, Helmut. *St Luke: Theologian of Redemptive History*. London: SPCK, 1967.
Flint, Peter W., Jean Duhaime, and Kyung S. Baek, eds. *Celebrating the Dead Sea Scrolls: A Canadian Collection*. Early Judaism and Its Literature 30. Atlanta: Society of Biblical Literature, 2011.

Foakes-Jackson, F. J., and Kirsopp Lake. *The Beginnings of Christianity*. Vol. 1. The Acts of the Apostles. London: Macmillan, 1933.

Foss, Clive. *Ephesus after Antiquity: A Late Antique, Byzantine and Turkish City*. Cambridge: Cambridge University Press, 1979.

Foster, Paul, Gregory, Andrew, John S. Kloppenborg, and Jozef Verheyden, eds. *New Studies in the Synoptic Problem: Oxford Conference, April 2008: Essays in Honour of Christopher M Tuckett*. Bibliotheca Ephemeridum Theologicarum Lovaniensium. Leuven: Peeters, 2011.

Francis, Fred O. "Eschatology and History in Luke-Acts." *Journal of the American Academy of Religion* 37 (1969): 49–63.

Franklin, Eric. *Christ the Lord: A Study in the Purpose and Theology of Luke-Acts*. Philadelphia: Westminster, 1975.

Freedman, David Noel. "The Anchor Bible Dictionary." 5 vols. New York: Doubleday. 1992.

Fuller, Michael E. *The Restoration of Israel: Israel's Re-gathering and the Fate of the Nations in Early Jewish Literature and Luke-Acts*. Beihefte zur Zeitschift für die neutestamentliche Wissenschaft 138. Berlin: de Gruyter, 2006.

Garrett, Susan R. *The Demise of the Devil: Magic and the Demonic in Luke's Writings*. Minneapolis: Augsburg Fortress, 1989.

Gathercole, S. "The Heavenly Anatole (Luke 1:78–9)." *Journal of Theological Studies* 56 (2005): 471–488.

———. "Jesus' Eschatological Vision of the Fall of Satan: Luke 10, 18 Reconsidered." *Zeitschrift für die Neutestamentliche Wissenschaft* 94 (2003): 143–163.

Gaventa, Beverly Roberts. *The Acts of the Apostles*. Abingdon New Testament Commentaries. Nashville: Abingdon, 2003.

Geldenhuys, Norval. *Commentary on the Gospel of Luke*. Grand Rapids: Eerdmans, 1951.

Grassi, Joseph A. *Jesus Is Shalom: A Vision of Peace from the Gospels*. New York: Paulist, 2006.

———. *Peace on Earth: Roots and Practices from Luke's Gospel*. Collegeville, MN: Liturgical Press, 2004.

Green, Gene L. *Jude and 2 Peter*. Baker Exegetical Commentary on the New Testament. Grand Rapids: Baker, 2008.

Green, Joel B. *The Gospel of Luke*. Edited by Gordon D. Fee. New International Commentary on the New Testament. Grand Rapids: Eerdmans, 1997.

———. *The Theology of the Gospel of Luke*. New York: Cambridge University Press, 1995.

Haenchen, Ernst. *The Acts of the Apostles*. Philadelphia: Westminster, 1971.

Hamm, Dennis. "Acts 3:12–26: Peter's Speech and the Healing of the Man Born Lame." *Perspectives in Religious Studies* 11 (1984): 199–217.

Hanson, Paul D. *Isaiah 40–66*. Interpretation Bible Commentary. Louisville: Westminster John Knox, 1996.

Hays, Richard B. *Echoes of Scripture in the Letters of Paul*. New Haven: Yale University Press, 1993.

Hedrick, Charles W. "Paul's Conversion/Call: A Comparative Analysis of the Three Reports in Acts." *Journal of Biblical Literature* 100 (1981): 415–432.

Helyer, Larry R. "Luke and the Restoration of Israel." *Journal of the Evangelical Theological Society* 36 (1993): 317–329.

Hendriksen, William. *The Gospel of Luke*. New Testament Commentary. Baker, 1978.

Hills, Julian Victor. "Luke 10:18 – Who Saw Satan Fall." *Journal for the Study of the New Testament* (1992): 25–40.

Hobart, William Kirk. *The Medical Language of St. Luke; A Proof from Internal Evidence that "The Gospel according to St. Luke" and "The Acts of the Apostles" Were Written by the Same Person, and That the Writer Was a Medical Man*. Dublin University Press Series. Dublin: Hodges, 1882.

Hodgson, Peter C. *The Formation of Historical Theology: A Study of Ferdinand Christian Baur*. New York: Harper and Row, 1966.

Hoffmann, Paul, John S. Kloppenborg, and James M. Robinson. *The Critical Edition of Q: Synopsis Including the Gospels of Matthew and Luke, Mark and Thomas with English, German, and French Translations of Q and Thomas*. Hermeneia. Louvain: Peeters, 2000.

Howell, J. R. "The Imperial Authority and Benefaction of Centurions and Acts 10.34–43: A Response to C. Kavin Rowe." *Journal for the Study of the New Testament* 31 (2008): 25–51.

Hultgård, Anders. "La chute de Satan: L'arrière-plan iranien d'un logion de Jésus (Luc 10, 18)." *Revue d'Histoire et de Philosophie Religieuses* 80 (2000): 69–77.

Humphrey, Edith M. "'I Saw Satan Fall . . .' The Rhetoric of Vision." *ARC* 21 (1993): 75–88.

Jellicoe, Sidney. "St Luke and the Seventy(-two)'." *New Testament Studies* 6 (1960): 319–321.

Jervell, Jacob. *The Theology of the Acts of the Apostles*. New Testament Theology. New York: Cambridge University Press, 1996.

Jipp, Joshua W. "Paul's Areopagus Speech of Acts 17:16–34 as Both Critique and Propaganda." *Journal of Biblical Literature* 131 (2012): 567–588.

Johnson, Luke Timothy. *The Acts of the Apostles*. Sacra Paginas. Collegeville: Liturgical, 2006.

———. *The Literary Function of Possessions in Luke-Acts*. Society of Biblical Literature Dissertation Series 39. Scholars, 1977.

Johnston, George. "Christ as Archegos." *New Testament Studies* 27 (1981): 381–385.

Jonge, H. J. de. "The Chronology of the Ascension Stories in Luke and Acts." *New Testament Studies* 59 (2013): 151–171.
Just, Arthur A., Jr. *Luke 9:51–24:53: A Theological Exposition of Sacred Scripture*. Concordia Commentary. St. Louis, MO: Concordia, 1997.
Kaiser, Walter C., Jr. *The Uses of the Old Testament in the New*. Chicago: Moody, 1985.
Käsemann, Ernst. *Essays on New Testament Themes*. Studies in Biblical Theology. Naperville: Alec R. Allenson, 1964.
Kilgallen, John J. "Jesus, Savior, the Glory of Your People Israel." *Biblica* 75 (1994): 305–328.
———. ""Peace" in the Gospel of Luke and Acts of Apostles." *Studia Missionalia* 38 (1989): 55–79.
Kistemaker, Simon. *Exposition of the Acts of the Apostles*. New Testament Commentary. Grand Rapids: Baker, 1990.
Klassen, William. "A Child of Peace" (Luke 10:6) in First Century Context." *New Testament Studies* 27 (1981): 488–506.
Koet, Bart J. "Isaiah in Luke-Acts." In *Isaiah in the New Testament*, 79–100. London: T&T Clark, 2005.
Kraftchick, Steven J. *Jude, 2 Peter*. Abingdon New Testament Commentaries. Nashville: Abingdon, 2002.
Kristeva, Julia. *Sēmelōtikē: Recherches pour une sémanalyse*. Paris: Éditions du Seuil, 1969.
Kurz, William S. "Acts 3:19–26 as a Test of the Role of Eschatology in Lukan Christology." *Society of Biblical Literature Seminar Papers* (1977): 309–323.
———. *The Acts of the Apostles*. Collegeville Bible Commentary. Collegeville, MN: Liturgical Press, 1983.
Lane Fox, Robin. *Pagans and Christians*. New York: Alfred A. Knopf, 1987.
LiDonnici, Lynn R. "The Images of Artemis Ephesia and Greco-Roman Worship: A Reconsideration." *Harvard Theological Review* 85 (1992): 389–415.
Lindemann, A. "'. . . und auf Erden Frieden.' (Lk 2, 14): Zum Friedensverständnis im Neuen Testament." *Bibel und Kirche* 61 (2006): 138–143.
Litwak, Kenneth D. "Israel's Prophets Meet Athens' Philosophers: Scritural Echoes in Acts 17:22–31." *Biblica* 85 (2004): 199–216.
Loader, William R. G. "Christ at the Right Hand: Ps 110:1 in the New Testament." *New Testament Studies* 24 (1978): 199–217.
Lohfink, Gerhard. *Die Himmelfahrt Jesu; Untersuchungen zu den Himmelfahrts- und Erhöhungstexten bei Lukas*. Studien zum Alten und Neuen Testament. München: Kösel, 1971.

Lund, Nils W. *Chiasmus in the New Testament: A Study in the Form and Function of Chiastic Structures.* Peabody, MA: Hendrickson, 1991.

Lyonnet, Stanislas. "'La voie' dans les Actes des Apôtres." *Recherches de science religieuse* 69 (1981): 149–164.

Maddox, Robert. *The Purpose of Luke-Acts.* Vandenhoeck & Ruprecht, 1982.

Maile, J. F. "The Ascension in Luke-Acts." *Tyndale Bulletin* 37 (1986): 29–59.

Malina, Bruce J., and John J. Pilch. *Social-Science Commentary on the Book of Acts.* Minneapolis: Fortress, 2008.

Mallen, Peter. *The Reading and Transformation of Isaiah in Luke-Acts.* Library of New Testament Studies. London: T&T Clark, 2007.

Manson, William. *The Gospel of Luke.* New York: Richard R. Smith, 1930.

Marcus, Joel. "Jesus' Baptismal Vision." *New Testament Studies* 41 (1995): 512–521.

Marguerat, Daniel. *The First Christian Historian: Writing the 'Acts of the Apostles'.* Society for New Testament Studies Monograph Series 121. Cambridge: Cambridge University Press, 2002.

Marsh, John. *The Fulness of Time.* New York: Harper & Brothers, 1952.

Marshall, I. Howard. *The Acts of the Apostles: An Introduction and Commentary.* Leicester: InterVarsity, 1980.

———. *The Gospel of Luke: A Commentary on the Greek Text.* Edited by I. Howard Marshall and W. Ward Gasque. The New International Greek Testament Commentary. Grand Rapids: Eerdmans, 1978.

———. *Luke: Historian and Theologian.* Grand Rapids: Eerdmans, 1971.

Marshall, I. Howard, and David Peterson. *Witness to the Gospel: The Theology of Acts.* Grand Rapids: Eerdmans, 1998.

Marshall, Jonathan. *Jesus, Patrons, and Benefactors: Roman Palestine and the Gospel of Luke.* Wissenschaftliche Untersuchungen zum Neuen Testament 259. Tübingen: Mohr Siebeck, 2009.

Martin, L. H. "Gods or Ambassadors of God? Barnabas and Paul in Lystra." *New Testament Studies* 41 (1995): 152–156.

Marx, A. "La chute de 'Lucifer' (Esaïe 14, 12–15; Luc 10, 18): Préhistoire d'un mythe." *Revue d'Histoire et de Philosophie Religieuses* 80 (2000): 171–185.

Marxsen, Willi. *Der Evangelist Markus; Studien zur Redaktionsgeschichte des Evangeliums.* Forschungen zur Religion und Literatur des Alten und Neuen Testaments, n F, 49 Heft Der ganzen Reihe 67 Heft. Göttingen: Vandenhoeck & Ruprecht, 1956.

———. *Mark the Evangelist; Studies on the Redaction History of the Gospel.* Translated by D. Juel J. Boyce, W. Poehlmann, and R. A. Harrisville. Nashville: Abingdon, 1969.

Mattill, A. J. *Luke and the Last Things: A Perspective for the Understanding of Lukan Thought.* Dillsboro, NC: Western North Carolina Press, 1979.

———. "Naherwartung, Fernerwartung, and the Purpose of Luke-Acts: Weymouth Reconsidered." *Catholic Biblical Quarterly* 34 (1972): 276–293.

Mattill, Andrew Jacob. "Jesus-Paul Parallels and the Purpose of Luke-Acts: H H Evans Reconsidered." *Novum Testamentum* 17 (1975): 15–46.

McKnight, Scot. *Interpreting the Synoptic Gospels*. Grand Rapids: Baker, 1988.

———. "Jesus and the Twelve." *Bulletin for Biblical Research* 11 (2001): 203–231.

Merklein, Helmut. *Jesu Botschaft von der Gottesherrschaft: Eine Skizze*. Stuttgarter Bibelstudien. Stuttgart: Katholisches Bibelwerk, 1983.

Metzger, Bruce Manning. *Introduction to the Apocrypha*. New York: Oxford University Press, 1957.

———. *A Textual Commentary on the Greek New Testament*. 2nd ed. London: United Bible Society, 1994.

Metzger, Bruce Manning, and Bart D. Ehrman. *The Text of the New Testament: Its Transmission, Corruption, and Restoration*. New York: Oxford University Press, 2005.

Michael Wise, Martin Abegg Jr., and Edward Cook. *The Dead Sea Scrolls: A New Translation*. Translated by Martin G. Abegg, Michael O. Wise, and Edward M. Cook. Rydalmere, NSW: Harper SanFrancisco; Hodder Headline, 1996.

Miller, John B. F. *Convinced That God Had Called Us: Dreams, Visions, and the Perception of God's Will in Luke-Acts*. Biblical Interpretation Series 85. Leiden: Brill, 2007.

Minguez, D. "Die Himmelfahrt Jesu: Untersuchungen zu den Himmelfahrts- und Erhöhunngstexten bei Lukas." *Catholic Biblical Quarterly* 35 (1973): 397–400.

Mitchell, David C. *The Message of the Psalter: An Eschatological Programme in the Book of Psalms*. Journal for the Study of the Old Testament Supplement 252. Sheffield: Sheffield Academic, 1997.

Mittelstaedt, Alexander. *Lukas als Historiker: zur Datierung des lukanischen Doppelwerkes*. Texte und Arbeiten zum Neutestamentlichen Zeitalter 43. Tübingen: Francke, 2005.

Miyoshi, Michi. *Der Anfang des Reiseberichts, Lk 9,51–10,24*. Rome: Biblical Institute Press, 1974.

Mosse, Martin. *The Three Gospels: New Testament History Introduced by the Synoptic Problem*. Paternoster Biblical Monographs. Milton Keynes: Paternoster, 2007.

Motyer, J. A. *Isaiah*. Tyndale Old Testament Commentaries 20. Downers Grove: InterVarsity, 1999.

Moule, C. F. D. "Ascension: Acts 1:9." *Expository Times* 68 (1957): 20–209.

Moulton, James Hope. *A Grammar of New Testament Greek*. Vol. 1. Prolegomena. Edinburgh: T&T Clark, 1908.

———. *A Grammar of New Testament Greek*. Vol. 3. Syntax. Edinburgh: T&T Clark, 1963.
Mounce, Robert H. *The Book of Revelation*. New International Commentary on the New Testament. Grand Rapids: Eerdmans, 1998.
Mowery, Robert L. "The Matthean References to the Kingdom: Different Terms for Different Audiences." *Ephemerides Theologicae Lovanienses* 70 (1994): 398–405.
Müller, Paul-Gerhard. *Christos Archēgos: der religionsgeschichtliche und theologische Hintergrund*. Bern: Lang, 1973.
Müller, Ulrich B. "Vision und Botschaft: Erwägungen zur prophetischen Struktur der Verkündigung Jesu." *Zeitschrift für Theologie und Kirche* 74 (1977): 416–448.
Murphy-O'Connor, J. *Jesus and Paul: Parallel Lives*. Collegeville: Liturgical Press, 2007.
Nave, Guy D., Jr. "No Pax Romana: A Lukan Rejection of Imperial Peace." *Theologies and Cultures* 2 (2005): 56–72.
Neyrey, Jerome H. *The Social World of Luke-Acts: Models for Interpretation*. Peabody: Hendrickson, 1991.
Nielsen, Anders Eyvind. *Until It Is Fulfilled: Lukan Eschatology according to Luke 22 and Acts 20*. Wissenschaftliche Untersuchungen zum Neuen Testament 2.126. Tübingen: Mohr Siebeck, 2000.
Nolland, John. *Luke 1–9:20*. Word Biblical Commentary 35A. Dallas: Word, 1989.
———. *Luke 9:21–18:34*. Word Biblical Commentary 35b. Dallas: Word, 1993.
———. *Luke 18:35–24:53*. Edited by Lynn Allan Losie Ralph P. Martin. Word Biblical Commentary 35c. Dallas: Word, 1993.
O'Toole, Robert F. "Luke's Understanding of Jesus' Resurrection-Ascension-Exaltion." *Biblical Theology Bulletin* 9 (1979): 106–114.
Ohly, Lukas. "Kontrast-Harmonie: Ein Beitrag zur Theologie der Himmelfahrt Christi." *Neue Zeitschrift für systematische Theologie und Religionsphilosophie* 49 (2007): 484–498.
Olsson, B. "The Canticle of the Heavenly Host (Luke 2:14) in History and Culture." *New Testament Studies* 50 (2004): 147–166.
Orchard, Bernard, and Harold Riley. *The Order of the Synoptics: Why Three Synoptic Gospels?* Macon, GA: Mercer University Press, 1987.
Osborne, Grant R. *The Hermeneutical Spiral: A Comprehensive Introduction to Biblical Interpretation*. Downers Grove: IVP, 1991.
——— "History and Theology in the Synoptic Gospels." *Trinity Journal* 24 (2003): 5–22.
———. *Matthew*. Zondervan Exegetical Commentary on the New Testament. Grand Rapids: Zondervan, 2010.

———. "Redaction Criticism." In *New Testament Criticism & Interpretation*, edited by David Alan Black and David S. Dockery, 197–224. Grand Rapids: Zondervan, 1991.

———. "Redaction Criticism and the Great Commission: A Case Study toward a Biblical Understanding of Inerrancy." *Journal of the Evangelical Theological Society* 19 (1976): 73–85.

———. *The Resurrection Narratives: A Redactional Study*. Grand Rapids: Baker, 1984.

———. *Revelation*. Baker Exegetical Commentary on the New Testament. Grand Rapids: Baker, 2002.

Oster, Richard. "The Ephesian Artemis as an Opponent of Early Christianity." *Jahrbuch für Antike und Christentum* 19 (1976): 24–44.

Padilla, Osvaldo. *The Speeches of Outsiders in Acts: Poetics, Theology and Historiography*. Society for New Testament Studies Monograph Series 144. Cambridge: Cambridge University Press, 2008.

Page, Sydney H. T. *Powers of Evil: A Biblical Study of Satan and Demons*. Grand Rapids: Baker, 1995.

Pao, David W. *Acts and the Isaianic New Exodus*. 2.130. Tübingen: Mohr Siebeck, 2000.

———. "Waiters or Preachers: Acts 6:1–7 and the Lukan Table Fellowship Motif." *Journal of Biblical Literature* 130 (2011): 127–144.

Parsons, M. C. *The Departure of Jesus in Luke-Acts: The Ascension Narratives in Context*. JSNT Supplement Series 21. Sheffield: JSOT Press, 1987.

Payton, James R., Jr. *Irenaeus on the Christian Faith: A Condensation of against Heresies*. Eugene, OR: Pickwick, 2011.

Pelikan, Jaroslav. *Acts*. Brazos Theological Commentary. Grand Rapids: Brazos, 2005.

Pennington, Jonathan T. *Heaven and Earth in the Gospel of Matthew*. Supplements to Novum Testamentum 126. Grand Rapids: Baker, 2009.

Pennington, Jonathan T., and Sean M. McDonough. "Introduction." In *Cosmology and New Testament Theology*, edited by Jonathan T. Pennington and Sean M. McDonough, 1–4. Library of New Testament Studies 355. London: T&T Clark, 2008.

———. eds. *Cosmology and New Testament Theology*. Library of New Testament Studies 355. London: T&T Clark, 2008.

Perrin, Norman. *What Is Redaction Criticism*. Guides to Biblical Scholarship. Philadelphia: Fortress, 1969.

Pervo, Richard I. *Acts: A Commentary*. Hermeneia. Minneapolis: Fortress, 2009.

———. *Profit with Delight: The Literary Genre of the Acts of the Apostles*. Philadelphia: Fortress, 1987.

Petersen, Norman R. *Literary Criticism for New Testament Critics*. Minneapolis: Fortress, 1978.
Peterson, David. *The Acts of the Apostles*. The Pillar New Testament Commentary. Nottingham: Apollos, 2009.
Peterson, Erik. *Theologische Traktate*. Munich: Kösel, 1951.
Pinnock, C. H. "Acts 4:12: No Other Name Under Heaven." *Theology in Scotland* 10 (2003): 19–28.
Plötz, K. "Die Areopagrede des Apostels Paulus: Ein Beispiel urkirchlicher Verkündigung." *Internationale Katholische Zeitschrift/Communio* 17 (1988): 111–117.
Plummer, Alfred. *A Critical and Exegetical Commentary on the Gospel according to St Luke*. New York: Charles Scribner's Sons, 1896.
Porter, Stanley E. *Verbal Aspect in the Greek of the New Testament, with Reference to Tense and Mood*. Frankfurt am Main: Peter Lang, 1989.
Ramsay, William Mitchell. *The Bearing of Recent Discovery on the Trustworthiness of the New Testament*. New York: Hodder & Stoughton, 1915.
Reese, Ruth A. *2 Peter and Jude*. The Two Horizons New Testament Commentary. Grand Rapids: Eerdmans, 2007.
Reid, B. E. "Puzzling Passages: Luke 2:14." *Bible Today* 32 (1994): 369–369.
Reid, Robert Stephen. *Preaching Mark*. St Louis: Chalice, 1999.
Repo, Eero. *Der "Weg" als Selbstbezeichnung des Urchristentums: Eine traditionsgeschichtliche und semasiologische Untersuchung*. Annales Academiae Scientiarum Fennicae. Helsinki: Suomalainen Tiedeakatemia, 1964.
Rese, Martin. *Alttestamentliche Motive in der Christologie des Lukas*. Gutersloh: Gerd Mohn, 1969.
Rhee, Victor. "The Role of Chiasm for Understanding Christology in Hebrews 1:1–14." *Journal of Biblical Literature* 131 (2012): 341–362.
Robertson, A. T. *A Grammar of the Greek New Testament in the Light of Historical Research*. New York: George H. Doran, 1919.
Rowe, C. K. "Luke-Acts and the Imperial Cult: A Way through the Conundrum?" *Journal for the Study of the New Testament* 27 (2005): 279–300.
Rowe, C. Kavin. *World Upside Down: Reading Acts in the Graeco-Roman Age*. Oxford; New York: Oxford University Press, 2009.
Rusam, D. "Sah Jesus wirklich den Satan vom Himmel fallen (Lk 10.18)? Auf der Suche nach einem neuen Differenzkriterium." *New Testament Studies* 50 (2004): 87–105.
Sánchez, Héctor. *Das lukanische Geschichtswerk im Spiegel Heilsgeschichtlicher Übergänge*. Paderborner Theologische Studien. Paderborn; Zürich: Schöningh, 2001.
Sanders, James A. "Isaiah in Luke." *Interpretation* 36 (1982): 144–155.

Schmid, Josef. *Das Evangelium nach Lukas. Regensburger Neues Testament.* Regensburg, Germany: Friedrich Pustet, 1960.

Schnabel, Eckhard J. *Acts.* Edited by Clinton E. Arnold. Zondervan Exegetical Commentary on the New Testament 5. Grand Rapids: Zondervan, 2012.

———. *Early Christian Mission. Vol. 2: Paul and the Early Church.* Early Christian Mission 2. Downers Grove, IL: InterVarsity, 2004.

Schneider, Gerhard. *Die Apostelgeschichte 1: Einleitung, Kommentar zu Kap 1,1–8,40.* Fribourg, Switzerland: Herder, 1980.

Schürmann, Heinz. *Das Lukasevangelium, vol. 1: Komentar zu Kap 1:1–9:50.* Herders theologischer Kommentar zum Neuen Testament. Freiburg im Br: Herder, 1969.

Schwindt, R. "Bibelhermeneutische Überlegungen zur Himmelfahrtserzählung Apg 1,4–11." *Studien zum Neuen Testament und seiner Umwelt* 35 (2010): 161–176.

Scobie, Charles H. H. "Origins and Development of Samaritan Christianity." *New Testament Studies* 19 (1973): 390–414.

Scott, James M. *Geography in Early Judaism and Christianity.* Society for New Testament Studies Monograph Series 146. Cambridge; New York: Cambridge University Press, 2002.

———. *Geography in Early Judaism and Christianity: The Book of Jubilees.* Society for New Testament Studies Monograph Series 113. Cambridge: Cambridge University Press, 2002.

Shade, Walter Robert, III. "The Restoration of Israel in Acts 3:12–26 and Lukan Eschatology." Ph.D. diss., Trinity Evangelical Divinity School, 1994.

Shauf, Scott. *Theology as History, History as Theology: Paul in Ephesus in Acts 19.* Beihefte zur Zeitschrift für die neutestamentliche Wissenschaft. Berlin; New York: de Gruyter, 2005.

Sleeman, Matthew. *Geography and the Ascension Narrative in Acts.* Society for New Testament Studies Monograph Series 146. New York: Cambridge University Press, 2009.

Sloan, David B. "The Understanding of the Psalms in Luke-Acts." Ph.D. diss., Trinity International University, 2012.

Sloan, Robert B. "'Signs and Wonders': A Rhetorical Clue to the Pentecost Discourse." *Evangelical Quarterly* 63 (1991): 225–240.

Smalley, Stephen S. "Redaction Criticism." In *New Testament Interpretation*, edited by I. Howard Marshall, 181–195. Exeter, England: Paternoster, 1977.

Smith, James. *The Voyage and Shipwreck of St Paul.* Grand Rapids: Baker, 1978.

Smith, Robert H. "Eschatology of Acts and Contemporary Exegesis." *Concordia Theological Monthly* 29 (1958): 641–663.

———. "History and Eschatology in Luke-Acts." *Concordia Theological Monthly* 29 (1958): 881–901.

Sorensen, Eric. *Possession and Exorcism in the New Testament and Early Christianity*. Wissenschaftliche Untersuchungen zum Neuen Testament 157. Tübingen: Mohr Siebeck, 2002.

Spencer, F. Scott. *Journeying through Acts: A Literary Cultural Reading*. Peabody: Hendrickson, 2004.

———. *The Gospel of Luke and Acts of the Apostles*. Interpreting Biblical Texts Series. Nashville: Abingdon, 2008.

Stein, Robert H. Luke. *New American Commentary*. Nashville: Broadman, 1992.

———. *The Synoptic Problem*. Grand Rapids: Baker, 1987.

Stempvoort, P. A. van. "Interpretation of the Ascension in Luke and Acts." *New Testament Studies* 5 (1958): 30–42.

———. "Interpretation of the Ascension in Luke and Acts." *New Testament Studies* 5, no. 1 (1958): 30–42.

Sterling, Gregory E. *Historiography and Self-definition: Josephus, Luke-Acts and Apologetic Historiography*. 5 vols., Supplements to Novum Testamentum. Leiden: E. J. Brill, 1992.

Stock, Augustine. "Chiastic Awareness and Education in Antiquity." *Biblic Theology Bulletin* 14 (1984): 23–27.

Stott, John R. W. *The Spirit, the Church, and the World: The Message of Acts*. Downers Grove: IVP, 1990.

Streeter, Burnett Hillman. *The Four Gospels: A Study of Origins*. New York: Macmillan, 1925.

Strelan, Rick. "Strange Stares: Atenizein in Acts." *Novum Testamentum* 41 (1999): 235–255.

———. *Strange Acts: Studies in the Cultural World of the Acts of the Apostles*. Beihefte zur Zeitschrift für die neutestamentliche Wissenschaft. Berlin: Walter de Gruyter, 2004.

Stuhlmacher, Peter, ed. *The Gospel and the Gospels*. Grand Rapids: Eerdmans, 1991.

Swartley, Willard M. *Covenant of Peace: The Missing Peace in New Testament Theology and Ethics*. Grand Rapids: Eerdmans, 2006.

———. "Politics and Peace (Eirēnē) in Luke's Gospel." In *Political Issues in Luke-Acts*, 18–37. Maryknoll: Orbis Books, 1983.

Sweet, A. M. "The Fall of the Angels." *Bible Today* 32 (1994): 15–20.

Sylva, Dennis D. "The Meaning and Function of Acts 7:46–50." *Journal of Biblical Literature* 106 (1987): 261–275.

Talbert, Charles H. *Literary Patterns, Theological Themes, and the Genre of Luke-Acts*. Missoula: Society of Bibical Literature-Scholars, 1974.

———. "Redaction Critical Quest for Luke the Theologian." *Perspective* (Pittsburgh) 11 (1970): 171–222.

Tannehill, Robert C. "The Composition of Acts 3–5: Narrative Development and Echo Effect." *Society of Biblical Literature Seminar Papers* (1984): 217–240.

———. *The Narrative Unity of Luke-Acts: A Literary Interpretation, vol. 1: The Gospel according to Luke.* Foundations and Facets New Testament. Philadelphia: Fortress, 1986.

———. *The Narrative Unity of Luke-Acts: A Literary Interpretation*, Vol. 2. Minneapolis: Augsburg Fortress, 1990.

Tertullian, Marcus Minucius Felix, and Rudolphus Arbesmann. *Tertullian's Apologetical Works and the Octavius of Minucius Felix*. New York: Fathers of the Church.

Theobald, M. "'Ich sah den Satan aus dem Himmel stürzen.' Überlieferungskritische Beobachtungen zu Lk 10, 18–20." *Biblische Zeitschrift* 49 (2005): 174–190.

Theobald, Michael. "'Ich sah den Satan aus dem Himmel stürzen . . .': Überlieferungskritische Beobachtungen zu Lk 10, 18–20." *Biblische Zeitschrift* 49 (2005): 174–190.

Thompson, Alan J. *The Acts of the Risen Lord Jesus: Luke's Account of God's Unfolding Plan.* New Studies in Biblical Theology. Nottingham: Apollos, 2011.

———. *One Lord, One People: The Unity of the Church in Acts in Its Literary Setting.* Library of New Testament Studies 359. London: T&T Clark, 2008.

Thornton, Timothy C. G. "Stephen's Use of Isaiah 66:1." *Journal of Theological Studies* 25 (1974): 432–434.

Thrall, William Flint, and Addison Hibbard. *A Handbook to Literature.* New York: Odyssey, 1960.

Throckmorton, Burton Hamilton, ed. *Gospel Parallels: A Synopsis of the First 3 Gospels.* Thomas Nelson, 1967.

Tiede, David L. *Prophecy and History in Luke-Acts.* Philadelphia: Fortress, 1980.

Tuckett, C. M., ed. *Luke's Literary Achievement: Collected Essays.* Journal for the Study of the New Testament Supplement 116. Sheffield: Sheffield Academic, 1995.

Turner, Max. *Power from on High: The Spirit in Israel's Restoration and Witness in Luke-Acts.* Journal of Pentecostal Theology Supplement. Sheffield: Scheffield Academic, 1996.

Twelftree, Graham. *In the Name of Jesus: Exorcism among Early Christians.* Grand Rapids: Baker, 2007.

Vernant, Jean-Pierre. "The Encyclopedia of Religion." In *Artemis, vol. 1.* Edited by Mircea Eliade, 420–421. 16 vols. New York: Macmillan, 1987.

Wainwright, Arthur W. "Luke and the Restoration of the Kingdom to Israel." *Expository Times* 89 (1977): 76–79.

Wall, Robert W. "The Finger of God: Deuteronomy 9:10 and Luke 11:20." *New Testament Studies* 33 (1987): 144–150.
Wallace, Daniel B. *Greek Grammar beyond the Basics: An Exegetical Syntax of the New Testament*. Grand Rapids: Zondervan, 1996.
Walton, John H. *Genesis*. The NIV Application Commentary. Grand Rapids: Zondervan, 2001.
Walton, Steve. "'The Heavens Opened': Cosmological and Theological Transformation in Luke and Acts." In *Cosmology and New Testament Theology*, edited by Jonathan T. Pennington and Sean M. McDonough, 60–73. Library of New Testament Studies 355. London: T&T Clark, 2008.
Williams, David J. *Acts*. New International Biblical Commentary. Peabody: Hendrickson, 1990.
Wilson, S. G. "Ascension: A Critique and An Interpretation." *Zeitschrift für die neutestamentliche Wissenschaft und die Kunde der älteren Kirche* 59 (1968): 269–281.
Winter, Bruce W., ed. *The Book of Acts in Its First Century Setting*. 5 vols. Grand Rapids: Eerdmans, 1993–1996.
Witherington, Ben. *The Acts of the Apostles: A Socio-Rhetorical Commentary*. Grand Rapids: Eerdmans, 1998.
Witmer, Amanda. *Jesus, the Galilean Exorcist: His Exorcisms in Social and Political Context*. Library of New Testament Studies 10. New York: T&T Clark, 2012.
Wolfe, Kenneth R. "The Chiastic Structure of Luke-Acts and Some Implications for Worship." *Southwestern Journal of Theology* 22 (1980): 60–71.
Wolters, Albert M. "Anthrōpoi Eudokias (Luke 2:14) and 'Nšy Rṣwn (4Q416)." *Journal of Biblical Literature* 113 (1994): 291–292.
Wright, N. T. *The New Testament and the People of God. Christian Origins and the Question of God 1*. Minneapolis: Fortress, 1989.
———. *The Resurrection of the Son of God. Christian Origins and the Question of God 3*. Minneapolis; London: Fortress, 2003.
Yamazaki-Ransom, Kazuhiko. *The Roman Empire in Luke's Narrative*. New York: T&T Clark, 2010.
Zwiep, Arie W. *The Ascension of the Messiah in Lukan Christology*. Supplements to Novum Testamentum 87. Leiden: Brill, 1997.

Langham Literature and its imprints are a ministry of Langham Partnership.

Langham Partnership is a global fellowship working in pursuit of the vision God entrusted to its founder John Stott –

> *to facilitate the growth of the church in maturity and Christ-likeness through raising the standards of biblical preaching and teaching.*

Our vision is to see churches in the majority world equipped for mission and growing to maturity in Christ through the ministry of pastors and leaders who believe, teach and live by the Word of God.

Our mission is to strengthen the ministry of the Word of God through:
- nurturing national movements for biblical preaching
- fostering the creation and distribution of evangelical literature
- enhancing evangelical theological education

especially in countries where churches are under-resourced.

Our ministry

Langham Preaching partners with national leaders to nurture indigenous biblical preaching movements for pastors and lay preachers all around the world. With the support of a team of trainers from many countries, a multi-level programme of seminars provides practical training, and is followed by a programme for training local facilitators. Local preachers' groups and national and regional networks ensure continuity and ongoing development, seeking to build vigorous movements committed to Bible exposition.

Langham Literature provides majority world preachers, scholars and seminary libraries with evangelical books and electronic resources through publishing and distribution, grants and discounts. The programme also fosters the creation of indigenous evangelical books in many languages, through writer's grants, strengthening local evangelical publishing houses, and investment in major regional literature projects, such as one volume Bible commentaries like *The Africa Bible Commentary* and *The South Asia Bible Commentary*.

Langham Scholars provides financial support for evangelical doctoral students from the majority world so that, when they return home, they may train pastors and other Christian leaders with sound, biblical and theological teaching. This programme equips those who equip others. Langham Scholars also works in partnership with majority world seminaries in strengthening evangelical theological education. A growing number of Langham Scholars study in high quality doctoral programmes in the majority world itself. As well as teaching the next generation of pastors, graduated Langham Scholars exercise significant influence through their writing and leadership.

To learn more about Langham Partnership and the work we do visit **langham.org**

www.ingramcontent.com/pod-product-compliance
Lightning Source LLC
Chambersburg PA
CBHW070234240426
43673CB00044B/1791